S0-FDT-027

WITHDRAWN
NDSU

THE GREATEST MAN UNCROWNED
A STUDY OF THE FALL OF DON ALVARO DE LUNA

NICHOLAS ROUND

THE GREATEST MAN
UNCROWNED
A STUDY OF THE FALL
OF DON ALVARO DE LUNA

TAMESIS BOOKS LIMITED
LONDON

Colección Támesis
SERIE A - MONOGRAFIAS, CXI

© Copyright by Tamesis Books Limited
London, 1986
ISBN 0 7293 0211 3

DISTRIBUTORS:

Spain:
 Editorial Castalia,
 Zurbano, 39,
 28010 Madrid

United States and Canada:
 Longwood Publishing Group, Inc.,
 51 Washington Street,
 Dover, New Hampshire 03820, U.S.A.

Great Britain and rest of the world:
 Grant and Cutler Ltd.,
 55-57 Great Marlborough Street,
 London W1V 2AY

Depósito legal: M. 11566-1986

Printed in Spain by Talleres Gráficos de SELECCIONES GRÁFICAS
Carretera de Irún, km. 11,500 - 28049 Madrid

for
TAMESIS BOOKS LIMITED
LONDON

*For Alan Deyermond
in friendship and esteem*

> «... era el mayor hombre sin corona que por estonçes se fallaua.»
> (PEDRO DE ESCAVIAS: *Repertorio de príncipes*)

> «He was getting up his last 'effect'; but he never finished it.»
> (MARK TWAIN: *A Connecticut Yankee in King Arthur's Court*)

NOTE

Publication of this book was made possible through grants from the Carnegie Trust for the Universities of Scotland and from the University of Glasgow. To them both, and to Professor John Varey, who has brought it through the final stages of its way into print, my particular thanks are due.

N. G. R.

June 1984

CONTENTS

	Page
PREFACE	XI
ABBREVIATIONS	XIII
1. PATTERNS OF INSTABILITY: CASTILE 1419-1453	1
2. THE LINEAMENTS OF CRISIS	32
3. EASTER	67
4. DEPENDENCE, DEROGATION AND DIVINE RIGHT	87
5. A FORM OF TRIAL	130
6. «CONVERSI SUNT IN VANILOQUIUM»	169
7. LEGACIES	211

MAPS
(facing pp. 242-243)

I. THE CASTILIAN KINGDOM AND ITS NEIGHBOURS IN THE TIME OF JUAN II.

II. CENTRAL CASTILE FROM BURGOS TO TOLEDO.

BIBLIOGRAPHY	243
INDEX	257

PREFACE

This book is not offered as the full-scale study which the figure of Don Alvaro de Luna still requires. It attempts only to deal with the violent and enigmatic circumstances in which his career came to an end. But a treatment in depth of that single episode can, in itself, deepen our understanding of fifteenth-century Castilian history generally, and of Don Alvaro —the dominant figure of its middle period— in particular. The fully adequate political biography of him which has yet to be written may prove a little easier to write on that account.

The origins of The Greatest Man Uncrowned *lie in part of a D. Phil. thesis dealing with members of the Díaz de Toledo family. These pages subsequently formed the basis of a paper, read to the 1976 meeting of Historians of Medieval Spain, on 'Don Alvaro de Luna: the Trial and the Background'. The rather longer draft from which that paper was excerpted eventually served as the outline for the present book. I am grateful to all those colleagues who have dealt kindly with it in these earlier forms. Dr. Angus MacKay, in particular, not only discussed its general perspectives at great length, but unselfishly lent an as yet unpublished typescript, without which I should have had no hope of making sense of the economic background. Professor P. E. Russell, at strategic moments, encouraged the work's successive transformations. Professor A. D. Deyermond, who believed in its existence as a book before I did, has been characteristically generous of time and trouble in providing detailed comments.*

A very much larger number of colleagues made my task easier by supplying particular references or general discussion when these things were needed. For one or the other of these reasons, I have to thank Professor Eloy Benito Ruano, Professor A. L. Brown, Dr Peter Davies, Dr Paul Donnelly, Professor Nigel Glendinning, Professor Miguel Angel Ladero Quesada, Professor Derek Lomax, Dr David Mackenzie, Dr Guadalupe Martínez Lacalle, Miss Patricia Odber, Professor Wim Phillips, Professor Brian Tate, Dr Gareth Walters, and Professor Lewis Warren. Like so many other British Hispanists, I also remember with gratitude the kindness in these matters of the late Professor Harold Hall.

Library staff in many places, but especially those of Glasgow Universi-

ty Library, have been indispensable in bringing the work to a conclusion. Miss Isabelle Brough has typed it without flinching at second and third thoughts in my manuscript. The British Academy provided a research grant for work in Spain, and Glasgow University provided a period of study leave, both at the moments when they were most needed. I must thank them all.

Finally, to my wife Ann I owe a double thanks: for the forbearance with which she has accepted Don Alvaro as a long-term presence in our household, and for the judgment with which she has enriched the work. Her reactions to the text at each stage of its writing have improved it in many matters of detail; still more, it has had the benefit of her overall historical sense. If I have managed here to think and write as a historian, the achievement is as much hers as mine.

NICHOLAS ROUND

Milngavie, August, 1982

ABBREVIATIONS

A) *MS collections and catalogues:*

AGS DdC	Archivo General de Simancas. Diversos de Castilla.
AGS *DdC*	Archivo General de Simancas. Printed catalogue: *Diversos de Castilla (Cámara de Castilla) 972-1716* (Madrid, 1969).
AGS *EMdR*	Archivo General de Simancas. MS catalogue: *Escribanía Mayor de Rentas. Contadurías de la Razón. Libros de Rentas ordinarios y extraordinarios.*
AGS M y P	Archivo General de Simancas. Mercedes y Privilegios.
AGS *PR*	Archivo General de Simancas. Printed catalogue: *Patronato Real (834-1851),* vols. I-II (Valladolid, 1946-9).
AGS QdC	Archivo General de Simancas. Quitaciones de Cortes.
AGS *RGS*	Archivo General de Simancas. Printed catalogue: *Registro General del Sello,* vol. I (Valladolid, 1950).
AHN	Archivo Histórico Nacional, Madrid.
BN	Biblioteca Nacional, Madrid.
RAH (CS)	Real Academia de la Historia, Madrid. Colección Salazar.
Sal Inds	A. de Vargas Zúñiga and B. Cuatrero y Huerta, eds., *Indice de la colección de Don Luis de Salazar y Castro* (Madrid, 1949 onwards).

B) *Periodicals and series:*

AEM	*Anuario de Estudios Medievales.*
BAE	Biblioteca de Autores Españoles (Madrid, 1846 onwards).
BHS	*Bulletin of Hispanic Studies.*
BAH	*Boletín de la Real Academia de la Historia.*
CCE	Colección de Crónicas Españolas, ed. Juan de Mata Carriazo (Madrid, 1940 onwards).
CHist	*Cuadernos de Historia* (Anexos de la revista *Hispania*).
CODOIN	*Colección de Documentos Inéditos para la Historia de España.* 112 vols. (Madrid, 1842-1895).
HID	*Historia, Instituciones, Documentos.*
HR	*Hispanic Review.*
JHP	*Journal of Hispanic Philology.*
JWH	*Journal of World History.*
MLR	*Modern Language Review.*
MTM	*Miscelánea de Textos Medievales.*
P&P	*Past and Present.*
RABM	*Revista de Archivos, Bibliotecas y Museos.*
REP	*Revista de Estudios Políticos.*
RFE	*Revista de Filología Española.*

C) *Printed sources:*

Abr H	*Abreviación del Halconero.* Excerpted in 'Estudio preliminar' to Lope Barrientos, *Refundición de la Crónica del Halconero,* CCE, 9 (Madrid, 1946).
BUS	Vicente Beltrán de Heredia, *Bulario de la Universidad de Salamanca (1219-1549),* 3 vols. (Salamanca, 1966-7).
CAL (C)	*Crónica de Don Alvaro de Luna,* CCE, 2 (Madrid, 1940).
CAL (F)	*Crónica de Don Alvaro de Luna,* ed. J. M. de Flores (Madrid, 1784).

ABBREVIATIONS

CCG	[*Cuarta crónica general*]. *Continuación de la Crónica de España del Arzobispo Don Rodrigo Jiménez de Rada por el Obispo Don Gonzalo de la Hinojosa*. CODOIN, 106.
CD	[*Colección diplomática*]. *Memorias de Don Enrique IV de Castilla. Tomo II. Contiene la colección diplomática del mismo Rey compuesta y ordenada por la Real Academia de la Historia* (Madrid, 1835-1913).
C Halc	Pero Carrillo de Huete, *Crónica del Halconero de Juan II*, CCE, 8 (Madrid, 1946).
CJII (CODOIN)	Alvar García de Santa María, *Crónica de Juan II*. CODOIN, 99-100.
CJII (R)	*Crónica de Juan II*, in *Crónicas de los reyes de Castilla*, vol. II, ed. Cayetano Rosell. BAE, 68 (Madrid, 1877).
Cortes (AC)	*Cortes de los antiguos reinos de Aragón y Valencia y Principado de Cataluña* (Madrid, 1896-1916).
Cortes (LC)	*Cortes de los antiguos reinos de León y Castilla* (Madrid, 1861-1903).
Foulché-Delbosc, *CC*	R. Foulché-Delbosc, ed., *Cancionero castellano del siglo XV*. Nueva Biblioteca de Autores Españoles, 15 and 22 (Madrid, 1912-1915).
Palencia, *CEIV*	Alonso de Palencia, *Crónica de Enrique IV*, vol. I, trans. A. Paz y Melia. BAE, 257 (Madrid, 1973).
Palencia, *Déc*	Alonso de Palencia, [*Décadas*]. *Alphonsi Palentini Historiographi Gesta Hispaniensa ex Annalibus Suorum Dierum Colligentis* (Madrid, 1834).
Partidas	Alfonso X of Castile, *Las Siete Partidas del muy noble rey Don Alfonso el Sabio glosadas por el Licenciado Gregorio López*, vols. I-II (Madrid, 1843-4).
Pérez de Guzmán, *G y S*	Fernán Pérez de Guzmán, *Generaciones y semblanzas*, ed. Robert Brian Tate (London, 1965).
Ref Halc	Lope Barrientos, *Refundición de la Crónica del Halconero*, CCE, 9 (Madrid, 1946).
Sánchez de Arévalo, *HH*	Rodrigo Sánchez de Arévalo, *Historiae Hispanicae Partes Quatuor*, in Andreas Schott,

	ed., *Hispaniae Illustratae seu Rerum Urbiumque Hispaniae, Lusitaniae, Aethiopiae et Indiae Scriptores Varii,* vol. I (Frankfurt, 1603).
Valera, *C Abr*	Mosén Diego de Valera, *Crónica abreviada de España,* excerpted in *Memorial de diversas hazañas. Crónica de Enrique IV, ordenada por Mosén Diego de Valera,* CCE, 4 (Madrid, 1941).
Zurita, *AA*	Jerónimo Zurita, *Los cinco libros postreros de la segunda parte de los Anales de la Corona de Aragon: compuestos por Geronimo Çurita Chronista del Reyno* (Zaragoza, 1579).

CHAPTER 1

PATTERNS OF INSTABILITY: CASTILE 1419-1453

The act of capital punishment is inescapably a paradox; it proclaims the vindication of right through force, of legality through ultimate violence. The judicial killing of Alvaro de Luna, Master of Santiago and Constable of Castile, in the main square of Valladolid on June 2nd 1453 was a deed rich in contradictory overtones, yet none was more central than this. Don Alvaro, for almost forty years King Juan II's closest friend, for the greater part of that time his chief minister, died «by the King's command». Yet the authority which could sanction such commands was not merely vindicated in the present by the ceremonial taking of a life; it was itself ultimately grounded in an earlier killing, without the patent of legality. And this was a matter of relatively recent history; the very oldest of the spectators that day in Valladolid might just have been its contemporaries. Juan II ruled in Castile —as his cousins Juan and Alfonso now ruled in Navarre and Aragon— because their great-grandfather, Enrique of Trastámara, had stabbed his half-brother King Pedro to death at a parley outside the castle of Montiel in the spring of 1369. Pedro had been «the Cruel»; at all events, both before and after his death the propaganda efforts of the Trastámara line had been dedicated to presenting him as such. Yet however uniformly ballad and chronicle might protest his tyranny, there could be no doubt about the means by which the rival dynasty had supplanted him. Enrique's campaign had culminated in murder; no less anomalously, it had been sustained by an appeal to the rebellious and acquisitive drives of the Castilian nobility. Both he and his successors faced the problem of curbing those very forces to which they owed their position. In constitutional terms, the Trastámara dynasty had to find a way of legitimizing an authority which their founder had done his best to subvert.[1]

---

[1] The narrative and constitutional framework for late mediaeval Castilian history must derive, in great part, from historians associated with the University of Valladolid. LUIS SUÁREZ FERNÁNDEZ, *Nobleza y monarquía*, 2nd edn (Valladolid, 1975) revises and restates some guiding themes; the same author's *Historia de España antigua y media* (2 vols, Madrid, 1976), vol. II, provides a

Of its nature, the problem was not one which could be directly acknowledged. But its pressure is evident in the writings of dynastically-minded historians, from Pero López de Ayala's denigration of King Pedro to the ideological regalism of certain mid fifteenth-century authors.[2] The practical attempts of the Trastámara kings to establish a secure foundation for their authority met with more varied success. Their nadir was reached in the mid 1380s, when Juan I, badly shaken by a military defeat in Portugal, in which his English dynastic rival had an ominous hand, had to turn in some anxiety to the *Cortes* for urgently needed political as well as financial support. But his deference to this assembly of the estates was short-lived; they never, in fact, achieved that right to redress of grievances prior to taxation which seemed so tantalizingly within their grasp. Nor did they manage to establish, as they were briefly promised, a permanent delegation of their own within the royal Council. Instead, the *Consejo,* its noble and ecclesiastical membership reinforced by trained lawyers in the royal employ, secured a place as a rival, and much more effective centre of policy-making. Alongside it, Juan I also developed the *Audiencia* —again the province of specialist *letrados*— as a supreme tribunal of civil appeal.[3] These institutional advances were accompanied by the eclipse of the dynastic threat from England, disengagement from the Portuguese war, and a successful policy of monetary deflation. The *Cortes,* meanwhile, began its long decline into ineffectuality, with a shrinking membership and a receding autonomy, leaving the rulers of Castile to face, without an effective buffer, the real rivals to their power.

These were the nobility, a group whose membership and circumstances both undergo decisive changes in precisely that period which we are now considering.[4] Some of these changes are merely fortuitous; it so

---

similarly updated narrative. JULIO VALDEÓN BARUQUE, *Enrique II de Castilla* (Valladolid, 1966), SUÁREZ FERNÁNDEZ, *Juan I, rey de Castilla* (Madrid, 1955), *Historia del reinado de Juan I de Castilla,* vol. I (Madrid, 1977), and EMILIO MITRE FERNÁNDEZ, *Evolución de la nobleza en Castilla bajo Enrique III* (Valladolid, 1968) offer differing but complementary emphases. Of works in English, P. E. RUSSELL, *The English Intervention in Spain and Portugal in the Time of Edward III and Richard II* (Oxford, 1955) is important for the early period; two recent works of synthesis are J. N. HILLGARTH, *The Spanish Kingdoms 1250-1516* (2 vols, Oxford, 1976-8) and ANGUS MACKAY, *Spain in the Middle Ages. From Frontier to Empire* (London, 1977). All these influences, especially the last, will be apparent in this chapter.

[2] See ROBERT BRIAN TATE, *Ensayos sobre la historiografía peninsular del siglo XV* (Madrid, 1970), esp. pp. 121-2.

[3] SUÁREZ FERNÁNDEZ, *Historia de Juan I,* pp. 337-45. The beginnings of this administrative strategy belong to the previous reign; see VALDEÓN BARUQUE, *Enrique II,* pp. 351-63.

[4] SUÁREZ FERNÁNDEZ, *Nobleza y monarquía,* pp. 21-97 and MITRE FERNÁNDEZ, passim may be supplemented by SALVADOR DE MOXÓ, 'De la nobleza vieja a la nobleza nueva. La transformación nobiliaria castellana en la baja Edad Media',

happens that a great number of ancient families die out around this time. Others have an economic basis; like other areas of Europe, Castile had suffered an inflationary crisis in the half-century following the Black Death, and families which had lived, substantially, off the labour and rents of the peasantry had to look to other sources of income. They found these in the form of various dues and exactions, some of them matters of seigneurial right, others usurped from the Crown or from local municipalities. But they found them above all in the most potent of all the agencies which were currently reshaping the Castilian aristocracy —in the grant of *mercedes* by the Trastámara kings as an incentive or a reward for political allegiance. This had been, notoriously, the practice of Enrique II, Pedro's rival, and much as he might wish these donations undone, he could not cancel as king the gifts and promises he had made as pretender. Nor could his successors, Juan I and Enrique III, reverse the tide. As the latter's troubled minority drew to a close, it became clear that, rather contrary to probability, the dangerous if tiny group of magnates linked to the monarch by actual kinship had died out. But the other recipients of the *mercedes enriqueñas* were, just as clearly, the new aristocracy of the land. Their holdings reinforced by the younger Enrique, they were in a position to consolidate or diversify their territorial domains by marriage, negotiation, purchase or war; they could draw cash from the royal tax-revenues, conceded or usurped; they could found entails which would keep these concentrations of wealth within their families; they were beginning to dominate, and to regard as similar appanages the major offices of the king's court and household, as well as the crucial military and territorial commands.

The reshaping of the aristocratic estate along these lines was inherently not a peaceable or a stable phenomenon. The central problem, therefore, for the Trastámara kings was an especially complex one. They had to arrive at an adjustment, satisfactory to themselves, with a menacingly thrustful and assertive sector of society whose members were perpetually at odds with one another. Not surprisingly, they often appear to have missed the wood for the trees, attacking the short-term task of taming this or that noble faction, but postponing or ignoring the more elusive issue of how to cope with a factious nobility as such. That issue was a real one, none the less, and it presented itself to such a king as Juan II —the legatee, from 1406 onwards, of the process which we have been discussing— in two complementary contexts. One was that of the king's traditional obligation to seek counsel; the other involved his various options for direct political action.

It is obvious enough that the two belong together; the counsel which

in *C Hist*, 3 (Madrid, 1969), 1-210, and 'La nobleza castellana en el siglo XIV', *AEM*, 7 (1970-1), 493-511. See also MACKAY, *Spain*, pp. 174-6.

the king sought related to matters of policy, and the institutions from which he sought it —*Cortes* and *Consejo*— saw themselves as having a policy-making role. The former still recalled the ancient principle that high and difficult matters *(ardua negotia)* demanded the widest possible consultation.[5] But by the 1420s, if not before, the *Cortes* was no longer in any state to furnish this.[6] Increasingly by-passed by both clergy and nobility, who had more effectual avenues of access to the king, its representation of the third estate had dwindled to fewer than a score of municipalities. This inadequate constituency was narrowed yet further in practice as these towns, though still legally within the royal domain, fell under the *de facto* control of local magnates. As a counter-strategy the Crown began to pay delegates to *Cortes* their expenses; before long it would be heavily involved in their nomination. Above all, the *Cortes* was not and never had been a continuing institution. Without a standing delegation in the Royal Council —and that prize, though briefly dangled before them again in the early 1420s, was more elusive than ever— the *Cortes* delegates could hope for no influence over the developing line of royal policy. It was the *Consejo* which had continuity.

And within the *Consejo* the third estate as such had no representative place. «Dukes, Counts, prelates, noblemen, knights», together with the Doctors of Laws who staffed the senior levels of royal administration —these were the men who supplied the king with day-to-day advice on government. Such a body, no doubt, could meet the traditional requirement of *consilium*— «because it is alleged that we undertake things as projects of our own, and without taking counsel, which is not the case». It could do so if only because virtually any form of consultation could be made to qualify.[7] If the *Consejo* was qualified in any more special sense, this was only partly to do with the training and experience of its

---

[5] WLADIMIRO PISKORSKI, *Las Cortes de Castilla, 1188-1520* (Barcelona, 1930), p. 106; cf. GAINES POST, *Studies in Medieval Legal Thought* (Princeton, 1964), p. 375.

[6] On the decline of the *Cortes* see PISKORSKI, pp. 36-9, 45; also VALDEÓN BARUQUE, «Las cortes castellanas en el siglo XIV», *AEM*, 7 (1970-1), 634-5, 640, and «Las cortes de Castilla y las luchas políticas del siglo XV», *AEM*, 3 (1966), 293-326. BARTOLOMÉ CLAVERO, «Notas sobre el derecho territorial castellano, 1367-1445», *HID*, 3 (1976), 149-50, insists that the meetings of town-delegates alone, which typified Juan II's reign, were mere «assemblies», not *Cortes*. The distinction is in some respects defensible, but it has not proved relevant to most of what follows here. On *Cortes* and *Consejo* in the 1420s see SUÁREZ FERNÁNDEZ, *Historia*, vol. II, pp. 489-90.

[7] For the definition of Council membership quoted see JOSÉ LUIS MARTÍN, *La Península en la Edad Media* (Barcelona, 1976), p. 721. Cf. Juan I's denial of acting without counsel (*Cortes* of Valladolid, 1385, in *Cortes (LC)*, vol. II, p. 333). On *consilium* generally see POST, pp. 273-4; on its theory and practice in 15th-century Castile, MACKAY, *Spain*, pp. 156-7; on the *Consejo* itself, DAVID TORRES SANZ, *La administración central castellana en la baja Edad Media* (Valladolid, 1982), pp. 181-211.

members. Their backgrounds —military, legal, administrative— were certainly relevant both to the routine business which the Council was competent to transact on its own, and to the larger matters on which it advised the king. But the real importance of the *Consejo* as a body was that it enabled the king to carry on a process of consultation, not indeed with his kingdom at large, but with the dominant interests within it.

In selecting the membership of the *Consejo,* then, he was both defining these interests as he saw them, and taking the first steps in his strategy for handling them. In broad terms, two choices lay open to him. He could, in the first place, take the balance of forces among the major noble families more or less as it stood, and select his Council with that in mind. Naturally the *letrados* and royal officials would have a place there, but noblemen and upper clergy would predominate, and within this group those families which enjoyed *de facto* power would be most likely to be represented. In developing policies, distributing *mercedes,* and resolving lawsuits, such a Council would tend to reinforce that pattern of dynastic advantage among the nobility which was reflected in its composition. Favoured clients and junior relatives of the leading magnates, or of the monarch himself, would be allowed advancement, but always within this predefined *status quo.* Theoretically, this strategy would lead to uncontentious policies and domestic peace; in practice, as often as not, it meant that the ambitions of noble families not initially favoured were furthered by actions beyond the law. These would culminate in the use of armed force, and would continue, if successful, until the new balance of power won recognition in a reconstituted *Consejo.* But whether or not the outcome tended towards stability, the role of the Crown in this model was inherently limited and passive. The king who set himself merely to respond to the dominant pattern of interests might learn to live with the ambitions of his ebullient nobility, but his degree of control over them was unlikely to increase.

The other possible strategy arose when the king discerned and sought to further a distinctive interest of his own. In that case, he was unlikely to acquiesce in whatever choice of advisers the current state of power-politics might dictate. Rather, he would select as official or unofficial counsellors those who seemed closest to his own mind. Thus new men and new lineages appeared in the *Consejo,* while established magnates found themselves excluded or ignored. By contrast, the importance of the *letrados* was much increased; directly dependent on the king, these members gave the Council both its continuity of practices and its day-to-day responsiveness to the royal purpose. But they were less likely to take the lead in actual policy-making than were figures of another kind: noblemen, perhaps of secondary rank, but personally close to the king and commanding his confidence. From this situation of *privanza* comes the Spanish term *privado,* at once more neutral and more accurate than the English «favourite». But the general run of the nobility were bound to see this style of government as the product of a capricious indulgence of royal preference. For it led inevitably to policies in which they were almost certain to discern a threat to their own position. It was not simply that the royal interest, thus articulated, might clash directly with that of one set of magnates or another, breaking up the larger concentrations of power, withholding or reclaiming *mercedes,* meeting extra-legal depredations by force. There was also a tendency to strengthen the institutional supports of the Crown —the appeal-courts, for example, or the fiscal system— in ways which implied a redefinition of what the magnates as a body might expect from the monarch, and *vice-versa.* This was bound to promote a sense of disturbance, and eventually to provoke resistance. There was, of course, no question of the nobility being displaced from their predominant role in Castilian society; the objective state of that society offered no means by which this end could be furthered, nor did the cultural formation of Castilian kings allow them even to envisage it. What was very much in dispute, on the other hand, was the nature of the constitutional relationship between the nation's rulers and its dominant social estate.

In matters of counsel and policy, then, the king might adopt a largely acquiescent approach to existing political realities among the nobles, or he might exercise a larger measure of choice and initiative on his own behalf. The former option did not guarantee stability; the latter made conflict certain, but held out the hope of a royal power better adapted to handling these crises. During the adult reign of Juan II, from 1419 onwards, the tension between these alternatives was focussed about the figure of the great *privado,* Alvaro de Luna. The detailed story, complicated as it is by the shifting fortunes and alliances of a whole supporting cast of magnates and their clients, makes for a long and, it must be admitted, extremely tedious account. It will not be necessary here to do more than summarize its main phases.[8]

We may begin with the pattern of established interests confronting Juan II as he reached his majority. Two phenomena were of importance to this. One was the group of lineages constituting the new nobility, whose fortunes had been consolidated through the *mercedes* of the past half century. The other was the family of Juan II's uncle and one-time Regent, the late King Fernando I of Aragon. Fernando's successful generalship on the Andalusian frontier and his shrewd political manage-

---

[8] The narrative is given most succinctly by SUÁREZ FERNÁNDEZ, *Historia,* vol. II, pp. 489-527; more fully in the same author's contribution to *Historia de España,* ed. Ramón Menéndez Pidal, vol. XV (Madrid, 1964).

ment had not only secured the crown of Aragon for himself and his line; they had enabled him to build up massive interests and appanages in Castile itself for his three younger sons. It was their intention, supported by Fernando's heir Alfonso V of Aragon, that the young Castilian ruler should respond first and foremost to their place in the existing patterns of power. And so, for a time, he might have been constrained to do, but for two disruptive factors: rivalry between the brothers, and the initiative of his gentleman-in-waiting, Alvaro de Luna. In the course of the 1420s, Don Alvaro first exploited the divisions between the Infantes of Aragon, then rallied a faction of his own against them, and finally turned that opposition into a national defiance of intervention from beyond the borders. At the same time, he succeeded in establishing his own *privanza* as the central political fact of Castilian life. It was not a smoothly uniform rise to ascendancy; on one occasion, in 1427, he was actually excluded from the Court, only to be recalled within months, when it became clear that nothing could be made to work without him. But all the time he was laying the foundations of his power —the titles and *mercedes,* the office of Constable, the alliances with individual magnates, the capacity to make or break royal officials. The war with Aragon and Navarre to which his policies led in 1429-30 was inconclusive, but for Don Alvaro the major prize was to have isolated the Infantes already from significant support within the kingdom. The spectacular military expedition into the Valley of Granada which followed in 1431 was almost a formal celebration of Castile's newly-forged unity.

Yet the forging was, in several respects, as fragile as it was recent. The military emergency of 1429 had been a financial emergency too; the Crown had met it with a tactical debasement of alloy coinage, and consequent devaluation of the money of account.[9] A sequence of political arrests, and of plots suspected or revealed gave expression to the mutual suspicions which still divided the *privado* and the magnates. Even the triumphal progress of the Granadine foray was shadowed by a *cause célèbre* of this kind in the headquarters city of Córdoba.[10] Nor were these merely temporary shortcomings. If any period of Don Alvaro's ascendancy warrants description in terms of a «system of government», it must surely be the years 1431-38, when with the Infantes either absent or quiescent, he was in a position to order the kingdom as he saw fit,

---

[9] ANGUS MACKAY, «Las alteraciones monetarias en la Castilla del siglo XV: la moneda de cuenta y la historia política», in *En la España medieval: Estudios dedicados al profesor D. Julio González González* (Madrid, 1980), p. 245. For this and other details of monetary history, I am grateful to Dr. MacKay for permission to consult and quote, while it was still in typescript, his study *Money, Prices and Politics in Fifteenth-Century Castile* (London, 1981).

[10] The case of Egas Venegas of Córdoba (*CJII* (CODOIN), 100, pp. 274-5; *CJII* (R), pp. 494-5; *CHalc*, p. 92; *Ref Halc*, p. 115) offers a good example of Don Alvaro's security methods in action.

in the royal interest and in his own. The effects were, perhaps, less dramatic than might have been expected. There were certainly some notable achievements in foreign policy in these years. The diplomatic and commercial conditions of trade with northern Europe improved as a result; so did the flow of booty and tribute from the Granada frontier, where Castilian military pressure was, on the whole, well-sustained. But despite these profitable undertakings, the downward drift in value of the *maravedí* continued, albeit in a controlled fashion. In domestic affairs, there were a number of reforming ordinances, though they scarcely add up to a general overhaul of institutions. It is hard to evaluate the many further reforming petitions emanating from the *Cortes*. The anti-seigneurial tone of some suggests that the assembly, which was summoned fairly regularly during these years, may have been amenable to Don Alvaro's political management. Even so, the delegates also found a good deal to complain of in the way the royal administration was working. The protestations of disaffected magnates later in the decade imply that on balance, and despite these reservations, the years of Don Alvaro's ascendancy did witness a certain tightening of royal control. But this was still having to be maintained in some part by extraordinary security measures; it was evident that Don Alvaro still did not trust the magnates, nor they him. His pre-emptive arrest, in August 1437, of the head of the great Manrique clan was a major blunder; the ever-widening feud which it triggered was to end by putting his whole regime in jeopardy.

Those who, in the next few years, ranged themselves against Alvaro de Luna included most of the greater nobility not directly tied to him by marriage-alliance or by clientage. At their head stood the Infantes of Aragon, whom he had most unwisely recalled to act as a third force in the situation. A further adversary soon emerged in the person of Juan II's teenage heir, Prince Enrique, whom the prospect of a marriage with his cousin Blanca of Navarre, and the attractions of independent action, had won over to a provisional alliance with the rebels. The coalition had two aims: to end Don Alvaro's personal sway over the king, and to end his domination of the kingdom. That the former ascendancy was the bedrock of the latter they understood well enough; their difficulty lay in comprehending the nature of Luna's *privanza* in itself. There were sinister rumours that he held the king bewitched, or even that he might be his sexual partner.[11] Both suspicions, insofar as they were not mere propaganda, implied the domination of a weak personality by a stronger one. Let Luna be removed, therefore, and replaced by sound advisers, and the problem, so the rebels assumed, would solve itself. Thus, when they secured an upper hand, first in negotiations at Castronuño late in 1439, and then in armed conflict at Me-

---

[11] *C Halc*, pp. 331-2.

dina del Campo in May of 1441, their immediate demand was for Don Alvaro to be expelled from the Court. His second and third exiles on his estates are the result of these demands. But the rebels, their vision perhaps limited by their sense of their own role in the state, failed to grasp the political dimension inherent in the Constable's personal *privanza*. Thus, following the sentence of Castronuño, the king was still able to isolate himself at the head of a small group of Luna partisans, many of them permanent officials. These men could see to it that policies remained consistent, and could keep open Juan II's lines of communication with his *privado* until the turn of events allowed the latter to reappear. The capture of King Juan at Medina gave the rebels a second chance, and their prompt exclusion of a number of officials showed that they had learned a little from past experience. Not that the major figures of Don Alvaro's administration could be kept away for long; all the signs are that it proved impracticable to carry on government business without them.[12] But the Constable himself, this time, was condemned to a six-year exile. A new *Consejo*, of fixed membership and strongly aristocratic bias, was installed; there were determined attempts to hold the currency stable. At the heart of this programme there was to be a curtailment of the king's own powers; he was made virtually the puppet of a regency whose dominant figures were to be the Infantes of Aragon.

These were desperate remedies; their underlying assumption was that if the king would not depart voluntarily from Alvaro de Luna's pattern of government —to which, in the rebels' own theory, he had been constrained— then he must be constrained again. Knowing that their coalition embodied the greater part of the noble estate, the Infantes had no doubt of their entitlement to put pressure on the king. Nor could their ability to control the sources of formal *consilium* be doubted; apart from the closed *Consejo*, they could manage a *Cortes* no less effectively than Don Alvaro's regime had done. But the longer any power-bloc dominated the making of royal policy, and the larger that bloc was, the more apt it was to make enemies among its own supporters. Where demands were being made by all, some were bound to go unsatisfied. Such discontents, when they arose, could all too easily unite about the issue of the Infantes' style of government. To constrain the king in a tactlessly pressing way was to create a natural rallying point for opposition —the restoration of the king's full liberty. Time, therefore, was not on the side of the Infantes. When King Juan of Navarre, the senior of the brothers, put his cousin and namesake under close arrest

---

[12] *C Halc*, p. 419 records the exclusion of all royal officials «both great and small». But salaries were still paid, and several officials were back at their posts within weeks (see the documents in *CJII* (R), pp. 587-606).

in the summer of 1443, it was the signal for a chain-reaction of political intrigue. The crucial link was forged when the Crown Prince reached an understanding with the exiled Constable. Juan II was able to escape from his captors in something less than a year; by the spring of 1445 he was leading a grand coalition of magnates, Crown Prince and Constable against the Infantes and their remaining supporters. On the field of Olmedo in mid May, the most decisive victory of the fifteenth-century civil wars was won. The younger Infante, Enrique Master of Santiago, died of wounds. Juan of Navarre fled the country. The interregnum in Don Alvaro's power was at an end.

But this was to be no return to the relative stability of the 1430s. True, the total victory was a rare prize. So was the Mastership of Santiago; the revenues of the Order, which Don Alvaro had enjoyed by default during the Infante's periods of exile, were now to be his right. But like the victors of 1441, he owed his victory to a coalition so amorphous as to present a problem in itself; bluntly, he owed too much to too many people. In particular the Crown Prince, his aspirations astutely guided by a *privado* of his own, Juan Pacheco, Marquis of Villena, was determined to make his presence felt as an independent power in the land. By 1446 elaborate negotiations were needed to disentangle the interests of the Luna-Juan II faction from those of the Pacheco-Prince Enrique grouping. There was also a problem of more literal indebtedness. The turmoil preceding Olmedo had been disruptive, the campaign itself a costly one. The *Cortes* held at Valladolid in 1447 was unusually articulate and indocile; its record bristles with querulous petitions. Supplies were voted and embarrassments averted in the end; they always were. But the *Cortes'*, message came over clearly: the land was inadequately governed; altogether too much of the revenues and the power had fallen into the hands of the insubordinate nobility, and there could be no question of making good these losses out of the regular taxes.[13] Since the magnates who were disrupting the governmental and fiscal system were also, through their *mercedes,* its main beneficiaries, it was not perhaps misdirected that Don Alvaro should involve himself in new conflicts with them. He did so, none the less, with an unhelpful and perhaps desperate heavy-handedness. A clutch of arbitrary arrests (including those of several former close allies) gave the signal, in May 1448, for a bout of renewed civil strife.

That meant renewed expense, and the finances of the Crown were not healthy. It seems likely that tactical debasement was employed as a remedy, as it may also have been used in 1445, but this solution was by now beginning to be part of the problem. Don Alvaro's personal fortune, of course, was immense. But neither he nor the king could have

---

[13] *Cortes (LC),* vol. III, pp. 496-503.

expected to have to meet quite the multiplicity of crises which now demanded their involvement. There were insurrections of the nobility, of course; that much was predictable, though the range of them, from Murcia to León, was alarmingly wide. There was a sequence of reverses along the Granadine frontier; there was a new Navarrese invasion; there was an especially ugly popular rising in Toledo, aimed partly at the Constable and partly at New Christian converts from Judaism. The same few years saw the eclipse in Portugal of that faction on which Don Alvaro had up to now depended for a good deal of external support. Taken together, these events made it seem unlikely that his power would outlast the decade. That it did so was due to three factors. The first was the decision of Pacheco (and hence of the Crown Prince) that it would be to their advantage to take some of the pressure off the Constable; to overthrow him now would be to inherit his problems. The second factor was Don Alvaro's own formidable energy and resource, not least in fomenting unrest in Juan of Navarre's kingdom, to the immediate relief of Castile's eastern frontier. The third element in enabling him to take a grip of the situation once more was Juan II's unswerving commitment to his *privado;* in this sense, Don Alvaro's government survived because it was almost inconceivable that there should be any other. Certainly it is hard to discern in his post-Olmedo rule any other line of policy than that of coping with emergencies by the most effective means at his disposal, or any achievement beyond the feat of mere survival. But at least by 1451 or 1452 his survival in power was scarcely in question any more. Then came the sudden withdrawal of royal favour, the arrest, the execution.

The splendours and miseries of Don Alvaro's career, thus summarized, have qualities of dramatic contrast and suspense, but not much by way of coherence. The modern historian, especially if his first interest is in underlying patterns of social development, is bound to feel a certain impatience with the whole story. Each turn of fortune implies merely a fresh distribution of *mercedes;* the nobility, with different faces, go on gaining all the time. Yet even in such accounts there is likely to be some positive judgment on Don Alvaro as a promoter of policies: «he sought to reinforce the power of the monarch, freeing him from the tutelage of the higher nobility.»[14] Such judgments are, in one sense, commonplace, in that any *privado* who knows what is good for him will try to act in his patron's interest. Are they, in the case of Alvaro de Luna, any more true than that? Did he, designedly and to some effect, «increase monarchical authority»?[15]

Any reply to this question has to relate, first and foremost, to Don

---

[14] MARTÍN, *La Península*, p. 721.
[15] HILLGARTH, vol. II, p. 307.

Alvaro's period of unchallenged ascendancy in the 1430s. The evidence of the preceding decade, when his main preoccupation was with gaining power, and of the post-Olmedo period, when the greater part of his energy was devoted to maintaining it, is bound to be less clear. As we have observed already, there are indicators in the 1430s which can be taken in either sense, but that same decade furnishes us with our main witness to Don Alvaro's reforming purpose. This is a long digression in praise of the Luna regime, inserted in Alvar García de Santa María's *Crónica de Juan II* for the year 1431. It may actually have been written in that very year; it cannot be much later than 1435, when Alvar García wrote what were to be the last chapters of his chronicle.[16] He was, of course, a salaried official historian and the element of panegyric in his account cannot be disregarded. But he does more than offer the Constable the kind of formal praises in which a member of the nobility would take pleasure —praise of his personal attributes and virtues, his family, his loyalty and signal services to the king. All this is present, of course, but essentially as a prelude to something else —an appreciative outline of Don Alvaro's administrative system. This too, perhaps, presents the ideal working of that system, rather than its less perfect reality. Even in that aspect, though, it tells us how Alvaro de Luna wanted his government to be perceived, and how some Castilians at least felt that such a régime ought to work. Where the *Crónica* enjoys independent support, we may fairly regard it as a reliable account of what Don Alvaro was trying to achieve.

The key to it all, in Alvar García's view, is the allocation of offices. Don Alvaro, he claims, did not sell these for gain, nor did he use the enormous patronage delegated to him by the king merely to advance clients of his own. Naturally there were some members of his extensive household who qualified for preferment, but other offices went to «other persons who were worthy to fill them». A particular group of examples, described by Alvar García in terms which strongly suggest some use of official documents, concerns taxgathering posts. By detaching these from the gift of the magnates, and linking them instead to the major tax-farms, Don Alvaro is said to have increased and stabilized the royal revenues. His habit of taking upon himself much of the business of government is presented as fulfilling Juan II's zeal for justice in his domains, but also as freeing the latter to indulge his love of sound, religious learning. Yet Alvar García is anxious to assure his readers that all was done constitutionally: «all matters connected with justice, or with the royal

---

[16] CODOIN, 100, pp. 302-11; the sections of most interest occupy pp. 308-11; discussed briefly by HILLGARTH, vol. II, pp. 309-10. For the date of composition see FRANCISCO CANTERA BURGOS, *Alvar García de Santa María* (Madrid, 1952), pp. 124-6.

finances, or with anything else, went through the Council.» This body, he explains, was divided into two sections, one dealing with grants and instructions, the other with matters of justice. Business of the former type was scrutinized by two veteran *letrados* of total integrity, Doctors Periáñez and Diego Rodríguez, on whose reports the Constable unquestioningly relied. They were associated in their work with the *contador mayor*, Fernán López de Saldaña, «the Constable's man and, at his behest, a member of the Council». The executive, as contrasted with the deliberative, functions of government were supervised by a more remarkable figure than any of these —the Relator, Doctor Fernán Díaz de Toledo. There follows a fulsome account of his prodigious industry, his total lack of venality, and his involvement in every level of business from special commissions of justice to the validation of royal letters. «For», Alvar García concludes, «with the above-mentioned Doctors to organize and advise on business, and this latter Doctor to put it into execution, the Constable did his utmost to give the king a good account of the great trust which he placed in him.»

The governmental tradition which is being rejected here was evidently in the habit of filling vacant positions by a combination of noble patronage and some form of sale of office. This practice, of course, was perfectly compatible with a close and literal adherence to established norms of procedure. By contrast, the system favoured by Don Alvaro is represented as relying on selection —the most suitable person is picked out, given full control over this or that sphere of government, and expected to carry out the work effectively. The specific institutional reforms mentioned by Alvar García are relatively minor, but there can be little doubt that, in this model of government, traditional procedures counted for less than efficiency and personal style. Thus the part played by each of these trusted subordinates in his own office parallels the role of the *privado* himself in furnishing the king with more directly political *consilium*. If the picture offered by Alvar García is accurate, Don Alvaro did not —or did not only— impose his arbitrary personal will on the government of Castile; he also imprinted upon it, as a more basic contribution altogether, his own personal manner of ruling.

One striking feature of Alvar García's account is that it is not at all a political anatomy of the Luna regime. The *Consejo secreto* —the essential vehicle of Don Alvaro's political counsel to his master— is not mentioned here.[17] Nor does the chronicler, in this passage, add much to our understanding of Don Alvaro's manipulation of interest-groups among

---

[17] See *C Halc*, p. 69 (Secret Council accepts truce with Aragon-Navarre, 1430); pp. 240-1 (regulations for its business, December 1436); p. 270 (Juan II denies Don Alvaro's domination but admits to summoning him to the *Consejo secreto* «in matters of great moment», 1439).

the nobiliy, through *mercedes,* alliances, intrigues, and main force. The chapter, after all, is about Don Alvaro's «great services» to the king, and it might have been harder to present these necessary parts of his system in such a light. For Alvar García, the areas in which Don Alvaro's methods actually strengthened the Crown were the control of *mercedes,* the fiscal system, justice, and office-holding. It remains to be seen what other support exists for these claims.

The first seems the hardest to justify. However thoroughly the «fechos de gracia e de expediente» might be vetted, the major problem about royal grants was that there were, and had been for at least sixty years, far too many of them. The Crown had enriched the new nobility at the cost of its own resources, and the concentrations of power thus created were constantly being deployed so as to extract yet more. The *Cortes* complained about this from time to time because it was the taxpayers of the third estate who came under pressure as the king's wealth declined. But for Don Alvaro at this stage in his career, *mercedes* were an essential instrument of policy, a means of securing and rewarding supporters. The most that can be claimed is that the policies were calculated, and that, on Alvar García's evidence, the general flow of royal outgoings was being systematically monitored. This is of a piece with other signs of an improvement in financial record-keeping in Castile at the time. We know from the *Cortes* of 1436 that the *contadores mayores* were carrying more chests of documents around with them than current business required, and that an archive of sorts for such papers existed in the *Casa de las Cuentas* in Valladolid. The registers of Simancas, though still fragmentary until the late 1440s, imply that already by that date, the *contadores* had developed a strict and thorough system of documentation; even Alvaro de Luna had to comply with it.[18] It seems at least possible that these practices began, or received some special impetus, during Don Alvaro's early ascendancy, with the labours of Periáñez and his colleague playing some part in this.

A stimulus to wider fiscal reforms was provided by the financial crisis of 1429. It seems too appropriate to be a mere coincidence that the earliest documents enabling us to reconstruct any kind of annual budget for Castile should date from that year. From then too, according to Ladero, dates a long memorandum to Juan II on all aspects of fiscal

---

[18] The archival problem of 1436 is in *Cortes (LC),* vol. III, p. 270; for the *contadores'* procedures see AGS, QdC, 1.10 and 1.284 (payments withheld because recorded in wrong tax-area); 1.345 (payment deferred pending enquiry into disputed surname); M y P, 1.778 (5th April, 1445: Alvaro de Luna, receiving a grant formerly enjoyed by the late queen, required first to show proof of her death, and to make his oath to the king). The royal edict of October 1433, limiting the salary and commission payable to officials is of a piece with these policies (MS Madrid, BN, 9427, fols. 1-30).

reform.[19] The suggestions put forward in this study include much curtailment of seigneurial power and a reduction in official hostility towards Jews as tax-farmers. Of special interest is the paragraph dealing with the unsatisfactory manner in which tax-collectors are appointed; its substance is exactly paralleled by what Alvar García has to say on the subject. But by 1431, it would seem, effective steps had been taken to put the matter right, for Alvar García is able to list this among the Constable's actual achievements. It is hard to avoid concluding that Don Alvaro had commissioned the original study, and that he was quick to act upon its findings. In both respects his concern to maximize the royal revenues would be very evident. Alvar García adds that he did indeed raise their level; in modern times, Ladero has concluded from his general study of royal finances that royal income rose substantially in the 1430s, thanks to Don Alvaro's purposive efforts. Alvar García, of course, was writing before the longer-term effects of Don Alvaro's debasement of the alloy coinage had become apparent; the resulting devaluation of the money of account meant that a higher total in *maravedís* could mask a fall in real value. Ladero, indeed, takes this point, but the shortage of data on real money values at the time means that his figures have to be regarded as provisional.[20] The more detailed studies of this question undertaken by Angus Mackay point authoritatively to a rather different conclusion. The nominal value of royal income rose; the real value fell. But it fell less sharply than the real value of the money of account. Thus, while everybody did badly, the Crown did less badly than those who received grants from it in devalued *maravedís*.

---

[19] MACKAY, «Las alteraciones», p. 245 (see also his account in *Money, Prices and Politics*) stresses the significance of the 1429 crisis. The reforming *Memorial* of that year (AGS, DdC, 4.35) is in MIGUEL ANGEL LADERO QUESADA, *La Hacienda Real de Castilla en el siglo XV* (La Laguna, 1973), pp. 328-45. See especially p. 335 (tax offices filled at request of magnates, who receive bribes out of taxes in return for these nominations; cf. ALVAR GARCÍA, *CJII* (CODOIN), 100, p. 308).

[20] LADERO QUESADA, *Hacienda*, p. 43 evaluates royal income in Castilian gold *doblas*, and indexes known totals, taking the 1429 figures as a base. MACKAY, *Money*, gives data permitting more accurate indices, in terms of Aragonese gold florins and —more relevantly still, since it can be compared with the devalued *maravedí*— of silver. Their figures for 1429, 1430 and 1444 can be summarized as follows.

	Gross royal income (maravedís)	Ladero's index (gold doblas)	MacKay's index (gold florins)	MacKay's index (silver)	Devaluation of maravedí (silver)
1429	60.8 millions	100	100	100	100
1430	57.6 millions	95	92	96.5	101
1444	73.6 millions	122	83.5	85.5	70.5

See also MACKAY, «Las alteraciones», pp. 247-8.
 Some of the increase in revenue may be due to a gradually rising population (but see below, n. 52).

Juan II, then, would have improved his position relative to those who drew their income from him. That, doubtless, was the differential on which Don Alvaro chiefly had his eye. To that extent there is some basis for saying that his fiscal policies strengthened the Crown. Because of the problems of debasement, and because of the continuing outflow of *mercedes*, it remains a fiscal achievement, rather than one of overall economic management. But there were to be periods later in the century when the Crown would learn by bitter experience the consequences of not achieving even that.

As these experiences would make very clear, fiscal effectiveness and the pursuit of royal justice went hand in hand. An impoverished Crown, weak where the magnates were strong, could not make its writ run in all parts of the kingdom; a monarch whose writ did not run could not collect his revenues. Alvar García's panegyric of Don Alvaro touches on the theme of justice in a largely incidental way, but it is perfectly clear what sort of general picture is being drawn. The *Crónica* mentions the king's great zeal for justice, the specialist role of one section of the Council, and the involvement in legal affairs of the incorruptible and vastly efficient Relator. The impression created is that the pattern of central institutions presided over by the Constable was fully adequate to the needs of the kingdom in this regard. Plainly it was important for the authority of the Crown that such an impression should be shared by the nation at large. But if we turn to the *Cortes* petitions of the 1430s, we shall find that the view was scarcely a universal one.[21] There is, for example, a running series of complaints about the *Audiencia* —an institution not mentioned by Alvar García at this point. These give the strong impression that the *Audiencia* itself was regarded as something well worth having, but that it was not felt to be working as well as it should be; it ought to be added, perhaps, that this is a fairly constant perspective in the *Cortes* records throughout the first century of the *Audiencia*'s existence. In general, only a minority of the complaints about the legal system allege outright misconduct in office; there is a greater concern with establishing procedures and securing regular attendance by properly paid judges. One or two reflect a suspicious response to the increasing professionalism within the legal system. The Relator, for example, was several times reproached for his habit of presenting petitions to the *Consejo* in summary form. But when the *Cortes* delegates

---

[21] For the following see *Cortes (LC)*, vol. III: location and staffing of *Audiencia*, p. 117 (Zamora, 1432), etc; bribery of magistrates, p. 183 (Madrid, 1433); summonses improperly issued by *Audiencia* judges, pp. 300-2 (Toledo, 1436), 331-2 (Madrigal, 1438); *Audiencia* judges working for private patrons or as advocates, pp. 299-300, 302-3 (Toledo, 1436); absenteeism in *Audiencia*, pp. 304 (Toledo, 1436), 334-5 (Madrigal, 1438); simplifying Chancery procedures, pp. 332-4 (Madrigal, 1438); *Consejo* petitions, pp. 265 (Toledo, 1436), and 325-6 (Madrigal, 1438); against subtleties of law, p. 303 (Toledo, 1436).

wanted a commission set up to simplify the confusions created by «subtleties of law», it was to the Relator's close colleagues Periáñez and Diego Rodríguez that they turned. From all of which one might conclude that the third estate had some confidence in the system, but had reservations about its working.

Most people's experience of justice, however, was at the more basic level of day-to-day personal security. A comment of great interest in this connection is that of the falconer-chronicler Pero Carrillo de Huete: «the kingdom was in such tranquility that no-one, great or small, dared to rob, or if he did, it was immediately remedied with justice.»[22] Carrillo, though anything but partisan, was a close personal dependent of the king, and he was writing about the year 1434 —perhaps the most tranquil of Don Alvaro's rule. But his testimony, however we may hedge it about, is still striking. Even if true only in part, it would mean that large numbers of Castilians derived some benefit from Don Alvaro's enforcement of royal authority. Those who benefited least would be those who lived under seigneurial jurisdiction —a sector of society whose numbers had greatly increased over the past couple of generations as a result of territorial and other *mercedes*. Like the other rights which could be granted, the right of local jurisdiction was open to abuse for profit, but as long as the proprietor's title was a genuine one, there was little his oppressed vassals could do about it. Petitions to the Crown, though notionally in order, rarely produced action; rebellions were quickly put down.[23] On such matters the monarch and those who believed in a reinforcement of his power were at one with the rest of the noble estate; there is no sign that Alvaro de Luna, in his zeal for royal authority, ever concerned himself particularly with the victims of seigneurial abuse. Where a territorial lord usurped some area of royal or other jurisdiction without benefit of *merced,* the case was different, and the Crown would intervene if it could; there are *Cortes* petitions of the 1430s which imply some hope of action on such matters.[24] Against the more blatant attempts by magnates to set themselves and their protegés above the law, the Crown, in its own interests, had to react vigorously, and there is clear evidence that it was Don Alvaro's policy to do so. Alvar García gives several examples from the years when the Constable was consolidating his power. The most notable case is that of the Salamanca malefactor

---

[22] *C Halc*, p. 176; see the discussion in HILLGARTH, vol. II, p. 309.
[23] See VALDEÓN BARUQUE, *Los conflictos sociales en el reino de Castilla en los siglos XIV y XV*, 2nd edn. (Madrid, 1976), pp. 140-74. The family of Alvaro de Luna's second wife, Juana Pimentel, had a notoriously bad record of seigneurial abuses, dating from the previous generation (pp. 118-24).
[24] *Cortes (LC)*, vol. III, passim, e.g. pp. 148-9 on enforced vassallage of migrants to seigneurial lands (Zamora, 1432); p. 223, on abuses against municipalities (Madrid, 1435); p. 316 on the same (Madrigal, 1438). HILLGARTH, vol. II, p. 307 notes Don Alvaro's use of *corregidores* to remedy local abuses.

Martín de Rueda, rescued from the gallows by his noble protectors, and condemned a second time after a retrial. The fact that the offending magnates here were the Count of Castro and Juan of Navarre himself confirms the seriousness with which this aspect of royal policy was pursued. Alvar García draws the political consequence with his usual clearsightedness: «At this, some of the magnates who were at the Court were even more affronted, and banded themselves together against the Constable, for they realized that he was encouraging the king to do justice, which did not please them.»[25]

Alvar García states that Don Alvaro, unlike other *privados*, took no reward for preferment to offices. A few years later, the Constable's adversaries were to claim that he did, though the allegation, relating specifically to legal offices, may be no more than a rhetorical topic of «justice denied». A more significant disagreement arises over the calibre of Don Alvaro's appointments generally. For Alvar García, they resulted in an improvement in the quality of the royal service; the dissident magnates of 1441 saw only «new men, insufficiently worthy, not Castilians».[26] It is, in fact, hard to find significant numbers of foreigners on the royal payroll, though Don Alvaro's own eventual background was Aragonese. If the reference is not to the exotic and comparatively small company of *caballeros moriscos,* it is tempting to see it as evidence of an early prejudice against *conversos* of Jewish descent. But the phrase used for Castilian nationality here is «naturales destos reynos», which admits of no such exception; *conversos,* Jews, and Moors alike, if born in Castile and not subsequently expelled, were always that. The charge, though repeated several times in propagandistic texts of the period, remains wholly enigmatic. The question of personal adequacy for office was perhaps a subjective one. But the accusation that the Constable brought «new men» into the royal service is, in itself, perfectly compatible with Alvar García's account. The note of controversy arises from the very different view which Don Alvaro's enemies took of it.

The trouble with «new men» was twofold. Where the offices in question were, as in the passage under discussion, those of the king's «chamber and household», such appointments were seen as infringing the monopoly which the upper nobility felt to be theirs by right. But Don Alvaro does not, in fact, seem to have made far-reaching changes of this kind. The ceremonial «great offices», to many of which the leading

---

[25] *CJII* (CODOIN), 99, pp. 438-9; see also pp. 432-3 for an earlier instance of prompt action against a client of the powerful Enríquez family.

[26] LUCIANO SERRANO, *Los conversos D. Pablo de Santa María y D. Alfonso de Cartagena* (Madrid, 1942), p. 291. The entire document, a manifesto issued by Juan of Navarre and his partisans at Arévalo in January 1441, is of great interest (pp. 289-303). For the *caballeros moriscos* recruited from the early 1430s, and numbering about a hundred by the 1450s, see AGS, QdC, 1.17-73.

families of the Trastámara nobility had by now established a quasi-hereditary claim, remained with them for the most part. So too, incidentally, did the principal military commands.[27] A minor aristocrat, Fernán Alvarez de Toledo, rose rapidly to eminence, and to the title of Count of Alba de Tormes under Don Alvaro's sponsorship, but his was an exceptional case. The real complaint was that the Constable controlled access to the king's intimacy («el allegamiento e amor de su persona»). And here the more fundamental resentment against «new men» becomes apparent. Those who were present at Court because they had the Constable's favour, those who held less prestigious but more functional office because he had singled them out, were bound to him by ties of loyalty and gratitude: «men who were the Constable's, or became his for that reason», as the same complainants wrote regarding legal and fiscal posts. The accusation is repeated and amplified elsewhere, in one instance with startling and circumstantial detail: «And furthermore it is well-known that he has many blank copies of royal letters, signed with your name, to use for his own purposes and give all offices which fall vacant, by his own hand, to whoever he pleases.»[28]

This is not so much a contradiction of what Alvar García has to say about the filling of offices as the mirror-image of that account, seen, this time, from the perspective of the Constable's opponents. We may well believe that Don Alvaro, if he did not take payment in cash or kind, was rewarded for these acts of patronage in the currency which interested him most —effective control over what was done. For the outcome of this supremacy over appointments— perceived negatively as the tyrannical power of one man —was an administration with a certain homogeneity of commitment and purpose. Instead of reflecting a confused balance of the different claims and pressures on the king, with appointees beholden to a dozen secondary patrons, the service of the Crown became —or, at least, was now capable of becoming— a coherent vehicle for a single line of policy. The issue of blank nominations —a clear indication that Juan II approved this development— need not be taken as a sign of weakness. It may just as well be evidence that the king recognized, as his chronicler Alvar García did, the positive aspect of what was going on. The possibility that it might function, in the end, to his advantage but

---

[27] HILLGARTH, vol. I, p. 401. For the origins of office-holding patterns among the major *linajes* see MITRE FERNÁNDEZ, pp. 130-4; for the remarkably stable tenure of military commands see the tables of holders in ROGELIO PÉREZ-BUSTAMANTE, *El gobierno y la administración territorial de Castilla (1230-1474)* (Madrid, 1976), vol. I, pp. 241, 243, 292, etc.

[28] C Halc, p. 327, whose version (pp. 320-33) of these *capitulos* issued by the rebel coalition in March 1440 differs in several details (but not in this one) from that in CJII (R), pp. 560-2 (evidently revised after Don Alvaro's fall). Cf. also SERRANO, p. 292.

to the detriment of Don Alvaro had not, at this stage, occurred to anyone.

The disposition to see the administrative system as a whole, rather than as an accumulation of loosely-connected functions and functionaries, is apparent in several ways. Notable among them are the comprehensive set of ordinances on legal and other offices promulgated at Segovia in 1433 and the further series issued at Guadalajara three years later.[29] A strongly unifying factor of a different kind was the involvement of the Relator in the issue of royal documents of every sort. Fernán Díaz's ratification, though not in theory indispensable, became in practice the standard formula to indicate that a piece of business had passed through the proper channels. Ratification as such was, of course, no novelty, but this unique prominence of a single official must have done much internally to standardize procedures, and externally to present an image of the Crown's service as a unified undertaking. It was so perceived even by those who did not care for the results; when the rebels of 1440 were complaining that all the royal officials and *letrados* were of the Constable's party, the Relator was the one functionary who was mentioned as an individual.[30] The nature of the work which he and the other senior *doctores* undertook meant, among other things, that the king was constantly in their company —an inner circle to whose number the *contadores mayores* and a few junior secretaries should probably be added. Obviously it was to Alvaro de Luna's advantage that such figures should be well-disposed towards him; others would find this pernicious. But irrespective of either attitude, these «great servants» were —it was their job to be— possessed of an awareness of the overall governmental process: its scale, its shape, its complexities. It would be surprising if this did not, in the outcome, contribute to Juan II's own sense of what it was to be a king.

And it has to be said that Don Alvaro's patronage saw to it that these exacting positions were filled by some remarkable men. They and their subordinates, though seldom to the fore in the chronicles of the time, often turn out to have been characters of notable individuality and talent. But their collective achievement is perhaps best measured by the systematic body of public records which they left behind them, and still

---

[29] See the table of contents in *Leyes e hordenanças que fizo el señor Rey don Johan* (MS Madrid, BN 6720), fols 5r-v (Segovia ordinances, mostly on remuneration); 7v-8r (Guadalajara regulations of 15th December 1436). The latter were evidently felt to be important enough for inclusion in all three main chronicles of the reign (*C Halc*, pp. 236-45; *Ref Halc*, pp. 206-13; *CJII* (R), pp. 529-32).

[30] *C Halc*, p. 327, *CJII* (R), p. 561. For the importance of senior officials like Fernán Díaz see MacKay, *Spain*, pp. 155-6. Don Alvaro's own post of *notario mayor de Castilla* gave him a measure of official control over the filling of notarial offices (see Suárez Fernández, *Historia de Juan I*, p. 336).

more by the fact —related to that feat of record-keeping— that a viable administration survived the economic and political chaos of the 1460s. What the Catholic Monarchs were able to do with Castilian government was done with the government which Alvaro de Luna had made and staffed.

He did not, of course, discover or exploit for the first time the sources of recruitment which made this possible. The emergence of the university-trained *letrados* into the royal service belongs to a previous century, with Juan I's administrative reforms of the 1380s marking a crucial stage in the process. By the time of Juan II, both Castilian universities —always primarily legal academies— were well-attuned to the demand for qualified personnel. Had Alvaro de Luna wanted to keep the *letrados* out of government, he would have been too late to succeed; Periáñez's initial appointment, for example, certainly antedates Don Alvaro.[31] The Constable's real contribution lay in the new opportunities which his system created for these legally-trained functionaries with their primary loyalty to the Crown as employer. The moment was especially opportune for one group in particular —the many New Christian families who became eligible for university training with the flood of conversions following the great anti-Jewish pogroms of 1391.[32] Those able to embark on such careers were likely to come from families which already had a certain wealth and standing, and with this, in the tradition of the Jewish *aljamas,* a measure of cultural amplitude could also be assumed. Whether a particular respect for the study of law was carried over in any form from one religion to the other is altogether harder to determine. But we may be reasonably certain of one attitude which would be widely shared among *conversos* in this position. The mediaeval Castilian Jew had lived in a relationship which was partly one of exploitation, but also in part protective, with the Crown itself, or with some magnate to whom the Crown had conceded a given sector of its rights over the Jewries; the *converso* found himself, unprecedentedly, without any such

---

[31] He was already signing royal documents in 1398 *(Cortes (LC),* vol. III, p. 108). Alonso de Cartagena noted in the mid 1430s that Castilians with some education had the habit «ab ipsa antiquitate» of making their way at once to the royal court (ALEKSANDER BIRKENMAIER, «Der Streit des Alonso von Cartagena mit Leonardo Bruni Aretino», in *Beiträge zur Geschichte der Philosophie des Mittelalters,* 20, no. 5 (Münster, 1922), p. 163. BELTRÁN DE HEREDIA, *BUS,* vol. I, p. 244 points out that in Valladolid, study at the University could often be doubled with employment in the king's service.

[32] See YITZHAK BAER, *A History of the Jews in Christian Spain,* vol. II (Philadelphia, 1961), pp. 95-110; 272-5. The new-found eligibility of *conversos* for certain avenues of training and office-holding seems to me more pertinent here than alleged contrasts in disposition and capacity between *converso* and Old Christian; contrast, however, FRANCISCO MÁRQUEZ VILLANUEVA, «The converso problem: an assessment», in *Collected Studies in Honour of Américo Castro's Eightieth Year,* ed. Marcel P. Hornik (Oxford, 1965), p. 318.

link. It was a natural reaction to be conscious, to a degree unusual even in that society, of the need to win and to retain patronage. Trained and specialist service under the Crown supplied an especially satisfactory response to that need.

What proportion of royal officials were *conversos* we simply do not know; their number in the early fifteenth century was liable to be perceived as higher than it actually was, just because large numbers of *conversos* were appearing simultaneously for the first time.[33] But there were certainly notable examples —the Relator for one— among the officials preferred by Alvaro de Luna. Again, Don Alvaro was not the first to make such appointments; Pablo de Santa María of Burgos was Chancellor before the great *privado* ever appeared on the scene. But his concern for efficacious government by officials with no prior attachments except to himself and the Crown meant that he was notably free of prejudice in this matter; it was possible, later in Juan II's reign, for Don Alvaro's name to become linked in the public mind with the employment of *conversos*.[34] Given the natural tendency of families to fall into a common pattern of employment, the appointments of this kind for which he was responsible were to supply the royal service in Castile with a still more significant element of its later composition. They also helped to form its distinctive ethos. The bond between these *converso* families and the administrative service, their attachment to the king as patron, and their conscious desire for the strengthening of royal government were all reinforced, as the century advanced, and it became apparent how much the *conversos* had to lose.

To trace the connections between *letrados* and *conversos* in office and the cultural movement of Juan II's reign would carry us well beyond the immediate question of Alvaro de Luna's attempted reinforcement of royal authority. The Constable did play a personal part in that movement, but it can scarcely be set down as a direct product of his policies; if anybody's initiative counted here, it was that of the king. Yet the literary and scholarly activities carried on under Juan II's aegis by lawyers and officials, the more educated of the clergy, and an untypical minority of the noble estate, have in this context an unmistakably ideological aspect. The central ideal of the scholar-king relates in the first instance to the doctrine of Justinian's *Corpus* that the monarch must be eminent in both arms and laws, so that he may both rule in person and understand the activity of ruling. This was the teaching which Alvar García, as *Cortes* representative for Burgos, commended to Juan II

---

[33] CECIL ROTH, *The Spanish Inquisition* (New York, 1964), pp. 28-9; 32-4.
[34] The association is made repeatedly by Marcos García de Mazarambroz, spokesman and ideologue of the 1449 anti-*converso* revolt in Toledo (ELOY BENITO RUANO, *Los orígenes del problema converso* (Barcelona, 1976), pp. 103-32 passim, esp. p. 105).

in 1425.[35] The eventual delegation of government to Alvaro de Luna, while Juan spent his time in study, is less a denial than a displacement of this ideal, for it was the king's conscious intention to diffuse instruction among his subjects. And this was to be, above all, legal and ethical instruction *(sciencia moral);* they were to learn, by way of the culture promoted by the Crown, the nature of their duties to it, to one another, to themselves. This programme was bound to conflict with the outlook of most of those —the nobility— to whom it was chiefly addressed. In practice their notion of duties was different; in principle they regarded book-learning as unbecoming in men of their station. Thus the «arms and letters» debate and the minority status of Juan II's variety of high culture have ideological overtones too.[36] Apart from its roots in material self-interest, resentment against Don Alvaro's style of government may also have stemmed from the tendency of some of its supporters to appeal to a general theoretical framework which most magnates felt to be either beneath their dignity or above their heads.

Perhaps this ideology came nearest to their own concerns when it commended the war against Granada as a holy enterprise and an expression of unified national purpose. These claims —most fully expressed by a totally civilian figure, the scholar-poet and royal secretary Juan de Mena— made sense in terms of the nobility's military and doctrinal formation, as well as promising the kind of material advantages which interested them most. But the same outlook also served the short-term needs of the Luna regime for Granadine tribute and for something to keep the warrior estate occupied. In a less immediate perspective, too, they helped to redeem the Trastámara dynasty from any residual taint of imperfect legitimacy; kings who had a share in this providential mission must surely rule by the grace of God.[37] This aspect of Luna's

---

[35] *CJII* (CODOIN), 99, p. 354, referring, perhaps to *Institutes,* Proemium (see ERNST H. KANTOROWICZ, *The King's Two Bodies* (Princeton, 1957), p. 138n.) Some twenty years later, in Pero Díaz de Toledo's introduction to *Proverbios de Séneca,* we find the term *sciencia moral* used for ethical wisdom generally in a very clear exposition of Juan II's purposes as outlined here (MS Escorial, S II 10, fols 1r-3r).

[36] For some other implications see P. E. RUSSELL, «Arms versus Letters: towards a definition of Spanish fifteenth-century humanism», in *Aspects of the Renaissance: a Symposium,* ed. Archibald R. Lewis (Austin, 1967), pp. 45-58; also NICHOLAS G. ROUND, «Renaissance Culture and its Opponents in Fifteenth-Century Castile», *MLR,* 57 (1962), 204-15 and «Five Magicians, or the Uses of Literacy», *MLR,* 64 (1969), 793-805.

[37] See B. BEINERT, «La idea de cruzada y los intereses de los príncipes cristianos en el siglo XV», in *C Hist,* 1 (Madrid, 1967), pp. 57-8. Juan II's Granada campaign of 1431 is celebrated by Mena, *Laberinto de Fortuna* (1443), stanzas 147-53 (ed. Louise Vasvari Fainberg (Madrid, 1976), pp. 154-7); the frontier war is commended, perhaps contemporaneously with that campaign, in the *Dezir que fizo Juan Alfonso de Baena,* in JOSÉ MARÍA AZÁCETA, ed., *Cancionero de Baena* (Madrid, 1966), vol. III, 11. 875 ff., 1211-18, 1291-8, 1729-30, pp. 1190-3, 1202, 1205, 1220.

programme, again, was not an original one; Fernando of Antequera, the eventual king of Aragon and father of the troublesome Infantes, had built his reputation and his family fortunes on success in this area. Don Alvaro's own attempt on Granada in 1431 put that lesson into practice well before it received its full elaboration at the hands of literary propagandists. But we may take it that in this as in so much else he knew what he was doing.

A tightening of bureaucratic control and of the fiscal regime, an enterprising recruitment policy for the public service, and a coherent ideology all made for a certain ingathering of power about the persons of the king and his *privado*. Unmistakably Don Alvaro loved power and the sheer efficacy of power; when the veteran court-poet Villasandino, in a begging poem to Juan II, wanted to turn a neat compliment to the Constable, he could have hit on nothing more apt than this:

> Alvaro vuestro criado
> que mande que lo mandado
> por vos non sea dubdoso.[38]

But the paradox is also evident: had Don Alvaro affirmed his master's power beyond all doubt, or had he, in his own interest, turned the proper relationship of lord and vassal upside-down? Some of the means by which the efficacy of his arrangements was pursued and preserved were paradoxical too.

The ideal of royal justice presupposed a kingdom enjoying a certain stability. But one way of checking any opposition among the magnates was to keep them in a state of relative insecurity. Arrests on suspicion of plotting were one obvious technique, but this direct and sometimes pre-emptive police-work was supplemented in more devious ways. The rebels of 1441, in their manifesto of Arévalo, complained of Don Alvaro's manipulation of internal politics in these terms: «he formed many illicit leagues and alliances, some of them even directed against each other, in opposition to many people in these kingdoms, and the Crown Prince was a member of some of them.»[39] The hint of what a twentieth-century government would call «destabilization» rings credibly enough. What seems an altogether more far-fetched allegation in the same document turns out, after all, to have its own basis in fact. This is the claim that Don Alvaro disrupted the marriage plans of great and small alike to further his own dynastic ends. It looks like the clearest instance in the Arévalo document of a scandalous charge inserted for propaganda effect. Yet in 1442, Juan

---

[38] «Let Alvaro your servant order that what you have ordered should not be in doubt» (FOULCHÉ-DELBOSC, *CC*, vol. II, p. 422; see also pp. 404-15 for poetic petitions by Villasandino, addressed to Don Alvaro). See, too, INGRID BAHLER, *Alfonso Alvarez de Villasandino: poesía de petición* (Madrid, 1977).

[39] SERRANO, p. 295.

Pacheco, the Crown Prince's *privado,* was to secure a decree of nullity on the grounds that in 1436 —when he was still a mere nonentity at Court— he had been forced into a marriage with the Constable's cousin.[40] It is hard to imagine that Pacheco required much forcing while Don Alvaro's fortunes were still at their peak, but it remains remarkable that the latter should have concerned himself with so apparently marginal a figure. More disturbing charges altogether appear in another rebel document of 1440-1 —the blatantly propagandistic *Capítulos* sent to Juan II in March of the former year.[41] Apart from illegal appropriations and the violation of clerical privileges, this manifesto lists a series of murders and attempted murders, some carried out by Don Alvaro's orders, one of them at least the work of his own hand; some of this violence, it is alleged, actually occurred in the king's presence. The *Capítulos,* which also accuse Luna of introducing homosexuality to the Court, and of bewitching the king, are not, it is true, the most reliable of sources. Poisoning, alleged in one of these cases, was an offence of unique infamy, easy to allege and hard to disprove; the fact that another killing is said to have been carried out «under the guise of justice» suggests that it was possible to take a different view of at least some of these events. But it is much harder to dispose of the notion that Don Alvaro was willing, if the need arose, to use ruthless and arbitrary means to protect both his personal position and his system of rule. If such methods did help to safeguard the former, they could bring the latter into damaging disrepute.

In matters of this sort there can still be dispute as to the facts. Other manifest contradictions in Don Alvaro's methods are scarcely open to doubt. For example, the sensible division of labour within the *Consejo* described by Alvar García is by no means the whole of the story; even when supplemented by reference to the secret Council, it remains incomplete. Following a trend initiated by Juan II's regents, and accelerated by the Infante Enrique during his brief ascendancy in 1420, Alvaro de Luna adopted a policy of inflating the membership of the Council. Its numbers rose from 30 to 75 in a mere five years, and they continued to rise.[42] The effect of all these nominations was to rob membership of all its political significance; it quickly became a titular distinction, sometimes with salary rights attached. The arrangement had its advanta-

---

[40] PILAR LEÓN TELLO, *Inventario del Archivo de los Duques de Frías,* vol. II (Madrid, 1967), p. 27; cf. SERRANO, p. 294.

[41] *C Halc,* pp. 325-32, as follows: tax usurpations, p. 325; ecclesiastical abuses, p. 326; Count of Luna poisoned, p. 329; Sancho Fernández, *contador,* killed «so color de justicia», p. 330 (in fact, executed in Burgos, ibid., p. 63); other arranged killings, pp. 329-30; an esquire murdered, a servant beaten, in the king's presence, p. 332; homosexuality, p. 331; black magic, p. 332.

[42] CONDE DE TORREÁNAZ, *Los consejos del Rey durante la Edad Media,* vol. I (Madrid, 1884), pp. 159-60; 172-6.

geous side; it provided a wide-ranging consultative panel —especially of lawyers— on which king or *privado* could draw at need, and it allowed the latter to manage conciliar business, through his permanent officials, with much greater flexibility. But its main effect was to reduce the *Consejo*, the main formal channel of *consilium*, to a parallel level of impotence, though for very different reasons, to that of the ailing *Cortes*. The resulting vacuum would be filled by Don Alvaro himself and the men of his choice. Here, surely, his methods were those of personal rule, disrupting the very institution by which the Crown's position might best be fortified. Disconcertingly, it is only in 1440-2, when Don Alvaro's opponents —the supposedly anti-monarchical faction— have control, that detailed regulations are issued for a Council of fixed membership and procedures.[43]

There is a similar case to be made against him on the basis of his financial policies. Recent work by MacKay has made it possible to speak with more precision of the history of currency debasement in Castile at this time.[44] It seems clear that the alloy coinage was debased, and the money of account consequently devalued, as a deliberate response to the financial crisis of 1429. This is precisely the stage at which Don Alvaro's control over the kingdom was first fully established; the practice of debasement seems to have continued until 1441, when the anti-Luna faction took power. The next year witnessed a sustained though sometimes confused effort on the part of government to bring the situation under control. This was partially successful, but in 1445 debasement was apparently resumed. That year and 1449 —both of them also marked by military crises— were particularly bad from this point of view; thereafter, the downward movement of the *maravedí* was held in check until the monetary disasters of the 1460s. The message of all these correlations seems clear enough: Don Alvaro, especially but by no means exclusively in response to emergencies, practised debasement as an instrument of policy; his opponents did not. It is not too hard to see why he should have done so. By this technique, the Crown could make a profit out of the nation; indeed, it could do so twice over. First, there was the intrinsic profitability of each new issue of coinage —a means of immediate relief from the pressures of spending in any kind of crisis. Then in the longer term, there was the relative advantage gained over every client of the Crown who was paid —as the great majority were—

---

[43] Regulations issued by Enrique IV in 1406 were readopted in May 1440 (TORREÁNAZ, p. 148). On 14th June 1442 a revised *Ordenanza del Consejo Real* appeared (MS Madrid, BN, 13107, fols 146r-151v). Don Alvaro's regime had shown interest in purely procedural efficiency, e.g. in the rules of 20th May 1432 for the *Consejo de la justicia* (MS Madrid, BN, 13259, fols 94v-95v).

[44] For this and the following paragraphs, the basis is supplied by MACKAY, *Money*, greatly amplifying the same author's *Spain*, pp. 179-80. See also his «Las alteraciones», pp. 245-8.

in *maravedís,* the now devalued money of account. This tended to promote a shift, favourable to the Crown, in the balance of power and resources between king and magnates. No outcome could be more relevant to Juan II's political problems, but the advantage was only available while the real value of the tax-revenues fell more slowly than the *maravedí* itself. As long as Don Alvaro ruled, it did. But that feat in itself depended on the continued possibility of improving the level of return from taxes —something which was, in several ways, problematic. This apart, repeated and cumulative debasement brought obviously damaging results for the economy at large. In the longer term the Constable was not making the Crown notably more secure; he was borrowing rather than buying time.

These drawbacks were aggravated by his failure to stem the continuing outflow of *mercedes* —a failure whose origins are in part economic and in part political. A devalued *maravedí* left everyone worse off, except in the short term the Crown, and among these losers there were bound to be some whom it was politically indispensable to compensate for their losses. Don Alvaro and his immediate clients would expect it, naturally. But so would all his actual and potential allies. They had seen their grants from the Crown shrink in real value; if they were to derive any benefit at all from their association with Don Alvaro, they would at least expect to make up the difference in fresh *mercedes.* This merely added to a strain on royal resources which had been building up throughout the Trastámara period. The alienation of Crown properties which had founded the fortunes of the new nobility was already a topic of protest and concern. But the alternative of annual cash grants from tax revenues was beginning to be just as much of an incubus. Whether they were issued in relation to some more or less concrete form of service, or took the form of straightforward annual bonds *(juros),* these payments went a long way towards eroding any notional advantage which the Crown might gain from greater fiscal efficiency. As a proportion of the ordinary revenues —those which the Crown could collect without the assent of the *Cortes*— such grants loomed less large in the mid 1440s than they had done in 1429. But the real value of the uncommitted balance left to the Crown had risen very little in that time.[45] Between debasements and *mercedes,* the Crown's room for manoeuvre was beginning to look embarrassingly small.

---

[45] See below, pp. 58-59. MACKAY, *Spain,* p. 180 analyses pledged payments in 1429; an extensive but still incomplete record for 1447 is in SUÁREZ FERNÁNDEZ, «Un libro de asientos de Juan II», *Hispania* (Madrid), 68 (1957), 323-68. A very rough comparison suggests that, by 1447, payments for «maintenance» took a much larger share (the Crown Prince now had an allowance of his own), military grants took a lesser proportion (1429 had been a year of military crisis); salaries —mostly fixed— had dwindled in importance, and *mercedes* showed a small proportionate rise.

The answer to the problem might be to cut back *mercedes* and other Crown payments, but that was the short way to make new enemies, and thus incur new sources of military expense. Or there might be an attempt to raise extra taxes, but that again could provoke popular unrest. Or the debasement could be halted, but that in itself was an awkward process, not by any means guaranteeing a return of confidence in the currency. Again it seems that Don Alvaro, in pursuit of short-term advantage, ran the risk of leaving the monarchy in a worse state than that in which he found it. The insoluble problems could be shrugged off for the term of his personal ascendancy; the Crown would have to deal with all that at some future date. Again, his opponents, who did at least attempt to halt the slide in the *maravedí,* emerge as the more responsible party.

Yet each of these shortcomings in Don Alvaro's rule must seem a good deal more explicable once we begin to set it in context. His arbitrary methods were deployed not against a band of ardent constitutionalists, but against a warrior aristocracy whose outlook and practice have been described, with some justice, as «gangsterism».[46] His manipulation of the Consejo was opposed, and the pattern of a closed Council upheld against it, not because under the latter arrangement the Crown would be quit of illicit pressures, but because one particular pressure-group believed that it would do better that way. Currency debasement, which, in his first period of government at least, he handled with a certain restraint, was practised by many monarchies in the belief that it worked to their advantage —as indeed, temporarily, it did. His opponents did not do it because, as a body, they did not stand to gain by it. Their zeal for the economic well-being of the realm may be judged from their appetite for *mercedes* once in power. What the *Cortes* of 1442 meant by control over grants was «that expenditure should not exceed revenue»; what the Infantes and their co-regents meant was that they were to be the ones who approved the king's donations.[47] Don Alvaro's deficiencies, in a word, illustrate the patterns of instability with which he had to contend; they are not so much problems caused by his rule as manifestations of his failure to solve existing problems. He remains, then, an arresting but enigmatic figure, whose significance, as Valdeón observes, has yet to be worked out. The balance of arguments examined here must, ultimately, fall in his favour; it would seem that he did equip the Crown to cope with its difficulties rather better than hitherto, and that such a

---

[46] Valdeón Baruque, *Conflictos,* p. 149, following Postan and Malowist on parallel phenomena elsewhere in Europe.
[47] See the petition on abusive *mercedes,* and the reply outlining the system of scrutiny by regents and councillors in *Cortes (LC),* vol. III, pp. 401-2.

result formed part of his purpose. But it is far harder to say how substantial a part it formed, or how great a difference it made.

Such, then, are the debates to which any study of Don Alvaro must address itself. One thing which makes these questions hard to resolve is the lack of agreement on the proper historical framework within which such a study would acquire its fullest meaning. How we are to regard and evaluate Don Alvaro must depend on how we elect to regard this period of Castilian history as a whole.[48] We have the traditional option of seeing the fifteenth century in terms of wreck and rescue, with the Reyes Católicos supplying the latter element, and Juan II's reign, as a result, assigned to the former. Or we may follow Menéndez y Pelayo and Silió in seeing Don Alvaro as a tragic precursor of Fernando and Isabel —whom we are not thereby committed to seeing as these particular historians saw them.[49] We may emphasize the contribution of peculiarly Castilian circumstances —the emergence of the *conversos,* the Granada war— in shaping Don Alvaro's fortunes. Or we may look for explanations which connect with general European phenomena, especially in matters of institutional and economic development —the rise of the lawyers, for example, or the importance of sheep-farming as a basis for wealth. We may want to insist on the Peninsula, rather than its central kingdom, as the theatre of Don Alvaro's activities, stressing the involvement with Portugal as Suárez Fernández has done, or, following a tradition which extends from Zurita to Vicens Vives, bringing to the fore the Aragonese dimension of the great *privado*'s struggle with the Infantes. We may, indeed, wish to explore the question of his wider international involvements —his supposed treasures in Venice, his standing in the Anglo-French conflict— in the light of what is now known about Castilian diplomacy or maritime trade.

One inescapable emphasis will concern Don Alvaro's relations with the nobility; these, surely, will have to stand at or near the centre of any possible account. Yet here, too, there are several possible perspectives to be considered. The merely personal and anecdotal idiom of most contemporary chroniclers is something which we may well want to set aside —until the skill with which that idiom is sustained in a masterpiece like the *Crónica de Don Alvaro de Luna* reminds us, disconcertingly, that the whole record is, among other things, one of personal activities and involvements. The sense of the evolution of the nobility as a group,

---

[48] The task is not greatly advanced by such a purely narrative treatment as DIDIER T. JAEN, *John II of Castile and the Grand Master Alvaro de Luna* (Madrid, 1978). For the studies discussed below see the Bibliography to the present volume. Only those few items which are not self-explanatory are separately annotated here.

[49] MARCELINO MENÉNDEZ Y PELAYO, *Antología de poetas líricos castellanos,* vol. II (Madrid, 1944), p. 7. CÉSAR SILIÓ, *Don Alvaro de Luna y su tiempo* (Buenos Aires, 1939), p. 274.

explicitly developed in the work of Suárez Fernández, Mitre, and Moxó, brings in its wake a notable refinement of concepts. It enables us to see Don Alvaro's opponents as a dominant social estate of fairly recent evolution, seeking to arrest, at a point advantageous to themselves, the developments that had brought them into prominence. The play of individual interests, and the fortunes of dependent groups —minor *caballeros* such as Don Alvaro himself once was, *letrados* and officials, the citizens represented in *Cortes*— would become ancillary to this major theme. So would the relationship between the nobility and the Crown itself. But here a new alternative arises. We are here approaching the notion of social class; ought it not to be deployed in something like its full potential meaning? To treat the nobility as a dominant estate is surely inadequate; they need to be presented as a ruling class. In that case, the institutions of government, the Crown included, have to be seen as part of the means by which the rule of the nobility was maintained, and their interest, as against that of other classes, upheld. It is often all too easy to treat the evidence for this as if it were too obvious to be worth a comment. Should we not, then, accept, with Martínez Moro, that the issue is not, as Suárez represents it, «nobility *versus* monarchy»; it is «nobility *and* monarchy», and the disputes between the two are mere matters of adjustment in a lasting and fundamental alliance?[50] Quite so, and yet the precise adjustment which was made defines much more than the detailed nature of that alliance. It was itself the actual constitution of Castile in this period; it was the framework which, not merely for the parties directly concerned but for the kingdom as a whole, made certain developments possible and ruled others out of account. It matters, surely, to understand it; at the time it mattered enough for people to fight and die over it.

Yet can this kind of history be adequate? Can Don Alvaro's role ever be understood without any reference to the wider life of Castilians, more especially of those who had no part in the governing alliance of Crown and client nobles? The study of royal finances, as undertaken by Ladero Quesada, is inescapably relevant to the Constable's story, but that study leads outwards into every department of Castilian economic life. It becomes necessary, then, to look, as MacKay has done, at the conditions of that life from year to year, or at the intricate history of money values and price movements.[51] There may even be a case for taking into account, as the substantive history of Castile in these years, the history of social moods and movements to which Valdeón Baruque has

---

[50] Jesús Martínez Moro, *La renta feudal en la Castilla del siglo XV: los Stúñiga* (Valladolid, 1977), pp. 18-19.
[51] MacKay, «Popular Movements and Pogroms in Fifteenth-Century Castile», *P&P*, 55 (1972), 33-67 adds distinctively and importantly to the same author's later studies.

made his recent contribution. It is probably still true that we know far too little about the existence and experience of the mass of ordinary Castilians in Don Alvaro's lifetime to indicate how any developments at this level may have affected his fortunes.[52] But we may still, by retaining an awareness of this dimension, hope to offer an exact account of what it is that we need to know.

Perhaps we shall not do justice to the figure of Alvaro de Luna unless we learn to place him simultaneously in all these different contexts. The best justification for taking a closer look at his condemnation and death may, indeed, be this: that these extraordinary events, by demanding to be assessed in terms of all these potential settings, can make us aware of the inherent complexity of fifteenth-century history, the human and social substance in which its often problematic data are bodied forth, the enduring nature of its many paradoxes.

---

[52] See JOSÉ LUIS MARTÍN, «La sociedad media e inferior de los reinos hispánicos», *AEM*, 7 (1970-1), pp. 555-76 —necessarily more tentative for Castile than for the better-documented Aragonese realms. On something as basic as population, for example, we have —excluding the much-debated estimate of households for 1482— no reliable figures before the 16th century (HILLGARTH, vol. II, pp. 6, 500). Some assertions seem well-founded in terms of what is known about Castile, and about Europe at large —that population had fallen with the great plague of the mid 14th century; that, despite later plagues, it tended to increase after 1400. But any detailed account of how population interacts with other factors at this time must be largely conjectural. (See also JAIME VICENS VIVES and JORGE NADAL OLLER, *Manual de historia económica de España*, 3rd edn (Barcelona, 1964), pp. 223-5; JAIME SOBREQUÉS CALLICÓ, «La Peste Negra en la Península Ibérica», *AEM*, 7 (1970-1), 67-101; MITRE FERNÁNDEZ, «Algunas cuestiones demográficas en la Castilla de fines del siglo XIV», *AEM*, 7 (1970-1), 615-21; JOSÉ ANGEL GARCÍA DE CORTÁZAR, *La época medieval* (Madrid, 1973), pp. 389-91.)

CHAPTER 2

THE LINEAMENTS OF CRISIS

«And at this time, since the Master of Santiago... realized that the house of Estúñiga was the only family left in the kingdom capable of harming him, and the one towards which he bore the greatest enmity...»

Thus the *Crónica de Juan II*, introducing its account of events in 1452-3. It goes on to describe Don Alvaro's abortive plot against the Count of Plasencia, chief of the Estúñigas, and the latter's counter-intrigues, which were to culminate in the Constable's arrest.[1] The emphasis here is explicable in terms of the chronicle's main source at this point —the detailed record of these events kept by the Count's most trusted agent, Mosén Diego de Valera. The relationship between the 1517 text of the royal chronicle, and Mosén Diego's account as it survives in his *Crónica abreviada* of 1481 is not straightforward; each contains details not present in the other. But the influence of Mosén Diego's recollections, and still more of his way of seeing events, is unmistakable. The phrases just quoted expand and explain what appears in the *Crónica abreviada* as the baldest of assertions: «The Master... was taking steps to have the Count of Plasencia imprisoned.» But it is an explanation in the same individualistic terms: Don Alvaro is overweeningly ambitious, anxious for his own security, personally vengeful. Instead of the deep-seated political conflict which ought, one feels, to precede an event as momentous as Don Alvaro's fall, we are offered a melodramatic spectacle of rivalry among aristocrats.

Few of the chronicles of the time furnish us with very much more than this. Friendly or hostile to Don Alvaro, they seem all alike in their inability to transform a record of intrigue into the testimony of a crisis. Or if crisis there be, they regard it as synonymous with Don Alvaro's personal struggles, first against the nobility, and ultimately against the king. The substantive conflict, it is taken for granted, lies on this level and on no other. And in one sense, of course, such a view is perfectly

---

[1] *CJII* (R), p. 677; also pp. 677-8 passim; VALERA, *CAbr*, p. 323 and pp. 322-7 passim.

defensible. That the handful of families making up Castile's warrior élite could monopolize the attention of chroniclers was scarcely surprising when they also enjoyed a near monopoly of political initiative. The hundred or so persons who, not being direct employees of the Crown, are known to have drawn incomes from royal sources in the late 1440s, the smaller number whom we can assume to have figured in missing portions of the record, the few thousand relatives and other clients whom we can plausibly add, controlled a decisive share of Castilian land and wealth and power. Their use or abuse of these assets was the political life of the period. Next to his influence over the king, the relationship which mattered most to Don Alvaro was his management of these people who, alone in Castile, had the resources and authority to thwart and possibly supplant his power. The chroniclers are not at fault in giving attention to the detail of this relationship; their weakness lies in their failure to analyse it, as Alvar García had analysed the nature of Don Alvaro's rule in the 1430s. For the later part of Juan II's reign, modern historians have had to do their interpretative work unaided.

It has not proved altogether easy. To attribute Don Alvaro's fall to a growth in the power of the nobility, as José Luis Martín has done, or to «nothing more complex than his final loss of favour with the king», as Hillgarth puts it, explains very little unless we also know why these matters came to a head in 1453. Suárez Fernández touches the root of one's dissatisfaction with such accounts when he points out the major paradox involved.[2] In 1449-50, with his grip on events in Castile badly shaken, the Constable's fall from power seemed imminent, but did not happen; in 1453, with his control largely reasserted, it did. Suárez assumes that the hardening of attitudes among the nobility of recent years had put Don Alvaro permanently at risk, and that this shift, in its turn, responded to a change in the Constable's governmental style: «He had begun with great schemes for monarchical reform; he was ending now as a mere partisan, defending his own material interests.»

Even this version of events, however, though it has some basis in fact, can scarcely be used to account for Don Alvaro's fall. In the first place it is not specific to 1453, being just as applicable, if not more so, to the years immediately after Olmedo. The hopes of a nationwide harmony which that victory had fostered barely survived the year; the structure of political alliances which Don Alvaro was building up in the late autumn was essentially that of a «king's party», ranged against the Crown Prince and his supporters.[3] Effectively, the dispute was between

---

[2] MARTÍN, *La Península*, p. 722; HILLGARTH, vol. II, p. 314; SUÁREZ FERNÁNDEZ, *Historia*, vol. II, p. 522, and *Nobleza y monarquía*, pp. 175-6.
[3] In the agreement of 5th September 1445 between Don Alvaro and the Count of Haro, loyalty was promised both to the king and to Prince Enrique (MS Madrid, BN, 638, fols 15-17). Contrast the mutual defence pact between the

Alvaro de Luna and Juan Pacheco, the Prince's *privado,* and the settlement of differences patched up at Astudillo in the spring of 1446 was all too blatantly a carving of the spoils between them. Not even the negotiators could have had much confidence in this dubious accommodation, and it left behind an ominous residue of expendable clients and disillusioned allies. Worst of all from this viewpoint were the arbitrary and botched arrests of May 1448; they scandalized the constitutionally-minded, alienated old supporters of many years' standing, revived the pro-Aragonese cause in arms, and launched Castile upon the military crisis of 1449-51. If they were an attempt to appease Pacheco, they failed; if they were aimed at extracting a financial profit from the victims' estates, they were scarcely worth the trouble they caused. But with the pattern of Don Alvaro's activity as a «mere partisan» thus firmly established, we are still some years away from his fall. The most that we can assert is that certain later decisions of his —the demand for a forced levy which provoked the Toledo uprising of 1449; the eventual gambler's throw against the Estúñigas— are broadly in line with these earlier activities.

Such a record, certainly, is far removed from the planned and responsible use of power outlined for us by Alvar García, writing in the 1430s. Yet it is hard to see a shift of this sort as making very much impact on the magnates. They had accused Don Alvaro of wholesale infringement of existing laws and liberties as early as 1425.[4] Nor was he in his early days any less ruthless as a political manipulator than he afterwards became; the skilfully woven web of obligations and alliances, the preemptive security measures, the sure thrust to dominate the centres of power had been his stock-in-trade all along. His personal wealth and splendour were not recent acquisitions. Whether these things were done, as Alvar García had believed they were, with an eye to the service and strengthening of the Crown, or whether they served only Don Alvaro's appetite for wealth and eminence mattered little to the Castilian nobility. What irked them was his dominance, not the relative purity or impurity of his motives. From this standpoint, no special circumstance prevailed after 1445, except that for a time his control seemed less absolute, his touch less sure. All the more reason, therefore, why he should have been toppled then rather than later. But as regards 1452-3, it is still not at all obvious why he should have found the magnates uniquely hostile —if,

---

Count and the *Adelantado* Diego Manrique (17th December 1445), embracing the families of Velasco, Manrique, Mendoza, Sarmiento, Enríquez, Estúñiga, Sandoval and Pimentel. Here the commitment is to Alvaro de Luna «por nuestro especial señor y amigo» (fol. 14). The worsening political situation after 1445 can be followed in SUÁREZ FERNÁNDEZ, *Nobleza y monarquía,* pp. 165-74.

[4] *CD,* p. 3 (letter of Alfonso V of Aragon to Pero Núñez de Herrera, June 1426).

indeed, they were— or why he should have thought it so urgently necessary to bring the Estúñigas, in particular, to heel.

It is possible, of course, that he required no special incentive. It must have been at some time in the late 1440s that he confided in the young Constable of Portugal: «that he never closed his eyes in sleep nor opened them to care without some thought of his death, for he was troubled by fear of conspiracies, and by his own conscience.»[5] All that we know about Don Alvaro suggests that he was a man of strong impulses, masked by a deceptive mildness of manner. To keep up such a reputation over long years of taxing and perilous crises can take its toll of judgment. There may have been an element of paranoia behind some of the miscalculations of his last few years; certainly his conduct at the time of his arrest fell short of his habitual self-command on a number of crucial occasions. That said, we have to recognize that, up to the very end, he did in fact show himself to be fully capable of handling opposition among the nobility. To over-emphasize the element of personal instability would be to do less than justice to Don Alvaro's firm grasp of the political realities that faced him.

Among the opposition nobility of 1452-3, it is possible to discern three distinct though sometimes overlapping factions. The first of these consisted of irreconcilable former partisans of the Infantes of Aragon. Tamed for a time at Olmedo, this group had revived in militancy within a very few years, becoming much more formidable after the arrests of 1448, when its most prominent members had managed to escape. But the Navarrese invasion of 1449 and the troubles of the next two years were to be its last serious effort in Castile. Most of its leaders were by now abroad —Juan of Navarre in his own kingdom; the Admiral of Castile and lesser dissidents in exile at the Aragonese court. Their state of clientage in relation to the eastern kingdom was a double disadvantage politically: Aragonese finance for a military invasion was no longer automatically to be had, and it did the faction no good to be known as the dependents of a foreign power. Besides, their demand for the restoration of their estates and revenues in Castile threatened the men now in possession. In the case of the Navarrese king's enormous losses, especially —they came to over four million *maravedís* in royal taxes alone— it would have altered the balance of power in a way unacceptable to many others, besides Alvaro de Luna.[6]

A second opposition party was the Crown Prince's following, formi-

---

[5] CONDESTÁVEL D. PEDRO, *Coplas del menosprecio e contempto de las cosas fermosas del mundo,* ed. Aida Fernanda Dias (Coimbra, 1976). p. 48.

[6] ZURITA, *AA,* fols 11-12 (Lib. XVI, Cap. IX); for the scale of the Navarrese king's claims see LADERO QUESADA, *Hacienda,* pp. 261-3. For a slightly different view of the constraints on the Crown Prince's party, see SUÁREZ FERNÁNDEZ, *Nobleza y monarquía,* p. 173.

dable above all for the political skills of its leading figure, Juan Pacheco, Marquis of Villena. But they too had their limitations. Pacheco and his associates had profited greatly from the dispossession of the Infantes' party, which made collaboration on this front difficult. Besides, their hopes were closely bound up with Prince Enrique's legitimate expectations. While quite willing to make life difficult for Juan II and his *privado*, they were unlikely to seek the total dislocation of royal government. It was not in their long-term interest.

The third group, though a good deal more diffuse in character, was free of such inhibitions; both these facts made it, from Don Alvaro's viewpoint, much the hardest of the three to handle. It consisted of those former allies of king and Constable who had become alienated from them as a result of the latter's policies since 1445. Some, like the Counts of Alba and Benavente, imprisoned in 1448, had suffered direct attack; others, like Alba's friend, the Marquis of Santillana, were bound by personal ties to one or other of Don Alvaro's victims. The Count of Benavente, Don Alvaro's brother-in-law, had by this time escaped from prison. Profiting from a spell of exile in Portugal, he had established contact with Prince Enrique, on whose behalf he was busy negotiating a second marriage with a Portuguese princess. Santillana, too, made common cause with other dissidents from time to time, but there is a case for regarding this unusually cultured and reflective nobleman as representative of an «opposition of principle», genuinely affronted by Don Alvaro's illegalities. He seems, at all events, less of an unabashed opportunist than Alvaro de Luna's close associate, Archbishop Carrillo of Toledo. Trusted by the Constable almost to the end, Carrillo had already begun to hedge his own position in 1450 when he arrived at a secret understanding with Pacheco and the Prince.[7] It was to this third opposition that the Estúñigas belonged.

We can only guess at their motives.[8] The Count of Plasencia had certainly been impressed by Mosén Diego de Valera's principled stand

---

[7] *CD*, pp. 38-40 (Count of Benavente in Portugal); JOSÉ AMADOR DE LOS RÍOS, *Vida del Marqués de Santillana*, ed. Augusto Cortina (Buenos Aires, 1947; 1st edn. Madrid, 1852), pp. 68-72 (Santillana and Don Alvaro); LEÓN TELLO, *Duques de Frías*, vol. II, p. 48 (Carrillo and Pacheco).

[8] For sources of friction detailed here see *CJII* (R), pp. 659-60 (the Mosén Diego incident, also in VALERA, *CAbr*, pp. 318-22); *C Halc*, p. 473 (Astudillo); BENITO RUANO, «Lope de Stúñiga: vida y cancionero», *RFE*, 51 (1968), 42-4 (Astudillo; tensions with Lope); 44-5, 96 (grant to Lope in 1453 —a commitment honoured after Don Alvaro's death); *CAL* (C), p. 258 (castle of Burgos); MARTÍNEZ MORO, pp. 100-1 (holdings in Burgos); 42, 67-70, 103 (in Seville); LADERO QUESADA, *Hacienda*, p. 263 (Don Alvaro's Seville holdings); SUÁREZ FERNÁNDEZ, *Nobleza y monarquía*, p. 172n (his troubles there in 1449); NICOLÁS CABRILLANA CIEZAR, «Salamanca en el siglo XV: nobles y campesinos», in *CHist*, 3 (Madrid, 1969), 257, 259 (Salamanca enquiries; the Count's involvement, p. 261; no sanctions against him when the commission reports in March 1453, p. 276); the background also explored in JEANNE BATTESTI-PÉLÉGRIN, *Lope de Stúñiga. Récher-*

against the arbitrary measures of 1448, for he offered Mosén Diego protection and employment. But he already had more concrete reasons for dissatisfaction with Don Alvaro; the Estúñiga family interest had been poorly served by the Astudillo settlement of 1446. There had been some reference to payments due to them since the wars of 1439-41, and the dispute between Don Alvaro and the Count's brother Iñigo over the town of Montemayor had been referred to arbitration. But this did not satisfy the Count, or, apparently, Iñigo's son, the poet Lope de Estúñiga, whom we find, within a few months, applauding the resistance to king and Constable of the Navarrese-held fortress of Atienza. The Estúñigas had Navarrese roots, of course, and had lost money when Don Alvaro's policies obliged them to abandon their estates across the border. There were other sources of friction, too. It seems that the poet Lope was imprisoned for a time. In 1451, Don Alvaro opposed the appointment of the Count of Plasencia as governor of the Castle of Burgos; this was a city where the Estúñigas, with an income of 144,000 *maravedís* in local taxes, probably felt they had a legitimate stake. They had long aspired to one, too, in Seville, where the Constable's own financial involvement was very considerable indeed, and his political hold, as events in 1449 had shown, none too secure. Now, in 1451, the death of the Marshal Sancho de Estúñiga had brought substantial rents there under the direct control of the Count of Plasencia. A rather different occasion for hostility arose in the villages around Salamanca. There, the Count had been heavily involved, after the manner of most fifteenth-century nobles, in abusive extensions of seigneurial control. He cannot have been best pleased with Don Alvaro's direction of royal policy when the protests of local authorities in the region were met by the establishment of comissions of enquiry, in 1450, and again in September 1452. The latter at least might be seen as part of the pattern of pressure on the Estúñigas which the chronicles imply in the autumn of that year. Yet it seems a mild enough instance, and it was followed in January 1453 by a wholly friendly gesture to Lope de Estúñiga, to whom the king, at Don Alvaro's suggestion, granted an annual 70,000 *maravedís* in compensation for his losses in Navarre.

    The record, then, is one of many minor tensions, but it is not unmixed; it still seems some way removed from the zeal to destroy the Estúñigas as a major force which our narrative sources portray. We cannot be certain, therefore, that the Count of Plasencia was right in thinking that the Constable had planned, that autumn, to take him prisoner in a raid on his stronghold of Béjar. It would favour such a view if we could be sure that the source of his information was the *contador* Alonso

ches sur la poésie espagnole au XVème siècle (Aix en Provence, 1982), vol. I, pp. 217-47.

Pérez de Vivero, but the *Crónica de Juan II* is uncertain on this point.[9] What is clear, though, is that the Count had some cause to feel chafed by Don Alvaro's power, and to believe that the latter would not be averse to reminding him forcibly of who was in charge in Castile. The reminder would have been in place as far as Don Alvaro was concerned because the Estúñigas were extremely rich —richer than any great family in Castile except the Constable's own, and possibly the Mendozas.[10] In that sense the royal chronicle is perfectly right; if any family had the resources to harm him, it was this one.

Nevertheless, he seems to have been well able to hold his own not merely against any single family, but against any one of the major nuclei of opposition. His danger lay, rather, in the possibility that they might combine against him, as had happened briefly in 1449. Around the turn of the year 1452-3, two separate sets of negotiations were in train to bring this about. One of these, described in great detail by Mosén Diego (pp. 323-7) and the *Crónica de Juan II* (ed. Rosell, pp. 677-8) was initiated by the Estúñigas, allegedly as a counter to hostile moves by the Constable. Their approach to Prince Enrique proved unfruitful; the Prince replied evasively, having, as we shall see, ideas of his own. But with various independent magnates —Santillana, Benavente, the Count of Haro— they were able to agree on a scheme to kill or capture Don Alvaro in Valladolid, where the royal entourage was based in late December 1452. The plot had to be postponed, though, until the court returned there early in the following spring, by which time Don Alvaro's suspicions had been thoroughly alerted. Meanwhile, on 10th February in Naples, the envoys of the Crown Prince were laying very different proposals before the king of Aragon (Zurita, Lib. XVI, Cap. IX, fols 11v-12r.). Enrique's plan was for a *coup d'état,* backed by Aragonese troops, to put himself and Pacheco at the head of Castilian affairs. Up to a point —the point where their own interests began to be affected— they would then take a positive line over the claims of the exiles. Aragon could recoup its expenses out of the vast treasures to be confiscated from the fallen *privado.* Not surprisingly, King Alfonso wanted very much fuller details

---

[9] *CJII* (R), p. 677: «créese que por Alonso Pérez de Vivero»; VALERA, *CAbr*, p. 323 is vaguer: «de quien bien sabía el secreto.»

[10] Cash incomes from a parallel range of royal sources, abstracted from MARTÍNEZ MORO and from SUÁREZ FERNÁNDEZ. «Asientos»: Count of Plasencia, just over 900,000 *maravedís*; Estúñiga family, just over 1,500.000 *maravedís* (in 1454); Mendoza family, 1,550,000 *maravedís* in 1447, but no individual total rivals the Count of Plasencia; Alvaro de Luna, 1,100,000 *maravedís*; Luna family, 1,660,000 *maravedís* in 1447. LADERO QUESADA, *Hacienda,* p. 263 documents a personal income for Don Alvaro from Crown sources of some 5.2 millions in 1453; to this add perhaps a million more in the *asientos,* income as Master of Santiago (unknown, but clearly very large), and more again from private sources. With all this, compare the Estúñiga cash income from all sources at roughly the same date, computed by MARTÍNEZ MORO, p. 107 at about 3.5 millions.

of these arrangements before committing himself. In the end, of course, the whole scheme was overtaken by events.

Both plots, then, were abortive; neither, indeed, was particularly realistic in the first place. Their most interesting feature is their coincidence in time. The Estúñiga plot is represented —credibly if not quite certainly— as a response to Don Alvaro's own move against the Count of Plasencia. But it also appears relevant that Enrique and Pacheco thought the time ripe for a concerted effort against the Constable. Don Alvaro, if he did actually plan to take the Count captive, may have thought so too. But we are no nearer to knowing what factor in the situation just then could have led him or anyone else to such a conclusion. The mere fact of endemic opposition among the magnates —an occupational hazard as long as Don Alvaro was in power at all— cannot account for his relations with the Estúñigas taking so dramatic a turn for the worse.

Nor can it be made to account for the events of 1453. It is true enough that the Estúñigas played a decisive part in his arrest, but this did not result from their rather ineffectual scheming with their fellow-magnates; it came about only after they had been coaxed into renewed activity of their own. Moreover, the unique aspect of what occurred in 1453 was not the fall of Alvaro de Luna; he had fallen from favour before, when his enemies had secured the right conjunction of forces against him. But after 1427, 1439 and 1441, he had been able to restore his position; this time he was executed. Both in the persuasion of the Estúñigas and in the final condemnation of the Constable, the vital role was played by the king. On this the most widely-differing of our sources are agreed. Both the *Crónica de Don Alvaro,* which makes Juan II an arbitrary and hysterical betrayer of his lifelong friend, and the royal chronicle, with its account of the due and justified exercise of authority, leave the king's responsibility beyond doubt. And, in general, this is the formula by which our early narratives account for Don Alvaro's ultimate fate. It was his enemies among the nobility —assisted, according to hostile sources, by his overweening arrogance —who made him vulnerable. But it was his friend and sovereign who undid him. The wrath of the prince was death.

This, to a public which knew fifteenth-century princes, was a credible and satisfying explanation. But it merely replaces one area of obscurity by another. What made Juan II react so violently against his friend of thirty years' standing? Is it possible to relate what can now be known of his motives to less subjective factors? Once again, we are not greatly assisted by the tendency of our narrative sources to narrow their explanations to matters of individual influence and temperament. When they do venture a more general mode of explanation, it is in terms of Fortune (as with Alonso de Cartagena or his pupil Almela) or of the hidden designs of Providence (the view preferred by Mosén Diego and Fernán Pérez de Guzmán).[11] It would appear that clerical observers were less disposed to present Don Alvaro's end as the manifest will of God than were hostile laymen, striving to make a party point. This contrast certainly underlines the intensely political nature of the event, but brings us little nearer to its actual causes. Of these, most of what was known then, or can be known now, must derive either from more or less informed rumour, or from official propaganda. If the «paper full of all manner of blasphemy and disloyalty» issued by Don Alvaro's partisans in May 1453 had anything to say about the king's motives, most people knew better than to repeat it.[12] By contrast, the general tenor of Juan's reply, and of his open letter to the municipalities after Don Alvaro's execution, finds a ready echo in the works of such relative outsiders as the Andalusian *alcalde* Pedro de Escavias and the Basque nobleman Lope García de Salazar, as well as in the *Cuarta crónica general*. All of these record the king's resentment, so amply expressed in the official apologia, against Don Alvaro's absolute control over royal business. It seems to have been common knowledge that the Constable did exercise this kind of sway; forty years later, to take only one of numerous examples, a witness who had lived on the fringes of Juan II's court recalled that everybody said that Don Alvaro's word was law in both court and kingdom. But this charge of *apoderamiento* lies at the heart of the whole enigma of Juan II's conduct. He had, after all, put up with this kind of thing for years. Why not now?

An answer much canvassed by popular rumour, according to Pedro de Escavias, was the alleged influence of Juan II's queen, Isabel of Portugal «whom the king loved very much, and who was ill-disposed towards the Constable». At first sight, this hostility looks surprising; it was Don Alvaro himself who had arranged the Portuguese marriage in 1447, brusquely overruling Juan's own preference for a French princess. But the story in its most circumstantial form was fully equal to this objection.[13] Fernán Pérez de Guzmán twice alleges that Don Alvaro's

---

[11] *Rubrica additio ex summa Episcopi Burgensis*, appended to *CJII* (R), p. 693; DIEGO RODRÍGUEZ DE ALMELA, *Valerio de las historias de la sagrada escritura, y de los hechos de España* (Madrid, 1793); p. 259; VALERA, *CAbr*, p. 327; PÉREZ DE GUZMÁN, *G y S*, p. 43.
[12] See *CD*, no. XXXVII, pp. 68-73 (Juan II's reply of 22nd May); his letter of 18th June is no. XLI, pp. 80-92; also PEDRO DE ESCAVIAS, *Repertorio de Príncipes de España*, ed. Michel García (Jaén, 1972), p. 343; LOPE GARCÍA DE SALAZAR, *Las bienandanzas e fortunas*, ed. Angel Rodríguez Herrero (Bilbao, 1955), p. 59; *CCG*, CODOIN, 106, p. 135; PÉREZ DE GUZMÁN, *G y S*, p. 43. The 1497 witnesses in LEÓN DE CORRAL, *Don Alvaro de Luna según testimonios inéditos de la época* (Valladolid, 1915), pp. 57-60.
[13] ESCAVIAS, p. 343; VALERA (Juan's envoy to France) supplies background to the marriage, *CAbr*, p. 314; see also PÉREZ DE GUZMÁN, *G y S*, pp. 40, 43;

apoderamiento extended to the attempted regulation of the royal couple's sexual life: «nor did he let him spend time with the second queen, his wife, or have intercourse with her when he wished.» In Santillana's *Coplas* directly inspired by the Constable's fall, we find a generalized version of the same charge («You made him hate the comforts of wife and children»), strongly underlining its anti-natural aspect. Alfonso de Palencia, as we might expect, elaborates this theme, linking it with Don Alvaro's loss of those youthful charms which had favoured his original advancement. This in its turn evokes Palencia's earlier hint of a homosexual bond between the two men —a colourable enough notion in itself, but neither totally convincing nor especially informative. The more specific charge, though, finds less tendentious support in other sources.

There is, in the first place, the decidedly uneasy attitude of Don Alvaro's own chronicler. If he was, as seems probable, Gonzalo Chacón, he had reason for his unease; he later married one of the Queen's waiting-women. He places the beginning of Isabel's hostility as late as 1453, and blames it, as he blames most things, on the machinations of Alonso Pérez de Vivero. Before this he has twice gone out of his way to heap praise on the Constable for enabling the royal pair to spend time together, in 1450 and in 1452, when the pressure of state business was very great. Yet he also represents Don Alvaro as writing from his prison at Portillo warning the king's advisers to keep their master, for the sake of his health, from too much indulgence of his carnal appetites.[14] Plainly this was a sensitive topic on which Chacón wanted to give his hero the best of both worlds. And even Palencia, in his account of Juan II's last days, grants that Don Alvaro restrained the king's desires for both sex and food «using coercion when persuasion failed him... anxious, above all, to prolong the king's life». Juan's indulgence once free of these restraints, Palencia insists, hastened his death. Other observers, much earlier in the reign, had remarked on the Constable's puritan reputation. According to the poet Juan de Torres, Love found no welcome at Don Alvaro's house. There are also several relevant pieces of sworn testimony in the Mendoza-Pacheco litigation of 1497, where the dispute

---

Marqués de Santillana, *Coplas*, stanza 13, Foulché-Delbosc, *CC*, vol. I, p. 499: «Los dones que la natura / otorga a todo animal, / en que toda criatura / recibe gozo espeçial, / solaz de muger e fijos / le feziste aborrecer»; Palencia, *Déc*, p. 31; also pp. 2-3 (*CEIV*, pp. 31, 9).

[14] *CAL* (C), pp. 307, 252, 287, 425; for Chacón as author, pp. 436-7 and Carriazo's *Estudio preliminar*, pp. xxv-xxviii; Palencia, *Déc*, p. 56 (*CEIV*, p. 53); Juan de Torres, *Pregunta a Juan de Padilla*, Marqués de Fuensanta del Valle and José Sancho Rayón, eds, *Cancionero de Lope de Stúñiga* (Madrid, 1872), p. 163. Torres was a retainer of Don Alvaro (see Nicasio Salvador Miguel, *La poesía cancioneril: El «Cancionero de Estúñiga»* (Madrid, 1977), pp. 231-6), and described him to the Italian Guinforte Barzizza as «summae sapientiae virum» (Andrés Soria, *Los humanistas de la corte de Alfonso el Magnánimo* (Granada, 1956), p. 198); Corral, pp. 68-72.

over Don Alvaro's lands turned upon the legality of his execution. Witnesses spoke of the Constable's rudely arousing Juan and Isabel after an unsanctioned night together, and of his declaring to her publicly «I married you. and I'll unmarry you». Most striking of all is the statement of Alonso Gutiérrez de Corral, a former servant of the Relator, Fernán Díaz de Toledo. He recalled his master «one day after dinner» telling in somewhat shocked tones of a sharp altercation between Constable and queen because she had come to court against his orders. There seems no reason to doubt this, though there are hints in the same material of other causes of friction, including disputes over property. At all events, Isabel is known to have had a hand in the incitement of the Estúñigas to a fresh coup against Don Alvaro. Mosén Diego (p. 327) and, following him, Palencia (p. 44) and the royal chronicler (p. 678), all affirm that she sent one of her ladies, the Countess of Ribadeo, as a confidential messenger. All seem to be agreed, though, that she did so at the king's suggestion rather than for any motive of her own. We cannot be certain how all these factors combined together.

There are fewer ambiguities about the other specific form of personal dominance which is most commonly said to have irked Juan II: the series of stringent domestic economies imposed on him by Don Alvaro. Both Palencia and Fernán Pérez refer to this in terms which echo Juan's own protestations of May and June 1453. The king had declared that: «I was often left without daily maintenance for my royal table, and indeed for those few old and constant retainers of mine.»[15] He had complained, too, that Don Alvaro's economies prevented him from giving alms as he would have wished. That charge also finds its way into the sworn testimony of 1497: «not letting him have money, nor possess it, not even to give in alms, although he wanted to». And there is an entertaining story of how the Constable, in 1450 or thereabouts, tried to overrule the king's gift of a suit of clothes to a Sevillan knight, and being unsuccessful, stormed at his royal master in terms whose unconscious irony defies translation: «Pues reniego de la puta que me parió si en este año vestís otro tal.» Juan II's privations may have been strictly relative —the usual scale of royal maintenance allowed for a generous margin— but it would appear that they were not wholly imaginary.

The exception among our sources in this matter of Juan II's motivation is, naturally enough, the *Crónica de Don Alvaro de Luna*. Here the heroic Constable is guilty of no offence at all. Everything stems from the plotting of the *contador mayor*, Alonso Pérez de Vivero, and from Juan II's own moral spinelessness. The literary genius with which this view is presented blurs and bedazzles any attempt at objective historical clarity.

---

[15] *CD*, no. XXXVII, p. 70; also no. XLI, pp. 81-2; cf. PALENCIA, *Déc.* p. 36 (*CEIV*, p. 39); PÉREZ DE GUZMÁN, *G y S*, p. 43; CORRAL, pp. 65-6.

The vacillating, nerve-wracked Juan II is so vividly pictured that the chronicler's assumptions about his motives go unquestioned. Alonso Pérez, the arch-traitor, is consciously represented as a type of Judas Iscariot; his ever-present perversity can thus be taken for granted without need of explanation.[16] Only when we step outside the author's frame of reference does it become possible to assess Alonso Pérez's actual responsibility. No other source regards him as the sole catalyst of Juan II's change of mood; if anyone plays that role elsewhere, it is the queen. Nevertheless, Fernán Pérez accepts Don Alvaro's suspicion that the *contador* «was plotting with the king to have him exiled and destroyed». And the *Crónica de Juan II* states that the Constable's abortive move against the Count of Plasencia at the end of 1452 was revealed «as it is thought, by Alonso Pérez de Vivero». Mosén Diego's vaguer formula —«somebody who was well-informed of the secret»— could refer to anyone, from the king downwards. There is a sharper dispute as to how far either Juan II or his *contador* was aware of the Estúñigas' countermoves. Don Alvaro's chronicler makes both men privy to the unsucessful plot to kill the Constable in Valladolid in the early months of 1453; the *Crónica de Juan II* insists that, even though the *coup* was planned to take place in the name of Prince Enrique, «he knew nothing of this; much less did the king».[17] Clearly, someone has done some remodelling of these events, and the indications are that it is the *Crónica de Don Alvaro*. If, as several of our accounts confirm, Juan II subsequently had trouble in convincing the Estúñigas that he genuinely did want Don Alvaro out of the way, he could scarcely have been conspiring with them earlier. Yet there is also the less tendentious statement in Don Alvaro's chronicle —supported, to some extent, by patterns of local landholding— that the city of Valladolid was dominated jointly by Alonso Pérez and the Estúñigas. Could a *coup* there have succeeded without the *contador*'s involvement? Palencia makes some sense of all this by regarding Alonso Pérez, «the hidden enemy of his former patron, the Master of Santiago», as actively involved, while the king was merely aware of the plot. But this does not help us to determine whether the *contador* was the inspirer of Juan II's hostility to Don Alvaro, or merely its agent. The balance

---

[16] *CAL* (C), p. 295; also pp. 295-357 passim; cf. PÉREZ DE GUZMÁN, *G y S*, p. 43; also, above, n. 9.
[17] *CJII* (R), p. 678; on the *bandos* of Valladolid see *CAL* (C), pp. 324-5; cf. J.R.L. HIGHFIELD, «The Catholic Kings and the Titled Nobility of Castile», in *Europe in the Late Middle Ages*, ed. John Hale, Roger Highfield and Beryl Smalley (London, 1965), pp. 364-5 and refs. See also PALENCIA, *Déc*, p. 44 (*CEIV*, p. 45); CORRAL, p. 70 (also pp. 74-6); GARCÍA DE SALAZAR, p. 60: «la ventura suya... pusole en la voluntad de ser en la fabla del Rey don Juan, que era contra el el Maestre e Condestable.» Either of the two obvious emendations (*dezir* for *de ser; el* for *el el*) would disturb Lope García's delicate ambiguity: the king had his way; Alonso Pérez suffered for it; we cannot know which of them was responsible.

of opinion among the witnesses of 1497, however, favoured the latter view; no fewer than ten of them declared that Juan II had ordered Alonso Pérez to «see to it that the Constable's acts were remedied and punished», and that it was this, rather than private enmity, which led to his murder. Perhaps the shrewdest verdict is that of Lope García de Salazar who, though not close to these events, had a clear awareness of the balance of power and initiative between overlord and official: «... his fortune, once his rise was complete, made him desirous of enjoying King Juan's confidence, [where he learned] that the Master and Constable was the king's enemy.» Alonso Pérez might, as Don Alvaro's panegyrist maintains, have been the Constable's protégé, but he held his post and his pay from the king.

Thus, if he did support the projected *coup* in Valladolid, he may still have done so less from personal initiative than because he knew the king's secret mind. But he cannot, at this stage, have revealed it to the Estúñigas. To do so was Juan II's next concern. At this point, certain other similarly dependent figures make their appearance.[18] Although our accounts differ on points of detail, it seems clear that Juan II's first approaches to the Estúñigas involved two such personages. One was the king-at-arms, *Castilla* —kings-at-arms and heralds were in a very strict and exclusive sense royal functionaries. The other was the Relator's son, Luis Díaz de Toledo. Luis Díaz, who had been promised the reversion of his father's offices in 1447, belonged to a family of officials who had risen, like Alonso Pérez, under the Constable's aegis, but who now stood or fell, as he did, by the king's favour. We might also note an even closer parallel to Luis Díaz's social background —*converso*, New Castilian, office-holding— in that of Mosén Diego de Valera, son of the public prosecutor Alonso García Chirino, and a fierce opponent of Don Alvaro since 1448. Mosén Diego, of course, was the Count of Plasencia's man, not the king's. And it was still true, as late as the end of March 1453, that the only official who enjoyed the king's full confidence in the matter of the Constable's impending arrest was Alonso Pérez de Vivero. We know this from Juan II himself, who declared in one of his anxious

---

[18] *CJII* (R), p. 654; VALERA, *CAbr*, p. 327; PALENCIA, *Déc*. p. 44 (*CEIV*, p. 45); For their discrepancies see below, p. 45. For Luis Díaz and his father's offices, AGS, M y P, 7.129; Luis Díaz may also have attracted the king's notice and favour as a minor poet (see the exchange of verses with him in FERNANDO DE LA TORRE, *Cancionero y obras en prosa*, ed. A. Paz y Melia (Dresden, 1907), pp. 159-60). It is also possible that he shared *Castilla*'s professional interests; a «Ludovicus Bachelarius» translated BARTOLUS, *De Insigniis et Armis* for Santillana (MS Madrid, BN. Res. 125, fol. 17r; see MARIO SCHIFF, *La Bibliothèque du Marquis de Santillane* (Paris, 1905), pp. 252-3). On Mosén Diego, see MARIO PENNA, ed., *Prosistas castellanos del siglo XV*, vol. I, BAE, 116 (Madrid, 1959), pp. c-cii. See also *CD*, no. XXII (Juan II to Alvaro de Estúñiga; 1453, n.d.), p. 41; SÁNCHEZ DE ARÉVALO, *HH*, p. 233 («viros religiosissimos atque doctissimos» advising Juan to show Don Alvaro less favour).

notes to the young Alvaro de Estúñiga: «... his [Alvaro de Luna's] dominance in this court is great, and I have nobody whom I can trust with this matter except for the *contador*.» But it does look as if a nucleus of at least potential hostility towards Alvaro de Luna —more than potential, if we are to credit Sánchez de Arévalo's account of the conduct of «certain most religious and learned men»— had already begun to develop among those royal officials whose appointments and activities he had controlled for so long. Their subsequent conduct certainly squares with this assumption. But as to what part Alonso Pérez, or Luis Díaz, or the latter's father may have had in inspiring the king's new outlook, we cannot yet be certain.

It would be easier to evaluate each of these factors if their chronology were clearer. The mission of Luis Díaz and *Castilla,* the king's first confidences to his wife, and her promise to send the Countess of Ribadeo to the Estúñigas, are all placed by the royal chronicle in 1447. This must be due to a corrupt text, for the same chronicle has the Countess deliver her message —which finally convinces the Estúñigas of Juan's resolve— in 1453, after the Valladolid plot. This is where both Mosén Diego and Palencia locate Juan II's earlier appeals, though the former does not mention Luis Díaz, and the latter refers to two separate embassies, not one. Despite these minor confusions, the whole set of negotiations seems firmly tied to the early spring of 1453. Yet the king's hostility to Don Alvaro may well have begun earlier than this.[19] Palencia tells us that Juan II found it impossible to conceal his feelings «for so long», but omits to say how long. García de Salazar, by contrast, sees it as providential that the king could keep secret his dealings with «certain favourites of his, of low estate, and with certain knights» for «two years or more». We do not know his source for this estimate, but it does square with the recollection of the 1497 witness that the incident of the courtier's clothes happened in or around 1450. The queen's involvement is harder to date. The birth of Prince Alfonso on 11th November 1453 confirms her intimacy with her husband at about the time of the Valladolid plot, but we know all too little of the preceding months or years.

We may still wonder, though, whether any of these factors —the Queen's hostility, the stringent economies in court expenditure, and the emergence of an anti-Luna faction among the officials— was enough to overturn a lifelong partiality on Juan II's part, or to undermine Don Alvaro's position as the combined might of his most powerful enemies had so recently failed to do. Yet if we ask what each factor implies about the state of Don Alvaro's governmental system in 1452-3, a much more

---

[19] PALENCIA, *Déc*, p. 31 (*CEIV*, p. 31); GARCÍA DE SALAZAR, p. 59; CORRAL, p. 66; for Prince Alfonso's birth see PALENCIA, p. 55 (*CEIV*, p. 53).

intelligible picture emerges. We can begin to glimpse the outlines of a crisis different in kind from the political and military challenge of 1449-52, and from the purely personal drama of Juan II's conscience and affections. Don Alvaro might still be able to destroy his opponents' capability, but his own system of rule was manifestly less and less capable of working to promote its chosen ends. If anything could threaten Juan II's attachment to Don Alvaro, it was the knowledge that the latter could no longer make effectual those policies which he was supposed to be implementing on the king's behalf. And by 1452-3 this was becoming all too apparent. The alleged sources of Juan II's resentment are less important in themselves than as the essential clues to all the interlocking reasons which now impugned the competence of Don Alvaro's rule.

Thus we may take it that his interference in Juan II's marital life was not a mere aberration of personal tyranny; some kind of political motive must also be at work if the thing is to make sense at all. It is unlikely that any such motive operated in the very early years of a match which the Constable himself had arranged. The *Crónica de Juan II,* it is true, furnishes a possible cause of tension then in the rumours attaching to the death in February 1445 of Isabel's aunt, the dowager-queen Leonor of Portugal.[20] Queen Leonor, and Juan II's first wife María (both of them sisters of the Infantes of Aragon) had died within a few days of one another, and with some common symptoms, though in widely separated localities. There had been stories of poison, the *Crónica* records, adding: «... it is even alleged that, in the indictment which King Juan caused to be drawn up against the Constable, it was discovered who had given these ladies poison, and by whose command.» No surviving document, however, confirms the charge, and the chronicle's cautious formula seems to disclaim any first-hand knowledge of that elusive *proceso*. The balance of probabilities, indeed, is against the Constable's involvement. The symptoms common to the two victims —purple weals on body, arms, hands and face— would be compatible with some forms of poisoning, but other indicators like vomiting and gastric trouble are not recorded. A common natural cause seems equally possible, though it would seem more likely if the two women had died in the same place. Leonor of Portugal, moreover, was said to have died of the enemas which were given to her in treatment; these caused fainting-fits, and may very well have aggravated her condition. But the real objection to

---

[20] *CJII* (R), p. 625; *C Halc*, pp. 529-30 rejects suspicions attaching to Pedro of Coimbra, attributing her death instead to inept medical treatment. If she, like her sister, was suffering headaches, the standard remedy of Don Alvaro's personal physician (enemas of olive oil and oil of violets, taken in the early morning) could well explain her fainting-fits (MARCELINO V. AMASUNO, *El «Compendio de Medicina» para D. Alvaro de Luna del Doctor Gómez de Salamanca* (Salamanca, 1971), p. 20).

the dual charge is that it is politically absurd. The whole point about poison was that it made for an inconspicuous killing; it was self-defeating to contrive, by identical and spectacular means, the almost simultaneous deaths of two great personages in closely parallel circumstances. Don Alvaro had been accused of poisoning before; if he did employ this weapon now, one would expect at least an elementary discretion in its use. The need was reinforced by the supposed occasion of the murder —the furtherance of the interests of Leonor's brother-in-law Dom Pedro, the Portuguese Regent, who had brought about her exile in Castile. Don Alvaro and Dom Pedro were close allies, but in obliging his ally to the extent of poisoning a relative, the Constable would have been risking, now or in the future, his whole relationship with the House of Avis and its kingdom. Consummate discretion was called for; what we have, if the charge is true, looks more like utter carelessness.

It is probable, even so, that the story did achieve currency in 1453, and it is not hard to see what its value as propaganda would have been at that point. The death of the other queen, María of Castile, had certainly served Don Alvaro's interests, not least by enabling him to arrange Juan's second marriage. Rumours of poison attaching to this case would have gained in topicality with his fall, but they would also have placed the union of Juan and Isabel in an embarrassing light. At this point, the death of Isabel's aunt assumed a special interest. In the period of Dom Pedro's political eclipse, between 1447 and 1449, his enemies at home had spread the story that he had arranged to have her poisoned; if he had done so through some agent in Castile, then surely his ally the Constable must have been privy to it. There was a certain plausibility, then, in linking the latter's name with Queen Leonor's death too. It was also highly opportune to do so, for it provided Queen María's end with associations other than Juan's Portuguese marriage, and managed to imply that Don Alvaro made a habit of poisoning queens. Hence the royal chronicle's vague but extremely sensational account.[21]

By 1453, however, the marriage of Juan and Isabel had long ceased to serve Don Alvaro's diplomatic aims.[22] Already by the time of its celebra-

---

[21] PALENCIA, *Déc*, p. 28 (*CEIV*, pp. 28-9) suggests that Don Alvaro feared both a reconciliation between Juan II and Queen María, and a love-affair between the king and Queen Leonor; he adds that Juan, was privy to both crimes. It is hard to make any sense of this, or of his statement that the poisoning of Queen María produced a slow fever (*CJII* (R) describes an illness of only four days). PALENCIA was out of Castile at the time (see *CEIV*, p. x); his account looks like a rhetorical working-up of later gossip. So does his confused attribution to poison administered by Don Alvaro of Queen Isabel's post-natal depression following her daughter's birth in April 1451 (*Déc*, pp. 31-2; *CEIV*, p. 35).
[22] SUÁREZ FERNÁNDEZ, *Historia*, vol. II, p. 522 (fall of Pedro of Coimbra); *CD*, no. XVII, pp. 38-9; no. XIX, p. 40 (Afonso and the Prince).

tion in June 1447, Pedro of Coimbra, the key figure in his dealings with Portugal, was losing his hold over his young nephew, Afonso V. In May 1449, Dom Pedro met his end, fighting as a rebel on the field of Alfarrobeira. King Afonso, enjoying for the first time his full powers as a monarch, was unlikely to take it as axiomatic that Don Alvaro was his best available ally in Castile. Before long, the exiled Count of Benavente was urgently canvassing the alternative of an understanding with Prince Enrique. On 19th March 1451 Afonso assured Enrique, through the Count, that the Portuguese crown had no prior arrangement with Alvaro de Luna. Shrewdly, though, he still declined any formal alliance with Enrique; such things were not necessary, he declared, between such close friends and kinsfolk. But the attractions of Enrique's support continued to increase. A written agreement had been ratified by 27th March 1453 for the Prince's marriage to Afonso's sister Juana, once his divorce from Blanca of Navarre had been made final. Afonso's need of allies in Castile was rendered more acute at this time by the sharp clash of national interests which was developing over Africa and the Canaries.

It was the Portuguese themselves who had brought things to a head. In 1448 Prince Henry the Navigator had bought out the proprietor of the island of Lanzarote, thus, in effect, reviving the old controversy over the title to the Canary Islands. Initially, even so, the practical dispute lay between Henry's semi-official expeditions on the one side and Sevillan free-lance traders and fishermen on the other; their respective monarchs were not involved, and need not have become so. But Juan II made Castilian claims explicit in 1449 by a grant of African coastline to the Duke of Medina Sidonia, and the high-handed treatment dealt out by the Portuguese to Castilian caravels in African and Canary Island waters proved impossible to ignore.[23] A series of such naval incidents from 1450 onwards evoked a strong Castilian protest in May 1452; this was renewed with further complaints in April 1454, after Don Alvaro's death. The wider context is furnished by the papal bulls issued by

---

[23] SUÁREZ FERNÁNDEZ, *Relaciones entre Portugal y Castilla en la época del Infante Don Enrique, 1393-1460* (Madrid, 1960), pp. 64-5 (grant to Medina Sidonia); FLORENTINO PÉREZ EMBID, *Los descubrimientos en el Atlántico y la rivalidad castellano-portuguesa* (Seville, 1948), pp. 148 (Lanzarote), 144-50 passim (naval incidents), 158-60 (embassy of 1454); C. R. BOXER, *The Portuguese Seaborne Empire 1415-1825* (Harmondsworth, 1973), pp. 20-1 *(Dum diversas)*; also EDGAR PRESTAGE, *The Portuguese Pioneers* (London, 1933), p. 47; BAILEY W. DIFFIE and GEORGE D. WINIUS, *Foundations of the Portuguese Empire, 1415-1580* (Minneapolis, 1977), pp. 92-5; PALENCIA, *Déc.* p. 57 (*CEIV*, p. 54); *CJII* (R), p. 692. For Saharan gold in Seville see J. HEERS, *Gênes au XVe siècle* (Paris, 1961), pp. 69-70 (quoted by MACKAY, *Money*); for the wealth of the city, ANTONIO COLLANTES DE TERÁN SÁNCHEZ, *Sevilla en la baja Edad Media* (Seville, 1977), pp. 285-6; for Don Alvaro's interests there, ibid., p. 379; *CAL* (C), p. 449; LADERO QUESADA, *Hacienda*, p. 263.

Nicholas V in the Portuguese king's favour, most notably by *Dum diversas* of 18th June 1452. This conferred the right to attack and conquer both Moslems and pagans, recognizing, in effect, the whole western Sahara and its coasts as the legitimate sphere of Portuguese military activity. Palencia, who had actually been in Rome at the time, was convinced that Afonso V sought nothing less than a monopoly of such enterprises: «... against the Moors of Morocco, and against all the other peoples, both Numidians and Ethiopians [i.e. Berbers and Black Africans] whose lands border on the Mediterranean Sea or the Libyan Ocean.» More, then, was felt to be at stake than the old dispute over the Canary Islands, or even maritime commerce generally. The question, as the references to blacks and pagans establish, was one of access to the supply-routes of West African gold. Even though the king of Castile had sent no expeditions into Africa and had no intention of doing so, this was still a significant threat to Castilian interests. It was enough to impel Juan II to make it an aim of the administration which succeeded Don Alvaro «not to allow the king of Portugal to make war in Barbary or Guinea». It was important enough for him to back the protest sent to Lisbon in April 1454 by threatening «war with fire and sword, as against an enemy».

Much of this evidence, it is true, refers to the months following Don Alvaro's death. But it also implies that the policy of defiance towards Portugal had been his in the first place. The first Castilian protest, after all, had been made in 1452, while he still ruled. The second was apparently sent, in April 1454, after a hint from the Portuguese that they would welcome negotiations. Presumably something had happened in the interim to make them a little less truculent; it is likely, then, that there had been some earlier show of Castilian firmness. The very confused chronology of the *Crónica de Juan II* itself points to this conclusion. It describes how Juan II summoned his new ministers when he was at Avila, on his way north from Escalona, and made it one of their policy aims to contest Portuguese attempts at southward expansion. It goes on to state that the embassy threatening Afonso V had returned with the latter's civil but evasive reply «at the time when he [Juan II] left Escalona». All these events are assigned to 1454. Yet the visit to Escalona and the journey north from there are as firmly tied to 1453, as the letter to Afonso (which has survived) is to the spring of 1454; it was dated from Valladolid —not Escalona— on 10th April. The error is best explained by the presumption that some other declaration of intent towards the Portuguese was, in fact, made in the summer of 1453. If that is the case, then the assertive policy adopted by Juan II must have been laid down already by Don Alvaro, for it is not plausible to think that it was improvised by the king in a matter of weeks after the Constable's fall. But one would, in any event, have expected such a policy from Don Alvaro, had he survived. The Portuguese threat was, above all, to the commerce of Seville, one of the great clearing-markets for the gold of the Sahara caravans. And in the Seville region Don Alvaro had an income from taxation of close on half a million *maravedís*. He also had an illegitimate son, Martín de Luna, who was in charge of the naval dockyard there. It was natural that he should oppose Portuguese aspirations, and that Afonso V should feel that a change of regime in Castile would be a change for the better.

Rivalry over Africa, compounded by Alfonso's new alignment with Prince Enrique, would have been quite enough to alter the Constable's view of the Portuguese connection. It may well, too, have changed his relationship with Queen Isabel. One very late source —the anonymous French *Histoire du Connêtable de Lune*— makes the African crisis decisive in bringing about the queen's hostility, and hence Don Alvaro's fall.[24] Its testimony may have been affected by its pursuit of useful political maxims: «Princesses are always more attached to their native country than to the kingdom into which they marry.» But the changes in Portuguese policy do offer a cogent reason why, from 1451 or 1452, Don Alvaro should have sought, whatever the risks involved, to limit Isabel's influence over her notoriously malleable husband. Nothing else does.

Don Alvaro, in other words, was forced to take this dangerous course by his lack of ultimate control over the international dimension of his strategy. He could not simply «take out» the king of Portugal by arrest or surprise attack, as he might have done with some rebellious count. The alternative —to cope with him as a permanent enemy— was bound to involve both risk and cost. A second area of weakness in the Constable's system is highlighted by Afonso's sponsorship of Prince Enrique. Based at it was on a personal bond, Don Alvaro's sway in Castile could never be absolute; as soon as Juan II died, its basis would be gone. With Juan now in his forties, it was evident to others besides Afonso of Portugal that the future lay with Enrique. Don Alvaro's long-term hopes had to lie in making his own preponderance over the other magnates so unassailable that the new ruler would be forced to reach agreement with him. This aim, however, was bound to be resisted on all sides. Hence the increasingly contradictory aspect of his rule since 1445. His aim was a pacified kingdom, and that, whatever his self-serving motives, meant a kingdom responsive to royal authority. But his longer-

---

[24] *Histoire du Connêtable de Lune, favori de Jean II, Roi de Castille & de Leon* (Paris, 1720), pp. 308-9. The anonymous MS Madrid, BN, 6185 (dated 1706) also attributes the Queen's hostility —though less specifically— to Don Alvaro's power, rather than to personal factors (fol. 10v).

term survival demanded policies so assertive that they must necessarily generate faction and disorder. It was the extreme form of a contradiction which had been present all along.[25] It was most obvious, no doubt, when his enemies were active in the field, as in 1449-51. But, obvious or not, it could do nothing but get worse, as the years went by and Enrique's expectations came nearer. To anyone at all who reflected on these matters —and we may take it that Juan II thought about them as much as any— Don Alvaro's utility to the Crown was correspondingly reduced.

Assertive policies were also expensive policies; indeed, it scarcely needed any extraordinarily contentious line of action on Don Alvaro's part to create a climate of budgetary difficulties. His irksomely tight control over Juan II's court expenditure is most effectively explained by the most straightforward of motives —the existence of a real economic crisis. It was not, after all, Don Alvaro who publicly contrasted Juan's financial record with that of his father, and demanded cuts in expenditure to produce a similar budget surplus. Nor was it the Constable who drew up a detailed code of restrictions on *ayudas de costa*— insisting, incidentally, that temporary servants of the Crown could not receive grants of clothing. It was, in each case, the *Cortes* of 1447, the general tone of whose petitions is one of acute economic alarm.[26] Signs of a worsening situation are evident in other desperate remedies adopted by Don Alvaro. In 1448, for example, the property of the arrested magnates was confiscated with an eye to paying off potential dissidents in a new distribution of spoils. It was this issue which drove Mosén Diego de Valera into opposition, but the move made sense to his colleagues in the *Cortes,* who would otherwise have had to find additional taxes. In January 1449, Don Alvaro sought to meet a military emergency by a hasty levy of a million *maravedís* from the city of Toledo, which promptly erupted in revolt. There was also the often tried and inherently damaging recourse of currency debasement. The very rapid devaluation of the *maravedí,* by more than 25% in the seven years from 1444, makes it seem highly plausible that this was being used as a means of relieving pressures on the treasury; MacKay believes that the likeliest dates for it are 1445, in the aftermath of the very costly Olmedo campaign, and 1449, when military needs were once more paramount. Between 1451 and 1453, by contrast, there seems to have been a notable stabilization

---

[25] See above, pp. 24-6.
[26] *Cortes* (LC). vol. III, pp. 505-6 (the general situation); 506-7 *(ayudas de costa).* For VALERA see *CJII* (R), pp. 659-60. On the Toledo revolt see BENITO RUANO, *Toledo en el siglo XV. Vida política* (Madrid, 1961), pp. 34-5, and *Orígenes,* pp. 41-2. Emphasis soon shifted to a purge of the *converso* officials who had helped to collect the levy, and thence to wider issues. But the initial complaint was that the demand infringed the city's privileges, and was too high for the poorer citizens. See the anonymous account in, AGS, D d C, 40.38, fol. 2v.

of the currency, which continued for several years thereafter.[27] But it is clear enough in general terms that the extreme courses to which the Constable was driven by financial difficulties went well beyond the occasionally tactless regulation of Juan II's domestic outgoings.

It is very much harder to establish whether economic affairs in the early 1450s were in a state of crisis which might help, in a more direct way, to explain Don Alvaro's fall. We can, for example, venture only the broadest of indications about the national economy in the decade following 1445. It has been suggested that the overall picture for the Castilian fifteenth century is of an expanding economy based on a gradually rising population. But we know little about the degree of discontinuity in either process, or about its incidence.[28] The widespread plague and dearth of the years 1434-8 may have created more than one such hiatus; any effects which this may have had on infant mortality would have made themselves felt in the size of the working population in the late 1440s. Naturally, this would cause graver problems if there was also some movement towards more widespread cultivation; if the trend was towards pastoral farming and away from agriculture, then the difficulties would be more manageable. But we do not know which of these tendencies predominated in Castile at the time; both have been suggested as characteristic of the century as a whole.

If we turn to indirect taxation as an indicator of economic activity, the evidence is still not straightforward.[29] There is an absolute fall of about

---

[27] Silver prices quoted by MacKay, *Money*, indicate a 27.6% devaluation in 1444-53; his year-on-year figures for coin prices allow a rough estimate of the proportion of that fall in each intervening year, as follows:

1444-5	5%	1448-9	20%
1445-6	10%	1449-50	15%
1446-7	15%	1450-1	20%
1447-8	15%	1451-3	—

The stabilization after 1451 seems unmistakable; the other figures give no clear evidence of MacKay's two «strategic» devaluations, but are compatible with these. Real values given below for revenues in these intermediate years must be seen as tentative; those for 1444 and 1451-3 have the full authority of MacKay's meticulous study.

[28] See above, Chapter 1, n. 52; also MacKay, «Popular Movements», p. 56; Valdeón Baruque, *Conflictos*, p. 146; García de Cortázar, pp. 400-2 (agrarian expansion typical of the 15th century); Hillgarth, vol. II, p. 6 (an opposite view of the whole period, 1300-1500).

[29] Ladero Quesada, *Hacienda*, pp. 43, 87; real values derived from MacKay:

	Total in maravedís		Real value indices		
	Ordinary revenues	Alcabala	Ordinary revenues	Alcabala	Other
1444	73.6 millions	65 millions	100	100	100
1453	80 millions	65.5 millions	79	73	116

a fifth in the real value of such revenues from the mid 1440s to the mid 1450s, but this is more than covered by a decline in the real value of the *alcabala,* the universal sales-tax. Other indirect revenues actually increase by some 16%. This would be consistent with a setback in population growth, accompanied by various instances of local or sectional prosperity. But it by no means imposes any such interpretation; the difficulties involved in collecting the *alcabala* may have been more important than any contraction of its base. The incidence of particular taxes can seldom be evaluated nationally; nor can the movement of prices, about which we know all too little. But some of the implications which can be pieced together for particular areas are striking.

For example, there are several disconcerting items of information from Seville.[30] Cereal prices there rose sharply in the late 1440s, while local customs dues in the area declined in real value by 10-15%. The evidence for other Andalusian districts follows no clear pattern, but it is of interest to find the tax-farmers of the region declaring in 1451 that without the Genoese merchants their revenues would be worthless. All this suggests that Alvaro de Luna did well to be anxious about the Portuguese challenge to Sevillan trade.

For the pastoral economy of the high Castilian plains, the crucial indicator is the *servicio y montazgo,* a tax levied largely in kind as a fixed proportion of transhumant livestock.[31] Its real value declined abruptly by about 17% from a peak in 1446-7 to the figure which the tax-farmers were willing to offer for it in 1449; there is no real sign of recovery in their tender for 1453-4. One wonders how this might relate to political rivalries in such areas as the southern Meseta. It seems probable that, in the initial phase, the struggles of Alvaro de Luna and the Pacheco interest could have been a contributory cause of smaller returns; warfare in other districts certainly had that effect on taxes. Thereafter, the quarrels between different magnates may have been exacerbated by the fall in the numbers of livestock. It is certainly tempting to see this background as relevant to the eventual detachment from Don Alvaro of Alonso Carrillo, the Primate of Toledo, who had strong family links with the *Mesta.* At the crucial time there were other econo-

---

[30] MACKAY, «Popular Movements», p. 66 (cereal prices); LADERO QUESADA, pp. 133, 144 *(almojarifazgo de Sevilla);* 129-30 (sharper decline in Murcia and Córdoba); 127 (incomplete data, pointing to opposite trend in Jaén). On the Genoese see HILLGARTH, vol. II, p. 43; COLLANTES DE TERÁN, pp. 215-6.

[31] LADERO QUESADA, p. 164. For the Carrillo de Acuña family see JULIUS KLEIN, *The Mesta: A Study in Spanish Economic History. 1273-1836* (Cambridge, Mass., 1920), pp. 81-3. For dearth around Toledo in 1453, see Juan II's letter of 9th May *(CD,* no. XXXIV, p. 60); also *CAL* (C), p. 424. The real value of the Burgos customs duties *(diezmos de la mar de Castilla),* fell by about 13% in 1447-54. By the latter date they were pledged in advance to the Count of Haro (LADERO QUESADA, p. 125).

mic strains in the Toledo region: an acute shortage of grain there in the early summer of 1453 must relate to poor harvests in the preceding year, and thus to an underlying source of unease existing in this area in the months immediately before Don Alvaro's fall. Very tentatively, we may advance the notion that the years around 1450 saw a decline in the relative self-sufficiency of Andalusia and New Castile. This would tilt the balance of economic importance towards the Old Castilian wheatlands and those magnates who held estates there. But the city of Burgos, heavily dependent on the export traffic in wool, would feel the effects of any serious decline in livestock —as, indeed, the relevant customs dues to some extent suggest. All this fits in uncommonly well with the politics of the Constable's eclipse. His own power, and that of the Order of Santiago were based south of the Guadarrama; the Estúñigas were a northern family. And Burgos, at the time, was clearly in a volatile state.

But the key to that episode did not lie in any local circumstance; it derived from the attitude of the monarch. And the problems which Juan II experienced with regard to his revenues were only secondarily concerned with the economic base; they were, rather, fiscal and political. Leaving aside such major windfalls as the papal grant of 1443 for the Granada war —it came to 100,000 florins, and was spent mostly on the Olmedo campaign— there were three main components in the royal income.[32] These were the *alcabala,* the mixed bag of other indirect taxes which the king was empowered to levy on his own behalf, and the subsidies voted by *Cortes.* Of these, the *alcabala* was usually the most substantial and always the most reliable; between 1444 and 1453, despite its fall in real value, its proportionate contribution to the total budget rose slightly, from 53% to 57%. The king's minor revenues increased in importance as well as in real worth; their percentage share of total income went up, in the same period, from 6.5 to 12.5. The *Cortes* subsidy was larger than this, but much less predictable; standing at 50 million *maravedís* and 40.5% of revenue in 1444, it declined to 30 millions and a 30.5% share nine years later. To collect the *alcabala* and other ordinary revenues, the king needed an efficient fiscal service, backed by the power to put pressure on defaulters; to get in his extraordinary subsidies, he had to be able to manage the *Cortes* firmly, but with a realistic eye

---

[32] LADERO QUESADA, pp. 43, 87, and table facing p. 218 (*Cortes* subsidies); MACKAY, *Spain,* p. 147 (papal contribution; tribute from Granada. The former came to 6.8 million *maravedís;* the latter to about 880,000 annually in the early 1440s —probably less later in the decade when new hostilities broke out; it was, of course, paid in gold). Another minor additional item was the tax paid by the Jews —perhaps rather more in mid-century than the 450,000 *maravedís* recorded for 1474 (AMADOR DE LOS RÍOS, *Historia social, política y religiosa de los judíos de España y Portugal,* vol. III (Madrid, 1876), p. 602).

to what taxpayers could provide. Neither task proved easy in the period we are now considering.

It was, for example, notoriously hard to realize the notional value of the indirect taxes. A certain amount of written-off revenue was, in any case, inevitable in any system based on tax-farming. The last of the sporadic attempts to recover such losses —the *cobro de albaquías*— had been made in 1427.[33] Of its nature, this exercise required the settlement of many old scores, and it could not be resorted to lightly. Significantly enough, the next attempt was made in 1454, the year following Don Alvaro's fall. Even after the debts of his major political adversaries —notably the Crown Prince and the Pacheco family— had been written off, it brought in 28 million *maravedís*. The depredations of these and other landowners, who appropriated the taxes levied in the areas they controlled, were another constant problem. The *Cortes* of 1447 had impressed upon Juan II the fact that, though taxes were too high, their full value was not being realized. None of the areas controlled by Prince Enrique, they declared, paid anything to the Crown; if he would pay up, other territorial lords would follow his example. If they refused, Juan II should confiscate and sell off first their income from the Crown, and then their lands.

Needless to say, Juan approved of this advice in principle; just as predictably, he did nothing of the kind. These seigneurial appropriations of taxes *(tomas)* remained a source of weakness in the revenues, and the *Cortes* of 1451 could only propose a remedy whose main effect would have been to institutionalize the disease. Seigneurial lands would be assessed for tax, and royal payments due to the landlords set directly against this assessment. The landowner, if he still had anything left to pay, would hand this balance over to the tax-officials; if the balance lay on the other side, then the king would make up the difference from his other revenues. Juan II's response was favourable but sceptical; who was going to beard the magnates in order to recover the sums still due? It was left to Enrique IV to introduce this *tasa de señoríos*, whose merit, if it had one, was that it cut out the middle-man. In this case, the middle-man happened to be the royal exchequer. This had, indeed, been the Crown's *de facto* position all along. For the principal drain on tax-revenues was neither the illegal *tomas* nor the shortfall in payments from the tax-farmers; it was the enormous and wholly legal array of earmarked payments —overwhelmingly to those same magnates who profited from the system in other ways. The free balance left after

---

[33] LADERO QUESADA, pp. 33-4 *(albaquías)*; *Cortes (LC)*, vol. III, pp. 496-503 (1447 proposals); LADERO QUESADA, pp. 78-9 *(tomas* and the 1451 *Cortes)*, 49 *(tasa de señoríos)*; SUÁREZ FERNÁNDEZ, «Asientos» *(mercedes* generally); MACKAY, *Spain*, pp. 175-6; MARTÍNEZ MORO, pp. 46-8 *(mercedes* in the income of the magnates).

these *mercedes* had been paid cannot have been much more than half the king's ordinary revenues.

Thus, despite the numerical preponderance of the *alcabala,* it was the *Cortes* subsidy which offered the king such freedom of action as he was able to enjoy. With adequate funds from this source, he could put sufficient forces into the field to cut down, if never to eliminate, seigneurial inroads into his ordinary revenues. Without such support, his free balances, already much eroded by *mercedes,* would dwindle yet more. The picture could be further complicated at any moment by major foreign or domestic warfare, which imposed a prior call on the king's disposable income. The *Cortes* delegates, then, were confronted with a problematic choice. They would naturally be anxious to keep the level of taxation as low as they could. But by making the king an offer substantial enough for his needs, they could increase fiscal efficiency on the ordinary revenue side, and so reduce his longer-term need of subsidies from them. In times of actual or impending turbulence, however, such as the late 1440s, even a very large subsidy might disappear on short-term military needs, with no such benefit to the third estate. The king, for his part, could generally manage the *Cortes* in a purely political sense, by intervention in its election, by the payment of delegates, by pressure on individuals, and by playing on the dilemma outlined above. But he too needed to exercise a delicate judgment; there were obvious dangers in going for a sum which taxpayers would find oppressive. One of these was that they would simply desert the *tierras de realengo* and go to live under the overlordship of one or other of the magnates. This happened often enough in the mid century to suggest that the Crown did not always get its calculations right.[34]

In 1445, the year of the Olmedo war, the *Cortes* had voted the largest subsidy ever —112 million *maravedís.* The next year's sum was a mere 20 millions, and the *Cortes* of 1447 made an attempt to have this accepted as the annual norm, unless reforms were made. In the end, they settled on 60 millions over two years, and this annual figure of 30 millions remained a standard one, despite devaluation, until 1452. In that year the grant was 25 millions, including $2\frac{1}{2}$ millions earmarked for repaying specific major debts, but with a promise of 35 millions in the following year. In other words, Juan II was getting rather more out of the *Cortes* than they were anxious to give him, and probably as much as the taxpayers at large could afford. Yet the sums were still small in

---

[34] See *Cortes (LC),* vol. III p. 690 (Córdoba, 1455: plague and dearth depopulating royal lands more rapidly than *señoríos);* VALDEÓN BARUQUE, *Conflictos,* pp. 143-4. For similar migrations in 1429-31, see above, Chapter 1, n. 24. Dissident magnates in temporary military control of an area could also levy its taxes in advance, to their own profit, as the Admiral's faction did in Palenzuela in 1451 (VALDEÓN BARUQUE, pp. 150-1).

relation to potential military demands, as the very much larger amount spent on the Olmedo campaign makes clear. The early 1450s in particular seem to have been years of real crisis in relation to extraordinary revenues. In 1451 a system of graduated payments was adopted, which brought many more Castilians (those with property worth between 60 and 150 *maravedís*) into the taxpaying orbit, while slightly easing the burden of those who were already there. It looks very much the sort of scheme which, devised to alleviate hardship without loss of revenue, ends by pleasing nobody. To judge from the fiscal nadir reached in 1452, it would appear to have thrown the collection of the subsidy into some disorder.[35]

Predictably, then, the *Cortes* were much preoccupied with the sums spent on *mercedes*. The assembly of 1447, whose gloomy view of the economy has been quoted already, concentrated on ways of reducing these payments. Those falling vacant in the next three years were to be halved; legacies and transfers were restricted; the king was to be cautious in making future grants; hereditary bonds *(juros)* were to have a lower priority when tax was collected. These rules, with others governing *ayudas de costa,* occupy almost a fifth of that *Cortes'* very large body of legislation.[36] In the event, they did little for the ailing treasury. When the *Cortes* of 1451 complained of military unreadiness on the Moorish frontier, Juan II could only plead poverty. There was an understandable desperation about this *Cortes'* request that no new *mercedes* should be granted for ten years. This, as the king pointed out, was hardly practicable, but the partial moratorium on *mercedes* which fell vacant was renewed for a ten-year period.

But the 1451 petitions also exhibit another tendency, which in some ways contradicts the drive towards economies. In 1447, the delegates had demanded that loans to the king from towns and cities should be repaid; that, of course, was fully within their area of interest. But now they began to concern themselves on behalf of the Crown's other creditors. There was a complaint that royal officials were not receiving their full salaries. And there was a similar concern for the prompt and proper payment of *mercedes* generally. These petitions reflect alarming financial strains —salaries were falling short by 10%, and other grants by up to a fifth. They also correspond to the charges made against Alvaro

---

[35] LADERO QUESADA, table facing p. 218; also p. 202 for the revised scales of 1451.
[36] MS Madrid, BN, 6720, fols 9v-12v lists 74 laws, of which 14 relate to these topics; see *Cortes (LC),* vol. III, pp. 495-574 passim, esp. pp. 506-14; also, for the 1451 *Cortes,* pp. 618-21; 577-8; 585-8. Juan II, in 1453, saw the limitation of royal grants as the first of Don Alvaro's *deservicios (CD,* no. XXXVIII, p. 75; see also no. XXXVII, p. 70, which presents the *Cortes* policy on vacancies as an instance of Don Alvaro's tyranny).

de Luna in 1453: «that he would not allow the king to make grants to those who served him».

This, then, is the background against which Juan II had to assess the value of his *privado*'s economic management. The data at his disposal, of course, would have differed in form and scope from the random array of items which now survives. Nor would he have looked at this information in the ways in which we now try to analyse it. But there were some figures of which he was bound to take notice. One was the size of the balance left to him out of each year's ordinary revenues, once earmarked payments had been made.[37] In 1429 this had come to 32% of a total of 61 million *maravedís*. The best estimate to be made for the late 1440s would amount to 54% of 76 millions in 1447. But when these figures are corrected for devaluation, the real value of Juan II's surplus turns out to have risen by only some 2% per year. It must have seemed a very marginal return for all the troubles involved in defending Don Alvaro's ascendancy during those eighteen years. We do not have the figures which would enable us to assess the position in 1453, but there is emphatic evidence of the way things were going in another statistic which the king would have found important —his total revenue from all main sources. In 1444, the *alcabala,* the minor dues (above, n. 29), and the *Cortes* subsidy (above, n. 35), combined to yield just under 124 million *maravedís*; in 1453, they provided 115 millions. Three factors help to explain this fall in real value of almost a third: the devalued *maravedí,* the difficulties of revenue-raising in a time of civil strife, and the reduced *Cortes* subsidy. But devaluation and debasement had been Don Alvaro's own strategies, and the policies which had courted strife were his policies. Even the management of the *Cortes* had been his responsibility. He had, in other words, conspicuously failed to match his earlier record of fiscal effectiveness.

We can plot this breakdown more exactly, using MacKay's detailed figures for devaluation, and the known totals for ordinary revenue —the *Cortes* shortfall, which merely underlines Don Alvaro's failure, may be

---

[37] LADERO QUESADA, p. 43 (ordinary revenues, 1429, 1444, 1453; 1447 figure derived *pro rata* from the last two). Real-value indices from MACKAY, (see above, n. 27). For pledged payments see MACKAY, *Spain,* p. 180 (1429), and SUÁREZ FERNÁNDEZ, «Asientos» (1447). The latter's total of 26.3 million *maravedís* omits the 70% of Estúñiga revenues —about 2.2 millions— which came from royal sources (MARTÍNEZ MORO), and, to judge from the Constable's holdings in 1453, further large payments to him (see above, n. 10). 35 millions seems a modest estimate for the full total. These figures yield the following table:

	Ordinary revenue (mrs)	Real value index	Free balance (%)	Real value (% of 1429)
1429	60.8 millions	100	32	32
1447	75.7 millions	81	54	44

set aside for the moment.[38] The percentage devaluation of the *maravedí* over any given period represents a saving to the Crown out of all payments made to other parties. By subtracting from this figure any percentage fall in real royal income in the same period, we can measure the Crown's eventual advantage. The devaluation figure also matters in its own right, since it represents the most readily perceived symptom of price-inflation. Over any particular period, we may, if we wish, work out notional annual rates as well, though in practice developments did not proceed with this kind of regularity. The resulting contrast between Don Alvaro's two periods of supremacy, in the 1430s and in 1445-53, is instructive and highly damaging to the Constable.

Between 1430 and 1444, the Crown gained an advantage of 18.8%, at an annual rate of 1.4%. Since devaluation was checked in the early 1440s, and tax-collection impeded by the wars of 1439-41, we may take it that most of the gain corresponds to the 1430s, and that the annual rate then was higher. Between 1444 and 1453, by contrast, the Crown's advantage was limited to 7.1%, a notional annual rate of 0.8%. Both the relevant variables —devaluation and the disruption of taxgathering through civil war— had done most of their work between 1447 and 1451, though there are no signs of actual recovery from either in the next two years. Moreover, devaluation over the whole period amounted to 27.6%, giving a notional rate of 3.1% every year; actual rates in the crucial years 1447-51 were of the order of 4 to 5%. Devaluation in the 1430s had apparently gone on at a somewhat lower rate than this. The Constable's second administration, then, was little more than half as profitable to the Crown, compared with his first. But it still contrived to whittle away the real value of *mercedes* at rates which were bound to make the holders more importunate in their demands on the king. It would scarcely be surprising if Juan II had begun to wonder whether his *privado* was worth saving any more.

By 1451, indeed, Don Alvaro himself seems to have realized the

[38] Rates of movements (first year of period as % base):

	Movement of real royal income (ordinary revenue only)		Devaluation of maravedí in terms of silver		Advantage to Crown	
	period	annually	period	annually	period	annually
1429-30	− 3.5	−3.5	+ 1	+1	− 4.5	−4.5
1430-44	−11.4	−0.8	−30.2	−2.15	+18.8	+1.4
1444-53	−20.5	−2.3	−27.6	−3.1	+ 7.1	+0.8

Figures derived from LADERO QUESADA, p. 43 and MACKAY (see above, Chapter 1, n. 20); year-on-year devaluation rates are based on the latter's annual coin prices (above, n. 27).

need for a new economic strategy. From that year onwards, all the coin prices monitored by MacKay level out once more; this must indicate that devaluation and the debasement of alloy coinage had been stopped at source. But the new policy was no more likely to win him friends. There must have been a good deal of speculation against the coinage going on —we have evidence that it happened even in the 1420s— and those who had counted on a declining *maravedí* would scarcely thank the Constable for his new-found zeal.[39] Moreover, the other essential ingredient of this policy was the tightening of control over *mercedes,* and this was unlikely to be understood or welcomed by those who lived off grants from the Crown. Juan II, too, may well have been genuinely indignant at the restrictions on what he felt to be his proper magnificence. The *Cortes* of 1447 would probably have understood, but the attitude of the *Cortes* was changing; by 1451, the earlier anti-seigneurial note had been replaced by a concern for the well-being of the holders of *mercedes* —overwhelmingly, that of the nobility. The process is carried further by the *Cortes* which met in Burgos in April 1453, just after the Constable's arrest.[40] On the limitation of *mercedes,* they merely urge the king not to give away the royal patrimony. But they also ask him to see that existing *mercedes* are paid. It is easy to see whose resources are expected to provide the ready cash; the assembly's only comments on the momentous arrest of a few days before are wholly complaisant.

Yet these delegates were in session by 8th April; they must have been summoned while Don Alvaro was still at the head of affairs. They were almost certainly men whom he believed he could trust to cooperate with his policies. Their shift to an identification with seigneurial interests and a latent hostility towards Don Alvaro may be seen as part of that increasing municipal dependence on local magnates which we know to have characterized the century as a whole. The process might well have been expected to develop apace in a decade which saw the Toledo revolt, a sharp decline in the Crown's economic resources, and perhaps a more general uncertainty about the Castilian economy.

By the early 1450s, then, Don Alvaro's fiscal problems were undermining, in newly disruptive ways, the structure of interests which had protected his position. Hard-pressed taxpayers, a gradually alienated *Cortes,* underpaid officials, the disgruntled holders of *mercedes,* were all less disposed to rally round him in any crisis. He still needed to build

---

[39] Speculative activity of the *tesorero* Juan Ramírez de Toledo recorded in his letter of May 1425 (MS Guadalupe, Archivo del Monasterio, Legajo 55). For the monetary complexities of the 1440s, see the disputes over Portuguese coinage circulating in Castile (*CJII* (R), pp. 690, 693). For the coinage after 1451, see the graph in MACKAY, «Las alteraciones», p. 244.

[40] *Cortes (LC),* vol. III, pp. 669-71. The delegates were in Burgos by 8th April (*CD,* no. XXV, p. 44). SUÁREZ FERNÁNDEZ's reference to «unas improvisadas Cortes» (*Nobleza y monarquía,* p. 182) cannot be justified.

up his own wealth and support —his insurance against a change of monarch— but that in itself gave colour to the charge that he restricted the king's munificence to his own profit and that of his clients. His ever more arbitrary efforts to break out of these constraints, and his shift to new financial policies in the years after 1451 were bound to offend more and more actual or potential allies —ultimately, of course, the king. It is to one particular group of allies— the royal officials —that we must now turn.

Juan II's much-elaborated claim that Don Alvaro had been in total control of all public offices and their occupants presents us with an immediate paradox. It might well lead us to expect a large-scale purge of those in royal employment to follow his fall; yet nothing so dramatic occurs.[41] Among a handful of apparent exceptions, a future royal secretary, Bartolomé de Zafra, was so militant on Don Alvaro's behalf that Juan II never forgave him, but Zafra, at this stage, was still a private employee of the Constable. Luis de la Cerda, lieutenant of the castle of Toledo, who was present in Burgos but hesitated to hand over his office to the king, was summarily arrested, but proved so free of suspicion that in June he was actually given charge of Escalona on Juan II's behalf. Anxiety to secure the city of Toledo may help to explain the king's treatment of the one high official to be summarily purged. This was the Licenciate Ruy García de Villalpando, Don Alvaro's sometime deputy in a Toledan magistracy, and the king's *asistente* in that city. Orders for his arrest and the sequestration of his goods and documents were issued on 15th April. Ruy García's background was peculiar, in that his family's original connections seem to have been with the King of Navarre. Doubtless this history reinforced his state of clientage where Don Alvaro was concerned; nor would the Licenciate's record of ineffectuality against the Toledo rebels have predisposed the rest of the officials to help him now.

The other officials, to a man it would appear, not only survived unscathed but collaborated enthusiastically in Don Alvaro's downfall. As we have seen, only a few of them had any inkling in advance, but their unanimity in the event does appear to confirm that their attitude to their former patron had changed in the past few years. Yet the most senior members of this group had been, in a very special sense, the

---

[41] On Don Alvaro and the royal officials see *CD*, no. XLI, p. 86; on Zafra, *CAL* (C), pp. 423-4; on La Cerda, BENITO RUANO, *Toledo*, p. 77; *CD*, no. XXIV, p. 42; *CCG*, pp. 136-7; on Villalpando, *CD*, no. XXX, pp. 55-6, but MS Madrid, BN, 13109, fol. 19v dates his arrest on 7th April; see also BENITO RUANO, *Toledo*, pp. 182-4. A Doctor Ruy García de Villalpando served in the king of Navarre's Council in 1429, and with his peace delegation to Castile in 1431 (MARÇAL OLIVAR, «Documents per la biografía del Marqués de Santillana», *Estudis Universitaris Catalans*, 11 (1926), 9); MANUEL DE BOFARULL Y DE SARTORIO, *Guerra entre Castilla, Aragón y Navarra. Compromiso para terminarla* (Barcelona, 1869), pp. 41-63).

Constable's men.[42] The Relator had been active at the heart of his governmental system since the 1420s; the rebel magnates of 1440 and the enraged plebeians of Toledo in 1449 had both denounced him by name as Don Alvaro's creature. His wealthy cousin, the *contador* Alfonso Alvarez de Toledo, had been a personal friend of the Constable, helping to engineer the latter's return to power in the 1440s. Closest of all had been Don Alvaro's former employee, Alonso Pérez de Vivero, appointed *contador mayor* in 1434, «of good character, loyal, and of good understanding for that office». He had proved his loyalty in difficult times. During Don Alvaro's second exile, he and the Relator had been part of «the Constable's league», keeping communication open between the king and his absent *privado*. In 1441, he had been kept away from the king's person for longer than most other officials; in 1443, Juan of Navarre had held him prisoner for a time. He had stood guarantor for the alliance between Don Alvaro and the Count of Haro in September 1445. Yet in 1453, Fernán Díaz's son was privy to the king's designs against Alvaro de Luna, Alonso Pérez was their principal agent, and the Relator himself helped to manage the judicial killing of his onetime patron. What had happened since 1445 to alter their lifelong alignment?

Some of the ingredients of an answer have been mentioned already. The officials were being kept short of pay, though the more reflective of them must have known that the mere elimination of Don Alvaro was not the remedy. The 4% or so of total revenue which went his way might cover their needs for a time, but could not cover the Crown's basic financial weaknesses. They might have been concerned, too, for their personal security. The fact that Mosén Diego was a public prosecutor's son had not saved him, in 1448, from being chased from court by the threats of Don Alvaro's military retainers. His offence, moreover, had been to take a public stand in favour of legality and public concord —much in line with the ostensible policies of the coalition which had won Olmedo. And whereas the Constable's falling-away from these professed intentions into the *Realpolitik* of the later 1440s would scarcely have moved the hostile magnates one way or the other, it may well have had its negative effect on the civilian lawyers of the administration.

In other respects, too, their experience had altered. During Don Alvaro's long exile after 1441, they had remained, for all or part of the time, at the king's side. That alone must have reinforced in their minds the fact that they were his officials, not the Constable's. Moreover, the greatest long-term prize they could hope for —the reversion of their

---

[42] On the Relator see above, Chapter 1, esp. notes 30, 34; on ALFONSO ALVAREZ, *CAL* (C), pp. 146-7; *C Halc*, pp. 211-2, 442; on ALONSO PÉREZ's character, *CJII* (CODOIN), 100, p. 390; his part in the 1445 agreement, MS Madrid, BN, 638, fol. 16r-v; other references to these three, below, pp. 172-9; 64; 202.

offices to their sons— lay, by definition, in the king's gift. The question of the royal sucession impinged on them too; every office which they or their families held would one day have to be confirmed by Prince Enrique. And all of them except those in full-time attendance on the king's person would have felt the enhanced attractions of seigneurial patronage at this time. Some of their offices, indeed, had become as devalued as the *maravedís* they were paid in.[43] Membership of the Council provides the best-known example, but the numerous judges of appeal were not far behind. Many judges, indeed, were busy diversifying their sources of patronage; the *Cortes* of 1447 had complained that most of the *Audiencia* members now lived with lords and would not serve their turn on the bench in Valladolid. The problem was not new, but the growing fiscal autonomy of the nobles in the late 1440s made such choices prudent. Other motives could occasionally play a part, as with the appeals judge Pero Díaz de Toledo, who took service with the Marquis of Santillana as both legal representative and literary collaborator. In all these ways, the administrative class felt themselves less automatically the clients of the Constable than had been the case a few years before.

Since the time of Amador de los Ríos, it has been traditional to suggest a further reason for this estrangement —a dispute over the treatment of the Castilian Jews.[44] In this view, Don Alvaro protected the Jewries, relying on their financial support; the *converso* families, seeking to supplant them, favoured a repressive policy, and so became his secret enemies. Three circumstances cast doubt on this ancient *canard*. First, the contribution which the Jewries could still make to Castilian economic life was as useful to the *converso* holders of Crown offices as it was to the Constable himself. Secondly, so far from keeping the *conversos* at a distance from power and influence, he was the personal sponsor of a great many New Christian bureaucrats, and had been so for years. Thirdly, the laws of Arévalo (1443), Amador's main evidence for Don Alvaro's allegedly pro-Jewish policy, had been promulgated at a time when the Constable's enemies were actually in the ascendant at court. The story has survived, one fears, because it serves, despite Amador's transparently liberal intentions, to shift responsibility for the disruption of Castilian affairs towards the existence of Jewish and *converso*

---

[43] See above, Chapter 1, n. 42 on *Consejo* membership; *Cortes (LC)*, vol. III, p. 450 (Valladolid, 1442) on the number of *oidores;* pp. 521-3 (Valladolid, 1447) on failure to serve and living with patrons. On Pero Díaz see below, pp. 180-2.
[44] AMADOR DE LOS RÍOS, *Judíos*, vol. III, pp. 31-59; CANTERA BURGOS, pp. 427-33. The tax-yield of the *aljamas* was relatively small (see above, n. 32), but wealthier Jews still farmed up to a fifth of royal revenues (LADERO QUESADA, «Los judíos castellanos del siglo XV en el arrendamiento de impuestos reales», *CHist*, 6 (Madrid, 1975), p. 431. For the date of the Arévalo edict (6th April 1443) see the text in AMADOR DE LOS RÍOS, vol. III, pp. 583-9.

minorities. With one significant exception, none of its elements ought to have survived Cantera Burgos' detailed refutation of 1952.

That exception is furnished by the revolt which broke out in the city of Toledo in 1449, which undoubtedly did have a serious impact on the administrative families. Not all of them, of course, were New Christians. Alonso Pérez, whatever the *Crónica de Don Alvaro* may have to say of his base origins, was, according to a witness with no motive for falsehood, «the son of a good man of Vivero, who was an *hidalgo*».[45] But the group also included such *conversos* as the de Toledo clan in its several branches, Doctor Franco's family, the Chirinos of Cuenca, and the Cartagena-Santa María family from Burgos. For such as these, the Toledo rebellion, with its explicit challenge to their right of office-holding, offered a test-case of Don Alvaro's priorities.[46] By using local *converso* officials to further unpopular policies, he had created a predicament for the whole caste; what would he now do to get them out of it? His response proved unsatisfactory; he failed to sustain his military pressure against the rebel city, and it was left to Prince Enrique to resolve the situation there. Don Alvaro, it was true, had the excuse of a kingdom-wide military commitment. And there was an obvious political advantage to him in the wide-ranging pardon issued to the Toledans in March 1451, since it helped to conciliate the Prince, who had taken the city under his protection. But *conversos* among the royal officials must still have felt that when it suited the Constable's wider purposes they were on their own. Henceforth, they would be less disposed to put themselves at risk for his sake.

On the morning of his arrest, Don Alvaro had harsh words to say of the *conversos*' ill-will towards him, and especially of Bishop Alonso de Cartagena, «my greatest enemy in this affair».[47] Yet his immediate suspicion of young Alvaro de Cartagena's offer to lead him to safety was, as his own chronicler admits, baseless. It was also of very recent growth; on his arrival in Burgos, Don Alvaro had actually chosen to lodge in the

---

[45] GARCÍA DE SALAZAR, p. 60. The mention of Alonso Pérez in Pedro Gerónimo de Aponte's *Adiciones* to the *Tizón de España* (MS Madrid, BN, 6043, fol. 162v), can scarcely overrule this testimony. WILLIAM D. PHILLIPS, «State Service in Fifteenth-Century Castile. A Statistical Study of the Royal Appointees», *Societas*, 8 (1978), 115-36, is properly cautious about the proportion of *conversos* among Juan II's officials.

[46] For the threat to *converso* office-holding see BENITO RUANO, *Orígenes*; also ALBERT A. SICROFF, *Les Controverses des Statuts de «pureté de sang» en Espagne du XVe au XVIIe Siècle* (Paris, 1960), pp. 32-62; ROUND, «Politics, Style and Group Attitudes in the *Instrucción del Relator*», *BHS*, 46 (1969), 289-319; for the pardon of 21st March 1451 see MS Madrid, BN 13108, fols 202-207v.

[47] *CAL* (C), p. 381 (contrast the chronicler's own view on p. 382); also pp. 333-4. This source implies that Pedro de Cartagena was living elsewhere at the time, or was, perhaps, merely the owner of this particular house (pp. 321, 374). But CORRAL, p. 73 makes it clear that contemporaries identified it as «Pedro de Cartagena's house.»

house of the Bishop's brother. Alonso de Cartagena, it was true, had aroused some suspicion a few days earlier by putting troops of his own on the streets at a moment of tension. And he was to play a prominent part in the negotiations which led to Don Alvaro's peaceful surrender, later that same day. But all this can be explained very adequately without the assumption of any special hostility to Don Alvaro.

The Cartagenas, after all, were closely identified with the merchant oligarchy of Burgos. They had an obvious interest in seeing the crisis resolved with a minimum of local disruption —the more so because, if Don Alvaro continued to resist, it would be Pedro de Cartagena's house which had to be stormed. Even before the crisis broke, however, they had to cope with a local situation of some delicacy.[48] Don Alvaro's enemies, the Estúñigas, were present in the city as an independent military force, thanks to their command of the castle. They were none too well-disposed towards *conversos;* moreover, they had both financial and political clients among the citizenry. Yet there was enough opposition to them to make it appear plausible that Don Alvaro might use the Burgos populace against the castle. In the event, the king's own declared hostility to Don Alvaro was enough to swing the mass of citizens towards a violently pro-Estúñiga mood. Against this background, the city's *conversos* had to tread warily. Only a few years earlier, the chief of the Toledo rebels, Pero Sarmiento, passing close to the city on his erratic progress into exile, had created a major panic among this, the most prosperous and established New Christian community in all Castile. What had happened in Toledo could still happen in Burgos. So it was a sensible precaution for Bishop Cartagena to deploy troops of his own when it looked as if Luna and Estúñiga partisans might clash on the city streets. And it was a matter of sheer self-preservation that, once the king's will was declared beyond all doubt, the Cartagenas, like virtually everyone else in Burgos, should make themselves conformable to it. As for Don Alvaro's outburst against the *conversos,* it must have removed any lingering incentive to help him in his time of need. The Bishop of Burgos did join the king at Escalona that summer, but not to plead for Don Alvaro; he went to settle a long-standing dispute with the Archbishop of Toledo. No doubt the Constable's eclipse helped to simplify such issues.[49].

The immediate crisis in Burgos, then, involved several interacting factors. In this it resembles the more general and more important crisis

---

[48] For the Estúñiga presence and financial holdings see above, n. 8; for their local support, *CJII* (R), p. 679; for the threat to the *conversos, CAL* (C), p. 374; for Don Alvaro's rumoured intentions see PALENCIA, *Déc,* p. 46 (*CEIV,* p. 47); for Pero Sarmiento's passage through the area, SUÁREZ FERNÁNDEZ, *Nobleza y monarquía,* p. 174.
[49] SERRANO, p. 203.

of which it forms a part. Since 1445, and more particularly since 1450, the coalition of interests on which Don Alvaro had based his power had begun to dissolve. He was no longer able to sustain a balance of forces within the kingdom such as would make his rule worthwhile for all the interests it purported to serve. In other words, we are witnessing, and Juan II, in withdrawing his favour was reacting to, an identifiable crisis of government.[50] The factors which mattered most before the Constable's actual fall were those which most directly sapped his sources of power: economic strains, the Portuguese dispute, the prospects of Prince Enrique, hostility among the *grandes*. But once the arrest had been made, the role of the officials was to prove decisive, not least because the removal of Don Alvaro now seemed to many of them essential for their own security. It was revealed as such by the Constable's most drastic political expedient to date —the murder of Alonso Pérez de Vivero.

---

[50] The change in the way in which Don Alvaro's power was now perceived by the king and those close to him is observed by *CCG*, pp. 134-5 (which sees his tighter control of government after Olmedo as the product of rapacity and arrogance), and by SÁNCHEZ DE ARÉVALO, *HH*, p. 233.

CHAPTER 3

EASTER

«To make the worse case appear the better» —the art of the classical rhetorician and the modern public-relations expert— was an essential skill for fifteenth-century chroniclers. Few needed it more than the author of the *Crónica de Don Alvaro de Luna,* and none understood the business better. In the last third of his narrative first-hand authenticity and dramatic tension serve the needs of an elaborate figural design. Don Alvaro appears as a victim, Christlike in his majestic innocence, betrayed and immolated at the liturgical climax of the Christian year. His story has its Last Supper and, in the person of Alonso Pérez de Vivero, its Judas Iscariot. The scriptural analogy, never forced in matters of detail, is sustained as an essential premise of all that is being described. It requires a positive act of reflection to expose the single glaring inconsistency which underlies all this. It was not, after all, Alvaro de Luna who on Good Friday 1453 fell victim to Alonso Pérez's treachery; it was Alonso Pérez who was murdered by Don Alvaro's agents.[1]

In their view he deserved it. He had been exposed as a party to Juan II's moves against the Constable; given his former close ties with the *contador,* it was natural that Don Alvaro should be enraged at this discovery. His chronicler, though, is not content to make that violent reaction seem understandable; he seeks to present it as fully justified. To this end, he represents Alonso Pérez as disloyal over a long period of time, and makes Don Alvaro aware of it long before their final confrontation. In themselves, these claims are plausible; the Constable's security depended on his getting to know such things in good time. But there is some heavy special pleading going on in the *Crónica,* as

---

[1] *CAL* (C), pp. 295-408 passim. For Alonso Pérez as Judas, see p. 295; the Constable's «Last Supper», p. 397; the murder, pp. 350-2; Alonso Pérez's earlier disloyalty, pp. 287, 307, 316, 327-30, etc.; the original plot against him, in Tordesillas, shelved, pp. 309-10; revived in Burgos, p. 345; reference forward to discovery of his dealings, p. 327. On the figural design of the *Crónica* see also RAYMOND R. MACCURDY, *The Tragic Fall: Don Alvaro de Luna and other Favorites in Spanish Golden Age Drama* (Chapel Hill, 1978), pp. 99-103.

it strives to show that its hero, so far from yielding to sudden anger, had been almost superhuman in his forbearance. We are told that the plan to dispose of Alonso Pérez in a simulated accident was formed before the Court moved to Burgos, but rejected by the ever-patient Constable. Yet can an identical opportunity really have presented itself in two different places? Again, there is good warrant in other sources for thinking that documentary proof of Alonso Pérez's involvement was obtained only on Good Friday morning; yet the *Crónica*'s mention of this episode is displaced to an earlier stage of the visit to Burgos. This leaves the actual murder oddly shorn of its most immediate motive. But then the chronicler's main concern throughout seems less to explain events historically than to convince by force of rhetoric.

The various hostile accounts of the murder, brief as they are, have rhetorical purposes of their own. Even Fernán Pérez de Guzmán, who supplies the correct motive, also passes judgment on Don Alvaro's culpable impatience *(Generaciones y semblanzas,* p. 43). Those who mention no motive at all seem merely to stress the act's inherent pointlessness. It is a foreign observer, Vespasiano da Bisticci, who makes explicit what these other accounts merely hint at: «... he failed to rule himself as he should have done, and took upon himself more authority than was proper, believing that he could do whatever pleased him.»[2] Instead of a noble-hearted forbearance, worn down by persistent malice, we are offered an exemplary picture of the rash pride which precedes a fall. Yet neither account helps us to understand the politics of the affair. To do that, we have to see the killing of Alonso Pérez as a rational act —a calculated if extreme risk which failed to come off.

When he arrived in Burgos, Don Alvaro may well have felt some generalized unease over his immediate prospects. It the situation in Castile was as I have described it, he would have been obtuse not to entertain such misgivings. The restive state of the city —manifested, for example in the affray in which the Bishop's troops took part— would have kept these anxieties alive. But outside the interested testimony of his own chronicle, there is little to suggest that the Constable had any inkling of the real threat facing him until 28th March, the Wednesday of Holy Week. That day saw a painful interview with Juan II, who confronted his *privado* with a crisis of confidence.[3] The magnates and the estates of the realm, he declared, were so hostile that Don Alvaro would have to leave the court. There was nothing novel, of course, in the

---

[2] VESPASIANO DA BISTICCI, *Vite di uomini illustri* (Milan, 1951), p. 234.

[3] *CAL* (C), pp. 360-5 places this conversation after the murder, and makes Juan II implausibly compliant. The other three accounts broadly agree, though PALENCIA, *Déc,* p. 45 *(CEIV,* p. 46) offers only a paraphrase. VALERA, *CAbr,* pp. 328-9, has fewer details than *CJII* (R), p. 680, though the latter clumsily inserts this incident as a flashback in its account of the following week.

nobility's ill-will, and there were hopeful precedents for this kind of tactical retreat. But the mention of the estates —the *Cortes* delegates, even now converging on Burgos— raised more serious issues. If they merely showed an inclination to favour the views of the magnates in their own home areas, then a troublesome session was in prospect. But these were men who sat in the *Cortes* at the king's bidding, and they tended to frame their political opinions in terms acceptable to him. Was Juan II, then, reporting what he had wished, or would have wished, to hear from them? If so, Don Alvaro was in deep trouble. And the turn which his conversation with the king now took was just as disturbing. The Constable suggested that, in his absence, Archbishop Carrillo of Toledo might preside over a caretaker administration; in other words, he sought a guarantee of at least benevolent neutrality towards his own interests. He was told, curtly enough, to mind his own business. Sooner or later, clearly, he would have to comply with the king's desire, and go. But he would be going with no assurance whatever of the king's goodwill.

By the morning of Good Friday he had been in this dilemma for some thirty-six hours. Meanwhile, and still unknown to him, the king's intrigue with the Count of Plasencia had taken a decisive step forward.[4] Late on Thursday night, the Countess of Ribadeo had reached the Estúñiga stronghold of Béjar with a personal message from the Queen. Within hours the Count's heir Alvaro de Estúñiga had set out with three companions on the hundred and twenty-mile ride to Curiel, an Estúñiga fief near Peñafiel in the Duero valley, about two thirds of the way to Burgos. But before they could arrive and begin to rally forces, early on Saturday afternoon, Alvaro de Luna had already struck at Alonso Pérez. The stimulus to this decisive action seems to have taken two forms.[5]

---

[4] VALERA, *CAbr*, pp. 327-8 is a first-hand account, but dates the departure from Béjar «viernes doze días de abril». By 12th April (which was not a Friday in 1453) Don Alvaro was already in custody. 12th April 1454, however, was Good Friday. VALERA evidently recalled setting out in the small hours of Good Friday (30th March in 1453), but worked out the date for the wrong year. The road to Curiel —rather longer than his estimate of 35 leagues— took until «sábado a comer»; allowing for a night's rest, this confirms Palencia's statement that it took 20 hours (*Déc*, p. 45; *CEIV*, p. 46). *CJII* (R), p. 678 compounds the error over dating, but adds some credible details not in *CAbr*. (A date of 23rd March, and a week spent waiting in Curiel would be compatible with Mosén Diego's account but seems less likely.)

[5] For the captured letter see *Abr H*, cap. 177, p. cxcix. Some of Juan II's messages to Estúñiga are in *CD*, pp. 40-1. Details confirming this story occur in *CAL* (C), pp. 347, 349; for the friar, see pp. 347-50 passim. In the more dramatic and perhaps less reliable account current in 1497, the friar names Don Alvaro, who complains to the king, is advised by him to leave the court, and erupts in anger; later, his men try to lynch the friar from the episcopal gaol (CORRAL, pp. 63-4).

Early that Friday morning, Don Alvaro's senior henchman, Fernando de Ribadeneira, had set out to make the rounds of the Stations of the Cross. On his way to a shrine outside the city wall, he met and recognized a serving-man of Alonso Pérez. The man's evasive conduct aroused suspicion; he was searched, and found to be carrying a dispatch from Alvaro de Estúñiga to the *Contador*. We do not know what it contained. Most likely it had little to say about the king; his own surviving messages to the young Estúñiga are scrupulously vague. Nor can the messenger have carried any report of Estúñiga's ride from Béjar, which had begun only hours before. But some preliminary planning had clearly been necessary, and it was Alonso Pérez's ill-luck to have that task fall to him. He, at all events, was irrevocably exposed as an enemy. We are told that the news of this conduct, on the part of a man for whom he had done so much, came as a profound shock to Don Alvaro. But after Juan II's behaviour of the previous Wednesday, he must have found the practical implications yet more alarming. He knew now that he could not do what he had done in 1440 and 1441 —leave the royal presence, knowing that his own agents still dominated the inner circle of the king's most trusted officials. Alonso Pérez's treachery made that impossible; hence Alonso Pérez would have to be put out of the way. And it must be done quickly, before the Constable was formally instructed to leave the court.

This urgency was underlined by a curious incident in Burgos Cathedral that same morning. The sermon of the day, delivered in the king's presence, was followed by an inflammatory harangue against Don Alvaro. The preacher, a Dominican friar, stopped short of mentioning his name, but his hostile intent was so blatant and so pointed that the embarrassed Juan II cut him short with a gesture of dismissal. The Constable, anxious to find out who had inspired the attack, protested at once to the Bishop of Burgos, who promised an immediate enquiry. Within hours, the Bishop was back, accompanied by the Relator —a welcome sign that the lines of clerical privilege were not being too restrictively drawn in this case. But they had an unsatisfactory story to tell. The friar, now in the ecclesiastical prison, would only say that he had been divinely inspired; Don Alvaro thought this unlikely, and said so. He urged the Bishop to examine him again «as his habit and the laws require». No doubt he would have liked to have the friar put to the torture, but the Relator's presence was a reminder that the law had its own reservations about this. We do not know what became of the friar. But it is not too hard to see what was in Don Alvaro's mind. If the preacher had not been acting on instructions from the king himself —and this would lend some point to his claim to divine inspiration— some other powerful adversary must be responsible. After that morning's disclosures, the obvious candidate was Alonso Pérez. And if the *contador* was, in fact, beginning to orchestrate a public campaign against Don Alvaro, the case for his immediate removal was greatly strengthened.

Exactly how these factors were combined is still uncertain, for the capture of Alonso Pérez's correspondence and the incident of the sermon are each attested by a single source. Yet the *Crónica de Don Alvaro,* our witness for the sermon, also confirms that Ribadeneira went round the Stations that morning, and that it was he who procured firm evidence of Alonso Pérez's guilt. The primary source for the other account, in the abbreviated *Crónica del Halconero,* can only be Ribadeneira himself. Can we, then, take his word for it that the news about Alonso Pérez came as a total surprise to Don Alvaro? Circumstantial evidence suggests that we can: it the Constable had known of his full danger when Juan II first mooted his dismissal, he would hardly have stayed his hand for two days. And if he was now to be sure of eliminating Alonso Pérez before the order to leave was made formal, he had to act upon the captured letter as soon as it reached him. The likeliest time for this would have been shortly after the interrupted sermon. At that point, indeed, the Constable's chronicler represents Ribadeneira as breaking some related news —the fact that the king had sent for Alvaro de Estúñiga. It seems probable that he did so in the context of the captured dispatch. And once the full discovery was in his hands, Don Alvaro's mind would have turned urgently towards action.

His first step, naturally enough, was to consult his followers.[6] Not, of course, on the point of substance; to leave Alonso Pérez alive was scarcely an option. The main problem was that of ensuring secrecy, given which, murder must now have seemed the safest of courses. It was agreed that Don Alvaro would petition the king for the dead man's son, Juan de Vivero, to have his father's offices. That should quieten any suspicions which the king might harbour. At best, if the *contador*'s sway over Juan II had merely responded to a passing mood, Don Alvaro might not have to leave the court after all. At worst, he could go and leave behind him no hostile figure in the king's close entourage. Or if Alonso Pérez had accomplices, what then? They would surely take the hint which his fate offered. And the rest of the world need know nothing.

The political judgment behind the scheme was shrewd enough; its weakness lay in its hastily improvised practical detail. The Constable's lodging had a tower with railings round the top; a section of these was to be loosened, and the *contador*'s body pushed over. A clamour would

---

[6] VALERA, *CAbr,* p. 329 and *CJII* (R), p. 678 mention a council held in Don Alvaro's lodging (implying a semi-formal consultation); *CAL* (C), pp. 350-1, describes a series of private conversations.

then be raised to the effect that Alonso Pérez, while talking with Don Alvaro on top of the tower, had fallen through the defective woodwork and met his death. There were technical features of this plan which could and did go wrong —another reason for doubting that it had been conceived long in advance. There were also serious and unavoidable flaws of principle. Acts of violence committed in the king's court were especially grave matters in law,[7] but there was no time to entice Alonso Pérez further afield. Nor was there time for Don Alvaro to remove himself to a prudent distance from the scene of the crime. Lastly, the plan involved an actual interview with Alonso Pérez, who was to be confronted with the evidence of his treachery. This risk, at least, was justifiable on two counts. It eliminated the remote chance that he was being framed by the Estúñigas for reasons of their own. And it was an insurance, should the crime become public, against the ultimate charge of killing by stealth. So, at any rate, it was done. Alonso Pérez was visibly shaken at the sight of his treasonable correspondence; Juan de Luna, the Constable's son-in-law, battered his head in with a mace, and shortly after sunset, his body was thrown off the tower.[8]

From the start, the cover-up went wrong. A cluster of servants idling at Pedro de Cartagena's door were the first to identify the body before Don Alvaro's men, rushing downstairs with loud cries about the pretended accident, could reach it. But even as it fell, the brains had bespattered an esquire who was watering his mule in the river at the foot of the tower; it was no longer a secret that the victim was dead already. Rumours of the fatal interview, and of the part played by Juan de Luna began to fill the city. The Constable kept up his chosen role, making an elaborate parade of sympathetic grief to young Juan de Vivero, and sponsoring the request to the king that the son should inherit his father's offices and *mercedes*. Juan II agreed to this; it was the least that he could do. When they met next day, he offered Don Alvaro no hint that he had any suspicions in the matter. But he no longer believed a word that the Constable said. More important still, he no longer wanted to.

This was what Don Alvaro could not grasp —the strength of Juan II's newly-awoken feeling against him. Even his personal chronicler, years afterwards, found difficulty in coming to terms with it; Alonso Pérez's confederates, he declares, were working upon the king in secret. Yet these shadowy figures —for the most part royal domestics— can scarcely have

---

[7] *Partidas*, vol. I, pp. 492-3, Pt. II, Tít. 6, ley III. Death was the penalty for any «man of honour» who killed another within a league of the king's person.
[8] The fullest account of the crime is in *CJII* (R), p. 680; further details and rumours in CORRAL, pp. 71-3. *CAL* (C) says nothing of the mace, declaring that Alonso Pérez's skull was broken during his fall. See also pp. 353-7 for the immediate aftermath.

exerted a major influence.[9] One would expect the king, rather, to turn for advice to his senior permanent officials. We have observed already that, as a body, they may well have been less securely aligned with the Constable than had been the case a few years earlier. Certainly they did not react to their colleague's death in the sense for which Don Alvaro might have hoped. They did not revert to their old loyalty to him, nor were they cowed into acquiescence. They seem, in fact, to have read the situation quite differently. After a *contador mayor* of twenty year's seniority had met his end in this fashion, literally anyone might be next. What was certain was that, with king and Constable at loggerheads, further victims would follow. The «killing-time» would go on until one side or the other won outright. But *privados* did not win such struggles outright; a restored security must depend on a prompt and total victory for the king. So the officials must have reasoned, and so it was that, from the crisis in Burgos at Easter to the execution in Valladolid on 2nd June, scarcely one of them broke ranks. They of all people were well-placed to know the nature of Juan II's resolve; their best interest lay in strengthening it.

This was an easier task than the single option left to Don Alvaro, now that he had lost the advantage of secrecy —the resumption of his old sway over Juan II by sheer high-handedness. Implausibly enough, he seems to have believed on Easter Saturday that he had been successful in this. Yet that same day a fresh royal envoy set out for Curiel, bearing the news of the murder and the most urgent summons yet for young Alvaro de Estúñiga to come to Burgos.[10] This message, arriving on Easter Day, found Estúñiga in some perplexity. Almost certainly the events in Burgos meant that the Constable now knew of his errand, and would try to hinder it; to achieve anything at all, he would need all the forces he could come by. But recruitment had gone badly; instead of the two hundred men at arms he had hoped for, he had been able to rally only forty, plus a handful of light cavalry. His best hope of additional support lay in calling out the Estúñiga faction in Burgos itself, but he had to get into the city first. A cautious advance seemed the safest response at this stage.

---

[9] *CAL* (C), p. 359 mentions the Mendoza brothers, later involved in Don Alvaro's arrest and captivity, but these are the only figures of note; the others are «algunos reposteros de cámara».

[10] Estúñiga's mission most fully in VALERA, *CAbr*, pp. 329-30, and the closely related *CJII* (R), pp. 678-9. The number of troops is given by Valera as 60 (40 knights and 20 light horse); the royal chronicle says 70 (40 and 30). Only *AbrH*, p. cc implies that Estúñiga managed to raise his planned 200 knights. Valera at least found time that Easter Sunday for other business: the *Cancionero de Román* (MS Madrid, Real Academia de la Historia, 2-7-2, fol. 383r) has a poem of his beginning «El quen este santo dia...» composed on that day (see BRIAN DUTTON, *Catálogo-índice de la poesía cancioneril del siglo XV* (Madison, 1982), p. 32).

Riding by night, and in great secrecy, the little troop made its way to a point some eighteen miles short of Burgos. There they left the highway to hide in a sheltered valley. From here onward, they ran the risk of meeting reinforcements on their way to join the Constable —though, in the event, the main body of these, under his son Pedro de Luna, was too late in assembling to reach Burgos in time. A more effectual danger to Estúñiga's force came from the Constable's light cavalry under Juan Fernández Galindo, who were scouring the countryside between the city and Curiel. Estúñiga, therefore, decided to go ahead in secret with a single companion, and was, in fact, able to slip into Burgos castle undetected. The other troops, under the historian Diego de Valera, remained in their hiding-place throughout Easter Monday, waiting for Estúñiga's summons to advance. It came after nightfall, and the soldiers set out on a blundering cross-country march which, more by luck than judgment, managed to evade Galindo's scouts. By the early hours of Tuesday, they too had entered the castle. They were joined there by supporters from within the city, bringing the total of new arrivals up to something like three hundred.[11] The first stage of Alvaro de Estúñiga's mission was complete.

Its second stage would depend on the continuing unpreparedness of the Constable and the strength of Juan II's purpose. In the first of these matters, luck was again on Estúñiga's side. Though never able to locate Mosén Diego's confused and wayworn troops, Galindo had been aware of their passage, and had formed a fairly accurate notion of their numbers; thus his report to the Constable on Tuesday morning was not an especially alarming one. Even so, Don Alvaro decided to find out what forces had entered the castle, and made enquiries of a frequent visitor there —the Bishop of Avila, whose sister was married to the garrison commander, Iñigo de Estúñiga. Bishop Fonseca, a talkative but unobservant prelate, had actually been deep in conversation with his sister when Alvaro de Estúñiga arrived, causing the latter some moments of alarm. But he knew no more now than the story which had been sedulously fed to him: that the younger Estúñiga had sent in a consignment of munitions from Curiel, with an escort of some seventy knights. The story, though it tallied with Galindo's, did not wholly satisfy Don Alvaro, who sent Gonzalo Chacón to the king that evening to ask for clarification.[12] But neither did there appear to be any special

---

[11] VALERA, *CAbr*, p. 331 says that there were 300 well-equipped men-at-arms in the castle; *CJII* R, p. 679 states that 200 were recruited from the city. The two figures can be reconciled if we add to the latter the men of Estúñiga's force, and some members of the original garrison.

[12] VALERA, *CAbr*, p. 330 puts Galindo's estimate of the approaching force at 70 men; *CJII* (R), p. 679 puts it at «up to 80 or 90»; *CAL* (C) offers no figure (p. 358). It also claims (pp. 361-4) that the Constable then agreed with the king

reason for alarm. It was beginning to look as if Juan II would prove biddable after all.

It did not look like that to Chacón, who found the king in an acute state of nervous anxiety, barely able to stammer out his limp excuses for what was going on. And indeed Juan II had been through a harrowing day. The welcome news of Alvaro de Estúñiga's arrival had been clouded by the weakness of his accompanying force. The king's first reaction was to write off the entire project. But Estúñiga flatly refused to return to Curiel; he had come, he declared, to kill or capture Alvaro de Luna, and would not leave Burgos alive without doing one or the other. If the king would not help, let him remain neutral. This was the way to talk to Juan II, as the Constable himself knew. A message soon came back, promising full co-operation. Towards evening it was followed by what Estúñiga most needed —a specific instruction, irretrievably committing the king: «Don Alvaro de Estúñiga, my *alguacil mayor,* I order you to arrest Don Alvaro de Luna, Master of Santiago, and if he resists, to kill him.»[13] These vacillations came close to justifying the Constable's desperate gamble; Juan II's resolution held by the merest thread. But hold it did, and his unease that evening is colourable both as the guilty reaction of someone with something to hide, and as the anxiety of a deeply irresolute man who has reached a decision at last.

Fuller details of that decision are given in another message to Estúñiga, whose date is certainly Tuesday 3rd April, but whose timing in relation to the order just quoted remains uncertain. The forces now in the castle were to take up positions early next morning, surrounding the house where Don Alvaro lay; they were not to move from there until they had arrested him and his principal followers. They were also to provide a screen of mounted scouts to cut off any fugitives who managed to pass the city gates. Meanwhile, Juan II, standing by in a neighbouring street, would rally the armed citizenry to lend their support.[14]

Two aspects of this plan call for some comment. It is notably ambiguous over what Estúñiga is supposed to do should Don Alvaro decline to come quietly. Juan II's briefer instruction, if issued later, may have been meant to clarify this. More notable still is the contrast between the active and demanding role assigned to Estúñiga's tiny force and the vaguely supportive function envisaged for the king. At first glance it would appear that Juan II was still being evasive. But other factors may

---

to go into voluntary exile for a time. Based on a displaced and adapted version of their interview of the previous Wednesday, this story appears very doubtful. By contrast, the account of Chacón's visit to the king (pp. 367-8) is totally convincing.

[13] VALERA, *CAbr*, p. 331. A virtually identical text appears in *CJII* (R), p. 679.
[14] *CD*, no. XXIII, p. 41. *Abr H*, p. cc states that the king ordered Estúñiga to storm the house, promising active support, but other sources, and the subsequent course of events, contradict this.

have been at work. It was far from certain that the townsfolk of Burgos would support the Estúñigas and the castle garrison against Don Alvaro. Who but the king himself could be certain of commanding their trust and ensuring their docility?

Such a role as the commander of a potential «third force» had other attractions. Alvaro de Estúñiga's defiant outburst must have struck a depressingly familiar chord with Juan II; had he escaped his domineering Constable only to let himself be bullied by the Estúñigas? But the fiery young captain's injudicious taunt that Juan II might stand aside from events if he wished pointed to a possible way out. He could, indeed, use the Estúñigas to topple Don Alvaro, but then discard them, arrogating to himself the question of how the fallen Constable was to be treated. As king, he was formally entitled to demand from the Estúñigas as much or as little by way of action as he might choose; they, on the other hand, had no right to demand that he should follow up their actions in the way which they happened to prefer. In undertaking to stand by at the head of the citizenry in arms, Juan II was preparing himself for just such a role as the arbiter of events. And this in turn strongly suggests that, at some time in the course of that anxious Tuesday, someone had reminded him that he was, after all, the king. The most obvious people to issue such a reminder were the permanent officials, who combined a strong personal attachment to the Crown with a background of regalist theory. We do not know whether Juan II did confide his troubles to any particular official on April 3rd, though it would have been both possible and natural to do so. What we do know is that his conduct from then onwards is marked by a growing sense of independent purpose.

And still Don Alvaro made no counter-move of his own.[15] Chacón brought in his ominous report, together with a personal warning from the royal Chamberlain; it inspired some discussion of an immediate flight, but other counsels prevailed. Another of his retainers brought rumours of the impending arrest and a plan for leaving the city; he was told not to panic. The Constable ate roasted pears, drank wine, listened to the king's new French musicians in the street below. Orders previously given that an additional guard of men-at-arms should spend the night on the premises were neglected; nobody thought to check whether they had been obeyed. That night, by all accounts, Don Alvaro slept better than some of his more anxious followers.

At dawn next morning Alvaro de Cartagena, son of the Constable's host Don Pedro, came beating at the door of his father's house with the news that an armed force was marching down from the castle.[16] First

---

[15] *CJII* (R), pp. 680-1 and *CAL* (C), pp. 368-72 offer distinctive but compatible accounts of the Constable's last night of freedom.

[16] *CAL* (C), pp. 373-87 gives one side of the military events leading to Don

reports suggested that this was the Estúñiga garrison on its way to attack the city's *conversos,* and Don Alvaro was quick to offer the Cartagena clan his protection. But it soon emerged that he, not they, was the target of the raid, for the attackers rallied to the cry of «Castile and the king's liberty!». The king, meanwhile, was in a nearby square, heading the muster of the citizens, and exercising his liberty in a manner not much to the liking of Alvaro or Iñigo de Estúñiga. A series of urgent messages warned them to attempt no frontal assault on Pedro de Cartagena's house, but merely to blockade it. Here again, Juan II may have been thinking chiefly of how the townsfolk might react; it was not the moment to risk affronting them by storming the home of a prominent fellow-citizen. But the Estúñigas, never very certain of the king's intentions, must have feared the worst. By this time they were involved in a brisk and lethal exchange of bowshot and arquebus. Yet it was the defenders of the house who were in the less tenable position, and who were even now being made painfully aware of it.

This was the moment when young Alvaro de Cartagena made his offer of a safe passage through the back-ways of the city —an offer at first suspiciously rejected by the Constable, then accepted, then abandoned in mid flight. This mistrust of the *converso* Cartagenas seems all the more puzzling when, only a few hours earlier, he had offered to take up arms in their defence. Yet the likeliest explanation is surely the one nearest to hand: that he felt betrayed by the failure of the Burgos *conversos* to do the same for him, and to come to his rescue. In fact, they were in no position to do so; they had been mustered since dawn, along with the rest of the citizens, under the king's direct command. But Don Alvaro, trapped in the besieged house, had no means of knowing this.[17] His judgment, in any case, was beginning to show signs of strain; the return to the Cartagena house was a decisive act of folly.

He returned to a military impasse. The defenders were too few to break out, and the attackers were not being allowed to break in. There would be no hand-to-hand fighting; the king, following out his chosen role, would not allow Estúñiga to bring in the prisoner himself, but insisted on a negotiated surrender.[18] In this none of the Estúñigas was

Alvaro's arrest, laying much emphasis on the non-arrival of expected reinforcements —the forces of Pedro de Luna (p. 371), and those of retainers quartered elsewhere in the city and unable to get through the hostile crowds. On the other side, VALERA, *CAbr,* pp. 331-2 (largely followed by *CJII* (R), pp. 679-80) has much to say of Estúñiga's frustrations.

[17] According to *CAL* (C), p. 387, details of the king's role reached the Constable only after his return from his abortive flight. On Don Alvaro and the *conversos* see above, pp. 63-5. *CCG,* p. 136 states that Pedro and Alonso de Cartagena, along with the city magistrates, had been summoned to assist the king.

[18] Accounts of the negotiations conflict with one another. *CAL* (C) describes

to be allowed any part. The opening moves seem to have been entrusted to the herald *Restre,* and indeed, the sending of a herald was the obvious way of establishing a cease-fire. But the herald could only state the king's demand for a surrender; he was not a suitable person to negotiate issues of substance. And the Constable was interested above all in the substantive issue of a safeconduct for himself and his companions. To some extent his insistence was a device to gain time —perhaps Pedro de Luna might yet turn up with a relieving force. In the end he did not, though the delay did enable the Constable to send out a number of letters, presumably soliciting support elsewhere. But he also seems to have placed some genuine trust in the legal validity of whatever document Juan II might grant him. Hence the long-drawn out negotiations over its terms.

As many as a dozen missions may have passed to and fro between king and Constable. In about half of them, the intermediary was Don Alvaro's chaplain. According to the *Crónica de Juan II,* these occupied the beginning of the process; the Constable's chronicler places them at the end. There is at least one reason for preferring the royal chronicle on this point; it provides us with a convincing reason why the chaplain's involvement in the negotiations should have been broken off. It seems that besides acting as a go-between for the king, he was also the bearer of the Constable's messages to third parties. Once this had been discovered, the king was most unlikely to regard him as an acceptable envoy. The main work of establishing the terms of the safeconduct then passed to a group of negotiators so shrewdly chosen that it seems almost certain that the king had selected them in advance.

Don Alvaro's military and aristocratic enemies were represented by Ruy Díaz de Mendoza, a junior member of the one great house to rival the Estúñigas in power and wealth.[19] The Constable's chronicler implies

---

the following: two embassies by *Restre* (pp. 387-9); one by Bishop Cartagena and Ruy Díaz de Mendoza (pp. 390-2); several by Don Alvaro's chaplain, issuing in the agreed safeconduct (pp. 392-3); one by Ruy Díaz and Perafán de Ribera, who make the arrest. *CJII* (R), p. 680, describes four or five embassies by the chaplain (who also carries other messages for Don Alvaro), one by the Relator alone, four or five by the Relator, the Bishop and Ruy Díaz, and one by these three with Perafán, which settles the terms of the safeconduct, on whose receipt Don Alvaro surrenders. VALERA, *CAbr,* pp. 332-4 offers a summary version of the royal chronicle's data, omitting, for example, all mention of the chaplain. PALENCIA, *Déc,* pp. 46-7 (*CEIV,* pp. 47-8) mentions all four negotiators, but intermingles both earlier and later events. *Abr H,* pp. cc-cci mentions only Ruy Díaz and another knight as intermediaries.

[19] Above, Chapter 2, n. 10, for Mendoza family income. Ruy Díaz himself held over 500,000 *maravedís* from the Crown in 1447 (LADERO QUESADA, *Hacienda,* p. 275). For his involvement with Alonso Pérez see *CAL* (C), p. 359; his hostility to the Constable is there dated only from 1453 (p. 320), but the chronicler describes a clash of personalities at the siege of Atienza in 1446 (p. 200), following earlier close collaboration.

that Ruy Díaz had been a party to Alonso Pérez's conspiracy, but his appointment now could hardly have been bettered as an exercise in political balance. He was joined, for the final stages leading to Don Alvaro's surrender, by Perafán de Ribera, military commander of the Andalusian frontier.[20] This plump, middle-aged, and decidedly unheroic figure —at some stage, a client of Don Alvaro— was no threat to anyone. But he carried enough rank to upstage Alvaro de Estúñiga, and to receive with dignity the great Constable's sword. The ceremonial primacy of the nobility was thus firmly assured. But the other two negotiators were neither members of that class nor, on their record, proven enemies of the Constable. They were, rather, king's men —strongly committed to Juan II's purposes, and disposed, if they could, to see these realized peacefully.

This would certainly have been the attitude of the Bishop of Burgos, Alonso de Cartagena. The most important and widely trusted of the local leaders present that day, he would have been anxious in the first place to spare his city the risks of a large-scale military engagement. His presence as a negotiator would also be useful to the king if Don Alvaro chose to invoke his own quasi-ecclesiastical status as Master of Santiago. The other envoy was the Relator, Fernán Díaz de Toledo, the senior royal official, and the one closest to the king. He may, indeed, have known of Juan II's hostility to Don Alvaro from a much earlier stage;[21] certainly, he would have been alarmed and alerted by the fate of his old colleague, Alonso Pérez de Vivero. But the reasons for his presence now were strictly professional; he had a fine legal brain, unrivalled experience in government, and two important tasks to perform.

The first was to deliver the official summons requiring Don Alvaro to surrender «at the king's command».[22] This formally indispensable errand is mentioned only by the royal chronicle, which also refers to four or five later visits, on which the Relator was joined by Ruy Díaz and the Bishop. In the *Crónica de Don Alvaro,* we have an account of a single visit, in which these two alone take part. This seems a typical piece of artistic simplification, but the interview described there has a compelling authenticity about it. The Bishop, it appears, tried to calm Don Alvaro's ruffled feelings, only to be snubbed, woundingly, as a wearer of «long skirts» and no gentleman. The fraying temper and the

---

[20] He had held this command —virtually a family inheritance— since 1436 (PÉREZ BUSTAMANTE, vol. I, pp. 390, 393; see also p. 376 for abusive poems on his girth and cowardice). For his membership of the Constable's household see CAL (C), p. 443.
[21] His son Luis Díaz certainly did; see above, p. 44.
[22] The procedure of formal *requerimiento* is particularly well described in C Halc, pp. 43-4 (also Ref Halc, pp. 81-2), where the Relator once again plays the main part at the surrender of Peñafiel in 1429.

reversion to social type as a military grandee are much of a piece with the rest of the Constable's behaviour under stress. He probably felt the same about the Relator, a *converso* like Alonso de Cartagena, and, as a Doctor of Laws, a wearer of long robes too. Don Alvaro's chronicle, indeed, subjects Fernán Díaz to the ultimate snub of not mentioning him at all, but it may have other reasons for this. The Relator's second task, given his unique experience as an inditer of royal documents, would have been to draw up Don Alvaro's safeconduct. And the official version of what this document contained stands in flat contradiction to the account given by the *Crónica de Don Alvaro*.

Both the royal chronicler and Mosén Diego de Valera describe the safeconduct as an autograph text, issued under the king's seal following a visit to Don Alvaro by all four of the royal envoys. All four duly returned as its bearers, whereupon the Constable, though not at all happy with the terms, made his surrender to Perafán and Ruy Díaz. Mosén Diego professes to have forgotten the detailed terms, but the *Crónica de Juan II* offers a brief paraphrase: «that the king gave him his royal word, as touching his person and his property, that he would suffer no offence or injury, or anything contrary to justice.»[23] By contrast, the *Crónica de Don Alvaro* insists that Juan II did concede the terms which the Constable, through his chaplain, had named. The king bound himself to this agreement by oath, signed it, and sealed it «with his secret seal». Don Alvaro then gave the document for safekeeping to Gonzalo Chacón —probably the author of this chronicle, and certainly the main source at this point. Its terms are reported as follows: «... received him into his protection, promising that he would not suffer death or injury or imprisonment... and extending this guarantee to cover his wealth and property.»[24] The agreement is to cover action by any of the king's agents against the Constable or any of his followers. After a long and ceremonious farewell to his household, Don Alvaro surrendered, on this understanding, to Juan II's returning envoys —as well he might have done, considering that they ruled out virtually all future action against him. It seems most unlikely that the king should have agreed to anything of the kind. Yet the Constable's supporters remained firmly convinced that he had, while Juan himself was equally adamant that he had not. The dispute was to reach its climax in the king's letter of 22nd May to the embattled Luna partisans, where he virtually challenged them to produce their evidence —«any such oath or safeconduct, supposing

---

[23] *CJII* (R), p. 680: «que el Rey le daba su fe real que en su persona ni en su hacienda no resciberia agravio ni injuria, ni cosa que contra justicia se le hiciese.» Cf. VALERA, *CAbr,* p. 333.

[24] *CAL* (C), p. 393: «e lo resçibía en su seguro, asegurándolo de muerto e de lisión e de prisión... e asimesmo a sus bienes e faziendas». For Juan II's disclaimer see *CD,* p. 71, no. XXXVII.

that I were shown to have given any». Both of the rival summaries contain formulae which might have been taken from actual texts or drafts; our problem, therefore, is to show how both could have come to exist and to be believed.

A closer scrutiny of the *Crónica de Don Alvaro* suggests that it cannot have made direct use of the document issued by Juan II.[25] Along with other written guarantees offered by the king, this final safeconduct is stated there to have been handed over to Gonzalo Chacón as part of Don Alvaro's winding up of his affairs. But within a very short time of the Constable's arrest, Chacón and other retainers were also detained by the royal forces, and «robbed of all that they had». The vital document, then, was in Chacón's possession for a matter of hours at most, and he can have had little chance to study it closely. For any later account, he would have needed to rely on memory. His memory, of course, could still be accurate. Juan II might have issued a safeconduct embodying the Constable's demands, but then had it confiscated and suppressed. The more limited formula which the royal chronicle prefers —perhaps borrowed from some earlier offer, rejected by Don Alvaro— would have been circulated later on as an official text. If this was done —and Chacón's arrest certainly provided the opportunity— it was a master-stroke to give the official version the extra authenticity of a royal autograph.

But we are not bound to accept this reading of events at all. In the course of these long-drawn-out negotiations, we can imagine all sorts of proposals and counter-proposals being exchanged. But the crucial interview was the last of the series —the one where Perafán de Ribera was brought in. At this meeting, Don Alvaro would have helped to draft the kind of elaborately comprehensive guarantee which his chronicle records. But it could not be accepted there and then; it would have to go to the king for ratification. Indirectly, the Constable's chronicler confirms that it did so, for he describes (pp. 393-404) a considerable lapse of time between the preparation of the safeconduct and the actual arrest. During this interval, Don Alvaro is portrayed as dining with his retinue, bidding them a suitably edifying farewell, and handing over the documents of the negotiations to the faithful Chacón. But these papers can have included only the draft of the final agreement, not its signed and sealed version; that arrived only with the arresting officers. Meanwhile, Juan II was having to reach a complex decision about Don Alvaro's draft. As it

---

[25] *CAL* (C), p. 403 («los seguros que el Rey le avía enbiado» handed over to Chacón); the arrest follows *de facto* with the return of Perafán and Ruy Díaz (p. 404), though only on p. 406 do we learn that the latter had Don Alvaro disarmed and confined to his room. For the treatment of his followers see p. 407. Young Estúñiga, acting through Mosén Diego de Valera, had offered them a safeconduct of his own (VALERA, *CAbr*, p. 333).

stood, it clearly would not do, but on what other basis could the Constable be induced to surrender? Eventually there emerged the notion of a guarantee against unjust treatment, to which Juan II was willing enough to swear, giving «his royal word». It was this amended document which the four negotiators took back to Don Alvaro. Its terms were not those which he had expected, but he was in no position to demand better.[26]

In the confused and anxious aftermath of the arrest, Chacón could hardly be expected to collate the new safeconduct with the draft in his possession. All he knew, as he sat in Burgos gaol that evening, was that he had been robbed of his papers and possessions and flung into prison. He could remember the terms on which Don Alvaro had expected to surrender, and was painfully aware that these had not been honoured in practice. From this it was entirely natural to conclude that the king had treacherously promised one thing and done another.

Whichever of these versions we accept, the ambiguous character of the official safeconduct boded Don Alvaro no sort of good. It offered him security against his immediate enemies, but none against legal proceedings by the king. It was the king, after all, who was empowered to define, in the last resort, what was or was not «against justice». That, at least, was the view which the regalist-minded lawyers of the administration were likely to take; one wonders if this potentially useful formula can have been the work of the Relator himself. Legal proceedings, of course, were very much in prospect, given what Juan II must by now know about Alonso Pérez's murder. And in the longer term it could be argued that the agreement left room for any future action on which the king might decide.

For the present, though, he was content to retain and reinforce his new-found grip on events. Once Ruy Díaz and his party had returned, and the arrest had been made, this meant protecting the prisoner from the citizens of Burgos, whose attitude to Don Alvaro had been abruptly transformed by the day's events. Having seen the king's change of heart, and the collapse of the Constable's power, they had become violently hostile to the fallen *privado*. His captors refused, for his own good, to conduct him across the city to the king's presence, lest he be assaulted on the way. In other respects the guarantees given him were harshly interpreted. His retainers were harassed and plundered; some, like Chacón, were gaoled. Whatever possessions he had on the spot were confiscated. And when the king did arrive at Pedro de Cartagena's

---

[26] *CJII* (R), p. 680 puts the point bluntly enough; the crucial factor, as the otherwise inadequate *Abr H*, pp. cc-ccii makes clear, was the hostility of the citizens. Both VALERA, *CAbr*, p. 333, and *CAL* (C), pp. 404-5 agree that, at the moment of the arrest, Don Alvaro and Ruy Díaz discussed this; presumably this was the context in which he acceded to the terms offered him. If so, however, his own chronicler either misses or suppresses the point.

house, he simply refused to see his captive.[27] An early, though suspiciously well-found, story suggests that he was following a maxim of Don Alvaro's own: «that he should never speak directly with anyone whom he had ordered to be arrested.» But Almela's simpler explanation is just as likely to be the right one: «after losing his former affection for him, he could not bear to see him.»

This was still the thing which Don Alvaro found hardest to believe. He preferred to cast about for third parties on whose intrigues and ill-will the crisis in his affairs might be blamed. Earlier in the day it had been the *conversos* and Bishop Cartagena; now, momentarily, these resentments came to focus on the embarrassed Bishop Fonseca of Avila.[28] From the king Don Alvaro still felt that he had something left to hope for, and these hopes, immediately before and after his arrest, found expression in a series of written appeals. We know, for example, of a petition drawn up in the last hours of his freedom, of a letter (possibly not the same) carried to the king by the Deputy Prior of Montalbán at some time on 4th April and used in evidence later, of a warning from Don Alvaro's prison of Portillo about the effects of sensual indulgence on the king's health.[29] And it is tempting to think that one of the handful of the Constable's verses surviving in fifteenth-century *cancioneros* represents another, more personal approach to Juan II:

> «A tu discreta ordenança
> inclino mi voluntat
> confiança.
> Luzero de la verdat
> usando de tu iusticia
> no consientas que maliçia
> pueda cuentra caridat,
> por esto con humildança
> pido atu santidat
> lealtança.»[30]

---

[27] *CAL* (C), p. 406; *Abr H*, p. cci; *CJII* (R), p. 681, including the maxim «que nunca hablase a persona que mandase prender». This was recalled by a witness in 1497 (CORRAL, p. 87) and paraphrased more sensationally by BISTICCI, p. 234: «che uomo che egli volessi fare more, nollo udisse mai.» Characteristically, the *Centón epistolario* (spuriously Burgos, 1499), p. 158, Letter CII picks up the tale. Contrast ALMELA, p. 259.

[28] VALERA, *CAbr*, p. 334; *CJII* (R), p. 681. So unfounded were Don Alvaro's suspicions that Fonseca actually hid Fernando de Ribadeneira, one of the most militant Luna supporters, during the subsequent hue and cry (*CAL* (C), p. 409).

[29] *CAL* (C), pp. 401 (the petition), 425 (letter from Portillo); *CD*, no. XLI, p. 88 (18th June 1453).

[30] *El cancionero de Palacio (Manuscrito no. 594)*, ed. Francisca Vendrell de Millás (Barcelona, 1945), pp. 280-1: «[My] trust [in you] has bent my will to your wise order. O morning-star of truth, display your [habitual] justice, and do not let malice prevail against charity; therefore I humbly beg your holiness [to act with] loyalty.» Some of the lines are ambiguous, but a reading of this sort would be consistent with Don Alvaro's poetic practice, as described in

With this and another dubious exception, though, we lack the text of any of Don Alvaro's appeals.

The second exception is an undated letter to the king, paraphrased by Zurita in the late sixteenth century, and transcribed in distinctive but compatible versions by Mariana and an anonymous seventeenth-century manuscript.[31] The letter dwells at length on Don Alvaro's services to the Crown, and on his failure to adjust to the mutability of fortune. Its main point, however, is an offer to repay certain monies which are due to the royal Exchequer. The two transcriptions mention a sum of ten or twelve thousand *escudos,* which suggests that this text must have been composed after 1534. And, indeed, it has the style of a consciously literary creation. Yet it could still be a remodelling of a genuine letter of Don Alvaro. Zurita gives the sum offered as ten or twelve thousand *doblas.* At somewhere between 2 million and 2.4 million *maravedís,* this would be the kind of quantity which Don Alvaro could lay his hands on without undue hardship; yet it was still large enough to interest Juan II. The *Crónica de Don Alvaro* has the Constable declare, just before his arrest, that the king is to have all the valuables he has with him, in compensation for «things he had acquired and possessed with less than total justice». The total of this conscience money is estimated at «up to twenty thousand florins», or just over 2.1 million *maravedís* —very close to Zurita's figure. The letter which we have could be a version of the petition which Don Alvaro wrote just after this and just before his arrest, though Mariana places it immediately after that event. It would not be surprising, certainly, if such an offer were rejected in the heavily ironic terms which both Mariana and Zurita report.

For the whole strategy of any such appeal was rendered otiose by the still unrealized extent of Don Alvaro's personal and political failure. Reminders of the past merely recalled to the king's mind a servitude from which he was happy to have escaped. Exhortations that he should exercise the virtues associated with royalty only reminded him that he at last had a choice as to how he should exercise them. The admission that Don Alvaro had been at fault in some things reinforced Juan's growing sense that his *privado* had been wrong in most matters. The offer of money could only underline the fact that there was more where that came from. A new range of options was opening before Juan II —a range in which Alvaro de Luna had no part. The constraints and enmities

---

CAL (C), p. 207: «he composed very lively and witty love-poetry, and often used it to declare mysteries concerning other great matters.»

[31] ZURITA, *AA,* fols 12v-13r (Lib. XII, Cap. IX); JUAN DE MARIANA, *Historia de España,* Lib. XXII, Cap. XII, in *Obras,* vol. II (Madrid, 1950), BAE, 31, p. 137; MS Madrid, BN, 6185 (dated 1706), fol. 11v («Papel de Don Alvaro de Luna al Rey Don Juan el Segundo.» Cf. *CAL* (C), p. 399. Money values derived from MACKAY; the sum in *escudos* would, of course, be meaningless before the 1530s.

which had pressed in upon him with the gathering crisis of Don Alvaro's policies could be dispersed at a stroke with the great *privado*'s removal. We do not know if Juan II was as aware of the political opportunities thus created as he evidently was of the personal relief, and the prospect of financial plunder. But the last of these factors alone made it essential to keep his prisoner secure.

With this in mind, he granted the custody of Don Alvaro's person not to young Alvaro de Estúñiga, but to Ruy Díaz de Mendoza and his brother.[32] To have given this charge to Estúñiga would have been to make him, dangerously, the arbiter of the whole situation. For besides having several hundred troops at his command, he was, for the moment, the hero of the hour in Burgos. Even those citizens who were not themselves his clients were bound to feel relieved that his foray of that morning had not been directed against them. And they were all sharply aware that he, unlike the Mendozas, had strong family ties with their city. It was in this mood that the «judge, magistrates, knights and squires» of Burgos actually offered to recover the prisoner by force of arms from Pedro de Cartagena's house and place him in Estúñiga's charge. The latter, however, rejected this proposal, reaffirming his duty to the king.

Several aspects of this affair remain obscure.[33] Mosén Diego de Valera, who tells the story, served the Estúñiga interest, and may have been inclined to exaggerate his patrons' standing in Burgos. Did the «knights and squires» of that city include its powerful merchants and such *converso* burgesses as the Cartagena family? Did any of those magistrates who joined in making the offer to Estúñiga do so under duress? Were the poorer townsfolk genuinely hostile to Don Alvaro? The bitter trading of insults which marked his departure a few weeks later suggests that they were. Yet the unanimity within the city may have been less than our narrative sources make it seem. The king took the precaution of setting an armed guard on the house where the Constable lay, but he still trusted the city council to provide it. This would certainly imply that not all the local magistracy were totally committed to supporting Estúñiga. Even so, there seems little doubt that he was widely preferred to the outsider Ruy Díaz. In keeping Don Alvaro out of his hands, Juan II was keeping the initiative in his own; that the decision tended to favour the prisoner's personal safety was probably incidental.

---

[32] VALERA, *CAbr*, pp. 334-5; *CJII* (R), p. 681; *CAL* (C). p. 406 assigns the more important role to Ruy Díaz.

[33] *CJII* (R) here follows Valera practically word for word; neither makes it clear who were the «justicia, regidores, caualleros e escuderos» in question. For Don Alvaro's acrimonious departure from Burgos see CORRAL, pp. 81-2. For the guard mounted on Don Alvaro's lodging see CANTERA BURGOS, p. 433. (I interpret this incident on somewhat different lines from Cantera himself.)

Meanwhile the king had urgent business to attend to; within four days the *Cortes* were in session.[34] Not that the *Cortes*, whose delegates had apparently made known their misgivings about Don Alvaro before the crisis broke, presented many problems. Their meeting lasted little more than a week, and the trend of their petitions can have caused Juan II little anxiety. He must have been particularly pleased when they formally expressed their satisfaction that he now intended «to carry on the rule and government of his domains in his own person». This was, he assured them, his intention. All the signs are that he was beginning to enjoy it.

---

[34] *Cortes (LC)*, vol. III, pp. 669-70. See also above, Chapter 2, n. 40.

CHAPTER 4

DEPENDENCE, DEROGATION AND DIVINE RIGHT

Don Alvaro's conclusive fall from favour created a situation such as Castile had not known for thirty years. The situation was a novel one precisely because it had yet to define itself. Always before, when Don Alvaro had been in eclipse, one faction or another of his enemies had been visibly in the ascendant; their dominance and his efforts to contest it defined between them the immediate political agenda. This time there was something very like a political vacuum, which the *Cortes* hoped the king would fill «in his own person». But there were a number of other interests whose representatives were very willing to fill it for him. Juan II's handling of these would provide the first clues as to what the new situation held in store.

He had already made it clear that none of the Estúñigas would be the guardian of the Constable's person or the legatee of his power. Their rewards were to be altogether more modest. The aged and vengeful Count of Plasencia could die happy, having encompassed his enemy's fall. When the report on seigneurial abuses in the Salamanca region came to be implemented, the Estúñiga family's depredations were tacitly allowed to stand. Relief from such pressures was welcome, but the impetuous young Alvaro de Estúñiga had almost certainly hoped for more. Since he was not after all to have custody of the prisoner he had done so much to secure, he now set himself a different and no less ambitious goal. This was to engineer the return to power in Castile of the Navarro-Aragonese party —a political coup which, if successful, would set its author firmly at the centre of Castilian affairs. The everpersuasive Diego de Valera was sent to Juan II to argue that contraries were best cured by contraries; peace should now be made with the eastern kingdoms, and the exiles there allowed to return.[1]

At first, Juan appeared to be convinced by this appeal. He authorized

---

[1] VALERA, *CAbr*, p. 336 (death of the Count); see also PALENCIA, *Déc*, pp. 56-7 (*CEIV*, p. 53); for Estúñiga's diplomatic initiatives, see VALERA, pp. 335-6; PALENCIA, p. 48 (*CEIV*, p. 48) attributes them to Valera himself; see also *CJII* (R), p. 682, CABRILLANA CIEZAR, p. 276.

Estúñiga to open a correspondence by proxy with the king of Navarre and with the exiled Admiral. It was a logical enough move; since neither side could readily afford a full-scale war, there was bound to be a settlement sooner or later. The removal of Alvaro de Luna meant that it could come about more quickly. But to replace his ascendancy by that of the Admiral and Juan of Navarre was not precisely what the king of Castile understood as «curing by contraries»; to him it must have seemed like more of the same thing. When the Admiral, taking Estúñiga's encouragement too immediately to heart, returned prematurely to Castile, he was sharply informed of his mistake and packed off once more across the border. Vigilance on the eastern frontier was not relaxed; on 10th April, for example, the king wrote to the captain of the fortress at Ayllón, congratulating him on his resistance to Aragonese raids (CD, no. XXVII, pp. 47-8). Clearly Juan II intended to control the pace of détente himself.

Mosén Diego de Valera attributes these unwelcome second thoughts to the promptings of other counsellors. But they also reflect that concern for his own untrammelled freedom of action which had marked Juan II's conduct since before the arrest. In any event, by the end of the fortnight or so for which the king remained in Burgos, Estúñiga was sufficiently disenchanted with his policies to entertain proposals from quite another quarter. They came from the Constable himself, who now urged Estúñiga to make one more attempt to supplant Ruy Díaz de Mendoza as his custodian. A new alliance of the Luna and Estúñiga families, cemented by a double marriage, would then seize the political initiative from the Constable's enemies (CAL (C), pp. 412-13). This bold project was well calculated to appeal to young Estúñiga's mood of frustrated daring; he in turn seems to have done his best to convince the king that he should be given charge of Don Alvaro. But Juan II was adamant and the plan came to nothing.

We do not know if Don Alvaro made any similar approaches to the Crown Prince and his supporters. But the fear that Enrique's opportunism might find such an alliance attractive seems to have been very much in Juan II's mind. Zurita, indeed, suggests that this was a main motive behind the rapprochement with Aragon. However that may be, the king lost no time in reassuring his son and heir that what had happened in Burgos was in his interest too. On 5th April, the day immediately following the arrest, he wrote to Enrique at great length, laying particular stress on his sequestration of the Constable's property. «It was», says Zurita's paraphrase, «his intention to arrogate to the Crown all that the Constable was found to have lost or to be due to lose.» Enrique was unlikely to miss the point that one day all this would be his.[2]

---

[2] ZURITA, AA, fol. 12r-v. Zurita dates this letter on the day of the arrest—

Don Alvaro's wealth, in fact, was rapidly coming to be a major factor in the king's own calculations. For this the Constable himself was partly responsible. His earliest appeals to Juan II had included the offer of a cash indemnity, and this, if it brought no other result, had encouraged the king to interrogate Gonzalo Chacón regarding his master's treasures. Don Alvaro, the conditions of whose arrest were, initially at least, fairly lenient, was quick to learn of this interest and to appreciate its implications. His wealth might yet prove useful in bargaining with the king, but if the latter could get his hands on it without a struggle, he would have no incentive to strike any bargain. Don Alvaro, therefore, set himself to make his treasures hard to come by. Using as messengers the personal pages who were still allowed to wait on him, he sent out letters to his supporters in the country at large —his wife Juana Pimentel, his son Juan de Luna and the other partisans who had escaped the net at Burgos, his other son Pedro who had never arrived there. His chronicler assures us that the content of these messages was never known; it is practically certain, though, that they were a direct incitement to revolt.[3] By 20th April it was known in the north that Don Alvaro's castle of Escalona was defying the king in arms. But enough of his letters had already been intercepted for this news to come as no surprise.

The Constable's wealth, of course, bore an obvious relevance to Juan II's choice between broad political strategies. He could adopt a defensive approach, accepting the protectorate of some powerful faction —the Estúñigas, the Aragonese exiles, the Crown Prince's party, or perhaps some alliance of them all. Or he could opt for the altogether bolder strategy of affirming the royal authority independently of all these. Quite evidently, Juan preferred the second option: wary of too close an identification with any one faction, carefully discouraging their coalescence into any larger union, he was working all the time to secure and extend his own freedom of manoeuvre. To this the ready money of the Constable's treasuries could obviously contribute; meanwhile there were less spectacular but still valuable gains to be made from the management in the royal name and interest of Don Alvaro's sequestered revenues and estates.

The formal justification for this lay in the serious criminal charge pending against Don Alvaro as the instigator of Alonso Pérez's murder. Doctor Zamora, the Public Prosecutor, had made a preliminary report on this by April 8th, and perhaps as early as April 5th; the dead man's

---

which he regards, erroneously, as 5th, not 4th, April. The mistake may well derive from his having a dated text of the letter before him.

[3] *CAL* (C), pp. 411-12. The earliest royal response to the Escalona revolt appears in the letter to Toledo, written in Torquemada, on the road south from Burgos, on 20th April (*CD*, no. XXXI, pp. 56-8). An earlier note to Toledo (Burgos 15th April) makes no reference to the revolt (ibid., no. XXX, pp. 55-6).

relatives were also pressing the king for action.[4] In fact, Juan was in no hurry to begin criminal proceedings, but the work of sequestration went ahead promptly.[5] The earliest instructions to this effect date from 9th April; next day the Constable's personal treasurer was ordered to hand over all his papers to the royal officials. The process, once begun, was largely a routine affair. The order sent to Seville on 9th April, for instance, is a brief, businesslike document, drawn up by a relatively junior secretary, Pero Ferrández de Lorca. It is, too, self-evidently a *pro forma,* intended to serve also for «all the other cities, towns and villages of my domains».

The much longer letter to the city of Toledo which the Relator had drawn up on the previous day had been designed for a similarly wide circulation. But it had touched upon far more contentious issues. Most immediately, it had sought to outline and justify the king's actions against Don Alvaro. But it also called upon the citizens to oppose and if possible apprehend those active partisans of the Constable who were still at liberty. This order was potentially a problematic one because it clashed with those legal and quasi-legal sanctions by which Don Alvaro had sought to protect his ascendancy.

He had, in the first place, built up a far-reaching nexus of formal agreements with private individuals —alliances, loyalty oaths, acts of personal homage and the like. As long as he remained the king's friend, this system tended to reinforce the Crown's authority as well as his own. Now, however, it could give rise to real conflicts of allegiance: Luis de la Cerda, for example, seems to have been genuinely uncertain whether his oaths to the Constable permitted him to surrender his lieutenancy of the castle of Toledo.[6] His case, it is true, was an untypical one. Most people in Burgos —Ruy Díaz de Mendoza for one— seem to have regarded the king's change of heart as cancelling any ties which bound them to Don Alvaro. It was a natural enough reaction, however the Constable's chronicler might deplore it, and there was much to be said for simply allowing the whole apparatus of oaths and promises to wither away in this fashion. But the threat of a revolt favourable to Don Alvaro meant that his nationwide system of personal dependence

---

[4] The letter of 5th April (ZURITA, *AA,* fol. 12v) mentioned information laid by the Prosecutor. On 8th April the king referred to Dr Zamora's report, to Vivero family pressures, and to further enquiries in train *(CD,* no. XXV, p. 43; This text —surely by an error of transmission— dates the murder six days earlier, instead of nine).

[5] *CD,* no. XXVI, pp. 46-7 (9th April); for the order of 10th April to Don Alvaro's treasurer, Gonzalo García de Illescas, and for the formal writ of sequestration (11th April) see MANUEL JOSÉ QUINTANA, «Apéndices a la vida de Don Alvaro de Luna», *Vidas de españoles célebres,* in *Obras completas,* BAE, 19 (Madrid, 1898), p. 503. *Sal Inds,* 20 (Madrid, 1957) has a copy of no. XXVI, addressed to Soria.

[6] On Luis de la Cerda, see above, Chapter 2, n. 41; below, p. 224.

could not, after all, be disregarded. It had to be broken. With this in mind, the Toledo letter and the other documents addressed to the same purposes went far beyond the abrogation of particular private agreements. Nobody could be certain exactly what range of obligations Don Alvaro had created; better, therefore, to be safe rather than sorry, and to leave nothing out. It is the whole system of such ties which is abrogated in these texts, and which soon comes to be presented as a central instance of the Constable's abuse of power.

But here fresh problems arose. Much that Don Alvaro had done had been wholly legal, and by far the greater part of it had been done with the king's approval. How far was the latter now entitled to overrule legally binding private agreements, lawfully entered into, but now embarrassing to the Crown? Besides, the Constable's authority and that of his satellites was very often grounded in royal grants and enactments. How far could the king overrule previous commands or even laws of his own or his predecessors' making? What was being tested, in other words, was the extent to which the royal power was absolute. The dilemma was, if anything, more acute because of the history of the previous thirty years. Don Alvaro's actual infractions of the laws were essentially casual and marginal in the context of a long-term policy which had two consistent and closely-related themes. He had habitually identified his own interest with that of the king. And he had, just as tenaciously, furthered and favoured the affirmation of the king's sovereign will as the source of binding law. These cognate principles had been most memorably asserted eight years earlier on the field of Olmedo. There Juan II had virtually laid claim to the power of revoking whatever laws infringed his supremacy.[7]

But he could claim to have done this in *Cortes,* as the law required. At Olmedo, moreover, he had been backed by a powerful military coalition, assembled for the forthcoming battle. In 1453, though the *Cortes* offered its general encouragement, the problems posed by the continuing resistance of Don Alvaro's faction were dealt with essentially as an administrative matter.[8] Furthermore, Juan now lacked the practical argument of overwhelming force; that would become available only if he could persuade sufficient numbers of those bound to Don Alvaro

---

[7] *Cortes (LC),* vol. III, pp. 483, 493; see also MACKAY, *Spain,* pp. 138-9; LUIS G. DE VALDEAVELLANO, *Curso de historia de las instituciones españolas* (Madrid, 1968), p. 427; JOSÉ ANTONIO MARAVALL, *Estado moderno y mentalidad social* (Madrid, 1972), pp. 251, 253; CLAVERO, pp. 163-5; cf., ibid., p. 150n, for the technical element of constitutional inadequacy in this meeting (but also for the fact that, by this time in Juan II's reign, the term *Cortes* was being applied freely to assemblies of this type).

[8] For the ban on derogation outside *Cortes* see *Cortes (LC),* vol. II, p. 371 (Briviesca, 1387). The *Cortes* was still in session on 16th April (ibid., vol. III, p. 650), but none of our derogation documents invokes its presence.

that their obligations were now null and void. Most ominously of all, the claims of royal absolutism were now being advanced against the one man in Castile who had hitherto done most to promote them. In attempting to overcome both the practical challenge and the political paradox by administrative fiat, Juan II was subjecting regalist and absolutist theory to its severest test since Olmedo. His major advantage, of course, was the continuing solidarity of the body of lawyers and officials who had served that theory since the 1420s.

Their attempts to serve it now may be studied in the documents of the *Colección diplomática de Enrique IV*. Six items are especially relevant: letters to Toledo of 7th and 8th April; two dispatches for the captain of the fort at Ayllón; a letter of 14th April to the kingdom at large, urging resistance to the rebels, and the king's reply of 22nd May to the manifesto issued by the defenders of Escalona.[9] All these, except one minor Toledan letter, are signed by the Relator, whose experience, it is reasonable to think, must have carried weight in their drafting. Their most striking feature is an intensive use of formulae of derogation, purporting to override any legal barriers to action against Don Alvaro. Formulae of three kinds are involved. There is the invocation of some attribute of kingship, entitling the monarch to overrule the normal course of law. There are the actual words of dispensation or exemption. And there is the specification of exactly which provisions are nullified, and to whom this applies. Some documents add a fuller justification of the

---

[9] *CD*, no. XXIV (pp. 41-2) 7th April: to the captain of the Alcántara bridge in Toledo; no. XXV (pp. 43-6) 8th April: to Toledo and other cities on the arrest, and on the flight of Luna supporters; no. XXVIII (pp. 48-9) 13th April: to the captain of Ayllón; no. XXIX (pp. 49-55) 14th April, incorporating letter of 11th April: to the municipalities generally, against aiding the rebels, with a copy of an earlier letter to these, forbidding revolt; no. XXXVI (pp. 66-8) 16th May: to the captain of Ayllón; no. XXXVII (pp. 68-73) 22nd May: reply to the Escalona manifesto. The term «derogation», though not normally used in the documents analysed here, is an essential one for their interpretation. Its original meaning was «the partial abrogation or repeal of a law, contract, treaty, legal right, etc.» It is the «partial» element —the notion that the law could be dispensed with for the purposes of this troublesome case alone— which matters, and which makes this exercise of royal power seem especially notable. The *NED*, which gives the definition quoted above, cites a characteristic English 17th-century use: «New and subtile inuentions in derogation of the Common Law» (Coke, 1608). On certain of the formulae discussed below, see MARAVALL, *Estado moderno*, pp. 252-87 passim («no temporal superior», «vicar of God», «absolute royal power», etc.); also CLAVERO, pp. 151-4; JOSÉ LUIS BERMEJO, «La idea medieval de contrafuero en León y Castilla», *REP*, 187 (1973), 299-306; MARÍA DE LA S. MARTÍN PÓSTIGO, *La cancillería castellana de los Reyes Católicos* (Valladolid, 1959), pp. 27-8. A similar repertoire of formulae was used to validate royal laws made outside the full *Cortes* —the so-called *pragmáticas* (cf. BERMEJO, «Orígenes medievales en la idea de soberanía», *REP*, 200 (1975), pp. 288-9). These, indeed, became common under Juan II (VALDEAVELLANO, p. 443). But the use of the formulae in derogation of other laws throws the related constitutional issues into clearer relief.

proceeding, in terms of circumstance or principle. From all these elements, but especially from the last, it is possible to build up a picture of the doctrine of royal supremacy as Juan II and his senior officials accepted it, and sought to make others accept it, in the moment of its crisis.

A typical invocation, as in XXIV or XXV, will refer, not always in the same order, to the king's *propio motu,* his *cierta ciencia,* and his *poderío real absoluto.* The three phrases have separate histories, though they share a common background in Roman and canon law. The most narrowly formulaic of them, as its Latinistic spelling implies, is *propio motu* —a phrase strongly associated with that most influential of all mediaeval bureaucracies, the papal Curia.[10] It was common to find in papal bulls and provisions the statement that a grant or nomination was made «of our own accord, unprompted by any request from you or from anyone petitioning us on your behalf, but out of pure liberality on our part». *Motu proprio* —the form preferred in curial documents— must once have been a literal disclaimer of simony or duress; more usually it lacks all specific semantic force. So does *propio motu* in the usage of Juan II's chancery, which would appear to confine its occurrences to the tripartite formula of our present documents. Earlier uses, which go back at least to the years of Juan's minority, almost all relate to acts of derogation. An exception is the royal letter of 30th June 1441, delegating extensive powers to the regency imposed by the victors of Medina del Campo. Since it was very doubtful whether Juan was acting of his own volition, it made sense for him to protest the spontaneity of his actions. But this aptness was almost certainly coincidental; *de mi propio motu* in Castilian documents is hardly more than a legalistic punctuation-mark.

Cierta ciencia presents a more interesting case. Secular uses outside the Iberian peninsula, if they exist at all, are very rare. The Catalan jurist, Jaime Callís, observing that a monarch may overrule previous dispositions *de certa sua scientia,* refers to a note by Bartolus.[11] But it

---

[10] Cf. *BUS,* vol. I, p. 351 (Clement VI, 1343): «Motu proprio non ad tuam vel alterius pro te nobis oblatae petitionis instantiam, sed de mera nostra liberalitate», and passim, e.g. vol. I, pp. 481-2 (Clement VII, 1391); vol. II, p. 73 (Nicholas V, 1454). Fray MARTÍN DELAVAYEN, «De torrente voluptatis tue...» (Pamplona, 1514) —a broadsheet proclamation of papal indulgences— notes that the Latin formula *motu proprio* «es palabra del mayor favor que su sanctedad puede dar». (I owe this reference to a paper in the Grey Collection of Auckland Public Library to Dr R. J. Lyall.) For *propio motu* in Castilian documents see PÉREZ BUSTAMANTE, vol. II, p. 203 (1419); *CJII* (R), p. 596 (1441), and many other examples.

[11] JUAN BENEYTO PÉREZ, *Textos políticos españoles de la baja Edad Media* (Madrid, 1944), p. 342, quoting Callis, *Extragravatorium,* 7, 36: «Tamen Rex qui superiorem non cognoscit, et habet tantam potestatem in regno suo qualem Imperator in Imperio disponendo contrarium de certa sua scientia tollit praedictas dispositiones iuxta nota per Bartolus» [sic]. For Aragonese uses see *Cancionero*

is not clear whether Bartolus himself uses these words, or whether they derive from Callís' own background. In the years around 1400, certainly, the phrase *de certa sciencia et expresse* is well enough attested in Latin documents issued by the Aragonese crown. Its function there, however, is to reinforce royal commands, not to sanction acts of derogation. For early uses of this latter type, we have to turn to Castile, where what looks very like a direct translation of the same formula appears in the wills of Enrique II (1374) and Enrique III (1406). Both kings use it in revoking their earlier wills. The concept of «being of sound mind» may be relevant here, but Enrique II also claims to act *de cierta sciencia* when he declares his son and heir to be of age despite his tender years. These native precedents, even so, may well have been less influential than the example offered, from the 1360s onwards, by papal notaries.[12] Their use of the formula *ex certa scientia,* sporadic in the later fourteenth century, becomes slightly more frequent under the Aragonese Pope Benedict XIII. But it is under Martin V, to whom Castilian allegiance was transferred in 1417, and his successor Eugenius IV that a peak of frequency is reached. Pope Martin's chancery, moreover, seems to have been the first to refer to *certa scientia* in a context of derogation. Such uses remain a minority; the main function of this phrase in curial usage is always that of confirming previous enactments. But there were enough instances from 1419 onwards for Juan II's lawyers to take notice of them.

The theoretical overtones of *certa scientia* must have struck them as especially apt and satisfying. «The king's heart is in the hand of the Lord», declared the Book of Proverbs —a text which Alfonso the Wise had glossed in his *Siete partidas,* and which Juan II quoted more than once in vindication of his own authority.[13] His part was not to judge,

---

de Palacio, pp. 112 (1429), 117 (1434); ROGER BOASE, *The Troubadour Revival* (London, 1978), p. 129 (1393). For Castilian royal wills see *Crónicas de los Reyes de España,* vol. II, ed. Rosell, BAE, 68, p. 39 (Enrique II): «especialmente é de cierta sciencia»; p. 264 (Enrique III): «expresamente é de cierta sabiduría»; also p. 43.

[12] *BUS,* vol. I, p. 385 (Innocent VI, 1360; confirmatory use); vol. II, p. 125 (Martin V, 1419: first use for derogation). The pattern of papal uses in Beltrán's Salamanca and Valladolid documents is as follows:

	Confirmation/ provision	Derogation/ defect supplied	Literal use	Total uses	Number of documents in sample
Innocent VI to Clement VII (1352-94)	3	—	—	3	153
Benedict XIII (1394-1417)	6	—	—	6	342
Martin V (1417-31)	4	6	—	10	324
Eugenius IV (1431-47)	18	6	1	25	259
Nicholas V (to 1453)	4	—	1	5	77

[13] *Partidas,* vol. I, p. 385, Pt. II, Tít. 2, Ley III. The reference is to Proverbs,

he affirmed on one such occasion, «according to the utterances of men, but according to his conscience». This appeal to a privileged wisdom had both papal and imperial precedents.[14] A Pope's awareness of «the utility of the Church» was believed to entitle him to change ecclesiastical laws. Roman legal theory, as interpreted in the Middle Ages, maintained that only the Emperor could recognize the public good and, on the basis of that knowledge, actually alter the law. For it was said that the *princeps* «bore all the laws in his heart». Hence, too, other topics of imperial praise: the «prudence» of the ruler; the description of him as *philosophiae plenus*. That the «certain knowledge» involved in derogation was linked with these imperial attributes is evident from the passage of Callís already quoted: this power belongs specifically to those rulers who recognize no superior and are as emperors in their own domains. As we shall see, these were claims which Juan II and his officials had no hesitation in making on behalf of the Castilian Crown. *Cierta ciencia* is of a piece with them.

The king was most obviously laying claim to this kind of supremacy when he asserted his *poderío real absoluto*. Indeed, the special status of this particular attribute was made very clear in the autumn of 1440, when Juan II and Prince Enrique issued a joint authorization to the commander of the castle at Trujillo to hand over his charge to the Estúñigas. «We each of us exempt you», their letter declares «by virtue of our *propio motu* and certain knowledge, and I the king do so by virtue of my absolute power.»[15] Not even the king's heir had any share in this power. It was a position which the Trastámara rulers and their officials had been at pains to establish over a long period.[16] The earliest

---

21:1. Cf. *C Halc*, p. 268 (1439: Juan II addressing dissident magnates); *Cortes (LC)*, vol. III, p. 483 (1445: the *Cortes* delegates at Olmedo, saying what the king expected them to say); *CD*, no. XXXVII, p. 70.

[14] POST, p. 265 on the Pope, «perspecta ratione utilitatis ecclesie» (Stephen of Tournai; mid 12th century); WALTER ULLMAN, *A History of Political Thought: The Middle Ages*, p. 35 (the Emperors); KANTOROWICZ, p. 28n. on «omnia iura in scrinio pectoris» (quoted by Pseudo-Aquinas [Ptolemy of Lucca] among many others); POST, p. 298n. on royal «prudence» (Henry of Ghent; late 13th century); KANTOROWICZ, p. 455 and n. on «philosophiae plenus» (with comments by the post-glossators Andreas of Isernia and Lucas de Penna).

[15] *C Halc*, p. 351: «nos e cada vno de nos, de nuestro propio motu e cierta çiençia, e yo el dicho Rey de mi poderio avsoluto, lo alçamos».

[16] VALDEAVELLANO, p. 427 (quoting a privilege of 1393); see also *Crónicas*, ed. Rosell, p. 269 (will of Enrique III): «si alguna mengua... hay... yo de mi poderío real suplo»; *CJII* (R), p. 596: «poderío real libre ó absoluto»; cf. in the same series of documents, pp. 594, 603; *Cortes (LC)*, vol. III, p. 484. See also MARAVALL, *Estado moderno*, pp. 278-87; BERMEJO, «Principios y apotegmas sobre la ley y el rey en la Baja Edad Media castellana», *Hispania*, 35 (1975), 42. There are important links with other topics of our study (theocratic kingship; *princeps legibus solutus;* sovereignty); see MARAVALL, «The Origins of the Modern State», *JWH*, 6 (1961), 799; VALDEAVELLANO, p. 426; BERMEJO, «Soberanía», p. 290. The last-named, pp. 286-8, draws attention to the contrast felt to exist between

uses of the «absolute royal power» formula go back to the 1390s (though Enrique III's will, in 1406, speaks merely of *poderío real* in making good possible defects of law). Under Juan II this persistent, though often theoretical, self-assertion achieves a kind of token triumph in 1441, after the defeat of Medina del Campo. Most of the documents of that abject settlement which the victors of Medina forced upon the king were deeply coloured by the language of royal absolutism. Juan could even invoke his «free or absolute royal power» in the very act of signing away to the new regents that part of it which gave him discretion over *mercedes*. It was as if, even with the Crown under this kind of constraint, such language was now felt to be indispensable. At the Olmedo *Cortes,* four years later, and later still at the time of the dispossession of Don Alvaro de Luna, the same formulae were invoked to more effectual purposes.

The three basic elements of the invocation admit of little variety in the documents of 1453. It is normal, though still optional, for them to mention that absolute power is being called upon to deal with the particular matter under review *(poderío... de que quiero usar, é uso en esta parte)*. There is a reference in no. XXIX to *plenario poderío real absoluto,* recalling papal and imperial claims to *plenitudo potestatis*.[17] The extension of such a claim to kings in general had long been commonplace. Louis IX of France had asserted it, and one fourteenth-century Italian jurist had actually described the Pope as being «like a king in his kingdom because he has plenitude of power». Document XXIX also contains a simpler form of invocation: offences committed against the Luna faction are exempted from all penalty «by virtue and authority of this letter of mine».[18] This type of formula may well be older —Juan I had used a similar wording in 1381— and it is certainly less influenced by Roman and canon law than those which the mid-fifteenth century came to prefer. But the preference now is decisive: it is for invocations which are legally sophisticated, ideologically charged, and strongly formulaic.

The actual words of exemption are also formulaic, but in a somewhat different fashion. Four basic patterns occur, but the functional distinc-

---

the king's «ordinary» power, and the «absolute» power required for such cases as exemption, derogation, and autonomous lawmaking.

[17] *CD*, p. 53; see ULLMANN, *History*, p. 133; also KANTOROWICZ, p. 203, quoting Lucas de Penna: «et papa est quasi rex in regno propter plenitudinem potestatis.» The same terminology used for the power delegated to the regents in 1441 (*CJII* (R), p. 589): «plenario poderío é facultad para proveer... así como yo por mi propia persona lo pudiera hacer».

[18] *CD*, p. 53; perhaps merely an expansion of «por la presente» (ibid., and no. XXIV, p. 42), but see also F. LAYNA SERRANO, *Historia de Guadalajara y sus Mendozas*, vol. I (Madrid, 1942), p. 285: «Et por esta nuestra carta o por el dicho su treslado signado... vos quitamos» (Juan I, 1381).

tions between them are only loosely observed.[19] *Vos lo suelto é alzo é quito* confers release from oaths and acts of homage. *Quiero é mando que no pueda ser* and its analogues forbid the operation of legal sanctions which might otherwise obtain; some parallel phrases, however, refer to ties of personal obligation. *Vos do por libre é quito* is used indifferently to exempt from both obligation and punishment. *Revoco é caso é anulo* can also be used for oaths and homage, but its primary and literal function is to cancel laws or instructions previously issued. This last formula represents the most radical variety of derogation, and is —with one minor exception— the only one of its type to be expressed in the technical vocabulary of the law. The contribution of the *letrados* here is not, as it is with the formulae of invocation, primarily semantic and conceptual; it is, rather, a matter of style. What makes the words of exemption formulaic is the insistent amplification and repetition of synonyms.

This is wholly explicable, of course. The invocation was meant to overawe with the unique, lofty and opaque language of royal supremacy; the point about exemption was that people should know how they stood. Perhaps the simplest way of making this clear to them was illustrated by the formula granting exemption «once, twice, and three times»; this had long been a standard formula both in acts of homage and in their dissolution, and it is still employed in the documents of 1453. But Juan II's officials were not content with such primitive reinforcement as this or any other single formula had to offer. Hence their simultaneous use of several exempting phrases: the captain of Ayllón, for example, is released from his vassallage to Don Alvaro in these terms: «I lift and remove and take away [your obligation] once, twice, and three times, and I revoke it and make it null and of no effect, and I count you free and quit of it all and of every item of it.»[20] Less concentrated but even more comprehensive is Document XXIX, which sanctions resistance to Don Alvaro's partisans by way of nine separate exemption formulae. Such blanket coverage was the product of legalistic convention, but it was a convention with a highly relevant practical purpose. It ruled out any ambiguity in the reception of these documents and it enhanced their impact as propaganda.

Amplification for similar purposes is also characteristic of the way

---

[19] Examples from *CD*: *vos lo suelto*, no. XXIV, p. 42; *quiero e mando*, no. XXIX, pp. 53 (sanctions); 54 (obligations); cf. ibid., p. 54: «dicerno é declaro que... non pudieron ser fechos»; *vos do por libre*, no. XXVIII, p. 49 (both applications, but combined here with two other formulae); *revoco e caso*, no. XXV, p. 45 (both uses).

[20] *CD*, no. XXVIII, p. 49: «vos alzo é suelto é quito una é dos é tres veses é lo revoco é do por ninguno é de ningund valor, é vos do por libre é quito de todo ello é de cada cosa dello»; cf. CLAVERO, p. 154n. LAYNA SERRANO, vol. I, p. 285: «vos quitamos... una y dos y tres veses» (Juan I, 1381).

in which the arrangements subject to derogation are specified. Even the simplest of specifications casts a fairly wide net:

> notwithstanding any oath and act of homage which you may have made... to the aforesaid Master, or the aforesaid Count, or to any other person of whatever estate or position, eminence or dignity, whether by my command or in any other manner.[21]

Wider-ranging lists —no. XXIX presents a series of them— can run to a score of items or more:

> notwithstanding that you, or any one of you... have or may have any bond of blood, or birth, or affinity, or of any other kind with the said Don Alvaro de Luna, or the above-mentioned persons... and although you may... be bound and obligated to them by vassallage, or oath, or vow, or act of homage and promise, or any other tie of obligation, or contract, or duty of birth or upbringing and familiarity and alliances and confederations and combinations and associations, or friendships...

Again, these elaborate legal solemnities have their purely conventional side. But they also serve a more immediate practical intention: that of blocking all possible loopholes for Don Alvaro's remaining supporters. To that end, the widest possible range of models and precedents is being pressed into service.

Other instances of specification illustrate that process yet more clearly. Thus, in Document XXV, the provisions of unspecified royal documents are derogated wholesale, «taking them as expressly stated here, as if they were here transcribed word for word».[22] The practical dilemma is obvious enough: nobody could disentangle at short notice exactly what warrant existed for the Constable's authority in Toledo

---

[21] *CD*, no. XXIV, p. 42: «non embargante qualquier juramento é pleito omenage que tengades fecho... al dicho Maestre, nin, al dicho Conde, nin á otra persona alguna de qualquier estado ó condicion, preeminencia ó dignidad que sean, así por mi mandado como en otra qualquier manera»; cf. also no. XXIX, p. 53: «non embargante que vos ó qualquier de vos... avedes, ó ayades qualquier debdo de consanguinidad ó cognacion ó afinidad ó en otra qualquiera manera con el dicho Don Alvaro de Luna, ó con los suso nombrados... é aunque les... seades astritos é obligados por vasallage ó por juramento ó por voto ó pleito-menage é promision, ó otro qualquier vínculo de obligación ó contrato ó debdo de naturaleza é crianza é familiaridad é alianzas é confederaciones é compañías é sociedades ó amistades...»

[22] *CD*, no. XXV, p. 45: «aviéndolas aqui por espresadas é declaradas bien, así como si de palabra á palabra aquí fuesen puestas»; cf. *BUS*, vol. I, p. 331 (Clement V, 1301) and passim, esp. vol. I, p. 596: «etiamsi de illis et eorum totis tenoribus de verbo ad verbum specialis et expressa esset praesentibus mentio facienda» (Benedict XIII, 1405); Pérez-Bustamante, vol. II, p. 186: «asi como si fuese sellada con nuestro sello mayor» (Juan I, 1384); *CJII* (R), p. 522 (1436); Clavero, p. 150n. (examples of 1430, 1431), 151; Bermejo, «Soberanía», pp. 288-9. See also *CJII* (R), p. 592: «bien ansí como si no fuese por mí hecho» (1441); p. 594: «bien ansí como si de palabra á palabra aquí fuesen incorporadas y hecha dellas y de lo en ellas contenido expresa mencion.»

and its district. Yet the «as if» formula was very far from being invented for the purpose. In papal documents it is found from the early fourteenth century at least, with just this reference to a detailed text being taken as read. In Castile in the 1380s, it had been used by the royal chancery to make good particular legal defects («as if sealed with our Great Seal»). Above all, it had been a standard usage in autonomous royal lawmaking, whether the king was operating in a depleted (and therefore constitutionally suspect) *Cortes,* or issuing wholly independent *pragmáticas* of his own. There are examples of both kinds from the 1430s. In 1441, the same method had proved its value for derogation. In September of that year, Juan's enforced revocation of grants issued in the preceding period of civil strife proclaimed any such grant to be null and void «as if it had not been done or issued by me». And in a document of almost the same date, we find him derogating previous legal instruments «as if word for word» in terms which appear to be a halfway stage between the papal formula and the wording used in 1453.

In other respects, too, the documents of Juan II's self-assertion in 1453 echo those of his abject state after the defeat at Medina twelve years before. He was, after all, doing for himself now what the regents and the victors of 1441 had tried to do through his unwilling agency —taking apart the legal basis of Alvaro de Luna's power. He could not avoid now, any more than then, the issue which lay at the heart of the problem: the need to overturn previous enactments of his own. Indeed, there were times when this had to be specified, as in no. XXIX: «... and although for the above... you may have had my permission and authority and consent and express instruction, and although this may have been by letter from me, and by my special warrant, or in any other form.»[23] The accepted theory of royal powers of derogation could encompass all this. In 1441, royal letters had been overruled «even though they may have been signed and validated by oaths and solemn vows»; a year earlier, King and Crown Prince jointly had exempted the captain of Trujillo from those formalities which «the laws and ordinances of my realms, and the custom of Spain, and common law» required for the formal surrender of castles. This might seem latitude enough, but there was still a further problem, highlighted by no. XXV when derogating:

> ... any letters or covering letters or writs of mine, even though these purport to overrule earlier instructions and are issued later, with whatso-

---

[23] *CD*, p. 53: «é aunque para lo susodicho... ayades avido mi licencia é actoridad é consentimiento é espreso mandamiento, é aya seido por mi carta é especial mandado ó en otra qualquier manera»; cf. *CJII* (R), p. 596: «aunque sean firmados é valederos con juramento é voto solemne»; *C Halc,* p. 351. For Juan II underwriting with his own instructions oaths sworn to Don Alvaro see *CAL* (F), p. 436 (pardon to Rodrigo Manrique, Count of Paredes, May 1452).

ever penalties [they may contain] ... and with whatsoever clauses of derogation and *nihil obstat* and other assurances which there may be or might be, which may have been or may [in the future] be shown to you.[24]

The citizens of Toledo, to whom these words were addressed, might well, if they remembered recent history, have had just this difficulty in view. Obedience to the king now was all very well. But what if the balance of power shifted once more, and the king's intentions altered with it? What security had they then? A form of words as specific as this was needed to overcome such hesitations, and to make it quite clear that the citizens would not be arraigned in the future for obeying the king's present intentions. Whether it actually set the Toledans' minds at rest is another matter. They may well have recalled that such formulae were no novelty. The documents of the 1441 settlement had more than once gone out of their way to overrule «derogation clauses, and abrogations and derogations and other guarantees». The king had assured the regents then that he revoked such provisions together with «any letter or letters... written or issued by me, or issued or promised or written in the future». He had stated that he did so «insofar as they are or may in future be contrary to what you may declare and ordain». Thus both the derogation of derogation and its use in a prospective sense were established practices. Given the way in which the 1441 settlement had been summarily overturned four years later, they cannot have seemed particularly effectual ones.

Yet those best-placed to judge seem to have found some value in them. In March 1442, the Relator had been granted the right to renounce or bequeath the offices which he held. At the same time, he had secured from Juan II a written promise that this entitlement was to be absolute, notwithstanding either previous or subsequent royal enactments. The king affirmed that, should he confer any of these offices on anyone else (or should he have done so already): «... the letters in question... are inauthentic, and have been gained by importunity, and do not proceed from my will, even though particular mention may be made of this writ and of its contents.»[25] All this implies some confidence

---

[24] *CD*, p. 45: «qualesquier mis cartas é sobre cartas é albalaes aunque sean de segunda jusion é dende en adelante con qualesquier penas... é con qualesquier cláusulas derogatorias é non obstancias é otras firmesas que sean ó ser puedan, que en contrario desto vos ayan seido ó sean mostradas»; cf. *CJII* (R), p. 594: «cláusulas derogatorias, é abrogaciones y derogaciones y otras firmezas» (also pp. 592, 596); p. 596: «qualesquier carta o cartas... que por mí hayan sido hechos é dados, ó se dieren ó prometieren, ó se hicieren de aquí adelante»; ibid.: «en quanto son ó fueren contra lo que vos pronunciardes y ordenardes.»

[25] AGS, M y P, 7.129: «declaro las tales... ser obrrepçias e ganadas por inportunidad e non proçeder de mi voluntad aun que faga mençion especial deste mi alvalá e delo en él contenido.» Cf. the nomination of Fernán Gómez de Herrera as *oidor* in 1462 (AGS, QdC, 3.79): «e aunque... vaya ynxerto de verbo ad

in the formula, if not much in Juan II, on the part of the man who was to be his chief agent in drawing up the derogation documents of 1453. And as a matter of fact, Juan did keep his promise to Fernán Díaz. The most interesting feature of this private and specialized instance of derogation, however, lies in its reference to the king's will. It is as if an attempt were made to identify that will —or *propio motu*, to borrow the phrase used in formulae of invocation— with the particular orders now being sent out, and with nothing else. Exactly that attempt is made, on a far larger scale, in the documents of Don Alvaro de Luna's fall. It was administratively necessary to do so in order to cut through the tangle of earlier pro-Luna enactments. It was politically necessary because Juan II's will had so long been identified with that of his *privado*. And because it involved the premise that the king had the power to define his own will in this way —to identify *propio motu, cierta ciencia,* and *poderío real absoluto* in a single act— the attempt was, above all, doctrinally apposite, marking a significant stage in the growth of royal absolutism.

Appeals to that emergent doctrine were among the forms of justification offered for these acts of derogation. But they were not the only form, and they may not even have been the most impressive. The fact that after a month a second message had to be sent to the captain of Ayllón *a mayor abondamiento* —«in further confirmation» (*CD*, no. XXXVI, p. 67) renders all the talk of absolute power distinctly less convincing. The most direct way of justifying the king's present procedures was to point to the offences by which Don Alvaro had incurred his displeasure.[26] Thus the letter sent to Toledo on 8th April provides a fairly circumstantial account of the murder of Alonso Pérez, as well as some hints of that broader case in terms of *apoderamiento* which was to loom so large at the time of the Constable's trial. Document XXIX, drawn up a little later, alludes more vaguely to «the major scandals and perils and irreparable disadvantages» averted by the arrest of Don Alvaro. The implication is that he had been plotting to promote disorder; however that might be, there could be no doubt, within a few days of these words being written, that his family and supporters were offering armed resistance to the king. All these things contributed to a general climate in which extraordinary measures might well be thought appropriate. But the derogation of specific legal arrangements was felt to require some more particular line of explanation.

---

verbo este mi alvalá, por quanto por la presente declaro non proçeder de mi voluntad e ser ganados de mí por ynportunidad, non me seyendo fecha rrelaçion delo contenido en este mi alvalá.»

[26] *CD*, no. XXV, p. 43; no. XXIX, p. 50 (11th April). By 14th April, the date of the *sobrecarta*, Juan II seems to have had more definite evidence of rebellion.

At its simplest, this could be furnished by the claim that the arrangements in question had not been legally valid at all:

> I declare... that they could not have been made, and are of no effect, and ought not to be kept, because even if they could be heard and introduced in evidence, as far as the foregoing is concerned they would be and are rejected by all divine and human law and right, and especially by the laws of my realms, which expressly forbid it...[27]

Hitherto, Juan II had connived at Don Alvaro's use of private treaties as a technique of political control. But the laws of Castile did, in fact, forbid it. There were statutes of Juan I and Enrique II banning all «alliances and leagues, with oaths sworn on the sacrament, or with acts of homage... or any other guarantees». There was also —whatever one might make of more recent notions of absolute monarchy— a potential conflict of principle between any such alliance and the traditionally accepted authority of the Crown.

Thus the same document (no. XXIX) goes on to invoke the ancient role of the king as a feudal superior, to whom his subjects are bound by specific and personal acts of allegiance. Agreements made with the Constable are invalid because they contravene «the lawful and just oaths and acts of homage which all my vassals and subjects and natives of my lands have sworn to me».[28] The term *naturales,* used here, carries us over from the archaic model of feudal contract to that theory of allegiance which had by this date superseded it in Spain. «There are many forms of lordship, but that of *naturaleza* is over all,» Alfonso the Wise had declared, meaning that the subject's supreme loyalty was to the sovereign ruler of the land where he was born. In the following century Don Juan Manuel had explained how the duties of the *vasallo natural* included all those of the feudal vassal, and more besides. The matter was clearer still to Bishop Alonso de Cartagena, writing in the mid 1440s: «We call [our kings] natural lords so that from this sound

---

[27] *CD*, no. XXIX, p. 54: «dicerno é declaro... que aquellos non pudieron ser fechos, nin valen, nin deben ser guardados, porque en caso que se pudiesen entender, quanto á lo susodicho aquellos serian é son reprobados por toda ley é derecho divino é humano, é especialmente por las leyes de mis regnos que espresamente lo defienden»; cf. *Cortes (LC),* vol. II, p. 425 (Guadalajara, 1390), p. 529 (Madrid, 1392).

[28] *CD*, no. XXIX, p. 54: «é non menos contra los lícitos é justos juramentos é pleitos omenages que todos mis vasallos é súbditos é naturales me tienen fechos.» Alfonso el Sabio discusses the varieties of lordship in *Partidas,* Pt. IV, Tít. 25; see GARCÍA DE CORTÁZAR, p. 309, and, more generally on *naturaleza,* pp. 290-322; 441-79, passim. See also DON JUAN MANUEL, *Libro de los estados,* ed. Robert Brian Tate and Ian R. Macpherson (Oxford, 1974), pp. 175-6; ALONSO DE CARTAGENA, *Duodenarium,* Q. 1, cap. 1: «dominos naturales vocare solemus ut ex ipso tuto uso loquendi omnibus innotescat regi nostro ad populum, populoque ad regem inesse vinculum naturalis amoris quo nullum gratius, nullum diuturnius» (AHN, microfilm 1088; copy of MS 42 of Cathedral Library, Burgo de Osma).

way of talking all men may know that the bond between our king and his people, our people and their king is one of natural love, than which none is more dear and none more lasting.» It is no surprise, then, that Juan II should go on to denounce Alvaro de Luna's alliances in these terms also: «... and it would be against the fidelity and loyalty and lordship and subjection and reverence and *naturaleza* which are owed to me as their king and sovereign natural lord...»[29] What is a little more surprising is that, for the most part, these documents do not exploit natural lordship as the central argument for Juan II's right to engage in acts of derogation. The formula «king and natural lord» is prominent only in Document XXXVII, where the obligations as *naturales* of the defenders of Escalona are very much in view. Otherwise, this aspect of kingship is subsumed in a general picture whose implications range much more widely.

The arguments which we have examined so far were enough to dispose of those obligations which Don Alvaro had created on his own initiative. There remained those which had arisen out of orders and authorizations issued by the king himself. To some extent, it was still possible to cope with these without cancelling them outright; it was a question of how they should be interpreted:

> ... because in such a matter it was always understood, and is understood, and ought to have been and ought to be understood, that my royal person and majesty, and whatever pertains to my service and to the public good and peaceful state and tranquility of my realms, should be and was and is excepted and unimpaired and excluded and unharmed, as in the present case it is...[30]

Mediaeval jurists had long held that no king could sign away those things which were intrinsic to his royalty. As the great English lawyer Bracton had put it in the thirteenth century. «Those things which pertain to justice and peace... cannot be separated from the Crown since they actually constitute the Crown.» The issue was not neglected in Castile; the will of Isabel the Catholic was to refer to «those things which go with the royal lordship, and neither can nor should be separated from it». On one level, Juan II was making a similar point here.

---

[29] *CD*, no. XXIX, p. 54: «é asi mismo seria contra la fidelidad é lealtad é señorío é subjecion é reverencia é naturaleza á mi debidas, como á su Rey é soberano Señor natural.»

[30] *CD*, p. 53: «por quanto en lo tal siempre se entendió é entiende, é debió é debe ser entendido ser, é fué é es escebta é ilesa é sacada é salva mi persona é magestad real, é lo que concierne á mi servicio é al bien público é pacífico estado é tranquelidad de mis regnos, segund que lo es en el presente caso»; cf. KANTOROWICZ, p. 149n. quoting Bracton, *De Legibus:* «ea quae sunt iustitiae et paci annexa... nec a corona separari poterunt, cum faciant ipsam coronam»; MARAVALL, «Origins», p. 801, quoting Isabel's will.

But he was also asserting his own right to clarify the law.[31] That right had been recognized in the *Partidas* as the king's alone, and the *cortes* of Olmedo had reaffirmed the principle in 1445. But Alfonso the Wise had offered the essentially pragmatic reason that only the maker of the laws was capable of interpreting them. Juan II's complaisant assembly used the occasion to assert once more their master's theory of his own authority: «... and should there be any contradiction between some laws and others, the right to consider and determine it all belongs only to your Highness, as king and sovereign lord recognizing no superior in temporal affairs.» It would have been possible, then, for Juan II to claim that his actions in 1453 involved no derogation at all, but only a clarification of how the law stood. Yet he does not make that claim, or limit himself to that line of argument. And when he does approach the business of clarification, the language in which he and his officials elect to present it invokes a view of kingship which is capable of claiming very much more.

It does so above all through phrases like «the public good and peaceful state and tranquility of my realms». That formula recurs half a dozen times in our documents, with minor variations, and it connects immediately with the ideological background of the royal *cierta ciencia*. What the ruler who was «full of philosophy» and whose «heart was in the hand of God» was privileged to know was precisely this: the right action to be taken for the public good.[32] Nobody, insists the twelfth-century English *Dialogus de Scaccario*, may resist a royal decree made for the good of the peace. And only the king could define what constituted «his» peace. The view had been further developed by later mediaeval jurists along lines with which Juan II's officials, to judge by the terms which they employ here, must have been familiar. *Bien público* echoes the Roman lawyers' *res publica;* indeed, the direct calque *cosa pública* sometimes appears as an equivalent (e.g. *CD*, no. XXIX, p. 54). *Pacífico estado*, similarly deployed as an alternative to *paz*, recalls the *status regis et regni* which one tradition among jurists defined as the object of the king's unique knowledge.[33] That tradition is important in this context because it gave rise to the notion of «reason of state» as a total justification for all royal acts. In theoretical writers

---

[31] See *Partidas*, vol. I, p. 9, Pt. I, Tít. 1, Ley XIV, and contrast *Cortes (LC)*, vol. III, p. 489.

[32] See POST, p. 15; ULLMANN, *History*, p. 133 (quoting *Dialogus de Scaccario)*; above, n. 14. The power transferred to the regents in 1441 was essentially that of acting on their own perception of the «paz y sosiego de mis Reynos» *(CJII* (R), p. 589).

[33] *CD*, no. XXIX, p. 53; cf. POST, pp. 22 *(status regis et regni)*, 300 (on Henry of Ghent): «Reason that does not err... is the 'reason' of the *status* of the State, rightly interpreted by the supreme authority by reason of his public *status*.»

like the thirteenth-century theologian Henry of Ghent, this concept can form part of a lofty and generalized account of ideal monarchy; in the service of actual monarchs, it had an evident practical use. The men of Juan II's chancery do not press the point, but they were clearly aware of both advantages.

Rhetorical and pragmatic purposes are similarly at work together in other aspects of the language of sovereignty, as it is deployed in these documents. As rhetorical assertions of his exalted dignity, the repeated references to Juan II as «king and sovereign lord» had an obvious propaganda value. Whatever concrete pressures he might be having to endure, nobody but the king could talk like this. Significantly, when Don Alvaro's allies attempted a written defence of their own position, the only rhetoric available to them was the language of insurrection.[34] But to proclaim the king's sovereignty was also to identify the grounds on which he expected to be obeyed. These are implicit, for example, in the full version of the formula just quoted: «king and sovereign lord, recognizing no superior in temporal affairs».[35] This topic may have its origins in the attempts of the Hohenstaufen emperors to demarcate imperial and papal spheres of supremacy —the so-called «two swords» theory. Later, it was articulated by legal commentators, notably the Portuguese canonists of the thirteenth century. One of this group, Johannes de Deo, held that kings had no superior but the Pope; Vincentius Hispanus argued that in temporal matters they had none at all. Though not precisely what the emperors had originally intended, this view was evidently pleasing to kings, and it finds its way into the outlook of Alfonso the Wise. It goes on to gather fresh associations in Baldus and Bartolus: the king's *principalissimum principatum*, the all-inclusive character of his juridical personality, and the doctrine that he is «emperor in his own kingdom» are all linked with this formula. In other words, it becomes a central element in the identification of every secular ruler as the unique *princeps* of Roman legal tradition. It is in this light that we have to view its use by Juan II in addressing dissident

---

[34] If, that is, we are to credit Juan II's report of it (*CD*, no. XXXVII, p. 68). ALAN DEYERMOND, «'Palabras y hojas secas, el viento se las lleva': Some Literary Ephemera of the Reign of Juan II», in *Mediaeval and Renaissance Studies on Spain and Portugal in Honour of P. E. Russell*, ed. F. W. Hodcroft, D. G. Pattison, R. D. F. Pring-Mill and R. W. Truman (Oxford, 1981), pp. 11-12 offers another view.

[35] *CD*, no. XXV, p. 45: «Rey é soberano Señor non reconosciente superior en lo temporal», also no. XXXVI, p. 68. See MARAVALL, *Estado moderno*, pp. 252-4; ULLMANN, *History*, p. 140 («two swords»); POST, p. 342n. (Johannes de Deo); MARAVALL, *Estudios de historia del pensamiento español*, vol. I (Madrid, 1973), p. 65 (Vincentius Hispanus); POST, p. 483n. (quoting Alfonso el Sabio, *Espéculo*, I, 13); MARAVALL, *Estudios*, pp. 84-5 (Bartolus); KANTOROWICZ, p. 398 (Baldus). Use of the topic by Juan II in *C Halc*, p. 275 (1439); *Cortes (LC)*, vol. III, p. 484 (1445).

nobles in 1439, and its later use at the Olmedo *Cortes,* but especially its occurrences in 1453. In opting for this form of words, he and his officials were echoing a tradition rich in regalist and absolutist possibilities. They were, additionally, making a claim which had a particular bearing on the present case. Much of Alvaro de Luna's authority derived from his quasi-ecclesiastical status as Master of Santiago. In stressing that the king acknowledged no temporal superior, notice was being given that no attempt at an appeal to papal jurisdiction would be entertained.

A similar set of arguments for a unique authority centred upon the description of the king as «vicar of God». The history of this concept is broadly comparable with that of the «no temporal superior» topic, though somewhat more varied.[36] It had begun with a passage referring to the Roman emperor and his responsibilities in Seneca's *De Clementia,* later quoted by St Isidore of Seville. But it was the Hohenstaufen once again who made this regalist topic an essential part of their imperial ideology. Subsequently, it was taken up by religious writers like St Bonaventure (who used it to illustrate the principle of unity) and John of Wales, as well as by legal authorities like Johannes de Deo. From the thirteenth century onwards it is a familiar theme in Spanish sources.[37] In the wisdom literature of that period, the king is described on one occasion as «God's seneschal»; on another, he is reminded of his duty, occupying God's place, to imitate God in virtue. Of greater political relevance are the several uses of the topic in the *Partidas,* where Alfonso the Wise is usually careful to add that the king holds this exalted position for the purpose of promoting justice. A century later, in the will of Enrique II, this limiting emphasis on the ruler's responsibility is replaced by an insistence on the duty of all subjects to obey his divine vicariate.

[36] SÉNECA, *De Clementia,* I, 1: «in terris deorum vice» —a text used by Frederick II (KANTOROWICZ, p. 92n.); ST ISIDORE, *Sententiae,* III, 48; ST BONAVENTURE, *Queastiones Disputatae,* IV, a, 3 (both in JOAQUÍN GIMENO CASALDUERO, *La imagen del monarca en la Castilla del siglo XIV* (Madrid, 1972), pp. 18, 16); JOHN OF WALES, *Communiloquium,* I, 6, 108 *(Cortes (AC),* vol. XII, p. 69); JOHANNES DE DEO, *Libellus Dispensationum:* «qui non habent maiorem super se nisi papam loco dei» (POST, p. 342n.; this last will, of course, bear either a papalist or a regalist emphasis).

[37] *El libro de los cien capítulos,* ed. Agapito Rey (Bloomington, 1960), p. 1; *Castigos e documentos para bien vivir ordenados por el rey don Sancho IV,* ed. Agapito Rey (Bloomington, 1952), p. 91 —both post-Alfonsine; MARAVALL, *Estudios,* vol. I, p. 52 finds no pre-13th-century Spanish instances. *Partidas,* vol. I, p. 374, Pt. II, Tít. 1, Ley V: «Vicarios de Dios son los Reyes, cada vno en su Reyno, puestos sobre las gentes, para mantenerlas en justicia, e en verdad»; p. 376, Ley VII: «lugar de Dios, para fazer justicia, e derecho»; p. 449, Pt. II, Tít. 13, Ley I: «para fazer justicia e derecho, e merced.» Contrast Enrique II's will, (1374) in *Crónicas,* vol. II, ed. Rosell, p. 39: «la mayoria... que les dió... para que los obedesciesen todas las gentes de su señorio en lugar de Dios.» For examples from Juan II's reign see also MARAVALL, *Estado moderno,* p. 260.

Fifteenth-century uses highlight different implications according to the political and ideological needs of the moment.[38] Thus, when Marcos de Villalba at the Catalan *Corts* of San Cugat in 1419 described the king of Aragon as «vicar and image of God», he went on to remind the monarch that he had not been put in that exalted position to enjoy himself. Alonso de Cartagena, in his *Defensorium Unitatis Christianae,* addressed to Juan II in 1449, was similarly high-minded, but less abrasive. When he quoted the biblical text by which Christ had submitted himself to the secular power, he drew the lesson of the king's vicariate only to confute the rebels of Toledo. When he addressed the king as one who occupied God's place on earth, his aim was that Juan might be encouraged to set about the godlike task of restoring order in that city. Juan himself had long been familiar with the topic —possibly from the *Partidas,* since he refers, in a document of 1430, to «the place of God which I occupy in order to fulfil justice». In 1439, however, he had used the same formula for a rather different purpose —that of emphasizing the uniqueness of his own power, derived as it was «not from men, but from God, whose place the king occupies in all things temporal». The documents of 1453 provide examples of both types.

Where Juan II's main concern was to report and justify actions already taken —the arrest of Alvaro de Luna and the referral of his case to an enquiry by the Public Prosecutor— it was natural for him to adhere to the Alfonsine tradition of a vicariate primarily for the sake of justice. Thus on 8th April he refers to:

> ... the place of God which I occupy on earth, with regard to justice, to administer and exercise it, which is the proper and principal business of every Christian and Catholic king who seeks to pay his due and discharge his conscience.[39]

He writes in very much the same strain on 11th April, though he now adds a reference to his sovereign status. The relatively cautious tradi-

---

[38] *Cortes (AC),* vol. XII, p. 69; CARTAGENA, *Defensorium Unitatus Christianae,* ed. Manuel Alonso (Madrid, 1943), pp. 278-9 (quoting John, 19.11); 319; *CJII* (R), p. 478 (1430): «para complir la justicia»; *C Halc,* p. 267 (1439): «no lo ha [el poder] de los honbres, mas de Dios, cuyo lugar tiene en todas las cosas tenporales»; the same formula used by *Cortes* delegates at Olmedo *(Cortes (LC),* vol. III, p. 483).

[39] *CD,* no. XXV, p. 44: «al logar que de Dios tengo en la tierra, quanto á la justicia para administrar é exercer aquella, lo qual propia é principalmente pertenesce faser á todo Rey cristiano católico que quiere pagar su debdo é descargar su conciencia»; cf. no. XXIX, p. 50: «como á Rey é soberano Señor de mis Regnos é por el logar que de Dios en ellos tengo para los gobernar é mantener en verdad é justicia». Contrast p. 55 «muy alto, apartado é separado de todos los otros, como aquel que tiene lugar de Dios en la tierra», and no. XXXVII, p. 71: «é todos reconozcan é obedezcan é sirvan un Dios, é en la tierra á un Rey vicario suyo, é que su logar tiene.»

tion of the *Partidas* is abandoned, however, on 14th April, when a general warning is issued that nobody is to aid the pro-Luna rebels, whatever legal pretexts they may show. Here, by contrast, the stress is on the king's unique authority: «very high, set apart and separated from all others, as one who occupies God's place on earth.» And in the letter of 22nd May to the Escalona rebels, the royal vicariate —here, for the first time in our series of documents, presented through the actual term *vicario*— justifies not simply the king's acts of derogation but his demand for instant obedience: «... that all should acknowledge and obey and serve one God, and on earth one king, God's vicar, who occupies his place.» What is affirmed in these last two instances is not so much the king's divinely ordained responsibility as his divine right.

It was, of course, the pro-Luna rebellion which precipitated this step from Alfonsine to absolutist claims. Indeed, once the discovery of Don Alvaro's treasonable letters had given warning of the revolt, the step was a natural one for Juan II to take sooner or later. He was affronted and insecure, and liable to react by aggressive acts of self-assertion. It was also a necessary step in practice, since rapid and authoritative derogation of previous commands was required. But the language of these absolutist utterances already existed in the repertoire of the king's chancery, and the intellectual traditions which made them possible were present already in the background of the lawyers who served there. Only the crisis was new, turning these established habits of language and thought to fresh ideological uses.

The process is most clearly seen in the letter of 14th April. Strictly speaking, this is a *sobrecarta*, incorporating a copy of the warning sent to the Luna partisans three days earlier, lest «not being informed of the true situation» they should rise in revolt.[40] This earlier letter is measured enough in tone to suggest that Juan II still thought it possible that its recipients would not fight. In the interval something must have changed his mind. It is unlikely to have been the knowledge of Don Alvaro's secret correspondence, since it was presumably from this that the king already knew to whom to address his warning of 11th April. Nor was it, in all probability, news of the armed stand at Escalona, which one would not expect to have reached Burgos for some days yet.[41] Possibly Juan had received a discouraging report from some Luna stronghold nearer at hand —perhaps Portillo. We have no means of knowing. But the change of mood in the *sobrecarta* cannot be disputed. Its formulae of derogation are particularly explicit and elaborate, and these patently

---

[40] *CD*, no. XXIX, p. 50: «é porque podria acaescer que vos..., non informados de la verdad de lo susodicho... faríades algunos movimientos.»
[41] See above, n. 3.

urgent provisions are justified at unusual length. The first part of this justification seeks to show that the whole structure of Don Alvaro's alliances runs contrary to law, and to both feudal and natural obligations. These aspects we have examined already. What follows is of still greater interest —a long, ecstatic proclamation of the power and authority of kings (pp. 54-55). Here if anywhere, one feels, Juan II and his officials had raised their sights from immediate administrative needs to challenge the forces of opposition with a considered statement of their own view of kingship.

The transition to that view is furnished here —as it may very well have been in the actual historical development of these same ideas— by the concept of natural vassallage. Duty to the king as natural lord is to be preferred to «every other private good», since it is itself «a common good, and also more divine and more immediate».[42] It is the last of these terms, *proprio,* which comes closest to expressing the spirit in which the primacy of the natural tie had been acknowledged in Castile. What was in question was, in the first place, a bond of birth —Alonso de Cartagena's *vinculum naturalis amoris quo nullum gratius.* To call that tie «divine» was to go further, and to link it with the supernatural dimension traditionally ascribed to kingship. The sources of that tradition were in part biblical and Christian, in part imperial and pagan; its expressions in mediaeval Christendom were so universal as to defy summary.[43] The boldest of markers had been laid down by apologists of the emperors in their struggle with the papacy: that no power was closer to God than that of the emperor; that he was «God present upon earth». But even their opponents allowed that the judgments of secular princes were somehow «celestial». In Spain, long ago, Juan Gil de Zamora had presented the king as situated «between God and men, between heaven and earth».[44] As matters of habitual royal usage, a

---

[42] *CD,* p. 54: «... como á su Rey é soberano Señor natural [see above, n. 29], lo qual como sea bien comun aquel así como mas divino é mas proprio, debe ser antepuesto é preferido á todo otro bien particular»; cf. CARTAGENA, *Duodenarium,* above, n. 28.

[43] See, for the general picture, ULLMANN, *History,* passim; for extreme imperial claims, KANTOROWICZ, p. 63: «Usque ad Deum quippe erectus est... nulla potestas Deo... propinquior» (the so-called «Norman Anonymous»); pp. 91-2 *(deus in terris, deus praesens,* epithets derived from Vegetius *De Re Militari,* II, 5). POST, p. 352n., quotes a papalist acknowledgement that «Celeste enim dicitur arbitrium habere princeps secularis.» Cf. also ULLMANN, *The Medieval Idea of Law as Represented by Lucas de Penna* (London, 1946), pp. 51 (Baldus, «Deus in terris»); 53 (Lucas de Penna: «coeleste arbitrium»).

[44] *De Preconiis Hispaniae,* quoted by MARAVALL, *Estudios,* vol. I, p. 48; KANTOROWICZ, p. 93 observes a shift from early mediaeval «liturgical» kingship, to a late mediaeval «divine right», grounded in legal theory. The latter is the significant emphasis in Trastámaran Castile, whose kings had abandoned any coronation ritual since Juan I (VALDEAVELLANO, p. 431), and had not been anointed (except, possibly, for Alfonso XI) since the early twelfth century

whole series of related topics lay at Juan II's disposal; we have examined his use of some of them, and more still remains to be said. But to call the claims of natural lordship «divine» was to effect a subtle shift in the argument. It implied not that the king had to be obeyed because of *naturaleza,* but that the natural tie derived its binding force from what the king himself was. And that, in the context of this passage as a whole, would appear to be Juan II's emphasis here.

The term whose implications are first explored, however, is *bien común* —the natural tie envisaged as a commitment to the public welfare:

> in whose favour it is not only possible but a duty for the son to be against his father, and brother against brother, and husband against wife, and wife against husband, and kinsman against kinsman, and vassal against lord, and the household servant against the master who nurtured him, because all these, every one, are included in one's own homeland, and in the subjection and obedience and command of the king....[45]

Several levels of meaning are at work in this passage. Most immediately, some of its examples were topical ones: Alvaro de Luna's wife and sons and vassals and servants faced just this choice. A second obvious message was that feudal ties were subordinate to those of *naturaleza;* this was, by now, a commonplace in Castile, but it is here located in a broader context, deriving from Roman law —that of the prior claim of the *res publica* on all its citizens.[46] Many mediaeval jurists had been greatly struck by the statement in the *Digest* that a son, acting *pro patria,* might oppose or even kill his own father. Some had drawn the conclusion that, since feudal duty did not extend so far, the obligation to the *patria* was the greater. But the present passage seems to depend less on this syllogistic approach than on the general premise in Roman law that the public interest must come before the private. It amplifies that principle in terms which recall a familiar New Testament text, much as the Neapolitan jurist Lucas de Penna had done in the previous

---

(CLAUDIO SÁNCHEZ ALBORNOZ, «Un ceremonial inédito de coronación de los reyes de Castilla», in *Estudios sobre las instituciones medievales españolas* (México City, 1965), p. 749).

[45] *CD*, p. 54: «en favor de lo qual no solamente pueden, mas aun deben el fijo ser contra el padre, é el hermano contra el hermano, é el marido contra la muger, é la muger contra el marido, é el pariente contra el pariente, é el vasallo contra el señor, é el criado contra el que lo crió; porque todos estos, ansi los unos como los otros se incluyen so la propria patria, é so la sojubcion é obidiencia, é mandamiento del Rey.»

[46] See ULLMANN, *Lucas de Penna*, p. 54; KANTOROWICZ, p. 245; POST, pp. 443-4 (*Digest*, 11, 7.35; Odofredus, Johannes Teutonicus); KANTOROWICZ, p. 237n. (Andreas of Isernia: feudal duty overrules family ties, but duty to *patria* is superior again «quia plus tenetur patriae quam filiis»); p. 246n. (Lucas de Penna «pro patria filius in patrem, et pater in filium, ac vir in uxorem insurgere debent»; cf. also Matthew 10:35-6).

century, though whether in conscious imitation of him it is impossible to say. But the lawyers' tradition of an all-subsuming *patria,* the scriptural echo, and the logical axiom that the greater must include the less are all given a characteristic bias. The obligation exacted by the *patria* is at once identified as obedience to the king's will.

Indeed, were the passage to break off at this point, it would be possible to claim that king and *patria* are here regarded as one and the same. The literal sense of what follows, however, stops short of this: «... all these... are included in one's own homeland, and in the... command of the king, who is its lord and father and heart and foundation and head.»[47] Yet some of these figures of kingship work to identify ruler and realm more closely than their literal sense alone might suggest. An exception is *padre,* whose recent history in such contexts was, in any case, none too impressive: Juan I, at a difficult moment for himself, had used it to define his own relationship with his kingdom. By contrast, *fundamento,* though it appears to have been little used, had quite powerful implications if glossed in any absolutist sense. Most potent of all were the descriptions of royalty in terms of the heart —the seat of the soul— and the head —the source of conscious direction. Juan II had cited them already, at Olmedo, referring to the king as «head and heart and soul of the people». Alfonso the Wise had noted their especial aptness and their ancient origins. Both figures tended to encourage a sense of the king's corporate personality as somehow diffused throughout his realm.

As far as the heart was concerned, that implication was there already in Seneca's original aphorism —quoted with approval by Lucas de Penna— that the *princeps* was the soul of the state and the state his body.[48] It could be drawn also from Aegidius Romanus' maxim that kings should be the life and health of their domains, as souls were of bodies, or from the teaching of Alfonso the Wise that the monarch, like the heart, gave «unity to all the other members, to make a body of them». The topic of the king as head was impressively compatible with St Paul's teaching on the nature of the Church, as with those

---

[47] *CD*, p. 54: «todos estos... se incluyen so la propria patria é so... [el] mandamento del Rey, el qual es Señor é padre é corazon é fundamento é cabeza della»; cf. *Cortes (LC),* vol. II, p. 331 (Valladolid, 1385), and SUÁREZ FERNÁNDEZ, *Juan I,* pp. 87-8; also vol. III, p. 483: «cabeça e coraçon e alma del pueblo»; *Partidas,* vol. I, p. 468, Pt. II, Tít. 13, Ley XXVI; also p. 375, Pt. II, Tít. 1, Ley V: «corazon, e alma del pueblo»; «cabeça del Reyno»; on these, see FRANCISCO RICO, *El pequeño mundo del hombre* (Madrid, 1970), pp. 70-4.

[48] KANTOROWICZ, pp. 214-5; POST, p. 355 (quoting SÉNECA, *De Clementia,* I, 5, 1: «tu animus rei publicae tuae es, illa corpus tuum», and Lucas de Penna); also ULLMANN, *History,* p. 124; AEGIDIUS ROMANUS, *De Regimine Principum,* III, ii, quoted by GIMENO CASALDUERO, p. 84; *Partidas,* vol. I, p. 375, Pt. II, Tít. I, Ley V: «como el corazon es vno e por el reciben todos los otros miembros unidad para ser vn cuerpo»; cf. Ephesians, 1: 22-3.

other patterns of subordination which mediaeval thinkers perceived in nature at large. This sense of analogy finds a classic expression in the *Policraticus* of John of Salisbury: «In this we follow the best guide to living, Nature, who has placed all the senses of her microcosm, that is to say, her little world, Man, in his head, and thus subordinated all the other members to it, so that all may be moved aright.»[49] The commonplace equation of headship with rule can as easily inform the blunt authoritarianism of Aegidius («the head of the realm, by which the whole realm ought to be governed»), as it can the anxious public introspection of a Juan I on the king's duty to display «great diligence and thought». But the location of «all the senses» in the public head points in another direction —that of those topics of unique royal authority deriving from a unique royal knowledge of the public good which meant so much to Juan II in the present crisis. Moreover, it was a natural extension of the metaphor to link headship, in particular, with identity. It was common experience, after all, that individuals were known to be who they were because of their faces. So it is not surprising that Jacques de Révigny in the late thirteenth century, discussing possible conflicts between local and royal jurisdictions can quote the legal argument that «the Crown of the kingdom is the common *patria* because it is the head».[50] The metaphor of headship interposes no third term between king and *patria;* rather, it facilitates their identification. And so in our present text, the notion of an overriding public obligation, familiar to most Castilians as *naturaleza,* interpreted by those who knew Roman law in terms of *patria,* is merged once more with an outright and all-inclusive regalism.

It is to a statement of something like the full claims exacted by such a doctrine that the document now moves:

> ... to whom, in recognition and respect and service, all other temporal things give place, being insufficient, base and subject, and whom with all humility and reverence all his vassals and subjects and *naturales* ought to, and are bound and obliged to, obey, by the duty of nature and subjection and gratitude, and universal and singular and sovereign lordship, and very high, set apart and separated from all others...[51]

---

[49] JOHN OF SALISBURY, *Policraticus*, IV, 1 in *Opera Omnia,* ed. J. A. Giles (Oxford, 1848), vol. III, p. 219; see also POST, p. 363n; Aegidius Romanus, I, ii, (GIMENO CASALDUERO, p. 84); *Cortes (LC),* vol. II, p. 362.

[50] POST, p. 341: «corona regni est communis patria, quia caput.»

[51] *CD,* pp. 54-5: «en acatamiento é respecto é servicio del qual, todas las otras cosas temporales así como insineras é bajas é sugebtas cesan; é con toda humildad é reverencia todos sus vasallos é súbditos é naturales deben é son tenudos é obligados de obedecer por debdo de naturaleza é subjecion é reconoscimiento é universal é singular é soberano señorio, é muy alto, apartado é separado de todos los otros...»

It is clear that this is meant to recapitulate much that has gone before. «Vassals and subjects and *naturales*» correspond to the three models of royal authority put forward elsewhere in the document. The *vasallos*, of course, are feudal, bound to the king by individual acts of homage; all Castilians are his *naturales* from birth; in terms of his status as the *princeps* of Roman law, empowered to take thought for the «public good and peace and tranquility», his people are —in a significant Latinism— *súbditos*. Any one of the three, we have been given to understand, is enough to overrule any claim to allegiance which Alvaro de Luna might advance. But the full measure of the king's authority encompasses them all. This tripartite concern very naturally sets up a ternary rhythm of amplification; indeed, such a rhythm makes its appearance before the three modes of obligation come into view *(acatamiento/respecto/servicio; insineras/bajas/sugebtas)*, and continues when the focus of attention has shifted elsewhere *(muy alto/apartado/separado)*. At the heart of the passage, however, a more elaborate set of correspondences appears. Vassals, who have a contractual tie with their lord, are bound to him by *reconoscimiento*; he is their *singular señor* —the proper title of a feudal superior.[52] The bond for *naturales* is, of course, *naturaleza*, and the formula *soberano señor natural* has appeared a few lines above in this very document. As for the «subjects» of the *princeps*, their relationship with him is, etymologically *subjecion*, and his lordship over them is *universal*. But the order in which these elements occur is not that of a simple parallelism; their sequence changes from *feudal/Roman/natural* to *natural/Roman/feudal*, and again to *Roman/feudal/natural*. The impression created, then, is that the king's authority is threefold in its nature, but that all three natures are inextricably united in him. He is, in a word, three in one and one in three.

What follows, then, can scarcely come as a surprise: «... and very high, set apart, and separated from all others, as one who occupies God's place on earth, and is his image, and represents him there.»[53] The qualifying phrase *é muy alto, apartado é separado de todos los otros* is ambiguous in its reference. In the first instance it appears to describe *señorío*, but it might equally well relate to *aquel*, meaning the king himself. The fault could lie with a copyist, but anacoluthon of this sort seems to have been regarded as more tolerable in fifteenth-century prose than it was later to become. In this case it is even functionally appropriate. The broken grammatical sequence marks the king's separation from all other men, at the same time as the whole passage,

---

[52] Pero Díaz de Toledo refers to the Marquis of Santillana as his «singular señor» in the title of his translation of Plato's *Phaedo* (MS Santander, Biblioteca de Menéndez Pelayo, M. 96, fol. [1] v°).

[53] *CD*, p. 55, «é muy alto, apartado é separado de todos los otros como aquel que tiene lugar de Dios en la tierra, é es su imagen é lo representa en ella.»

by its sense, defines the connection that exists between them. The effect of the ambiguity is to make the king appear identical with his own *señorío* —to assimilate his individual person to his public personality. And that, after all, was a point of importance both in the derogation exercise itself and in the whole process which led up to Alvaro de Luna's execution. Among the accusations levelled at the king by the Escalona rebels in May, one which aroused an especially sharp response from Juan II's Councillors was the claim that things were being done *por forma de voluntad* —that is to say, out of personal malice.[54] From the outset, a conscious attempt had been made to establish just the opposite —to identify the «will» involved as a constitutional force, not an individual caprice.

That is what all the language of derogation has been about. The topic of the king as «vicar of God», which now makes its appearance, lent well-tried support to such a claim. So did the related concept that the monarch was also God's image; liturgical usage and the general habit of analogical thought both seemed to reinforce its purely political associations. Already in the twelfth century, John of Salisbury had quoted it as a common definition that the king was «a sort of image of the divine majesty upon earth». The topic had run its course from him to Don Juan Manuel; from John of Wales to the Catalan regalist Marcos de Villalba; from the pseudo-Aquinas to Juan II's own century and kingdom, as the work of Mosén Diego de Valera was to illustrate some years later.[55] According to another contemporary, Rodrigo Sánchez de Arévalo, it was the view of «all written laws, Gentile and Catholic alike». Yet the present use of this topic, unsurprising as it is, is given an especial potency by the final phrase *é lo representa en ella*. To a modern reader this looks like a mere synonym of *é es su imagen,* and so it might be, in strictly Nominalist usage. But the philosophical climate of fifteenth-century Castile was decisively Realist.[56] To say that the king «represented» God meant both that he was an image of God and that he acted for God; it brought together the two topics of *imago Dei* and *vicarius Dei* in a single, imposing formula.

---

[54] *CD,* no. XXXVII, p. 73. On the king's public and private personalities see below, pp. 146; 158-60.

[55] JOHN OF SALISBURY, *Policraticus,* IV (p. 219): «in terris quaedam divinae majestatis imago» (meaning the true *princeps,* not the tyrant); JUAN MANUEL, *Libro infinido,* ed. José Manuel Blecua (Granada, 1952), p. 29 (the whole section is very much in the tradition discussed here, including (p. 30) the *lugar de Dios* topic, and reference to Aegidius); *Cortes (AC),* vol. XII, p. 69 (John of Wales; Villalba); PSEUDO-AQUINAS, *De Regimine Principum,* I, 12 (apparatus to *Partidas,* vol. I, p. 375, and quoted by VALERA, *Doctrinal de príncipes,* in Penna, p. 187; SÁNCHEZ DE ARÉVALO, *Suma de la política,* ibid., p. 103. The topic is also taken up by Lucas de Penna (ULLMANN, p. 50).

[56] TOMÁS and JOAQUÍN CARRERAS Y ARTAU, *Historia de la filosofía española. Filosofía cristiana de los siglos XII al XV* (Madrid, 1943), vol. II, pp. 582-3.

This, then, is the rhetorical and ideological climax of the most sustained attempt to justify Juan II's acts of derogation. Not all the elements in its rhetoric as they have been analysed here need have been —or indeed, could have been— matters of conscious choice. It is scarcely to be thought that one or several senior lawyers of the chancery, or Juan himself for that matter, actually set out to order their material by interlocking threes so that the king must appear as the image of a Trinitarian godhead, or to exploit a syntactic breakdown for the sake of half-formulating a constitutional principle. It is unlikely, even, that they reflected much on the philosophical overtones of the verb *representar*; their concern —and the training of most of them— had to do with law, not logic. Two things, however, do emerge with some force. In the first place, a statement which proves to be unconsciously structured in this way is evidence that we are dealing with a coherent ideology —and one, moreover, which presses the familiar topics of royal supremacy to extreme conclusions. The passage as a whole comes closer to the imperial affirmation of the monarch as *Deus praesens,* or indeed to latter-day absolutism, than its literal terms would themselves imply. Secondly, it is clear that such a statement could only be made by men who passionately and profoundly believed in this view of kingship. It was not something improvised to meet the short-term demands of the moment, though its expression may well have crystallised as a result of these demands. The final touches are added to that process in the letter which Juan II addressed on 22nd May to the defenders of Escalona.

This too was, in its way, a document of derogation. Don Alvaro's supporters accused the king of treacherous dealing towards the Constable, and in particular of failing to honour the safeconduct issued to the latter at the time of his arrest. There was dispute as to the precise terms of this document —indeed, at one point, Juan II implies that he does not necessarily admit its existence. But most of his counter-arguments are unconcerned with such matters of detail. He begins by developing at some length the view that Don Alvaro's offences are too great, and his own claims to obedience too wide-ranging to admit of any such criticisms. It is in this phase of the argument that he adduces his own unique authority as «vicar of God» in terms which, as we have seen, come close to an assertion of divine right.[57] As for the safeconduct, he declares, Don Alvaro's dereliction of his bounden duty would be enough to render it void.

> ... and I, according to reason, and natural law, and divine law, and even positive law, even if I were not exempt from that as I am, would not

[57] *CD*, no. XXXVII, p. 71 (above, n. 39).

be obliged to keep, or to abide by any oath or guarantee made to him; because all those things are, and are meant to be, regulated according to right...[58]

Any document effectively protecting Don Alvaro would, it is argued, be repugnant to law. But in virtually the same breath Juan II proclaims himself exempt from the law. The notion of absolute monarchy is plain in view at last.

Once again there is a tradition at work.[59] It was the third-century jurist Ulpian who had first laid it down that «the monarch is not bound by the laws». His words had challenged the ingenuity of mediaeval theorists; John of Salisbury, for example, had portrayed the king as legally unaccountable, yet morally bound to observe both law and justice. Alfonso the Wise accepted that kings above all were bound to obey the laws, but again for reasons of ethical principle «since the laws are the king's honour and his creation». The English legal tradition was relatively quick to initiate the claim that positive legislation as well as natural law could bind a ruler; in Aragon, a later line of development suggested that, even though not bound by positive law, monarchs could commit an offence by infringing it. Bartolus and others distinguished between the worthy prince and the tyrant on the grounds that the latter overrode the law frequently and for no good cause; the former did so only in grave emergencies. Baldus put forward an ingenious verbal distinction: the king was not under the law but «in the law». The more robust monarchism of the emperor Frederick II declared that he actually was the law —*lex animata*. Since the animate was superior to the inanimate, Aegidius Romanus was to conclude, the king ought to be superior to the law. This is probably a less extreme view than it appears; Aegidius has a good deal to say about the moral obligations of princes, and the general rule which he adopts is in line with this: «Positive law is beneath the ruler, as natural law is above him.»

[58] ibid.: «et yo segund razon, nin derecho natural, nin divino, nin aun positivo, caso que del tal yo non fuese soluto, lo que soy, non seria obligado de le guardar nin observar juramento, nin seguridad alguna; porque aquellos todos son é entienden ser condicionados segund derecho...»

[59] *Digest*, 1, 3, 31: «Princeps legibus solutus est», quoted by POST, p. 259 (see also p. 272); JOHN OF SALISBURY, *Policraticus*, IV, 2, p. 221: «quod Princeps, licet si legis nexibus absolutus, legis tamen servus est et aequitatis»; commentary in KANTOROWICZ, pp. 95-6 and POST, p. 259; *Partidas*, vol. I, p. 10, Pt. I, Tít. 1, Ley XVI; on Bracton and the English tradition, KANTOROWICZ, p. 148 and POST, p. 469; PEDRO BELLUGA, *Speculum Principum* (BENEYTO PÉREZ, *Textos*, p. 308): «si princeps vel eius officiales, in iis regnis non tenentur ad iuris positivi observantiam, si contra ius faciunt possunt gravare»; views of Bartolus, Salutati, Innocent IV in POST, p. 261; BALDUS, *De Aliena Feud.*, 1 (apparatus to *Partidas*, vol. I, p. 10): «sic Princeps non propriè dicitur sub lege sed in lege positus; tantae enim celsitudini non potest lex imponi, cui Deus et ipsas leges subjecit»); for Frederick II's *lex animata* see KANTOROWICZ, pp. 129-31 and cf. ULLMANN, *Lucas de Penna*, p. 53; for Aegidius Romanus, III, ii, KANTOROWICZ, pp. 134-5.

Juan II had long been conscious of this tradition, and of its points of contact with the other topics of royal authority which he liked to quote.[60] Thus, at the time of the Olmedo *Cortes,* he had let it be declared that the power conferred on him by his divine vicariate was «so great, especially according to the laws of your realms that it holds sway over all laws and rights». That was a bold step indeed, but it set the scene for a solemn exercise in the revision, interpretation and making of laws in *Cortes.* The almost casual parenthesis in the letter to Escalona was potentially much more radical in its implications. The crucial words are «yo segund rason, nin derecho natural, nin divino, nin aun positivo, caso que del tal yo non fuese soluto, lo que soy, non seria obligado...». Now it is clear that *el tal,* from which Juan claims to be exempt, must embrace *derecho positivo;* that is to say, he will not consider himself bound by anything that the law actually says. Is it conceivable that the exemption should extend to natural and divine law too? In terms of anything which mediaeval theory has to offer, clearly not; moral obligations and the commandments of the Christian religion were binding upon all. Yet the formal ambiguity of the wording does mark out a «grey area» in these spheres also: if Juan II should have been guilty of any incidental deceit or other morally irregular practice in his dealings with the fallen *privado,* notice is tacitly given that he declines to be called to account for it. Even in terms of positive law, the assertion is startling enough. The letter thus far has devoted hundreds of words to proving that Don Alvaro has no case in law; now, in a mere phrase, Juan II makes it known that what the laws say is of no importance. They happen to say that the alleged agreement with Don Alvaro ought not to be honoured. But if they said just the opposite, it would make no difference to the king. He is not bound by them.

Are there, then, to be any legal limits on his absolute free will to keep or to derogate agreements as he wishes? The suggestion that they are to be «regulated according to right» implies that there still are such restraints. But the next few sentences make it very clear that these are envisaged as operating within an essentially absolutist frame of reference. If, Juan contends, he were to let the safeconduct override the grave allegations which have been made against Alvaro de Luna: «... it would be a great weight on my conscience, and an express denial

---

[60] See *Cortes (LC),* vol. III, p. 383: «el derecho del poderío el qual [sc. *del qual,* i.e. *del Rey*] es tan grande, especialmente segunt las leyes de vuestros regnos que todas las leyes e los derechos tienen [sc. *tiene*] so sí.» The almost identical wording in Juan's letter to rebel magnates in 1439 (*C Halc,* p. 267) allows the reconstruction of his meaning here; cf. VALDEAVELLANO, p. 427, and MACKAY, *Spain,* pp. 137-9.

of justice, which has been entrusted to me on earth by God.»[61] In other words, the interpretation *segund derecho* by which all agreements are to be regulated consists of the king's scrutiny of his own conscience. That scrutiny is to be undertaken in the light of the vicariate which he has received from God to dispense justice upon earth; necessarily, therefore, it will involve considerations both of natural right and of the actual state of the law. But in the last resort it is the king himself who «bears all the laws in his heart», who has «certain knowledge» of the «public good and peace» of his domains, and who, with the manifold and godlike authority of feudal superior, natural lord and Roman *princeps,* may do as he thinks necessary, creating obligations and dispensing from them at will.

It would scarcely be fair to Juan II to regard this outlook as cynically *ben trovato.* When he spoke of his «conscience», the issue foremost in his mind was probably the murder of Alonso Pérez, and the guilt which he would feel if he were to let its perpetrator go free. There is no reason to suppose that he was indifferent to these matters, even though other feelings had, by this time, come into play —rage at the defiance of Escalona; unslaked frustration after what Juan now perceived as the years of base subjection to his great minister. Nor can the king's response to the crisis at the level of constitutional theory be set down to any short-term calculation of political advantage. Juan II and his chancery had the option of playing down the theoretical issues, and of rallying political support by concentrating instead on the tale of Don Alvaro's misdeeds; there were enough Castilians about who had scores of one kind or another to settle with the Constable to make that course an attractive one. It was not followed. Instead, Juan and his officials found in the pressure of events the stimulus to articulate and make public their own working ideology of absolute kingship.

To do so was to appeal to principles which were still less than universally accepted, as the actual relations between crown and aristocracy in fifteenth-century Castile make very clear. It was, however, the particular background of training and experience shared by senior *letrados* which commended these principles to them, and through them to the king. That background began with a formation in basically Roman law, followed by a working life of day-to-day involvement in Castilian legal practices. This purview was sometimes broadened by contact with other systems —Aragon, the Curia— or by individual reading. But there was also an element of specifically political experience. Most recently this had meant a clearer sense of the uniquely intimate ties which bound senior administrators to the monarch himself, rather than to any other interest.

[61] *CD,* no. XXXVII, p. 71: «seria en grand cargo de mi conciencia é denegar espresamente la justicia que por Dios me es encomendada en la tierra.»

In a longer perspective, their experience ranged back through the years of Don Alvaro's ascendancy, taking in a good many instances of the practical assertion of royal as against seigneurial authority. Particular acts of derogation, for that and other purposes, necessarily formed a part of that experience. Such acts had assumed a critical importance on two recent occasions —that of Juan II's humiliation at the hands of the anti-Luna forces in 1441, and that of his and Don Alvaro's triumph at Olmedo four years later. But in 1441 the forms of derogation, so far from being invested with the royal «plenitude of power», were actually being used to strip Juan II of that power. And in 1445, despite much insistence on the king's inherent authority, the issue was about to be tested by force of arms, rather than by constitutional principle.[62] In 1453, by contrast, the power of derogation was actually being exercised on the king's own behalf, and real issues depended on its effectiveness. It was natural that the *letrados* should look to their own background in the law for definitions of what the king was entitled to do.

Legally, derogation was undesirable; administratively, it was useful. Castilian legal history reflected that tension.[63] Alfonso the Wise had observed that laws were more easily unmade than made; they ought not to be relaxed, therefore, without consulting «all the principal men of the land, the most honourable and the most learned». This requirement to take counsel was construed by Juan I in 1387 to mean that the only valid derogations were those enacted in *Cortes*. But it is clear from his own edict that kings of Castile, including Juan himself, had been in the habit of issuing derogations in the form of royal letters. Such letters were henceforth to be ignored, and the officials who drafted or signed them were to be dismissed. This was still how the law stood throughout Juan II's reign; it did not prevent the crown from carrying on very much as before. The *Cortes* of Valladolid, in 1442, petitioned for and obtained rulings «that the laws shall be kept notwithstanding any royal letters or covering letters». That is of interest because the 1442 assembly was dominated by the anti-Luna forces; it may well be that derogation by royal letter was felt to be especially associated with Don Alvaro's style of government. There were other reasons, though,

---

[62] MACKAY, *Spain*, p. 138 finds it impressive that the king's claims were being put on record irrespective of the outcome of the forthcoming battle. But these claims faced no immediate political test in 1445; in 1453, they did.

[63] *Partidas*, vol. I, p. 12, Pt. I, Tít. 1, Ley XVIII: «todos los homes buenos de la tierra, los mas honrados é mas sabidores»; *Cortes (LC)*, vol. II, p. 371: «Muchas veces... damos algunas cartas contra derecho»; this law quoted in 1455, PÉREZ-BUSTAMANTE, vol. II, p. 236; *Cortes* of 1442 in MS Madrid, BN, 6720, fol. 9r-v: «que se non pongan muchas exorbitançias en las cartas»; «que se guarden las leyes non embargante qualesquier cartas e sobrecartas»; see MARAVALL, «Origins», p. 799 and VALDEAVELLANO, p. 427; cf. also *CD*, no. XLI, p. 86. Some of Juan II's derogations were effected in *Cortes* (e.g. *Cortes (LC)*, vol. III, p. 547; Valladolid, 1447).

why the rule of «no derogation except in *Cortes*» could hardly be expected to work in practice. It was, after all, in the nature of those cases where derogation was most useful that they could not be held up until the next *Cortes*. Besides, the issue was blurred by the king's undoubted right to clarify the laws or to resolve conflicts between them, and by the question of whether the *Cortes* was the only body which could provide adequate counsel. Could not the *Consejo* suffice? Or indeed, was it not enough for the king to refer the issue to his following of expert *letrados?* This last group, meanwhile, had contributed in their own way to the continuing practice of independent derogation by the crown. They had, over the past two generations or so, largely transformed its vocabulary.

Much remains to be discovered about the early appearances of the various derogation formulae. But it is instructive to contrast the range of those which were common in the 1380s with the repertoire available to Juan II in 1453. The legislation of 1387 refers to two patterns: the use of *non embargante* («notwithstanding»), and the mention of particular rulings, normally introduced by the command «do not fail to do this because of the law...».[64] Also to be found in the 1380s are the «as if» mode of derogation, and the «once, twice, three times» formula for release from homage. None of these is wholly obsolete by 1453; indeed, the last two occur in documents of the Luna case. But their wording is entirely straightforward; there are no Latinisms and the meaning is always clear. They are concerned with the act of derogation itself, rather than with the powers and principles which have to be invoked in carrying it out. By contrast, the language of derogation in 1453 is greatly taken up with these latter issues, and it employs a much more technical, Latinistic vocabulary. Yet its elements are not, for the most part, very recent in date.[65] *Cierta ciencia* has a fourteenth-century use —very restricted, it is true. *Poderío real absoluto* can be traced to the 1390s; *propio motu* to 1419; *revocar* to 1406 at least. Several of the common topics of royal supremacy have an Alfonsine background, and though some, like «no temporal superior», do not appear in documents until fairly late, «vicar of God» was so used by the very first of the Trastámara kings. Juan II's *letrados,* then, did not invent the new

[64] *Cortes (LC),* vol. II, p. 371 («*non embargante*»); for examples of *ni lo dejedes de fazer por la ley...* see PÉREZ-BUSTAMANTE, vol. II, pp. 184 (1383), 186 (1384). For «as if», see above, n. 22; for «once, twice, three times», above, n. 20.

[65] See above, n. 11 *(cierta ciencia);* n. 16 *(poderío real absoluto);* n. 10 *(propio motu).* CLAVERO, p. 153n. sees the formula combining all three as extending from use in privileges to a more general legislative function in the late 1420s. See *Crónicas,* ed. Rosell, p. 269, will of Enrique III (for *revocar);* for Alfonsine precedents, this chapter, passim; for «vicar of God» used by Enrique II, see above, n. 37.

vocabulary of derogation; what they did was to bring it together from various more or less established chancery uses. The decisive period for this seems to be in the middle years of the reign; by about 1440, most of the elements were in place. The effect was to make derogation appear a more complex and imposing business, and to link it, even before the strongly regalist statements of 1453, with certain far-reaching notions of what the royal power could encompass.

These notions were grounded in Roman law —partly in those traditions of sacred kingship which blended both Roman and Biblical sources, but more fundamentally in the *lex regia*— the vesting of the Roman people's law-making power in the person of the emperor.[66] For Ulpian, quoted in the *Digest,* it followed that «What the *princeps* has approved has the force of law». Naturally this did not refer to the emperor's private feelings but to his public judgment, and even this, John of Salisbury was to maintain, was legally binding only «insofar as his view is compatible with just reflection». Francesc Eiximenis in the fourteenth century tells a story which turns on just this point: «We read that when king Pere of Aragon said to one of his servants 'The law goes as the king wills', a wise man who was present told the king 'Yes, but no man should be king who does not keep the law and serve it.'»[67] This is the voice of the Catalan 'pactist' tradition in constitutional matters. But even in Catalonia, it is the lapidary simplicity of the *Digest,* and no local scepticism, which finds its way into proverbial use. Views could be further polarized by rhetoric which exalted the powers of a particular sovereign: «nor is he subject to any law... he himself is the law... and what pleases him is law.» That was written about the Pope, but imperial and royal claims did not lag far behind. Juan de Lucena knew enough law to paint a more cautious picture had he chosen, but

---

[66] See KANTOROWICZ, p. 103 *(lex regia);* POST, p. 260 *(Digest,* I, 4, 1: «Quod principi placuit legis habet vigorem», quoted and explained); JOHN OF SALISBURY, *Policraticus,* IV, 2 (p. 222): «eo quod ab aequitatis mente eius sententia non discordet.» The maxim reached the Peninsula early; it was used in Catalonia before 1200 (MARAVALL, *Estudios,* vol. I, p. 60).

[67] FRANCESC EIXIMENIS, *Regiment de la cosa pública* (Barcelona, 1927), p. 69: «lla va la llei on vol lo rei»; for the Latin equivalent (already in Rodrigo Jiménez de Rada) and its Castilian derivative see BERMEJO, «Principios y apotegmas», pp. 31-47 passim. On papal absolutism, POST, p. 352n. quotes a canonist: «nec ei lex posita est... ipse est lex; et quod placet ei lex est.» JUAN DE LUCENA, *De Vita Beata,* in *Testi spagnoli del secolo XVº,* ed. Giovanni Maria Bertini (Turin, 1950), p. 108 (but the view is immediately challenged in Lucena's dialogue); for «necessitas legem non habet» in Gerson and Jean Petit see POST, p. 243. MACKAY, *Spain,* p. 142 sees *quod principi placuit* and *princeps legibus solutus* as the central concepts of Juan II's absolutism. Friar MARTÍN DE CÓRDOBA in a work dedicated to Alvaro de Luna himself, had argued that kings, by the power of God, «make and give and take away laws» *(Libro del regimento de señores,* ed. Fernando Rubio, *Prosistas castellanos del siglo XV,* vol. II, BAE, 171, (Madrid, 1964), p. 164).

he was probably voicing something like the popular view when he wrote «Just or unjust, the will of the prince is enough; what pleases kings is law.» By the time Lucena wrote that, Alvaro de Luna had been dead for several years. But is was earlier again in the fifteenth century that the great French lawyer Jean Gerson had maintained not just that rulers could break any laws which did not square with the public good, but that they ought to do so. This topic of *quod principi placuit* and its ancient twin, *princeps legibus solutus,* defined between them an ample scope for royal initiatives.

The principle which sanctioned their application to all the European monarchies was that «every king is emperor in his own domain».[68] This had originally referred only to the power to levy taxes; by the thirteenth century St Louis of France was claiming an imperial «plenitude of power», and Alfonso the Wise could insist that the powers of kings were identical with those of emperors, if not greater. Don Juan Manuel observed differences in the ways in which the two types of ruler were chosen, and added that kings could be subject to emperors —but that not all were. Legal commentators, from Vincentius Hispanus down to Bartolus, linked this topic with the refusal to admit any temporal superior; a king who could validly make both claims was «a *princeps* to himself». In these terms, Juan II certainly qualified, whether on his own estimate or on that of his advisers. «I rule my realms,» he announced in 1439, «... as emperors and kings and other princes have done... each in his own lands...»[69] Bishop Cartagena regarded the two forms of sovereignty as identical, but also thought that Castilian kings could do far more in their kingdom than could the emperors in the Roman Empire. This becomes less striking if the Bishop had in mind the Holy Roman Empire of Albert II, which he had visited in the late 1430s, but it is still remarkable enough. Alonso Díaz de Montalvo, a junior judge at Alvaro de Luna's trial, later incorporated the *rex imperator* topic in one of his legal textbooks. Another jurist of Montalvo's generation, Rodrigo

---

[68] See POST, p. 15 on «Rex est imperator in regno suo»; also above, n. 17 (St. Louis); *Partidas,* vol. I, pp. 376-7, Pt. II, Tít. 1, Ley VIII: «todos aquellos poderes... que los Emperadores han... en las gentes de su Imperio... essos mismos han los Reyes en las de sus Reynos, e mayores»; cf. also, p. 374 (Ley V), p. 376 (Ley VII); JUAN MANUEL, *Estados,* p. 168. See also above, n. 39 (Vincentius, Bartolus): *sibi princeps* is Sánchez de Arévalo's phrase, but within the tradition of Bartolus (MARAVALL, *Estudios,* vol. I, p. 85).

[69] *C Halc,* pp. 264-5: «rriego... mis rreynos... según que... lo acostunbraron... fazer los enperadores e rreyes e otros príncipes, cada vno en su enperio e rreyno e tierras»; CARTAGENA, *Duodenarium,* Q. 8, Cap. VII: «reges nostri plura mire in regno quam imperatores in imperio facere possunt», perhaps merely echoing the *Partidas* (above, n. 68), but see SERRANO, pp. 150-8 for Cartagena in Germany; ALONSO DÍAZ DE MONTALVO, *Repertorium quaestionum super Nicholaum de Tudeschis* (Seville, 1477), s. v. *rex;* SÁNCHEZ DE ARÉVALO, *Liber de Differentia Principatus Imperialis et Regalis:* «summus et verus imperator in regno suo» (in BENEYTO PÉREZ, *Textos,* p. 374).

Sánchez de Arévalo, defined the imperial status of Spanish kings in exactly the terms which Bartolus had used.

Sometimes these claims are reinforced by arguments asserting a special status for the Spanish kingdoms in particular.[70] Their ancient imperial tradition, evoked in the titles adopted by Alfonso VI and Alfonso VII of Castile-Leon, was carried a stage further by peninsular canonists in the thirteenth century. The Spaniards, they said, were the subjects of no empire; they were building their own, «snatched from the jaws of the enemy» in the course of the reconquest from Islam. Other kingdoms, it is true, had used imperial titles, and were quick to assert their independence now. But the special nature of the Spanish case was widely recognized. Statements of it found their way even into texts of the strongly pro-imperial Johannes Teutonicus: «the rule of the world has passed to the Germans, except for that of Spain.» Less surprisingly, Spaniards themselves shared and amplified this belief. Lucas of Tuy actually found support for it in the fact that the ancient Spanish legal codes were non-Roman. Juan Manuel disclaimed knowledge of the Pope's temporal powers «because I am from Castile, and the kings of Castile and their realms are freer of external control than any other land in the world». Rodrigo Sánchez de Arévalo denied that either France or Spain, despite their use of Roman law, was subject to the empire. Freedom from outside suzerainty was not, of course, the same thing as plenitude of power within the kingdom. But lawyers had associated the two for generations, and reminders of the one were bound to call to mind the other.

Such, then, was the pattern of topics and precedents. Any description of the actual channels of influence into which they were articulated has to rely very much more on guesswork. But we may be perfectly definite about one influence which Juan II and his officials could not but experience. The *Partidas* of Alfonso the Wise had been part of the law of Castile since 1348. A great deal of administrative work must have involved some use of them; much of the business of the *Cortes* of Olmedo, for example, was concerned with laws drawn from this compilation.[71] Both the king and his *letrados* must have been thoroughly familiar with them. And the *Partidas* were the most important single work through which the impact of Roman law and of its early mediaeval interpreters came to be felt in

---

[70] POST, pp. 462, 482, 483 (early imperial claims); pp. 454-5 (other kingdoms); p. 466 (the canonists); pp. 482-93 (Vincentius Hispanus); p. 458: «regnum ab hostium faucibus eruerunt» —echoed and applied to the kings of Aragon by PEDRO BELLUGA, *Speculum Principum*, quoted by BENEYTO PÉREZ, *Textos*, p. 376; POST, pp. 457-8 (interpolations in Johannes Teutonicus); MARAVALL, *Estudios*, vol. I, p. 65 (Lucas de Tuy); JUAN MANUEL, *Estados*, p. 258; also p. 85; MARAVALL, p. 85 (Sánchez de Arévalo).

[71] MACKCY, *Spain*, pp. 138-9. On the *Partidas* see EVELYN S. PROCTER, *Alfonso X of Castile* (Oxford, 1951), pp. 51-69; E. H. VAN KLEFFENS, *Hispanic Law until the End of the Middle Ages* (Edinburgh, 1968), pp. 159-221, passim.

Castile. Nowhere was this influence more potent than in the second *Partida,* whose concern is with kingship and the state. When Juan II speaks of his own royalty in terms that recall the second *Partida,* we need look no further for a source. And as we have seen, it happens often. Possibly this may reflect the *letrados'* familiarity with the work; equally, the reason may have been Juan's own fellow-feeling for another *rey sabio* who, as it appeared from the chronicles, enjoyed little success in practical affairs. At all events, it is scarcely too much to say that the whole presentation of royal dignity in these documents of 1453 is Alfonsine in origin. Yet it is not wholly Alfonsine in spirit. The topics —that of the royal vicariate is a very clear example— tend to be pressed to an extreme of regalism which goes well beyond the *Partidas.*

Alfonso's compilation represents only one moment of the long interpretative process, through which mediaeval jurists sought to give their Roman authorities contemporary meanings. The regalist outlook of Juan II's administration was also informed by other phases of that process. Sometimes these had found expression in ethical or political treatises. Works of this character had a fairly evenly-divided chance of influencing either the king's professional advisers or the king himself. John of Wales, for example, was a writer whom even an educated lay magnate like the Marquis of Santillana could know; John of Salisbury, by contrast, seems to have been only indirectly known, even among the professionals of scholarship.[72] But it was not the specialized nature of the *Policraticus* which could have kept Juan II from reading it; that specialism, after all, lay in a direction of some considerable interest to kings. The same was true of treatises which did circulate in the Castile of that time, like the *De Regimine Principum* of Aegidius Romanus, which had been translated into Castilian as early as 1344, for that most uncompromising of regalists, the future king Pedro the Cruel.[73]

It is far less likely that the more strictly professional kind of mediaeval legal scholarship exerted its effect on the issues of 1453 through any initiative of the king's. The genres through which this material was presented were the immediate product of formal modes of university teaching; they did not lend themselves to part-time reading by interested lay persons. By contrast, all the *letrados* were used to such texts,

---

[72] For John of Wales see RAFAEL LAPESA, *La obra literaria del Marqués de Santillana* (Madrid, 1957), p. 207n.; for *Policraticus*, PERO DÍAZ DE TOLEDO, prologue to Plato's *Phaedo* (MS Madrid, BN, Vitr. 17.4) fol. 3r-v, where errors in citation establish Pero Díaz's dependence on Walter Burley, *De Vita et Moribus Philosophorum.*

[73] JUAN GARCÍA DE CASTROJERIZ, *Glosa castellana al Regimiento de príncipes,* ed. Juan Beneyto Pérez (Madrid, 1947); see K. E. SHAW «Provincial and Pundit: Juan de Castrojeriz's version of *De Regimine Principum*», *BHS*, 38 (1961), 55-63; also HELEN L. SEARS, «The *Rimado de Palacio* and the *De Regimine Principum* tradition of the Middle Ages», *HR,* 20 (1952), 1-27.

having themselves followed university courses in law.[74] Neither of the two Castilian universities, it might be argued, was the most vital centre of European legal thought. But there was a long history of Iberian contacts with the University of Bologna, which was. This could be traced back as far as the Hispanic canonists of the early thirteenth century —themselves one possible influence on some of the positions adopted in our documents. Still more regular interchanges with Bologna developed after the foundation of the Spanish College there in 1367. It was not too hard, then, for lawyers in Juan II's service to keep in touch with relatively recent work abroad. That some of them did so is evident from that law of 1427 which forbade the use in Castilian courts of authorities more recent than Johannes Andreae in canon law or Bartolus in civil.[75] It seems that this ban was still effective in the mid-century, but it did not necessarily have the same impact on theoretical or private studies. The attitudes behind the derogations of 1453 would square very well with the notion that some *letrados* at least had been reading Lucas de Penna or even Jean Gerson. And we may be certain that they had all read Bartolus, whose works offered an important synthesis of some of the key topics of royal supremacy. They probably knew the work of earlier «post-glossators» too. But whatever the detailed picture, the absolutist tone of the 1453 documents is likely to have been informed by readings of this type. And it was the professionally trained *letrados* who supplied that information.

In so doing, they were in a sense «Europeanizing» the account of the royal estate which had become naturalized in Castile through the work of Alfonso the Wise. The incipiently absolutist mode of thought had already exerted an influence in the history of several other European monarchies. It is likely enough that the Castilian *letrados* and their

---

[74] See A. GARCÍA Y GARCÍA, *Estudios sobre la canonística portuguesa medieval* (Madrid, 1976), pp. 67-94 (Roman Law in the Peninsula); pp. 41-54 (university studies); pp. 90-1 (forms of legal treatises); pp. 108 (Vincentius), 113 (Johannes de Deo). Isabel the Catholic owned works of Baldus, Bartolus and Johannes Andreae, besides the *Partidas* (BENEYTO PÉREZ, «The Science of Law in the Spain of the Catholic Kings», in *Spain in the Fifteenth Century*, ed. Roger Highfield (London, 1972), p. 280); some of these may also have been owned by her father.

[75] VAN KLEFFENS, pp. 225-6; GARCÍA Y GARCÍA, «Bartolo de Saxoferrato en España», *AEM*, 9 (1974-9), 441; BENEYTO PÉREZ, *Science of Law*, p. 281. The satire against lawyers in the *Cancionero de Martínez de Burgos*, ed. Dorothy S. Severin (Exeter, 1976), pp. 45-56 includes among authorities cited in court only names permitted under the 1427 legislation, but GARCÍA Y GARCÍA, «Bartolo», pp. 441-2 finds later writers cited by 15th-century Spanish jurists. He also lists (pp. 448-52). 123 MSS of Bartolus in Spanish libraries, at least 25 being identifiably from Castile. Among other relevant «post-glossators», Baldus and Joannes Andreae are found in Spain copied with Bartolus (ibid., pp. 456-7), and Odofredus was later quoted —with these three— by Montalvo (BENEYTO PÉREZ, «Science of Law», p. 279); Lucas de Penna (ULLMANN, p. 13) was certainly well known among Spanish jurists of the following century.

master remembered some of these parallels.[76] The discouraging example offered by Richard II of England was perhaps not one of them, despite the close dynastic link with the Trastámaras. But the kings of France had a more impressive and tenacious history of self-assertion, stemming from their early commitment to the *rex imperator* principle. It may not be coincidental that Enrique II, who introduced the «vicar of God» topic into Castilian official documents with a newly authoritarian emphasis, had lived for years in exile in France. It certainly did not pass without notice that the Castilian kings too could claim descent from St Louis. Alonso de Cartagena, in a famous speech to the Council of Basle had made this point one of the grounds for Castilian precedence, and we may assume that Juan II was well aware of it. As for Castile's immediate neighbour, the Crown of Aragon, the situation there was complex.[77] The dominant tradition, especially in Catalonia, was one of limited monarchy. But the newly implanted Trastámara dynasty did display a preference, as at the *Corts* of San Cugat, for at least the rhetorical forms of regalism. And this counter-emphasis was to gain in importance as the century advanced; it becomes very marked indeed, for example, in the work of Cardinal Margarit. If the Castilian *letrados* looked to the eastern kingdoms for some general hint that their view of royalty represented the way in which things were moving, they need not have looked in vain.

A more powerful focus of outside influence than any so far considered was the papacy. The mediaeval Popes had made both an involuntary and a deliberate contribution to the growth of secular absolutism.[78] The themes and motifs of their supremacy had first been appropriated by their imperial rivals, before passing to other secular rulers as the defining topics of that doctrine. But the crucial link in this process was the

---

[76] KANTOROWICZ, p. 28 (Richard II); JOHN LE PATOUREL, «The King and the Princes in Fourteenth-Century France», in HALE, HIGHFIELD and SMALLEY, pp. 156-7; P. S. LEWIS, «France in the Fifteenth Century: Society and Sovereignty», ibid., p. 279; see also above, n. 41 (Enrique II); SÁNCHEZ ALBORNOZ, «Un ceremonial inédito», p. 753 (anointing and the power of healing in Alfonso XI's coronation rite); SUÁREZ FERNÁNDEZ, *Juan I*, p. 87 (French precedents for Juan I's reforms); CARTAGENA, *Proposición contra los ingleses*, in PENNA, p. 208.

[77] See above, notes 36 and 55 (San Cugat). Bishop Sapera's remark of 1416 that «Nobles... were only suited to execute orders devised by scholars» illustrates the potential for a *letrado*-based regalism (HILLGARTH, vol. II, pp. 183-4). By the 1460s, Juan II of Aragon was claiming to be accountable only to God (ibid., p. 271); for the contrast between Margarit, writing in mid-century, and the «pactist» Eiximenis see TATE, *Joan Margarit i Pau, Cardenal e Bispe de Girona* (Barcelona, 1976), pp. 206-8.

[78] ULLMANN, *History*, passim, supplies the background; see also GARCÍA Y GARCÍA, *Estudios*, pp. 244-5 on French *rex imperator* claims and the 14th-century papal «captivity»; J. M. LABOA, *Rodrigo Sánchez de Arévalo. Alcaide de Sant'Angelo* (Madrid, 1973); SERRANO, pp. 137-50 (Cartagena at Basle); FERNÁN DÍAZ DE TOLEDO, *Instrucción del Relator* in CARTAGENA, *Defensorium*, ed. Alonso, p. 347 (the Relator at Morella).

notion of the individual *rex imperator,* and this had been fostered in the first place by the papal interest itself, as a counterweight to imperial pretensions. The results as far as the French monarchy was concerned had not been entirely happy for the Popes. But it is in keeping with this history that some of the most emphatic statements of the Castilian king's unique position should come from persons closely associated with the papacy. Rodrigo Sánchez de Arévalo, for example, was to end his career at the papal court in Rome, and Alonso de Cartagena had led the Castilian delegation at Basle in a markedly papalist spirit. Earlier in the century, of course, the pontificate of the Aragonese Benedict XIII (Pedro de Luna) had brought the institutions of curial government into the Iberian Peninsula itself for a time; the Relator, as a young chancery clerk, had actually visited Benedict's court at Morella in 1414. It is hardly surprising, then, that several of the formulae used in our documents —notably those of invocation— should be apparent imitations of papal usages. Anomalously, the most striking of them all —the *cierta ciencia* formula— does not seen to have been especially favoured by Benedict; it comes into much more prominence under his Roman rival Martin V, to whom the allegiance of Castile was eventually transferred.

Such anomalies of detail are to be expected in a picture where much remains to be clarified by fuller research into Castilian chancery practices. Yet the main characteristics of that picture are surely clear enough. One of them is the sheer temporal range of those authorities and experiences which are laid under contribution. Another is the way in which older concepts are reinterpreted as part and parcel of more modern ones —feudalism as *naturaleza; naturaleza,* in its turn, as a function of absolute royal authority. A third feature is the integration of Castilian with wider European experience —not, indeed, in the form of any dramatic new development in 1453, but rather as an overall tendency into which the events of that year are inserted. A fourth, and a decisive one in practice, is the alliance between two distinct cultural modes. The culture of the *letrados* is fully professional —essentially the tradition of Roman law and its commentators. But it is placed at the service of Juan II's own culture. That culture is, in one sense, personal: its most deeply-felt concerns are those of self-discovery. But it is also inseparable from Juan's position as ruler; what he needs to discover is what he is and what he should now do *as king.* All these elements in the forging of an ideological statement in this one crisis are paralleled in the wider cultural movement of the reign. The ideological meanings of that movement generally are made that much the clearer.[79]

---

[79] For a general interpretation, in some respects debatable, see OTTAVIO DI CAMILLO, *El humanismo castellano del siglo XV* (Valencia, 1976), together with the review by the present writer in *BHS,* 56 (1979), 59-61; recently and most usefully, JEREMY N. H. LAWRANCE, *Un tratado de Alonso de Cartagena sobre la*

Sometimes, indeed, it is possible to trace a more precise set of connections.[80] The origin of the view that the *princeps* was God's vicar lay in the *De Clementia* of Seneca. The same author's *De Beneficiis* informed other aspects of mediaeval juridical thinking about kingship. The Italian Andreas of Isernia had observed that «Seneca was an excellent jurist, as those who have read him know». And Juan II had most certainly read him; he had had versions made by Alonso de Cartagena of a considerable body of Senecan works. These did not include the *De Beneficiis*, apart from excerpts in Luca Manelli's *Compilatio*, but the *De Clementia* was there in full, and there were generous selections, wrongly attributed, from the *Controversies* of Seneca the Elder, which could only add to the philosopher Seneca's reputation as a legal authority. As a cultural presence, he matters more to the scholarly movement fostered by Juan II than any other ancient writer. The versions made by Cartagena in the early 1430s had had a score of years to make their presence felt. It would be surprising if Seneca were far from the king's thoughts at this moment. Of the more specialist writers who were of concern to the *letrados,* the ones likeliest to be more than mere names to him were Baldus, Johannes Andreae, and most certainly Bartolus. Among less narrowly professional sources, John of Salisbury's *Policraticus,* though ideologically central for the growth of regalism, seems to have been unknown at first hand in Juan II's Castile.[81] However, the *De Regimine Principum,* wrongly but prestigiously attributed to Aquinas, had found its way into Santillana's library, and was probably available elsewhere too. As for Aegidius Romanus' work of the same title, its readership extended well beyond any narrowly professional circle.[82] One

---

educación y los estudios literarios (Barcelona, 1979). See also JUAN BAUTISTA AVALLE-ARCE, *Temas hispánicos medievales* (Madrid, 1974), p. 123 (on Europeanizing tendencies); ROUND, «The Shadow of a Philosopher: Medieval Castilian Images of Plato», *JHP,* 3 (1978-9), 35 (on cultural syncretism); above, Chapter I, n. 36 for further references.

[80] See above, n. 40 (SENECA, *De Clementia*); also *De Beneficiis,* VII, 4-6; KANTOROWICZ, p. 473n. (Andreas of Isernia). See also F. STELLA-MARANCA, *Seneca giureconsulto* (Rome, 1966; 1st edn Lanciano, 1926). Dating of Cartagena's Senecan translations: some, at least, before 1435 (ROUND, «Shadow of a Philosopher», p. 22n); MANELLI's *Compilatio* the first (MS Madrid, BN, 6765, fols 2r-v); *De Clementia* later than spring 1431 (ibid., fols 46v-47r).

[81] On John of Salisbury see above, n. 72; on Pseudo-Aquinas see SCHIFF, p. 202.

[82] SCHIFF, pp. 202-3; 209-10; 210-11; LICINIANO SÁEZ, *Demostración histórica del verdadero valor de todas las monedas que corrían en Castilla durante el reynado del señor Don Enrique III* (Madrid, 1796), p. 374 (Vasco Ramírez de Guzmán). Vasco Ramírez, who died in 1438, had dedicated to Juan II a translated *florilegium* including excerpts from Aegidius, Seneca and Vegetius (A. PAZ Y MELIA, «Biblioteca fundada por el Conde de Haro en 1455», *RABM,* 1 (1897), pp. 62-3. For Estúñiga's copies see SÁEZ, p. 374. In the period between Castrojeriz and Juan II's *letrados,* Pero López de Ayala appears to have read Aegidius and some related authorities, but not Pseudo-Aquinas («*Libro de Poemas*» o «*Rimado de Palacio*», ed. Michel García (Madrid, 1978), vol. I, p. 256; SEARS, p. 26).

fifteenth-century owner was the Toledan canon, Vasco Ramírez de Guzmán, who was on book-borrowing terms with the Relator. Another was the Marqués de Santillana, whose library included copies in Latin, French and Castilian. Less expectedly, the handful of books owned by young Alvaro de Estúñiga included both the Castilian translation of Aegidius and a Latin text. The latter could have been bought as an investment, less likely to depreciate than its price in cash; the former suggests that he actually wanted to read the work. Whether he did so around the time of Alvaro de Luna's arrest, and whether he found instruction there we cannot know. But it is overwhelmingly likely that Juan II and the Relator, to say nothing of the latter's colleagues, were familiar with Aegidius' book. Among much else to their purposes, they might have found there this: «It is therefore sometimes appropriate to bend the law... in an opposite direction, and to punish the offender more harshly than the law itself lays down.»[83] It seems a very relevant remark to what they were about to do with Alvaro de Luna.

---

[83] AEGIDIUS ROMANUS, III, ii (quoted by GIMENO CASALDUERO, p. 145); see also BERMEJO, «Principios y apotegmas», p. 38.

CHAPTER 5

A FORM OF TRIAL

In the third week of April, Juan II was ready to move from Burgos. The work of the *Cortes* was finished; the administrative side of the Luna case was well in hand. There remained its more practical aspect. Elsewhere in the kingdom, it was now clear, Don Alvaro's supporters were disposed to make trouble. It was likely that this would require the king's personal presence in the Toledo area, where lay the major Luna strongholds of Maqueda and Escalona. Yet there was no very desperate haste about Juan's southward progress.[1] He left Burgos on April 17th, but it was almost a full month before he crossed the Guadarrama passes, south of Segovia. Certainly he kept Toledo and its neighbourhood well in mind. On 20th April after reaching Torquemada, he wrote to the Toledans, urging them to move against Escalona and promising to send troops. From Portillo, eight days later, a further letter went out, upbraiding the city for its inaction, but offering both reinforcements and a visit in person, «which will, please God, be soon». The Toledans complained that they could neither pay nor feed an army in the field; on May 9th, Juan undertook to remedy these difficulties as best he could. The very speed with which posts came and went between Toledo and the royal presence illustrates the urgency with which the king viewed the situation there. Yet by May 9th, he himself had got no further than Arévalo.

There was, of course, other business to delay him.[2] For two or three days at the end of April, he had been involved in negotiations, outside

---

[1] He had not yet left on 16th April *(Cortes (LC)*, vol. III, p. 650); he was at Santa María del Campo by the 18th, and at La Asperilla in the Guadarrama on 16th May. For these and other details of his journey see QUINTANA, p. 503; PALENCIA, *Déc*, p. 49n.; *CD* nos XXXI-XXXIV, pp. 56-60.

[2] See *CAL* (C), pp. 420-1; *CJII* (R), p. 682; VALERA, *CAbr*, p. 336 (Portillo). Juan signed documents in Arévalo on 5th and 9th May, and would not have left on 10th May, which was Ascension Day. See also JUAN TORRES FONTES, *Itinerario de Enrique IV de Castilla* (Murcia, n.d.), p. 35 (Arévalo to Segovia in two days): *Ref Halc*, p. 69 (another day to La Asperilla); *CD*, no. XXXV, pp. 61-6 (the Prince's divorce).

the castle of Portillo, with Alonso González de León, the Constable's lieutenant in that place; the reward was its surrender and a booty of 27,000 *doblas*. The six-day halt at Arévalo from 5th to 11th May, and the royal party's subsequent slow progress in crossing the mountains —taking five days for a journey which could be done in three— may perhaps be explained by other events in that region. In the parish church of the hamlet of Alcazarén on 11th May, the administrator of the diocese, Luis de Acuña, pronounced the final divorce of Prince Enrique from his wife Blanca of Navarre, on the ground of non-consummation of their marriage. Both politically and personally, the business was a deeply embarrassing one. But we may well believe that Enrique's father found it convenient to be in the area at the crucial time, and to reassure himself that matters had gone smoothly at the last. If the Navarrese, for example, had elected to raise last-minute objections, there would be a new and plausible occasion for them to make trouble on the eastern frontier. With that danger removed, Juan II could at last turn his full attention to affairs south of the passes.

He had also had to give some thought to the disposal of his prisoner. Ruy Díaz de Mendoza had preferred to travel with the king, and had placed Don Alvaro in the charge of his brother, Juan Hurtado. It was arranged that the Constable and his escort should travel south by a separate route from the king's party and, as it seems, a little earlier.[3] One reason for this may have been the danger of unseemly popular demonstrations against the fallen *privado*. Certainly, Juan II would have found it hard to retain his regal dignity in the kind of atmosphere which one witness was later to recall as marking Don Alvaro's departure from Burgos:

> ... and as they were leaving by the city gate, those who were standing on the walls called out «This is Burgos, monkey-face; this is Burgos, not your place!» And he had heard that the Constable had turned his head towards the city, and taking his beard in his hand had said «May I never shave this beard nor cut my nails, but I'll have you ploughed and sown with salt, you cow-pen!»[4]

More humiliations of a similar sort awaited him where he was going. For he was being taken to Valladolid, to be lodged in the house of his victim, Alonso Pérez de Vivero, and if the dead *contador*'s clients made no demonstration against him now, they were certainly to do so

---

[3] *CJII* (R), p. 681 places the change of custodian immediately after the arrest; *CAL* (C), p. 414 gives the timing and reason as here. If he met Carrillo and his brother when they were going to meet the king at Dueñas (ibid., p. 417), Don Alvaro was already south of Dueñas, and so had left Burgos first.
[4] Eyewitness report in CORRAL, pp. 81-2: «ésta es Burgos, cara de mona, ésta es Burgos que no Escalona». See also *CJII* (R), pp. 682, 683, and *Abr H*, p. cci for Don, Alvaro's lodging in Valladolid and his reception there.

when he was brought back there for execution a few weeks later. The choice of residence, in any case, preserved a nice balance between vindictiveness and honourable captivity. It can have done nothing for Don Alvaro's morale, which had already suffered a severe blow of another kind on his way from Burgos.[5] Some distance south of the town of Dueñas, he had caught sight of a great man's retinue hurrying northwards; it was easily recognizable as that of his old ally the Archbishop of Toledo. Don Alvaro, indeed, had been eagerly expecting the arrival of Archbishop Carrillo, and the support from the latter which their distant kinship and long association seemed to him to warrant. But Carrillo brought no such support; he and his brother Pedro de Acuña turned aside from the direct route which would have brought them face to face with the prisoner and his guards, and pressed forward with their retainers to Dueñas. The message of Don Alvaro's isolation could not have been more plainly conveyed.

The brothers themselves, encountering the king and his party in Dueñas on 20th or 21st April, were at pains to reaffirm that message by their studied hostility towards the Constable. Its point was not lost either on Juan II or on the minor prisoners of the Luna faction whom he had brought along with him. In a desperate search for a fresh strategy one of them, Gonzalo Chacón, now petitioned for an interview with the king. The proposal which he had to put was that he should be given a chance to speak to Don Alvaro in order to find out «where his treasures were buried».[6] It was, of course, a palpable ruse; Chacón wanted to establish contact with his former patron for quite different reasons. Juan II was not deceived for a moment, and returned him to custody. But the appeal to the king's appetite for treasure was shrewdly judged. The insistence of the *Crónica de Don Alvaro,* in its closing chapters, on covetousness as the mainspring of Juan's actions may reflect Chacón's regret (if indeed he is the author) at having done his work all too well. It is unlikely that he actually planted the idea of financial advantage in the king's mind. Don Alvaro's own offers at the time of his arrest were probably to blame for that. Since then Juan II had been busily sequestering the Constable's estates and revenues; the gains which this brought in could only be welcome, especially with the prospect of a military campaign in New Castile. But Don Alvaro's confiscated income was a measurable quantity; the hoards of ready money laid up in his strongholds were a dazzling unknown. The temptation which Chacón dangled before the king at Dueñas was a powerful one. At

---

[5] *CAL* (C), pp. 414-17. Carrillo may have met the royal party in Dueñas late on 20th April (when the king had signed successive letters in Torquemada and in Dueñas itself), or on the 21st.

[6] *CAL* (C), pp. 417-19; ibid., p. 411 for an earlier approach by Chacón along similar lines.

Portillo, not much more than a week later, it was tangibly reinforced, without benefit of any intervention by Chacón. The negotiated surrender, on or before 28th April, of this, the first of Don Alvaro's major fortresses to be held in strength, brought Juan II at least four million *maravedís* in cash —possibly half as much again.[7] A further hoard of about a third of that size was recovered from the monastery of Santa María de la Armedilla. Taken together, these two windfalls approached and perhaps surpassed Don Alvaro's annual income from Crown sources. It is scarcely to be wondered at that Juan's attention should have been concentrated on the main prize of this sort —the treasure of Escalona. But Escalona was not to be wheedled out of the hands of any lieutenant; it was held by Don Alvaro's wife and sons, with the most fanatical of their supporters. The king was not going to get into it without a fight.

These financial concerns compounded the damage which the Constable's activity as the inspirer of an armed revolt had done to his prospects of royal clemency. No doubt he had calculated otherwise, reckoning that his partisans would be able to keep up their efforts for months or years if necessary, pending his release. That, after all, was what the Count of Alba's friends and relatives had been doing since 1448. But Alba —whose imprisonment, incidentally, had not been shortened by these campaigns— had not been so important a figure that his departure altered the whole pattern of Castilian politics. Nor had he murdered the king's *contador mayor*. More to the point still, he did not have inmense riches stored away in any castle. If Don Alvaro's relatives really meant to hold on to Escalona until he was set at liberty, there was one very obvious way of putting that prize beyond their reach. Compared with the expense and uncertainty of a protracted siege, it was a very attractive alternative —all the more so if it gave access to treasure on the scale foreshadowed by the Portillo hoard. By simultaneously provoking the king with armed resistance and tempting him with vast sums of money, the Constable's supporters were making it much more likely that Juan II would want to kill him.

There remained the question of whether the king could do it. But the experiences of the previous month had helped to form his response to that dilemma too. In the first place, there had been the novel experience of voluntarily doing without his *privado*. That in itself, and the consequent first steps towards a new political orientation at home and abroad, must have made any prospect of rehabilitating Don Alvaro

---

[7] *CJII* (R), p. 682, VALERA, *CAbr,* p. 336 value the Portillo treasure at 27,000 *doblas; Abr H*, p. cci puts it at 30,000, but gives no figure for the sum recovered from Santa María de la Armedilla, which the other two reckon at 9,000 *doblas*. In *doblas de la banda* (the likeliest units), the total would be at least 5.4 million *maravedís;* in *doblas castellanas* a third as much again. For Don Alvaro's income see below, pp. 229-32.

appreciably more remote. Besides, the message which Juan's officials had been putting out in his name day after day was that he could do virtually whatever he wished. He could overrule the contracts entered into by his subjects, and the orders he himself had issued; he could take any action the «peace and calm» of his kingdom seemed to him to demand; he was the image and the vicar of God in the temporal affairs of Castile; he was, absolutely, the King. It would be surprising if Juan II, who had signed letter after letter to this effect in the past month, and no doubt discussed their content daily with the Relator and other officials, had not by this time come to believe it all himself. Therein lay Don Alvaro's chief danger.

That is probably as far as we can go in assessing the King's attitude towards his captive when, about the time of his departure from Portillo at the end of April, he made certain dispositions concerning the Constable. In the first place, a new gaoler was designated; the Mendozas were at last set aside, and a member of the Estúñiga family preferred.[8] The Estúñigas had some claim to the appointment in terms of the part they had played at the time of the arrest, and more formally because the Count of Plasencia was hereditary Chief Justice of Castile. But the basis of the decision is just as likely to have been political. The Mendozas, who had first been given custody of Don Alvaro because of their freedom from compromising local attachments in Burgos, assumed another kind of importance when it began to look as if the Toledo-Escalona area might become a theatre of war. Another branch of the Mendoza clan divided power in the crucial northern sector of New Castile with Don Alvaro himself and the Carrillo-Acuña interest. With the Luna territories in revolt and the loyalties of Archbishop Carrillo at best uncertain, any snub to even a remote Mendoza connection would carry with it an element of risk. But now, following the Archbishop's arrival at Dueñas, Juan could feel tolerably sure of him, and the Mendoza brothers became expendable. To transfer the prisoner to Estúñiga custody would avoid taxing that family's patience unduly. Even so, young Alvaro de Estúñiga was still not the chosen custodian; perhaps the rashness of some of his earlier *démarches* was remembered against him. Instead, the charge was given to his cousin Diego, who had been involved in Juan's very first negotiations with the family on the Constable's removal. Diego would be just as suitable, given that the prisoner was to remain in the area of Valladolid —a city whose Estúñiga and Vivero connections were doubly ominous for Don Alvaro's long-term

---

[8] For the king at Portillo see above, notes 1-2. He stayed for perhaps two days (*CJII* (R); VALERA, *CAbr*), perhaps three of four *(CAL);* one of these was 28th April. On the Estúñiga office of *justicia mayor* see MITRE FERNÁNDEZ, pp. 130-1; on Diego de Estúñiga, VALERA, *CAbr*, p. 327; PALENCIA, *Déc*, p. 44 (*CEIV*, p. 45); the corresponding passage in *CJII* (R), p. 654 is wrongly dated.

fate. He was to be moved, however, from the Vivero house to a new and grimmer prison —his own castle of Portillo.[9] This was, of course, a great deal more secure than anywhere else he had been lodged so far; there was to be no spectacular rescue or escape. But security was only one consideration; the irony of the choice continued that pattern of personal humiliation which had been established by Don Alvaro's previous lodging. It appears, too, that the conditions of his imprisonment were now made harsher. According to his chronicler, an especially close guard was placed upon him after the king left Portillo. This is confirmed by several anti-Luna sources, including Fernán Pérez de Guzmán, who says that he was kept chained in a wooden cage. Fernán Pérez evidently wrote from hearsay, and was in any case disposed to believe tales of Juan II's cruelty. But we cannot discount his story. Behind it there lies something which is quite certainly true: the fact that Juan II had decided to handle his prisoner on a different basis. From now onward, Alvaro de Luna was to be treated not as a great nobleman on whom a grave suspicion had somehow fallen, but as a criminal awaiting judgment. Such was the spirit in which Juan now made his first definite moves towards bringing Don Alvaro to trial.

The nature of the proceedings taken against him has long been clouded by partisanship, as well as by certain purely verbal confusions. The most important of these centre upon the term *proceso*.[10] This can be either concrete or abstract in meaning. Concretely it is the written record of legal proceedings —sometimes an indictment or *procès verbal*, sometimes the official transcript or summary of an entire trial. Thus, when the royal chronicle describes how the king at Portillo, having had a *proceso* drawn up against Don Alvaro, now referred it to twelve doctors of law, the term can only mean the outline of an indictment. When the *Abreviación del Halconero* speaks of the Constable's *proceso* as the object of scrutiny in a later Council meeting near Escalona, it may well mean a report of the whole case so far. But it should not be inferred from any such passage that a full and formal record of Don Alvaro's indictment and subsequent trial ever existed. Certain sixteenth- and seventeenth-century commentators were a good deal exercised by this question, and even the Constable's modern biographer César Silió labours the point unduly. His conclusion, though, is almost certainly correct: there neither is nor ever was such a record. At some stage,

---

[9] *CJII* (R), p. 682; CARTAGENA, *Rubrica Additio*, ibid., p. 693; *Abr H*, p. cci; *CAL* (C), p. 419; see also PÉREZ DE GUZMÁN, *G y S*, p. 43 (on Juan's character, p. 44). Fernán Pérez has Juan II bring Don Alvaro with him from Burgos; our other sources disprove this (see above, n. 3).

[10] See *CJII* (R), p. 682; *Abr H*, p. cci. SILIÓ, pp. 251-3 summarizes views of Salazar y Mendoza, Loaisa and Fray Pedro de Abarca. See also *CAL* (F), pp. 455-76).

no doubt, there was a draft indictment, based on the information which the Public Prosecutor had been collecting since the death of Alonso Pérez. There were, for other purposes, other notes made of what was done or decided, some of which, directly or indirectly, have come down to us. But there was no *proceso* of the fuller sort. It was not, in the end, that kind of trial.

On the other hand, it was not quite the hasty and predictably hostile affair which the *Crónica de Don Alvaro* describes as taking place in the king's camp before Escalona.[11] That was not how it appeared to most other contemporary witnesses. *Proceso* in its more abstract sense of «legal proceedings as such» seems to them the natural word to apply to these events; it recurs in such diverse commentators as García de Salazar, Escavias, and Sánchez de Arévalo. The last-named makes no secret of his regalist sympathies *(facto legitimo processu)*; Escavias is more cautious and perhaps more sceptical *(fue hecho cierto proceso contra él)*. But all agree that Don Alvaro's execution was preceded by some kind of formal judicial activity. Fernán Pérez de Guzmán is more explicit as to what kind it was; three of the essential elements of a regular trial —the taking of information; consideration of the evidence; the issue of a verdict— were all present: «by reason of certain information which he had, and proceeding as in a matter whose facts were notorious, with counsel from the lawyers who were at his court, he issued his sentence that [Don Alvaro] should be beheaded.»[12] These were the elements which Juan II himself had singled out in the open letter to his kingdom at large which he issued on 18th June. First had come the collection of «sure and true information» on the Constable's misdeeds. Then this evidence had been discussed, both publicly in Council and by the «doctors and prudent men of my aforesaid Council», consulted under oath. Finally, the affair was brought to a conclusion by royal decree. In the light of the evidence taken and the public notoriety of the facts, says the king, «I ordered my justice to be carried out, and it was done by my command». At very great length, the letter of 18th June dwells on Don Alvaro's offences in order to justify the actions taken. Such justifications aside, it is worth enquiring how far these actions can be regarded as embodying any regular or defensible notion of legal proceedings.

Gaps and anomalies in our pattern of data make any answer to that enquiry difficult. The royal chronicle, for example, is consistent in its own terms but hard to reconcile with other evidence *(Crónica de Juan II,* ed. Rosell, p. 682). Before the king left Portillo, it informs us, the indict-

---

[11] *CAL* (C), pp. 425-6; even more dismissive is *Causa escrita a Don Alvaro de Luna* (MS Madrid, BN, 10774), fols 25v-26v (18th century). Contrast GARCÍA DE SALAZAR, p. 59; ESCAVIAS, p. 343; SÁNCHEZ DE ARÉVALO, *HH,* p. 235.
[12] PÉREZ DE GUZMÁN, *G y S,* p. 44; cf. *CD,* no. XLI, pp. 90-1.

ment against the Constable was passed to the «twelve famous doctors of the Council», who were formally sworn «to pronounce sentence as they found according to law». The king then set off for Maqueda, whose captain was Don Alvaro's trusted retainer Fernando de Ribadeneira. Resistance was fierce for a few days; then, rather surprisingly, it collapsed when the defenders were threatened with a formal charge of treason. Juan now turned his attention to Escalona, whose reduction promised to be a far harder task. With this in mind he decided to enquire what should be done with Don Alvaro, and summoned the twelve commissioners he had appointed. He ordered them, together with «all the bishops, knights and doctors who were present» —that is to say, the Council— to discuss the *proceso* and to determine a penalty. Those present asked for time to reach a decision, and in a full Council meeting two days later, the Relator announced the finding that Don Alvaro «ought, by law, to be beheaded». The king accordingly «gave orders for the sentence to be drawn up at once», and it was sent to Portillo for action by Diego de Estúñiga «who held the Master prisoner there».

This «official history» is not too hard to square with the official apologia of 18th June; on the one point where they clash —the order of consultation of the specialist lawyers and the full Council— the chronicler is probably in the right. Yet on the timing of events he must be wrong.[13] The *Colección diplomática* and the documents seen by Quintana make it possible to trace Juan's southward journey in fair detail. Leaving Portillo perhaps on 29th April, he was in Arévalo from 5th to 9th May; on the 16th, he was in the mountains at La Asperilla; by 22nd May, he was established at Fuensalida, his first base against the Luna fortresses. He remained there for at least a further five days. Letters from his camp outside Maqueda begin on 29th May and end on 7th June; it was after this that the royal army moved on to Escalona. Yet Alvaro de Luna had been executed in Valladolid on June 2nd. Taking the order for his execution from Fuensalida to Portillo, and making the necessary arrangements in Valladolid must have occupied several days. The decision to have him killed can hardly have been much later than 24th May, at which time Juan had neither taken Maqueda nor invested Escalona. He was still in Fuensalida.

Fuensalida is also identified as the scene of the crucial meetings by the most detailed of our surviving records —a late fifteenth-century paper from the Villena family archive.[14] This describes how Juan II, while in Fuensalida, summoned nine eminent lawyers (all named, along

---

[13] Datings from Quintana and the editors of Palencia's *Décadas* who also establish June 2nd as the date of Don Alvaro's execution (see above, n. 1).

[14] *CD*, no. XXXVIII, pp. 74-7. All later references here are to this edition. (Also printed in J. RIZZO Y RAMÍREZ, *Juicio crítico y significación política de Don Alvaro de Luna* (Madrid, 1865), pp. 415-19). See especially *CD*, pp. 75-6.

with two more who appear later in the document), together with two noblemen, Pedro de Acuña and Diego de Estúñiga. He addressed them all on the «disservices» which Don Alvaro had done him, and sought their advice, beginning with the Relator, Fernán Díaz: «and the said Relator asked his Majesty whether he knew that all that he had just told them was the truth, because he did not have to give any account of it, save to God alone.» It was all true, replied the king, and they might base their judgments on it. In that case, the Relator declared, «it was his view, according to the law, that Don Alvaro deserved the death penalty and the loss of his property.» The other *letrados,* «seeing that this was the king's will», readily agreed. But at a second meeting in the local church, with Doctors Franco and Zurbano, who had been absent earlier, there was «great argument». Its outcome was that the verdict should be given «as a mandate and not as a sentence». In this form, signed by those *letrados* who were Council members and witnessed by those who were not, the decision was issued and transmitted to Diego de Estúñiga. This version of events leaves out altogether any mention of arrangements made at Portillo; it has nothing to say of the two full Council meetings at Fuensalida, or of the two-day pause for consideration between them. All these elements imply a more measured and deliberate procedure. Are they, then, inventions of the *Crónica de Juan II?*

If so, we might account for them in either of two ways. The Galíndez de Carvajal version of the royal chronicle could have placed events in the wrong chronological sequence. Or there could have been a conscious attempt, when the chronicle was first written, to make some rather hasty and irregular proceedings look a little more respectable. Neither explanation would represent a unique case. But to opt for one or the other would also involve seeing the Villena document as wholly authoritative. And this, despite its very great interest, is hardly possible. For one thing, the document says nothing about the swearing-in of the panel of judges. Yet some such ceremony there must have been; presumably it took place before the summons to the king at Fuensalida. Also, the mention of Diego de Estúñiga raises a problem.[15] One other source, admittedly, places him in the Escalona area at this time. But this is the *Crónica de Don Alvaro,* whose account is notably vague at this point, for the very good reason that its author was no longer in any position to follow events in detail. Gonzalo Chacón was still in custody, and probably still in the north. As for Diego de Estúñiga, he had no business to be in Fuensalida at all. His predecessor as Don Alvaro's gaoler, Ruy

---

[15] See *CAL* (C), p. 429; on RUY DÍAZ, p. 414; Chacón lost touch with the king once the latter had left Portillo (p. 419); contrast *CJII* (R), p. 682 where orders for the execution are sent to Diego de Estúñiga in Portillo.

Díaz de Mendoza, had apparently been obliged to give up his charge when he could no longer remain by his prisoner's side. Diego de Estúñiga had been appointed to the post at the end of April; he still held it when the warrant for the execution arrived at Portillo. Where else should he have been in the decisive days of late May but at the castle of Portillo, presiding in person over Don Alvaro's close imprisonment? The Villena paper, then, makes better sense if we read it as a conflation of two quite separate meetings. The first, held in or near Portillo in the last days of April, would have included the king, the newly-commissioned *letrados* (or some of them), and Don Alvaro's new gaoler. The other layman mentioned, Pedro de Acuña, had joined the royal party at Dueñas. As a relative of the accused, but one whose loyalty to the crown was not suspect, he could well have seemed a suitable observer at such a preliminary session.[16]

Everything else which the Villena document describes, from Juan II's consultation of the *letrados* onwards, happens in Fuensalida. It has to be reconciled with the royal chronicle's account of two Council meetings separated by a two-day interval, with certain other references to the part played by Archbishop Carrillo, and with the inferences which have to be drawn from the king's letter of 22nd May to the defenders of Escalona. The time-limits for all this are extremely tightly drawn: Juan II can scarcely have arrived in Fuensalida before 18th May, and the decision regarding Don Alvaro cannot have been much later than the 24th. Of the intervening days, May 20th was a Sunday, when no official business was done. Yet it is still possible to build up a picture of events which has its own narrative and political logic.

In the first place, the lawyers' meetings described in the Villena paper were evidently not sessions of the Council. No prelates or noblemen were present —the two non-lawyers mentioned do not belong to the Fuensalida part of the story. Besides, not all the *letrados* mentioned were Council members themselves (*CD*, p. 77). Their decision, then, would have had to be ratified by the full Council. This, in effect, was what happened at the second of the meetings described in the royal chronicle. The events of the Villena narrative, therefore, must belong to the two-day gap between these meetings. They are, in fact, the main element in that process of «deliberation» for which the interval was meant to allow, even though the Relator's statement to the second

---

[16] AMADOR DE LOS RÍOS, *Judios*, vol. III, pp. 61, 62n. refers to the place of the *letrados*' meeting on successive pages as Fuensalida and Fuentidueña. Just possibly Amador may have seen some lost source naming Fuentidueña as the place of the *first* such meeting. Fuentidueña, though, is well to the east of Portillo, on the road to Aragon (see *C Halc*, p. 465). Juan II is unlikely to have gone almost thirty miles out of his way at this time; the name may have crept in erroneously because the castle of Fuentidueña was once held by Don Alvaro's bastard son, Pedro de Luna (*CAL* (C), p. 322).

meeting, as recorded by the *Crónica de Juan II,* cannot itself be equated with the report of these discussions.

That report, which would have been offered on behalf of the commissioners alone, would have been the starting-point for the Council's business. The statement in the *Crónica,* which was presented as the view of all the lay Councillors, whether present or not, reads like a summing-up of the Council meeting itself. There would have been obvious political value in such a show of unanimity at this decisive stage, and it was natural that it should be put on record in the royal chronicler's propagandistic history. But it confronted one ecclesiastical Councillor with a grave dilemma. Nobody had seemed more committed to Don Alvaro's ascendancy, and nobody owed more to it than Archbishop Alonso Carrillo —«next to God», says Chacón, the Constable's creature. For him, and perhaps for others, a loophole was found. The same chronicler records that «he left the Council and delivered no vote», because as a cleric he could not condone the shedding of blood.[17] Chacón was wrong about the reason; other prelates appear to have remained in the meeting. But the incident was also recalled in 1497 by the Archbishop's servant Juan de Vallejo:

> ... he had seen the old Relator come to the palace where Archbishop Alonso Carrillo... and other gentlemen and clergy were with his Majesty, and while they were there, the Relator said to the Archbishop, 'Go away, your Grace; this business is not for you', and so he left the palace and went away to his lodging, and some gentlemen and clergy went with him, and he had seen the Archbishop show some feeling of sorrow.[18]

Later, he learned that Don Alvaro's sentence had been pronounced that same day. Whether it had been at a Council meeting he did not know, though he had helped to arrange the furniture for the session, and had even placed the king's chair on its dais. But it is clear enough that these were the preliminaries to the second Council meeting. Just as clearly, the Relator was doing what the king would wish to have done in order to retain the support of Archbishop Carrillo —first by allowing him to leave without loss of dignity, and then by his pointed remark about absentee Councillors. This made it clear that Juan would not welcome any attempt to discredit Carrillo merely because he had not lent his name to the verdict against Don Alvaro. The whole matter was handled with much political skill.

For the precise dating of these events we have to rely on Juan II's letter to the Escalona garrison, whose own date of 22nd May is not in

---

[17] *CAL* (C), pp. 414, 426. See also *CJII* (R), p. 682. *Causa escrita,* fol. 26r-v suggests that both reasons obtained. *CJII* (R) implies and *Abr H,* p. cci states that other clerics were present; they were evidently expected to show at least passive solidarity with the verdict.

[18] CORRAL, p. 88; *palacio* here must mean Juan's lodging in Fuensalida; plainly, the story cannot refer to the camp before Escalona.

dispute. It is itself the reply to a «petition» —more accurately, a manifesto of defiance, sent by the rebels, and delivered by one Francisco de Trejo.[19] It does not appear that there had been any earlier exchanges between the two sides. The king's letter ends with a call to Escalona to surrender lest its garrison should be guilty of treason. This is precisely the kind of appeal which Juan II might be expected to make at the very start of his campaign. Its argument was a potent one; it was to prevail, for example, at Maqueda a fortnight later.[20] On this first occasion, of course, it did not succeed, but had it done so, the king would have been spared much trouble. We need, then, to consider the relationship to developments in Don Alvaro's trial of two items: the defiance carried by Trejo, and Juan's reply.

The former had protested against the Constable's captivity, but it had not mentioned the prospect of a death-sentence; it follows that the rebels did not yet know of this. They must have written, then, before the second Council, and before any news of the *letrados'* meetings at Fuensalida had time to reach them. Yet the tone of their manifesto, as reported by Juan II, was violent and desperate:

> And you also say... that you will summon to your aid... not only those who are my enemies, but the Moors, and the devils if you could, not only giving them what property you have from your husband and father [Alvaro de Luna]... but your very lives and selves, and that if all else fails you will set flame and fire to the property which you say I intend to take from you...[21]

Don Alvaro's supporters no doubt resented the harshness of his captivity in Portillo. They may well have been suffering some privation themselves; there was famine in the Toledo region that May. They were also faced with certain problems of a purely rhetorical nature. But the wildness of this language seems to require some more specific cause. Other aspects of their protest give some hint of what this might have been. They were, for example, particularly suspicious of Juan II's intentions towards his prisoner; they accused him of planning to act cruelly, wilfully, with «evil and mistaken counsel». As for the *letrados* who were giving him advice, the rebels attacked them with such ferocity that Juan's indignant Councillors added their own postscript to his reply, even though he too had defended them in the warmest terms:

---

[19] *CD*, no. XXVII pp. 68-73. See DEYERMOND (above, Chapter 4, n. 34). Can the author, denounced by Juan II (p. 69) as «that disloyal, evil, imprudent, mad, vain counsellor», have been Bartolomé de Zafra (above, p. 61)?

[20] The surrender of Maqueda (*CJII* (R), p. 682) was seen by observers of widely differing views as highly creditable to Fernando de Ribadeneira, who had held the place for Don Alvaro (*Abr H*, p. cci; *CAL* (C), p. 422).

[21] *CD*, pp. 68-9; for the famine see no. XXXIV, p. 60; also *CAL* (C), p. 424; for rhetorical considerations, above, Chapter 4, n. 34.

> I have not taken, nor do I take, counsel from persons of the kind you describe in your letter, but from God-fearing and authoritative persons, of good and sound conscience, good-living and religious men, learned and wise and well-tried, free of all avarice and suspicion, and properly devoted to my service...[22]

Behind all this there lies an urgent and bitter suspicion on the part of the rebels that something very much worse than what has happened already is just about to happen. The event which could, most obviously, have precipitated such a dark mood was the first Council meeting at Fuensalida, which offered the clearest of indications that the legal process against Don Alvaro was nearing its climax. The rebel manifesto would appear to have been sent to Juan II shortly after this meeting; if, as seems possible, it had actually been drafted a little earlier, its more violent passages would have been added after news of that first Council had reached Escalona.

Juan's reply, in its turn, has nothing to say of Don Alvaro's forthcoming execution. Instead, the king merely announces that he will make up his own mind:

> I shall give orders for provision to be made, and be caused to be made, and I shall act in all that matter, in the way in which, according to God's guidance and in the integrity of my own conscience, it belongs and is appropriate for every king's Majesty to act.[23]

The syntax is tortuous and the text perhaps corrupt, but it is evident that the final decision had yet to be made. The second meeting of the Council, therefore, had not yet taken place on May 22nd when this letter was written. Yet it contains unmistakable signs that something had happened which boded little good for Don Alvaro. Not once in his letter to Escalona does Juan II give him his titles of «Master and Constable»; he is always «your husband and father». This is a new departure since 16th May, when both titles were still in official use. They are, however, employed in the postscript which was added by «those of the king's Council». This was certainly composed after the king's letter, since at one point it refers to what Juan has written.[24] The explanation has to be that a decision had been reached but not yet promulgated. Juan knew that he was going to deprive Don Alvaro of his office as Constable, as he was fully entitled to do. It was less clear that

---

[22] CD, p. 72, both for this passage, and for the charges of cruelty, capriciousness and evil counsel. The postscript by «los del Consejo» is on p. 73.

[23] CD, p. 71; for the ideological implications of this appeal to «conscience», see above, pp. 117-18; also below, this chapter, n. 58.

[24] CD, p. 73; «su altesa... responde por su letra». The day of the month is left blank in this postscript, both in CD, and in the 18th-century transcription from which its text is taken (MS Madrid, BN, 13109, fol. 64v). I can find no significance in this omission.

he had the right to unmake a Master of Santiago, but he also knew that Don Alvaro's Mastership would soon be an irrelevance. Of the Council members, only those *letrados* who sat on the special commission would have shared that knowledge. It is highly probable that just this group of Councillors was responsible for the postscript. But until their decision concerning Alvaro de Luna had come before the Council they could not, when writing on behalf of the Council, take cognizance of its results. It follows that on 22nd May, when Juan's letter and its postscript were written, the *letrados* had met and made their recommendation, but it had not yet been ratified in Council.

With the aid of certain further details of Council procedure —that meetings were at eight in the morning and were held every day except on Sundays— we may now reconstruct the events leading to Don Alvaro's condemnation.[25]. The decision to try his case and the appointment of a twelve-man commission belong to the time of the king's departure from Portillo; we do not know how often the twelve *letrados* met in the next three weeks. But when Juan II reached Fuensalida, he found a situation there which was calculated to shorten his patience. Maqueda and Escalona were defiant and well-defended; the latter, in particular, looked strong enough to withstand any attack. Famine conditions in the country round about made the prospects for a besieging army very dubious indeed. Within the walls of Escalona there lay that unimaginably alluring treasure which the Constable had hoarded. But Juan found himself baulked by Luna intransigence now, as he had been baulked by Luna omnipotence in the past. The frustration is evident in his speech to the *letrados,* and in his letter to the rebels, with its long diatribe on Don Alvaro's arrogant usurpation of power, «as if *he* recognized no king and no superior» (*CD*, p. 70). But Juan's first response to these difficulties, naturally enough, was to ask if the commissioners had yet formed a view of the case. When this enquiry was discussed in Council, on the morning of Monday 21st May, there was a general desire for further consideration, especially among the empanelled *letrados*. The king's meeting with them, and their altercation with Franco and Zurbano followed later that same day —there was plenty of time for this. By evening, Juan had their recommendation that he should issue a mandate for Don Alvaro's execution. It was not exactly what he had wanted —he would have preferred them to deliver a sentence of their own— but it would serve.

Meanwhile, news of that morning's Council had travelled the few miles to Escalona. Very possibly, Juan had felt disposed to let it do so, hoping that it might encourage a prompt surrender. Instead, it had the

---

[25] Times of Council meetings (eight o'clock in summer; nine in winter), and days of business in *Ordenanza del Consejo Real* (1442), MS Madrid, BN, 13107, fols 148v, 150r.

effect of stiffening resistance, and perhaps of adding a note of furious aggression to a pre-existing statement of the rebel case. When Francisco de Trejo delivered that statement, probably on Monday evening, it was not the kind of message which Juan had looked to receive. The obvious business of the day at the Council meeting of Tuesday morning was the preparation of the king's reply and of the Councillors' contribution to it. By taking the rebel manifesto to the Council, Juan could hope to win sympathy and support for the strong action which he now knew he was about to take. At the same time, his letter of that day to Escalona included some powerful assertions of regalist ideology and a specific demand for the rebels to surrender on pain of high treason. It was worthwhile staying his hand if there was a chance that the enemy might be overawed by the sheer theoretical assertion of authority. It also gave hin time to work out, perhaps with the Relator, how former Luna sympathizers like Archbishop Carrillo could best be handled. Within days, however (by the morning of May 23rd if the royal chronicler's two-day interval between Councils is to be credited) Juan's course was settled for him. Escalona was not going to capitulate. Instead Carrillo was got out of the way, the Council meeting issued in the Relator's statement of how Don Alvaro stood in law, and the king gave the orders which would be taken north to Diego de Estúñiga.

In all this there is the same interaction of personal and public motives which we have observed in so many aspects of the drama of 1453. Of course, Juan II was angry that Don Alvaro's supporters had revolted, greedy for his treasures, racked by a long-suppressed resentment at his *apoderamiento*. All these responses accelerate the new phase of the crisis represented by Don Alvaro's trial. But the rebels themselves and those who might be tempted to join them are handled with evident political finesse; the pursuit of Don Alvaro's wealth seems to be highly relevant to an overstrained exchequer; the desire to be king in fact as well as in name merges into an ideology of kingship and the state. These things, rather than the emotional life of Juan II, are the movers of events. Yet, given their presence and their effect, it is necessary to ask again what room remained for justice. Did the form of Don Alvaro's trial, as we have been able to reconstruct it, offer him due process of law?

It did so in the first place —though even this has sometimes been denied— in the extremely limited sense that most of the procedures adopted were in accord with what the law required. There is little basis, for instance, for Salazar y Mendoza's complaint that the Council «did not pronounce sentence on the case or see it», much less for his contention that the Council was not even present.[26] Both *sentencia* and *proceso*,

---

[26] Pedro de Salazar y Mendoza, *Crónica de el Gran Cardenal de España, Don*

of course, are terms capable of a good deal of ambiguity. But the full Council did have a part to play, and possibly a somewhat less restricted one than the bare record in the royal chronicle might suggest. At the first of its two relevant meetings, after all, the king did invite discussion of the case, and presumably there was some response; at the second, other views had to be heard before the Relator was in a position to sum up «by the command and decision of them all». Yet the initiative in these meetings obviously did lie with the special commission of judges; it was they who required and were granted more time for consultation on the first occasion, and whose final report was decisive on the second. We have to think of that report as being read out by the Relator at the very start of the business, since it was his appointed task to «present a report of the item on which the Council is to advise». In the circumstances, it is not altogether surprising that no Councillor disagreed.

Referral to a specially appointed commission was a standard practice in serious cases against noblemen.[27] There were the recent precedents of the Count of Castro in 1429 and the Toledan rebel leader Pero Sarmiento, twenty years later. Under the law of 1442 on «legal cases touching persons of rank», this was one of three admissible procedures; the others were judgment by the *Alcaldes de Casa* and disposal by the king. Rizzo y Ramírez, then, is not justified in his claim that this law was disregarded in the Luna case, though its application was modified in one particular. Instead of two Doctors of Law, nominated by the king from among his Councillors and approved by their fellows, Juan II chose twelve *letrados*, not all of whom were Council members. In his letter of 18th June, justifying his conduct of the case, Juan makes something of a virtue of this breadth of choice.[28] Besides regular and resident members, he states that he also consulted Councillors who were «venerable and worthy... of good repute and sound conscience» but who did not reside at court, as well as «other famous lawyers» not in the Council. The 1442 regulations, in any case, were drawn up by an anti-Luna administration, which favoured a Council of limited membership. Since Olmedo the king had gone back to enlarging the number of Councillors without restriction; if this had an advantage, it was that it made wider consultation possible on issues of special gravity.

Pedro Gonçález de Mendoza, I, 19, (Toledo, 1625), pp. 70-92; also in *CAL* (F), p. 466. Contrast *CJII* (R), p. 682. For the Relator's functions in Council see *Ordenanza del Consejo Real*, fol. 149r.

[27] *C Halc*, p. 116 (Count of Castro); BENITO RUANO, *Toledo*, pp. 69-70 (Sarmiento). Law on «los hechos de justicia tocantes contra las personas de estado» in *Ordenanza del Consejo Real*, fols 146r-147r; cf. RIZZO Y RAMÍREZ, p. 216.

[28] *CD*, no. XLI, p. 90. For the range of policies on Council membership see above, pp. 25-6.

If challenged, Juan could have argued, with some plausibility, that he was over-fulfilling the requirement of the law, not subverting it.

His later intervention in the case is less straightforwardly defensible. In any objective sense it has to be seen as a form of pressure on the commissioners; this was, inescapably, a political trial. But a formal status of a somewhat more regular sort could be found for Juan's actions. In the first instance, he offered evidence to the judges. In the conduct of the case generally he was, as the sovereign and chief magistrate in his kingdom, «consulting» them, and hence entitled to oversee what they were doing. In the final outcome, again acting as the *princeps*, he determined the matter by his own mandate. None of these justifications, of course, was free of problems. As Rizzo points out, the action against Don Alvaro tended very obviously to the king's own profit; how, then, could his evidence not be suspect?[29] The difficulty with this line of criticism, however, is that in law the king was not simply an individual with his own interests to pursue; he was also the guarantor, the fountainhead, and in some accounts, the embodiment of the law itself. The problem posed by Juan's testimony, as by his intervention in general, was whether it involved the private or the public person. For the *letrados* who had to make that distinction it was not a matter of the king's state of mind —as it has tended to be for those later historians who have found against him. The question was one of law.

To some extent the law of 1442 offered guidance here.[30] Juan's eventual recourse to a mandate might be seen as his taking over the case himself —something which that law allowed him to do, provided that the *letrados* currently sitting in Council gave their advice and consent. When a case was judged by the king, the same law provided certain safeguards against the intrusion of his private will. The verdict had to be given in full Council, after a complete report of the case «so that it may be seen that it is not a matter of will, but that justice is being done to both sides». The decision also required approval by a majority of serving *letrado* Councillors. We may be reasonably certain that Juan had his majority among the lawyers, though the Villena record suggests that they were not at first unanimous. But we do not know how fully the Council was apprised of the details of the case. The Relator, whose duty it was to see to this, had been in trouble before for summarizing petitions from litigants in too brief a form. We lack the text of his initial report to the Council meeting of 23rd May. But

---

[29] RIZZO Y RAMÍREZ, p. 216. For the classic treatment of royal «duality», see KANTOROWICZ.

[30] *Ordenanza del Consejo Real*, fol. 147r. The reporting procedure is meant to cover judgments either by the *alcaldes de casa* or by the king. For complaints against the Relator's over-succinct summaries, see *Cortes (LC)*, vol. III, pp. 265, 325-6.

if it was anything like as succinct as his recorded summary of that meeting's views, it scarcely fulfilled the spirit and intention of the law:

> Sir, on behalf of all the gentlemen and Doctors of Law of your Council who are present here —and I even believe that all those who are absent would be of the same mind— they have seen and known those things and deeds which the Master of Santiago, Don Alvaro de Luna has committed in disservice to you, and to the detriment of the public weal of your realms, and how he has tyrannized and plundered your revenues, and they find that by law he ought to be beheaded... (*CJII* (R), p. 682).

It was this kind of abridgment of the complexities raised by Don Alvaro's case which his partisans in Escalona had feared when they claimed that Juan meant to proceed *por forma de voluntad*. His chronicler, too, strikes a similar note: «since will was sovereign, the sentence was signed.»[31] For Chacón this was a consequence of Juan II's flawed personality. Yet, whatever the truth of this, it cannot be the whole truth. The drive to conclude the case in the way the king wanted and in no other was implicit in the politics of the situation. This was no civil suit in which «justice to both sides» could be genuinely even-handed. The party ranged against Don Alvaro was, in the last resort, the king himself in his public person; the scale and substance of his alleged misconduct were, alike, grave. Persons arraigned in this form were not usually expected to be found innocent.

Many years later, in the much less politically-charged context of a commentary on the *Partidas*, one of the commissioners, Alonso Díaz de Montalvo, was to air his own second thoughts about the case.[32] Montalvo's main reservation is that the king had no jurisdiction over Don Alvaro who, as Master of Santiago, had ecclesiastical privilege. He adds that Juan II later sought absolution from Rome for this. Later, of course, was the right time to do it. In the summer of 1453 at least, Juan was particularly firm on just this point. His letter of 18th June accuses Don Alvaro of having sought «by concession from Rome» to make his son Master of Santiago after him. «The Holy Fathers», declares the king, «never meddled with the Mastership, or with anything to do with it; that has always been done by the Kings of Castile.» This is as close as Juan's regalism ever comes to open conflict with Church interests and it is

---

[31] *CAL* (C), p. 427. This follows a brilliant analysis of the inner debate between Juan's will and covetousness on the one part and his reason and conscience on the other. As imaginative literature it is admirable.

[32] ALONSO DÍAZ DE MONTALVO, gloss to *Siete partidas*, Pt. I, Tít. 7, Ley I, quoted by CORRAL, p. 30n., and in *CD*, p. 77n. SALAZAR Y MENDOZA deduced from this (wrongly) that Montalvo was not among the judges (*CAL* (F), p. 467). Published in 1491, the *Partidas* gloss is a late work of Montalvo. Contrast, on the Order of Santiago, *CD*, no. XLI, pp. 84-5. (Juan also accepted that the Order itself had a say in the Mastership.) See also the apparatus to *Partidas*, vol. I, pp. 166-7.

still not very near. The question of clerical privilege and the Military Orders was not a clear-cut one. The Order of Santiago could point to dealings with Rome which put their members on a par with regular clergy; the Kings of Castile could appeal to a long history of actual jurisdiction over the Order. It was a matter of some relevance that knights of Santiago could and did take wives —as Don Alvaro, of course, had done; for Johannes Andreae, the members of the Order were «married laymen». Whatever Montalvo may have come to think in later years, the weight of the legal advice available to Juan II at the time evidently fell on this side.

At the same time, there was little point in complicating matters by taking the case too far into this debatable territory. There are, it is true, several ecclesiastical charges listed in the letter of 18th June.[33] Don Alvaro is said to have interfered in elections to benefices, to have embezzled money from indulgences, to have monopolized to his own profit Castilian relations with the Holy See. But all this forms part of a propaganda exercise, designed to list every offence which could possibly have been imputed to the dead Constable. At the time of his trial, the only charges considered seem to have been secular matters. There was no lack of such misdeeds to be laid at Don Alvaro's door, and neither the king addressing the *letrados* nor the Relator speaking in Council needed to go beyond them.

Montalvo's second objection is that the Constable was neither summoned nor heard in his own defence. This was a clear breach of natural justice, but it had its precedents. Neither the Count of Castro nor Pero Sarmiento had been given a hearing, though as the one was in exile and the other leading a rebellion at the material time, this was scarcely to be wondered at. Yet if it came to that, Don Alvaro's supporters too were in open revolt. And he was known to have incited them; not all his correspondence with them had been secure.[34] Their manifesto of 21st May, though it came too late to be an influence on the commissioners, seems to have confirmed that the defenders of Escalona were acting on his instructions. Don Alvaro had not quite put himself in the position of the rebel Infantes when, at Alburquerque in 1430, they had fired

---

[33] *CD*, no. XLI, pp. 83-4 passim. See also pp. 81 (usurping Church lands), 82 (obstructing Juan's efforts to build the church at Miraflores), 85 (misappropriating ecclesiastical taxes). But these last —the *tercias*— had been assimilated to the king's secular revenues, amid much controversy, almost two centuries earlier (see PETER LINEHAN, «The Spanish Church Revisited: the Episcopal *Gravamina* of 1279», in *Authority and Power. Studies presented to Walter Ullmann*, ed. B. Tierney and P. Linehan (Cambridge, 1980), pp. 130-1.

[34] His page Morales (in later imaginative versions of his story, a pattern of loyalty) is said to have betrayed the messages which he sent out from Burgos (*CAL* (C), p. 412). For Don Alvaro as the direct inspirer of the Escalona rebels see *CD*, no. XLI, p. 89; for the Alburquerque incident and Juan's comments see *CJII* (R), p. 478.

on Juan II's own banner, and had been warned by him that he was entitled in law to condemn them out of hand. But the Constable had gone far enough in that direction to make a trial *in absentia* appear a colourable proceeding.

We may take Montalvo's word for it that the accused was never summoned before his commissioners; it is less certain that he had no opportunity at all to make his defence.[35] We do not have to give credence to all those witnesses who, in 1497, recalled that «he had been given a hearing so that he could plead in his own behalf». They had not sat in the tribunal itself, as Montalvo had; some of them may simply have been anxious to favour the Pacheco claims in the immediate lawsuit. But the testimony of one such witness is of more interest: «... the Constable himself said and replied to the things which they put to him and the charges they made against him, 'I am his Majesty's servant and his creature, and all that I have is his and he gave it me; let him do with me as he will'.»[36] Here, evidently, is a story intended to be favourable to Don Alvaro; it belongs to that traditional picture of undeserved suffering meekly borne whose most eloquent spokesman is the chronicler Chacón. Yet even within that tradition, whose purposes would be better suited by the claim that the Constable was denied a hearing, it was apparently accepted that he had the benefit of some sort of defence. Juan II in his letter of 18th June mentions having sent «certain members of my Council» to Don Alvaro at his own request, at some time after he had been taken prisoner. What he said on this occasion might have been used in evidence. Equally, someone may have gone to Portillo to question him on behalf of the commissioners. There was time enough for this between their appointment and the critical meeting at Fuensalida; in particular, the halt which the royal party made at Arévalo before Ascension Day would have allowed for at least one such visit.

Efforts to gather evidence from other sources were certainly made,[37]

---

[35] CORRAL, pp. 86, 87. Don Alvaro's daughter, María, now married to the Mendoza Duke of Infantado, was suing the Marquis of Villena (Juan Pacheco's heir) for former Luna properties. Thus the Mendoza interest lay in proving that Don Alvaro had not been fairly tried; the Pachecos sought to prove that he had (ibid., p. 9). The evidence analysed by Corral was assembled for the Pachecos. SILIÓ, p. 255, after seeing other papers of the same lawsuit, is inclined to reject almost all Corral's material as biased. Caution is often in order, but some items are less easily dismissed.

[36] CORRAL, p. 87; see also *CD*, no. XLI, p. 88.

[37] For the Prosecutor's report, see *CD*, no. XXV (8th April), p. 43; no. XXXVII (22nd April), p. 70; also p. 71 (further enquiries); no. XLI (18th June), p. 90 (again, further enquiries). On Maldonado's statement «en una probanza», see SALAZAR Y MENDOZA (*CAL* (F), p. 464); on Pero González, CORRAL, p. 87; see also MS Madrid, BN, 13109, fol. 66r. The 18th-century *Historia de la privanza y caída de Don Alvaro de Luna* (MS Madrid, BN, 6185), fol. 11v, states that the Constable «sought to make his defence», but may be merely guessing.

however problematic the question of Don Alvaro's own defence may habe been. There was, in the first place, the Public Prosecutor's report on the murder of Alonso Pérez. The first references to this, in early April, represent it as confined to that single charge, on which the king is said to have ordered «an enquiry to be made and certain information to be obtained». It was this enquiry, presumably, which gathered the evidence we know to have been given by Francisco Maldonado, the page sent to summon Alonso Pérez to his fatal interview. By May 22nd, the Prosecutor's report had apparently been extended to cover the general tale of Don Alvaro's usurpations of power. But Juan II also states, both then and in June, that he had ordered wider investigations to be made. We cannot be certain whether these were in the hands of the Prosecutor or of the commission as a whole. The testimony of the *contador* Pero González de Valladolid, «summoned by the king's command to say his say in that trial», as his nephew was to recall in 1497, almost certainly belongs to this phase of the enquiry. One would expect him to have been questioned about Don Alvaro's handling of the royal revenues. He was also one of those contemporaries who believed that the Constable had been heard in his own defence. That impression would perhaps have been more readily gained if Pero González himself had stood before a fully-constituted bench of judges. Another indication of how the case was pursued is the marginal comment in the Toledo copy of Juan's letter of June 18th, opposite the charge that Don Alvaro often lodged uninvited in the royal palace. «Note», it says «that it is proved with witnesses.» That witnesses were obtained on so minor a count is impressive —or would be so if we could be sure that the same had been done for the more serious charges. It is, for example, uncertain how much the commissioners were in a position to know about the horrific tale of the notary Gómez González de Illescas.[38] He had been imprisoned by Don Alvaro, and then had two sons held hostage in his place, but found, on paying their ransom, that one of them had been secretly murdered. Apparently, before his execution, Don Alvaro did confess that he had wronged Gómez González. Whether he admitted the murder we do not know, but the 200,000 *maravedís* of the ransom were repaid out of the confiscated Luna revenues. The first documentary evidence of all this, however, appears only ten days after the Constable's death. The story may not have come to light in time to influence the trial, though Juan II did, at some point, have it investigated and found it genuine. Whatever the truth of the timing

---

[38] QUINTANA, p. 504 reproduces Juan II's authorization of 12th June for payment of the indemnity; see also ibid., p. 491n.; RIZZO Y RAMÍREZ, p. 218n.; *CAL* (F), p. 437. Both Quintana and Rizzo find the tale incredible. Possibly the hostage died naturally but Don Alvaro still sought the full ransom. It was not, however, the only murder of which he was suspected (see below, n. 46).

of this one item, though, the commissioners plainly did have a certain amount of material to work on before Juan II addressed them at Fuensalida.

If this material is not greatly emphasized in our sources, it is because, in the event, it was not the decisive element. The evidence which did prove crucial came from elsewhere. To an extent it was common knowledge what Don Alvaro had been and what he had done. As Juan II declared on 22nd May, the Constable had behaved «in that manner which is notorious and known to everybody... and I know it more and better than anyone».[39] He repeated the assertion in very much the same words in the open letter of 18th June, remarking that this had made it superfluous to collect evidence (though he had done so), and that the *letrados'* judgment had been arrived at «according to the notorious and evident character of the facts». This, indeed, was one possible defence of the somewhat abrupt procedure finally adopted. That acute lay observer Fernán Pérez de Guzmán was able to make legal sense of the business in these terms; «proceeding as in a matter whose facts were notorious» *(como en cosa notoria)* is his description of how Juan II went about it. But this was scarcely the whole story. It was not the approach of the commission when first empanelled; they took specific evidence from the Prosecutor's report and from other sources. Nor was it to the notoriety of the facts that the Relator had addressed his remarks at the Fuensalida meeting; he and his colleagues had «founded», as the king had told them to do, on the latter's testimony as principal witness. The weight of what was common knowledge begins to make itself felt in Juan's own intervention, and in his subsequent disposal of the case by his own mandate. For when the king spoke of the charges against Don Alvaro as *cosa notoria,* he meant, first and foremost, that they reflected the facts as known to him.

Such a claim opens two further areas of doubt regarding the trial. Were the facts as presented sufficient to justify Don Alvaro's executino? And was Juan II's assertion of them conclusive as evidence? The Constable's judges have incurred much criticism for their ready assent to both propositions. Some of it, at least, is misdirected in principle.[40] Don Alvaro's chronicler, for example, derides the self-evident absurdity of proclaiming that the man being led to execution through the streets of Valladolid «had assumed power over the person of the

---

[39] *CD*, no. XXXVII, p. 72; cf. no. XLI, p. 90; also Pérez de Guzmán, *G y S*, p. 44.
[40] *CAL* (C), pp. 431-2; see also Salazar y Mendoza in *CAL* (F), pp. 468-9; the specific charges are: depriving the late Queen of the castle of Montalbán; usurping the church taxes in Osma and elsewhere; the affair of the Mastership of Santiago (above, n. 32). To these we may add the matter of the church at Miraflores (above, n. 33). It is not a very impressive list.

king». His irony is somewhat undermined by the fact that neither of the versions of the proclamation as we have it includes the words in question. Salazar y Mendoza finds only three charges of a specific nature in the letter of June 18th, and considers all of them too trivial for a sentence of death. So, indeed, they are, and most of the rest of that extremely long denunciation of Don Alvaro is too generalized and unsystematic to be of use in securing a conviction. But then, that was never its purpose, any more than it was the purpose of the proclamation in Valladolid. Both documents were issued after Don Alvaro had been condemned, and their aim was to make that condemnation seem acceptable, in the one case to the crowds watching the execution, in the other to the kingdom at large. Any understanding of what they have to tell us about the evidence on which Don Alvaro was condemned must start from there.

The proclamation, of its nature, cannot tell us very much. It exists in two versions —the shorter in the *Crónica de Juan II,* the longer, based on notarial copies, surviving most accessibly in Mariana's *History*.[41] The royal chronicle's pithier version could well derive from someone's aural memory. If so, the charge which it picks out would reflect what people remembered —as it certainly reflects what the Crown wished them to remember— of the reasons for Don Alvaro's fall: that he had been a «cruel tyrant and usurper of the royal crown». Insofar as it was a technical term, «tyrant» referred less to the harshness of his regime than to its lack of a legal basis. In the Roman legal tradition the mark of the tyrant was his habitual, as opposed to occasional, disregard of the law as it stood; for Alfonso the Wise, «tyrant» was virtually synonymous with «usurper».[42] It was the usurpation of

---

[41] *CJII* (R), p. 683: «Esta es la justicia que manda hacer el Rey nuestro Señor á este cruel tirano é usurpador de la corona real; en pena de sus maldades mándale degollar por ello»; also, with minor variants, in *Abr H,* p. cci. MANUEL DE FORONDA, «El tumbo de Valdeiglesias y D. Alvaro de Luna», *BAH,* 41 (1902), 179: «Esta es la justicia que manda hacer nuestro señor el Rey a este cruel Tirano: Por quanto el por orgullo de soberuia, e loca ossadia, e injuria de la Real Magestad, la qual tiene lugar de Dios en la tierra: se apodero de la casa, e palacio, e corte del Rey nuestro señor, vsurpando e ocupando el lugar que non era suyo, nin le pertenescia: E fizo, e cometio en desseruicio de Dios, e del dicho señor, e menguamiento, e abajamiento de su persona e dignidad, e estado de la Corona Real de sus Reynos: e en gran daño e desseruicio del Patrimonio Real e perturbacion, e menguamiento de justicia muchos e diuersos crimines, e excessos, e delitos, e maleficios, e tiranías, e cohechos. En pena de lo qual todo le mandan degollar. Por que la justicia de Dios, y del Rey, sea executada, e a otros sea exemplo: que non se atreuan a fazer, ni a cometer tales y semejantes cosas. Quien tal fiço, tal pena padezca.» (I have spelled out in full the contracted forms in Foronda's edition.) This was the text copied by a notary of Valladolid for Fray Alonso de Quiriales on 3rd June 1453. Also, with minor variants, in MARIANA, p. 138; SALAZAR Y MENDOZA *(CAL* (F), p. 462), and *Causa escrita,* fols 35v-36v.

[42] POST, p. 261 (the views of Bartolus, Salutati and Innocent IV); *Partidas,* vol. I, p. 379, Pt. II, Tít. 1, Ley X; cf. also, in the apparatus there, BARTOLUS,

power —Don Alvaro's *apoderamiento*— which was meant to be central in this reading of his fall. This is confirmed and amplified in the notarial version: the Constable has taken power over «the king's» household and court and palace»; he has done grave disservices to the royal estate, Crown and patrimony; he has perverted justice, and committed many other crimes and excesses. All this he has done arrogantly, «usurping the place which did not belong to him», and prejudicially to the king's person «which holds the place of God on earth». In effect, this is the charge of *apoderamiento* set in the context of regalist and absolutist ideology. Don Alvaro was dying because of the way in which that ideology construed his assumption of power in Castile.

The letter of June 18th was written after the execution but before the surrender of Escalona.[43] It concludes with a stern warning against aid to the rebels, but its primary intent is to justify beyond all dispute the king's treatment of Don Alvaro. Addressed to the kingdom at large, it envisages an audience of nobility, clergy and municipalities which will include some members capable of appreciating detailed points of law. Others, however, will be more impressed by the sheer accumulation of charges, while others again will respond most readily to whatever touches their own sectional interest. One of the reasons for the inordinate length of this document is its attempt to provide something for everyone. Another is the variety of sources on which the king's chancery officials draw to establish their definitive picture of Don Alvaro's misdeeds. The most obvious of such debts is to an earlier propaganda effort of their own —Juan II's letter of 22nd May to the Escalona rebels. This furnishes, often word-for-word, their general outline of the Constable's *apoderamiento*. A handful of more specific items may well have come directly out of evidence gathered for the trial. One particular section of the letter, as we shall see, is a paraphrase of the commissioners' own report. The compilers also filled out their tale from protests issued by Don Alvaro's enemies during the troubles of 1440.[44] The result is a piece of work which has no very clear overall argument and is, in some respects, anomalous. It seems strange that the king's

De Tyrannia: «Dicitur etiam tyrannus, qui vult occupare illud, quod est proprium Principis, et punitur poena mortis».

[43] *CD*, no. XLI, pp. 80-92; also *CJII* (R), pp. 684-91; GALÍNDEZ DE CARVAJAL (ibid., p. 274) reports its attribution to Mosén Diego de Valera. But Mosén Diego's pro-Aragonese activities had made him *persona non grata* with Juan II (PALENCIA, *Déc*, p. 48; *CEIV*, p. 48); besides, Juan needed no freelance propagandist to do work which his own officials could do.

[44] For example, the charge (*CD*, p. 82) of forcing members of the nobility to marry as he chose; cf. the rebel manifesto of 1441 (above, Chapter 1, n. 40). That text (SERRANO, pp. 289-303) and the 1440 *capítulos* (*C Halc*, pp. 320-33) include other charges paralleled in 1453, e.g. administrative supremacy (*C Halc*, pp. 327-8); promotion of «new men» (SERRANO, p. 291); cf. *CD*, pp. 86, 90.

officials should denounce Don Alvaro for having dominated the administration and surrounded Juan II with base and unworthy persons —presumably themselves. But these echoes of complaints from dissident noblemen of 1440 could still appeal to aristocratic ears, just as the various ecclesiastical charges listed might strike a chord with the clergy. A similar opportunism informs the attempts to blame Don Alvaro personally for recent economic constraints —on the king's household, on royal grants and almsgiving, on military resources for the Granada frontier.[45] In these respects the letter is primarily a political text, not a legal one.

Nevertheless, it does accuse Don Alvaro of a good deal of illegal conduct. Sometimes the activities concerned are against the law in some broad and general sense —sowing dissension, perverting justice, misappropriating tax revenues. Other charges involve more straightforwardly criminal acts —murders, imprisonments, thefts. But all these imputations, except for a very few financial items, are couched in such unspecific terms that their basis in concrete evidence —if they ever had any— cannot be assessed. One of the offences laid at Don Alvaro's door —the murder of Alonso Pérez— might seem a potential exception to this, but in the letter of June 18th that crime goes unmentioned. Though perhaps still present by implication, it has, by this date, been displaced as the central count against Don Alvaro by the broader theme of his usurpations of power.[46] That theme is certainly illustrated here in ways which involve grave infractions of the law. If Don Alvaro had indeed reached secret agreements with the king's enemies, as the letter alleges, he would, of course, have been a traitor.[47] Yet no concrete evidence establishes that he was one, or was proved so at his trial. We do know that the charge of forming illicit political leagues was true, and that there were statutes against it. But the cardinal element in this part of the case lay elsewhere; it was the claim that Don Alvaro had usurped things which were, in principle, inalienable from the royal dignity and estate. If true, this was *laesa majestas* and a beheading matter. Whether it was true or not was a question less of Don Alvaro's

---

[45] *CD*, pp. 81-2; 86; interestingly, Don Alvaro is said (p. 85) to have argued an economic case for disengagement from some Andalusian frontier positions.

[46] The letter refers back (pp. 88-9) to earlier royal statements (in which this crime is treated at length), and alludes (p. 90) to his «many killings». For stories of the murder of important opponents the Duke of Arjona and his son —see *C Halc*, p. 329; also GARCÍA DE SALAZAR, p. 29, and *Historia que escrivió el despensero mayor de la Reina Doña Leonor* (MS Madrid, BN, 773), fol. 117v. These last two differ over the method —poisoning or suffocation with a linen cloth— used to remove the Duke. More credible are the tales relating to more humble adversaries (above n. 38 and Chapter 1, n. 41).

[47] *CD*, pp. 87 (pacts with enemies, domestic and foreign); 82 (unlawful leagues; for examples see above, Chapter 2, n. 3; for legislation see Chapter 4, n. 80); 81 (usurping *inalienabilia*; cf. BARTOLUS, above, n. 42).

record than of how that record was to be interpreted. Hence the letter's insistent revaluation of Don Alvaro's methods in government; because his power is defined retrospectively as illicit, the account of these becomes a catalogue of abuses. The policy-making in his own person, the blurring of distinctions between his own household and the royal service, the sale of office, the reliance on instruments of derogation, the internal spy-system —all these and more are denounced.[48] Some are the normal repertoire of fifteenth-century government; others represent Don Alvaro's penchant for taking the shortest way with any obstacle. But all become the objects of attack now because Juan II has opted to take that view of them. For him, they are now the outward signs of a central disorder pathetically bodied forth even in the fact that «his house was... full of men of rank... and my royal palace was barren and empty and deserted». Don Alvaro's offence has been to have acted as if he were king.

This is yet more clearly the emphasis at work in the briefer summary of the charges which appears towards the end of the letter. The importance of this section is obscured by the sheer volume of other accusations in which it is embedded, and by the fact that it is made to repeat in two versions its charges regarding evil counsel and the exclusion of worthy persons from Court. Once these accretions are removed, however, it is plain enough what this passage is. It begins with the statement that the «Doctors of Law and prudent men» whom Juan had summoned to advise him under oath «all with one accord signed and gave me their advice, in which they said this...». It ends with a formulaic announcement of the penalties which Don Alvaro has incurred:

> for which reasons, the said Don Alvaro de Luna was deserving of death and the loss of all his goods and offices, of which I both could and should deprive him, and that for the sake of my conscience and the execution of my justice, I ought to give orders for this to be done.[49]

What we have here, then, is a close paraphrase —apart from the interpolations mentioned, the only changes involve tenses and the shift from third to first person —of the report of the Commissioners after their meetings in Fuensalida. And the view which they take is set forth

---

[48] *CD*, pp. 83 (own foreign policy); 87 (own servants prepare royal business); 82 (sale of office; spies); 86 (*cláusulas esorbitantes* in royal letters); 82-3 («his house full; mine empty» —a complaint later recalled, as a slight on royal *praeeminentia*, in SÁNCHEZ DE ARÉVALO, *HH*, pp. 234-5).

[49] *CD*, p. 90; *CJII* (R), pp. 689-90 from «los doctores é varones prudentes... los quales todos de una concordia firmaron é me dieron su consejo por el cual dijeron...», to «é que por descargo de mi conciencia é esecucion de la mi justicia lo debia mandar así esecutar.» The section from «é alongando de mi corte...» to «nin complideros para el servicio de mi real persona» I would regard as interpolated by the compilers of the letter.

very plainly. The facts of the case are accepted as notorious and grave. Don Alvaro's first guilt is his assumption of control over the king's person, and his wider *apoderamiento* over the royal household, government, patrimony and justice, all of which he has used for his own purposes «as if he were king and lord over it». This has been to the detriment of the king's «person, estate and dignity». There follow charges of tendering evil and interested counsel in order to preserve this dominance, of sowing discord in the kingdom at large, and of preventing access to the king by nobles, bishops, clergy, and men of learning. This second section concludes with a list of other excesses and criminal acts, all of which are said to have subverted the «peaceful estate» of Juan's realms. Don Alvaro, then, is found guilty of conduct damaging to the king's majesty and to the king's peace. The verdict follows from there.

All this is refreshingly cogent and concise, compared with the letter as a whole. But it shares with the longer document the defect of generality. The letter of 18th June was designed, as we have seen, to proclaim, not to prove, the case against Don Alvaro. But the commissioners in their report had also taken that case as proven already, and had gone on to say what it amounted to, and what should be done about it. We are still faced with the problem of their actual acceptance of those facts which the king presented to them as «notorious». What warrant did his statement at Fuensalida provide for that? Was their reaction to it a justifiable view of the evidence? The trouble is that, regarded as evidence, that statement seems to have been no less generalized and imprecise than all our other material. This effect, it is true, may well have been exaggerated in the Villena document, which preserves Juan's speech only in summary (*CD*, p. 75). But to a great extent the problem is traceable to the content of that speech itself. It is described as «an account of the great disservices which he had received» from Alvaro de Luna, and it is organized under four heads. Juan's first allegation was that Don Alvaro had not allowed him to confer *mercedes* on his servants. His second concerned the Constable's usurpation of power: «... over his royal household and over the cities and towns of his realms and over his revenues and rights and taxes, so much so that the king had no command whatever over his household or his realms.» The third charge was a vaguer one: «that he was secretly very active against the king's interests in other matters.» Last came the murder of Alonso Pérez, «a very loyal servant whom the king trusted greatly... his *contador mayor* and a member of his Council, whom he loved very dearly».

This fourth charge, at least, was specific and criminal; it was, for good measure, a *cosa notoria*. But there were problems involved in making it the basis of a public trial. That would bring into the open a great deal of the unedifying story of Juan II's evasive intrigues against his own *privado*. One or two of the commissioners probably knew enough about these, and others could guess enough, to realize the difficulties attached to any such course. Naturally, Alonso Pérez's fate carried its *ad hominem* message for every royal official; the king, particularly if he used the fulsome words of tribute to the dead man quoted in the Villena narrative, would have had this effect well in mind. The killing of one so high in the royal favour certainly marked out Don Alvaro as a public menace. But the murder charge remained a delicate affair. Again, there was something particularly promising for Juan's immediate audience in the complaint that he had not been allowed to give his servants as many grants as he would have liked. But the curtailment of royal generosity, though frustrating to those who lived by it, was scarcely actionable in itself. The third charge could mean anything or nothing; it probably referred to Don Alvaro's known complicity in the Escalona rebellion. Legally, of course, this put him in the wrong. But again, there were political difficulties: virtually any Castilian magnate would have done as much in the circumstances. Many of those who sat in Council had. They would not swallow without grave reservations the principle that a man of rank on whom the king's displeasure had happened to fall, but who had not yet been condemned at law, had no right even to set his properties in a posture of defence.[50] Their own constitutional tradition would have none of this, and however strongly Juan's constitutional notions might conflict with that tradition, he had to take account of it in practice. That meant that there must be some other ground for condemning Don Alvaro. Hence the whole case must stand or fall by its second count: the charge of usurpation of power. And that, in its turn, depended on one thing only: the weight to be attached to the king's own word.

One part of the claim which Juan II was to make so often regarding this evidence —that Don Alvaro's power in the kingdom had been a *cosa notoria*— was as true for other people as it was for him. Everyone had known that it was the Constable who exercised control over revenues and policies, who filled appointments with the candidates of his choosing, who ran the royal household. And everyone had assumed —as Juan himself had given them every reason to assume— that all this was in accordance with the king's own will. Had this not been so, Don Alvaro's position would have been a standing affront to the Crown, an instance of blatant *laesa majestas,* if not of outright usurpation. In

---

[50] For the aristocratic view see JUAN MANUEL, *Estados*, pp. 177-8: if a natural lord sought the death of a vassal other than by due process of law, the latter, by Spanish custom, was quit of natural obligation. The king might intend (as with Don Alvaro) to invoke the law. But the *grandes* did not believe in taking chances.

choosing now to treat this *apoderamiento* as criminal, Juan II was asserting that it had been against his will all the time. Such an assertion was virtually self-validating, for the difference between legitimate power and its illegitimate assumption turned upon the king's expressed attitude and upon that alone. If power did not come from an act of the king's will, delegating some part of his *poderío real absoluto,* it was a product of «self-empowering» (literally *apoderamiento*). And whether there had been an act of the king's will was known by what he said. Once Juan II had made his statement, there was little that the commission of *letrados* could do about it. The only alternative to believing him —and acting upon that belief— was to call him a liar. For the commissioners that was unthinkable; what made it so was the king's unique position in those traditions of law to which they all subscribed.

The dilemma which this posed was a question of the king's private and public personalities.[51] Juan of Trastámara, laying information before the judges concerning what he had thought and felt about Alvaro de Luna's activities might or might not have been telling the truth. The *letrados* were bound to be aware of this. But they also knew that they were not in a position to speculate on the matter. For Juan of Trastámara was also Juan of Castile, the *princeps* in law, to whom all the commissioners were, as magistrates, ultimately responsible. They could not, in principle, undermine his authority and their own by impugning his truthfulness; they could not, in practice, make him answer for his words, since no magistrate possessing *imperium* could be summoned before any court. Even so, the Relator reacted on their behalf by reminding Juan II that the dilemma was his responsibility and his only. He did so, in effect, by inviting the king to reaffirm his testimony as if on oath, «because he did not have to give any account of it, save to God alone».[52] At the same time, this made the *letrados'* dilemma inescapable. Nobody was going to accuse the *princeps* of perjury; their only choice was to accept his word.

---

[51] This aspect is missed by RIZZO Y RAMÍREZ (above, n. 29), and brushed aside by SALAZAR Y MENDOZA, in a passage quoted approvingly by SILIÓ, p. 254. For any man to judge the king was «most abominable, sacrilegious and absurd... scandalous and harmful, against God and divine and human law», said the *Cortes* of Olmedo *(Cortes (LC),* vol. III, p. 483). POST, p. 271 quotes the glossator Johannes Bassianus of Bologna on the immunity of magistrates.
[52] *CD,* p. 75: «é el dicho Relator preguntó á su alteza: ¿si sabia ser verdad todo lo que su alteza avia relatado? porque no avia de dar cuenta á otro alguno sino á Dios.» MACKAY, *Spain,* p. 140 sees these words as affirming the king's absolute royal power. Fernán Díaz may indeed have known Lucas de Penna's remark (ULLMANN, p. 51) that kings were morally answerable to God alone. Equally, he may have been aware of Aquinas' ruling that responsibility for a verdict based on the evidence lay with the witness, not the judge —a ruling, incidentally, supported in Jewish legal traditions (see MAX RADIN, «The Conscience of the Court», *Law Quarterly Review,* 48 (1932), 519).

In bringing about this result, Fernán Díaz may have had several motives. Grasping the essentials of the situation at once, he may have sought to rid it of any trace of ambiguity. That would have been an elementary protection for himself and his colleagues, if Juan II should later come to regret his decision. Equally, though, there may have been collusion between king and Relator to bring matters to the point where what the *princeps* wanted did, unavoidably, possess the force of law. The two had worked together for years; most recently, they had made the series of derogation documents linked with the Luna case the occasion for an exercise in affirming absolute royal authority. In declaring now that his attitude to Alvaro de Luna's ascendancy was not what it had been universally assumed to be, the king was merely carrying out the latest and most sweeping of these acts of derogation. No *letrado* who had been concerned with the process in its earlier stages could doubt his power to do so; it remained only for them to satisfy themselves that the act was an authentic one. In that sense, the ideological background is obviously relevant. Yet it seems unlikely that the Relator's words were intended as a straightforward assertion of absolutist principle. Although they will bear the meaning that the king, under God, may do as he will, a comment in this sense would not have been apposite in context. The question of Juan's entitlement to have Don Alvaro killed by his own mandate did not arise until the later meeting at which the dissent of Doctors Franco and Zurbano became known. At this stage the Relator's concern was to assure his colleagues of the formal validity of the king's statement. Behind that concern, it is possible to guess at a third motive. Besides self-interest and the furtherance of royal policy, the *letrados* were still conscious of a duty to the law, and to the forms of law.

The most explicit testimony of their outlook comes, once again, from Montalvo. Long before he published his critique of the trial, he had offered a defence of its propriety in his commentary on the *Fuero real* —a work which had been revised in the light of comments by the Relator himself.[53] This earlier treatment had concentrated on the king's alleged neglect of «due legal process in arriving at a condemnation» —a point which does not figure prominently in Montalvo's eventual

---

[53] Díaz de Montalvo, gloss to *Fuero real de España*, Lib. I, Tít. IV, quoted by Corral, p. 30: «licet Rex omisisset ordinem judicii in condemnando, hoc fecit cum consilio deliberato virorum litteratorum sui Consilii et de eorum consilio et informata sua regali conscientia, asserendo firmiter de certa scientia dicti Magistri crimina, cujus simplici verbo creditur in facto propter ejusdem magnam auctoritatem.» This is believed to be Montalvo's earliest work (though printed only in 1500); for its links with the Relator, see Fermín Caballero, *Conquenses ilustres: El Doctor Montalvo* (Madrid, 1873), p. 97. See also *Partidas*, vol. II, p. 168, Pt. III, Tít. 14, Ley VIII.

list of reservations. Presumably he felt that, whatever his later doubts, he had disposed of this one in a satisfactory way. In so doing, he stresses the fact that the king had taken advice from his *letrados,* and had sought spiritual guidance («informed his conscience»). But he finds the main basis for the king's irregular action in the weight of the evidence which he had to offer: «... firmly asserting of his certain knowledge the crimes of the aforesaid Master, his unsupported statement as to the fact is to be believed because of its great authority.» Proof in law, the *Partidas* had laid down, came from witnesses who could corroborate one another's accounts «and are such that, by reason of their persons or of what they have to say, they cannot be set aside». There was nobody to corroborate Juan II's statement, but it carried «great authority» on the other two counts. What he had to say was authoritative because here was a man testifying to his own motives and intentions, his evidence fortified by what amounted to an oath *(firmiter).* In this sense, the Relator's reminder that he would give account to God helped to diminish any potential gap between Juan's private and public selves. But his person —his public person this time— carried the authority of the *princeps,* the head of the legal system in which all these *letrados* were formed and employed. The interaction of these two modes of authority is symbolized by Montalvo's ambiguous use of the phrase *certa scientia.* Its primary meaning here is literal: Juan II was giving evidence of what he, and he alone, could know for certain. But its formulaic overtones are also strong, recalling that special authority which makes the monarch's decisions accord, by definition, with what ought to be done. Where *certa scientia* was in play, absolute royal power could scarcely be forgotten. Juan was not yet issuing commands, but when he came to do so, these, if issued in due form, would be identified by his present hearers as the law itself. Montalvo, casting about for a parallel to Don Alvaro's case, lights, significantly enough upon a Roman example. The Roman and regalist outlook of these *letrados* made it less than ever thinkable that they should question Juan II's binding definition of the true state of his relations with Alvaro de Luna.

Yet the mere awareness of the king's will did not abolish their commitment to the forms of law. That too was a second nature, imposed on them by background and training. A purely venal and subservient court could have cobbled together a damning indictment —even a circumstantial one— weeks before the Fuensalida meeting, with no need of all this elaborate charade. The Relator, if similarly corrupt, would surely have pressed home the demand for a sentence at every stage. Instead, his response to the king's renewed declaration was merely to formulate an opinion: «it was his view, according to the law, that [Don Alvaro] deserved the death penalty».⁵⁴ That form of words is still scrupulously adhered to in his report of the whole Council's finding: «they find that by law he ought to be beheaded...» This, of course, was in line with the compromise arrived at in the stormy meeting with Franco and Zurbano, when it was agreed that a sentence, issuing from the deliberations of a court, would not be in order, but that a mandate *(mandamiento)* giving royal authority for Don Alvaro's execution could properly be issued. The crucial statement in this form was the one which all the *letrados* signed, and which Juan was able to quote on 18th June as having been subscribed «with one accord». It was a unanimity which went less far than the unfettered sway of the royal will would have had it go: «the said Don Alvaro was deserving of death [and] ... I ought to give orders for this to be done.» The view of what the Constable deserved —the view conditioned by Juan's unsupported but uniquely authoritative evidence— was, ultimately, only a part of the background; he was to die because the king willed it.

At first sight this seems merely to make a bad case worse. Juan II was already a crucial witness in a suit whose outcome touched him nearly; now he was to be its arbiter as well. The whole process of trial by special commission was abruptly cut short. The material gathered for the purpose would never figure in any formal indictment. Don Alvaro would go to execution «without either pleading guilt or being found guilty in court», as Montalvo was to recall, uneasily, many years later.⁵⁵ Procedures which, even in their day, seemed questionable along these lines are bound to appear arbitrary now. But their shortcomings ought not to be overemphasized. The trial was certainly unusual in lacking both indictment and sentence —the documentary bases for any normal conviction. But there was no procedural vacuum. The king's own evidence took the place of a indictment; his mandate did the work of a sentence. Nor were these in any sense improvisations; the law provided for them, and the constitutional theories favoured by the judges made them seen appropriate. The controversial aspects of the Luna case do not stem from any flagrantly arbitrary act; they relate, rather, to three disputed issues on each of which Juan II and his commissioners took up a questionable but still defensible position. These were, in the order in which they affected the final phase of the trial, whether the king could be judge in his his own case, whether he could

---

⁵⁴ *CD*, pp. 75-6: «que le parescia segund derecho que era dino de muerte por justicia é de perder los bienes para la cámara é fisco de su alteza»; cf. *CJII* (R), p. 682; *CD*, no. XLI, p. 90: «é que... lo debia mandar así esecutar.» Contrast the formula by which the Count of Castro was sentenced in 1431: «por esta nuestra sentencia defenetiba lo declaramos, judgamos e pronunciamos así» (*C Halc*, p. 117; *Ref Halc*, p. 111).

⁵⁵ MONTALVO, gloss to *Siete Partidas*, quoted by CORRAL, p. 30n.: «ni confeso ni judicialmente convicto.»

properly be swayed by his own private knowledge of it, and whether he was entitled to conclude it by mandate in the way which he chose.

The manner in which these problems were approached was conditioned in great part by the nature of Don Alvaro's offences, as this was revealed during the trial. He had, Juan II claimed, so usurped power as to leave the king with «no command whatever over his household or his realms».[56] This was especially serious given the belief that not even kings themselves were entitled to make such grants to subjects that their capacity to govern was impaired. We know from the later evidence of Juan's open letter that the concept of inalienable royal rights was in question here. It arose again when Don Alvaro was accused of disrupting the king's peace and impeding his justice, since peace and justice were foremost among royal *inalienabilia*. All these accusations converged upon a charge of *laesa majestas*. Even the killing of Alonso Pérez lent itself to this. Andreas of Isernia had laid it down that to kill a member of the royal Council «because of any good counsel which he gave... touches the honour of the sovereign, and is punished as such». The specific atrocity, then, was subsumed in the wider offence of *laesa majestas* —in contemporary eyes a still more serious matter. By definition, this was a crime against the king's public person; there was, inevitably, a problem as to whether he ought also to act as its judge.

The extent to which Juan II did so was, of course, limited. He was left to determine that Don Alvaro should die, having been advised by his commissioners that the facts as they had heard them warranted his arriving at such a decision. He found himself so placed largely because they had been unable to agree on a verdict of their own. But they may very well have seen it as appropriate for him to act as judge precisely because the crime in question was *laesa majestas*. The defence of the Crown as an institution was a *causa regni*, in which the person presently embodying that institution had a duty to be active.[57] There were other reasons, too, which might obtain in particular cases. Lucas de Penna had said that the king might be his own judge when it was necessary to revoke acts of alienation that were «prejudicial to the royal dignity and Crown». That was very much Juan II's position now. He had underwritten many of Don Alvaro's alleged usurpations by acts of his

---

[56] *CD*, p. 75; cf. POST, pp. 400-1 (limits on grants); *CD*, no. XLI, pp. 81 (*inalienabilia* usurped), 90 (peace and justice disrupted); see also BARTOLUS (above, n. 42), BRACTON (above, Chapter 4, n. 30); ANDREAS OF ISERNIA (apparatus to *Partidas*, vol. I, p. 491, Pt. II, Tít. 16, Ley I). ALONSO DE CARTAGENA thought *laesa majestas* akin to heresy (*Defensorium*, p. 287); PERO DÍAZ DE TOLEDO saw it as the ultimate ingratitude (gloss to *Proverbios de Séneca*, MS Escorial, SII 10, fol. 49r).

[57] KANTOROWICZ, p. 169; ibid. n. for Lucas de Penna on revocation of matters «in praeiudicium dignitatis et coronae», and for Cino de Pistoia.

own. It was now necessary to undo those acts, and only Juan II could do it; therefore he could, and arguably should, sooner or later assume the role of judge. That some such train of thought was in the commissioners' minds seems to be borne out by Montalvo's use of the *certa scientia* formula, whose overtones of derogation can scarcely be a matter of chance.

Yet there were also jurists who supported the commonsense view that the king ought not to be judge in his own case. Cino de Pistoia, while recognizing the sovereign's right to take such cases in person, had seen it as normal that they should be referred to other judges. That view had been followed in practice by Juan II when he first set up the commission to try Don Alvaro. It needed less explanation than the alternative notion, and it was less dependent on specialized theories about kingship. Perhaps for that reason, Juan II in his public justification of the verdict against Don Alvaro dwells at length on the advice given by the *letrados,* and has less to say altogether about initiatives of his own.

The most important of such initiatives to date had been his testimony to the commissioners. The problem which this evidence had raised was, if anything, compounded when the *letrados* invited him to conclude the case by way of a mandate. To suggest that the king's mandate would be justified by the same evidence which could not support his commissioners in delivering a sentence was to imply that the evidence must carry a different weight for him than for them. This meant that he was being credited with a special insight into what his own evidence had been. And here the Luna case impinged on a controversy which had exercised a great many jurists. Was a magistrate, having private knowledge of the case before him, entitled —or indeed obliged— to take account of that knowledge? Or ought he to judge solely on the evidence which had been laid before him?[58] The former view could be supported by a uniquely powerful example —the trial of Christ before Pilate. Plainly something had gone very wrong in that instance, and the fault could be attributed to Pilate's failure to take account of his own knowledge and conscience. This was the view of Lucas de Penna, and it would appear to have been shared by Juan II and his *letrados.* The mention in the latters' report

---

[58] KANTOROWICZ, p. 396n. (Lucas de Penna; the *Decretum* gloss; the aphorism «non nisi per allegata iudex iudicet.»). Cf. on Juan II's conscience, *CD,* no. XLI, p. 90; no. XXXVII, p. 71; the latter, referring to the view now taken of earlier pledges to Don Alvaro, involves both Juan's knowledge of his own intentions and his ideology of kingship (see above, pp. 117-18). The king in his «private» person also continued to use the term in an ethical-religious sense; he actually consulted «religious persons on the matters which pertained to my conscience» (*CD,* p. 90). See, on the legal dilemma, RADIN, who mentions (p. 515) a precedent in Valerius Maximus, possibly known among Juan II's *letrados* (see SCHIFF, pp. 133-4).

of Juan's entitlement to act «for the sake of his conscience» suggests a broadly similar outlook. The king had acted upon what he alone was in a position fully to know. Yet here again, another approach was possible. The notion of the king or magistrate as possessing a double personality could be made to support the claim that he should look to the evidence alone. «A man's actions as a judge are one thing; his actions as a man are another», was how the Ordinary gloss to the *Decretum* put it. And the maxim that judges ought to judge only on the evidence had the additional prestige of being attributed to Christ himself. Juan II, of course, had already introduced his personal knowledge as evidence, thereby setting his *letrados* a problem in how they should react to that unsupported but authoritative statement. Eventually, they passed the task of reaching a definite reaction back to the king once more. But they did not, by so doing, abolish the problem; instead, they transformed it into the classic dilemma of the «conscience of the court».

As for the use of a royal mandate rather than a judicial sentence, that too was defensible in law. That such a mandate could be issued, and when issued be binding, had been the law of the land since before Castile was a kingdom.[59] Yet there was also a recognition that the *speciale mandatum regis* ought to be used with great caution —certainly that its objects ought themselves to be legal. Hence the extent to which Juan II, in declaring what his mandate was, still relied upon the views of his *letrados* to support and justify the action taken. There can be little doubt, even so, that a formal sentence from the commissioners themselves would have suited his propaganda needs a great deal better; if it had not been so, why the long wrangle among the lawyers before they fell back upon the alternative of a mandate? There may even have been some officially supported efforts to convince the wider public, after the event, that a sentence had, in fact, been issued. Certainly, there are some loose usages of the word *sentencia* by people who should have known better.[60] Mosén

---

[59] See VALDEAVELLANO, p. 440 (the *iussio regis* in the Asturian-Leonese kingdom). English lawyers under Charles I could find support in 15th-century authorities for limiting the power of the royal mandate. Precisely because «the king could do no wrong», they argued, unjust mandates could have no force. See, for example, JOHN FORSTER, *Sir John Eliot: a Biography. 1590-1632* (London 1865), vol. II, pp. 159-60.

[60] VALERA, *CAbr*, p. 337, seems especially disingenuous: «la qual sentencia el rey confirmó.» See also CORRAL, pp. 90-1 (Montalvo approached, on the Pacheco family's behalf, about 1460). The «sentence» was an elusive document; a copy circulating in the Relator's household vanished when someone who had borrowed it died «en tierra de moros» (ibid., p. 90). For further non-technical uses of the term, see *Abr H*, p. cci; PÉREZ DE GUZMÁN, *G y S*, p. 44. Lay observers who get the matter right include the author of *CCG*: «mandólo degollar por justicia» (p. 136), and one witness in 1497: «un mandamiento que era breve» (CORRAL, p. 90). *CAL* (C), pp. 427-8 suggests that both a *sentencia* and a *mandamiento* existed —a strange error.

Diego de Valera, for instance, knew something of the law, but still states that the Constable «was sentenced by agreement of twelve famous doctors of law», who signed the sentence —afterwards confirmed by the king— with their names. Montalvo, when asked if there had been a sentence, replied that there had, and that he had signed it, though he did not remember who held the original. This was within a decade at most of the actual trial, and it is hard to believe that Montalvo had forgotten what it was that he had signed. If these reports are not disingenuous, they are certainly in error; the Villena document, the Council report as preserved in Juan II's chronicle, and much of the controversy attending the trial, all make it very clear that a mandate was, in fact, used.

Its use was dictated by the fact that the *letrados* could not see their way to producing a sentence of their own on the basis of the evidence before them. The difficulty seems to have been a last-minute affair.[61] After the Relator had given his legal opinion on the effect of Juan II's evidence, and the other commissioners had concurred, they met their other two colleagues, Franco and Zurbano «to agree and decide on the form which should be adopted for the implementation of the aforesaid justice [in the case of Don Alvaro]». In other words, they were expected to produce a sentence. Since arguments between them only broke out at this stage, it is natural to assume that Zurbano and Franco were the dissentient voices; the latter is known to have been a direct and devoted protégé of the Constable. It is harder to guess at the detailed arguments which went on, but the question is likely to have turned upon the status of Juan II's testimony. Because of its source, it had to be credited; if credited, it was damning. But there was no escaping the fact that the commissioners had not been able to take the same sort of cognizance of it as they would have taken had it come from anyone else. At all events, the dissidents carried their point. The alternative of a mandate from the king himself was proposed and agreed; more surprisingly altogether, Juan II too acquiesced in it. No doubt this was because a sentence which neither Franco nor Zurbano had been willing to sign would have looked less convincing again. Yet this outcome still says much for the respect in which the king's *letrados* —and indeed the king himself— held the due forms of law.

There are indications, even so, that this respect had its limits.[62] Both

---

[61] CD, no. XXXVIII, p. 76. Franco and Zurbano, though in Fuensalida, had not attended the first meeting. On Doctor Franco see below, pp. 193-5.

[62] VALERA, *CAbr*, p. 337; *CJII* (R), p. 682 (twelve *letrados*); contrast *CD*, pp. 74-6. CABALLERO, *Elogio del Doctor Alonso Díaz de Montalvo* (Madrid, 1870), pp. 13-14, rejects Sánchez de Arriba's view that Montalvo refused to sign, arguing that royal sources emphasize the unanimity of the verdict. If there were other dissidents, that argument falls; the real evidence for Montalvo's involvement is that of the Villena paper and the 1497 lawsuit (CORRAL, pp. 90-1). On Doctor Juan Velázquez, see *CD*, p. 76, n. 4.

Mosén Diego and the royal chronicler are agreed that twelve *letrados* were appointed to judge the case; it is, indeed, a number which we should expect. The Villena document, however, names only eleven. The missing *letrado* is unlikely to have been Montalvo himself, as has sometimes been suggested. Nor can he have been Doctor Juan Velázquez de Cuéllar, whom Sigüenza believed to have signed the commissioners' report, perhaps with some reluctance; he had died seven years earlier. A more plausible, though still shadowy candidate might be that Doctor Juan Rodríguez who, according to Gil González de Ávila, was deprived of his town of Babilafuente: «because he refused to sign the sentence issued against Don Alvaro de Luna by those who persecuted him. For when they showed him the indictment he said that it did not provide sufficient reasons why that gentleman should die».[63] If Juan Rodríguez did voice his disagreement in these terms, he was going a great deal further than any of the other commissioners had dared to go. He was refusing to accept the king's own testimony at anything like its face-value, let alone accepting the added authority which stemmed from the unique position of the *princeps*. He was refusing to lend his name not merely to a sentence which might have been insecurely based in law, but to the recommendation for a mandate which the commissioners eventually issued. If he did carry his dissent to this point, then neither the loss of his property nor the disappearance of his name from what seems at least a semi-official record need surprise us. For his action would fall wholly outside what Juan II's sovereign authority was prepared to concede to the autonomy of the legal process.

In the event, though, rather more was conceded —certainly in the initial stages— than might have been expected. The overall procedure was neither hurried nor significantly irregular. The king's jurisdiction was boldly and broadly interpreted, in line with his general regalist claims. But there was the nucleus of a potential indictment in the prosecutor's report, and an attempt was made to gather further evidence. The accused may even have had some limited opportunity of defence. The charges were, for the most part, imprecise, but they tended to build into a substantial and coherent accusation of *laesa majestas*. The king's intervention at Fuensalida led to the by-passing of any formal indictment, and ultimately of any sentence in due form, but it did not involve the suspension of legal proprieties. It did have the effect of bringing the case into certain areas of unresolved debate, on the king's self-judgment, on the conscience of the court, and on the validity of the royal mandate. But the position

---

[63] *CD*, p. 77n., quoting GONZÁLEZ DE AVILA, *Historia de Salamanca*, III, 15. Holdings in the Salamanca area were, in any case, being adjusted following the report on seigneurial abuses there (see CABRILLANA CIEZAR, *passim*).

which was officially adopted on each of these, though obviously advantageous to the Crown, was perfectly tenable in law.[64]

More disturbingly, Juan's intervention undoubtedly put the commissioners under some pressure. The origins of that pressure were extra-legal —the king's eagerness for treasure; the defiance of Escalona— but it is harder to say how far it was itself improper. There was a broad hint to the *letrados* in the matter of royal grants, and there were grounds —well-founded, if we are to believe the story of Doctor Rodríguez— for fearing the king's displeasure. But the main constraint upon the commissioners was of a different order. It was now obvious that the king wanted Don Alvaro killed. His testimony against the Constable created the evidence which made that outcome legally imperative. For the cost of disbelieving the king was high, not merely because it meant incurring the royal wrath, but because it undermined the whole framework of constitutional assumptions to which the *letrados* subscribed. It was too high a price to be paid for the sake of any private patron. The one way in which the commissioners might still have resisted the king's decision was by pleading for clemency. But the prior attachments which had bound so many of them to Don Alvaro in earlier days had been on the wane for some years; since April, they had vanished altogether. After what had happened to Alonso Pérez, not many royal officials were going to plead very hard for the Constable.

What they did insist upon, even with the king impatient for a verdict, was an adherence to such legalities as the new and extreme situation seemed to demand. Juan's testimony was taken virtually upon oath; its implications were discussed at some length, and those *letrados* who stood out against a sentence got their way. In all of this the general lines of a procedure recognizable in Roman legal theory and compatible with Castilian statute were still observed. That did not, of course, inhibit the constitutional force which these *letrados* saw as inherent in the royal will. Nor did it alter the essentially political character of the trial itself. Juan II was anxious to have Don Alvaro executed, and the *letrados* thought that he was entitled to do it. Or at least they thought —and

---

[64] Professor W. L. WARREN informs me that aspects of the Luna case are paralleled in late mediaeval England. For example, the attempt to by-pass the process of indictment when the king testified of his own certain knowledge was also made by Edward III in the case of Archbishop Stratford. The outcome in that case was, of course, very different (see MAY MCKISACK, *The Fourteenth Century, 1307-1399* (Oxford, 1959), pp. 152-81). But the existence of this European dimension seems consistent with the European theoretical background explored here. ALONSO DE CARTAGENA, better-acquainted than most with the wider European context, gives a finely balanced summary of events: Don Alvaro was accused in due form by the Prosecutor; enquiry was made, and then the king «ordered him to be beheaded... keeping the form of justice» (*Rubrica Additio*, p. 693; in Latin as *Anacephaleosis*, ed. Andreas Schott, *Hispaniae Illustratae Scriptores Varii*, vol. I (Frankfurt, 1603), p. 288).

perhaps Juan Rodríguez found— that it was dangerous to dispute that entitlement. Their task was to see that the business was carried out with due regard for law. But they were not to be induced, and neither was the king entitled, to concoct the outcome of a normal trial when no such trial had been completed. The Luna case illustrates the effectiveness of Juan II's absolutism, but it also reveals the necessary compromises which that absolutism had to make with the legal doctrines which had helped to shape it.

CHAPTER 6

«CONVERSI SUNT IN VANILOQUIUM»

To the judges at Fuensalida it mattered a great deal that Alvaro de Luna was to die by mandate and not by sentence. Their concern can be seen as doing them credit. But Don Alvaro himself was unlikely to see it in this light, or to find the distinction a matter of great moment. The same applied to his relatives and clients. They had feared the worst —perhaps they had feared it more than he had— and now the worst had come about. It is not at all surprising, therefore, that the Constable's apologists then and since should have found little good to say of the proceedings against him.[1] For the chronicler Chacón, the fatal Council was an assembly of his hero's enemies «all intending and discussing his death»; the proclamation of his guilt was a lie, unworthy of that «clever and subtle-minded man», the Relator. Drawing upon this and similar sources, the *Causa escrita a Don Alvaro* derides the Council as a *conciliábolo,* and the verdict as the outcome of false and malicious testimony. Insofar as claims of this sort are worth weighing at all, their weight lies in the imputation of bias, rather than in any charge of improper conduct. This is not to concede that those who sat in judgment on Don Alvaro were, in fact, his personal enemies. Bias there undoubtedly was, but it informed the whole situation, not the previous attitudes of individual judges. Its source was the king. His manifest desire to have Don Alvaro put out of the way seriously restricted the options of both the special commission and the Council at large. Their choice, in effect, lay only between different ways of doing what the king wanted. They had scant possibility of resisting this course and, from the Constable's side, it must be said, small incentive to try.

From an early stage, however, Don Alvaro's supporters were prepared to judge the commissioners much more harshly than this. The first of such criticisms known to us appeared in the manifesto of the Escalona rebels, which was, as we have seen, composed before the crucial decisions regarding Don Alvaro had actually been taken. Although this document

---

[1] *CAL* (C), pp. 425, 431; *Causa escrita,* fols 26r-v, 45r.

has not survived, it evidently contained harsh words about the king's advisers. Both Juan II in his letter of 22nd May and some of those advisers themselves in a postscript to it take up and refute these comments (*CD,* pp. 72-3). The authors of the postscript present themselves simply as «the members of the Council» *(los del consejo del muy alto... Rey),* but the group under attack is defined with more precision in another phrase of theirs: «those of the king's Council who are with his Majesty». *Los del consejo... que con su altesa están* is virtually a formula for the active nucleus of Council members who accompanied the king wherever he went and transacted his business of government at daily Council meetings. That nucleus would, of course, include such nobles and prelates as might, from time to time, enjoy the king's favour. But its permanent members were the senior *letrados,* the great servants of the administration. It was on these and on persons closely connected with them that Juan II had drawn in setting up the commission which was to handle the Luna case. Though their business was not yet completed, their names, their task, and the extent to which they were directly and primarily the king's own men would all have been known to the Luna partisans. It was, we may take it, these *letrados* empanelled to judge Don Alvaro who were the main target for the denunciations which issued from Escalona. These must have been scathing indeed to have provoked this habitually self-effacing group into a public reply.

Disappointingly, the terms of that reply are too general to allow us to infer very much about the contents of the original attack. Juan II's own rebuttal, in the main body of the letter, is rather more informative. His advisers, he declares, are not «persons of the kind you describe»; they are: «God-fearing and authoritative... of good and sound conscience, good-living and religious men, learned and wise and well-tried, free of all avarice and suspicion...»[2] The rebels, then, appear to have charged Juan's *letrados* with lacking authority and legal expertise, with being corrupted by bribes, and with being «suspect», presumably in the sense that they were predisposed against Don Alvaro. All three charges reappear, much later, in Salazar y Mendoza's critique of the trial: the judges, he says, were «not even proper *letrados*»; they had been bought with money, and they were «notorious and open enemies» of the accused. Though the authority to which he refers at this point is only the rather vague one of «several chroniclers», it appears possible, at least, that Salazar y Mendoza had access to some record, direct or indirect, of what Don Alvaro's supporters actually said. It is harder to know whether we should make a similar connection between Juan II's insistence on the religious and moral probity of his counsellors and a fourth criticism

---

[2] *CD,* p. 72; cf. SALAZAR Y MENDOZA in *CAL* (F), p. 466; also pp. 469-70. The scriptural reference is to Titus, 1:10.

voiced by Salazar y Mendoza. This is the statement that the *letrados* judging Don Alvaro's case were «of different blood and lineage from his». It is reinforced a few pages later with a punning reference to St Paul: *Conversi sunt in vaniloquium, volentes fieri legis Doctores.* Had the defenders of Escalona denounced the Constable's judges as Jewish-descended *conversos,* hostile to him on that account? At first sight, this looks unlikely. Salazar y Mendoza's remark seems to have the characteristic slyness of many later allusions to these matters of purity of descent. It looks far more like a sixteenth-century inference from the list of names in the Villena document than an echo of any denunciation which might have been offered in 1453. But Salazar y Mendoza also states that the names of the judges cannot be found, and assumes —quite wrongly— that Montalvo was not among them. Plainly, then, he did not know the Villena record or its list. We cannot, therefore, exclude the possibility that he took his view of the commissioners' *converso* status from some other early source, now lost to us, and that, along with all the rest, it had formed part of the rebels' attack on them.

If that were so, it would not be especially remarkable in itself. Anti-*converso* feeling certainly existed in the Castile of the 1450s; it was specially rife against those New Christians who, like certain of the *letrados,* were professionally and publicly successful. Don Alvaro de Luna seems to have been relatively free of such racial and religious prejudice, at all events until the very end of his career. Then, as he stood at bay in the besieged house at Burgos, his sense of betrayal was quick to seize upon the *converso* issue as its focus. It may well be that his partisans, in the heat of the crisis, also found it natural to resort to this familiar theme, even though their objective warrant for so doing was as slight as Don Alvaro's had been. What would be of much greater interest would be any indication that their case was, in any sense, well-founded —that the commissioners, because they were New Christians, and because of Don Alvaro's record in this regard, actually were the more disposed to find against him. From this and other viewpoints, the list of commissioners as we have it is worth some further attention.

At its head, and with the most active role to play, stands the senior figure, the Relator, Doctor Fernán Díaz de Toledo.[3] The Relator came of a New Castilian *converso* family; his own branch of it was settled in Alcalá de Henares. His aged mother, Doña María de Toledo, was buried there in 1431. Of his father we know nothing at all, which suggests that he may well have died a Jew. If the task of establishing the family in

---

[3] On the Relator see the note by PEDRO DE SAINZ DE BARANDA to *Cronicón de Valladolid,* CODOIN, 13, p. 32, transcribing a late 15th-century *semblanza* (probably by Galíndez de Carvajal). On Doña María see MIGUEL DE PORTILLA, *Historia de la ciudad de Compluto, vulgarmente Alcalá de Santiuste y aora de Henares,* vol. I (Alcalá de Henares, 1725), p. 586.

the wider Castilian society fell to Fernán Díaz's generation, they made a notable success of it. His cousin and namesake the Archdeacon of Niebla had been a professor of medicine in Salamanca and a royal physician in Aragon, before serving Juan II in a similar role, and as chaplain of the Trastámara family shrine in Toledo cathedral.[4] He was also a canon there, and a highly successful businessman, who made a fortune from a diversity of interests in that region. His younger brother Juan Ramírez de Toledo held a series of financial offices, first under the Infante Enrique of Aragon, and then in the government service. The peak of his career came in 1440, when he and the great Jewish financier Abraham Bienveniste made a joint and successful bid to farm the major royal taxes of Castile.

A cousin of another branch was Alfonso Alvarez de Toledo, a former cloth-merchant from the town of Cuenca, who also entered the financial service of the Crown, not as a tax-farmer but as a treasury official.[5] From 1429, when he received a grant of 20,000 *maravedís* towards his expenses, we find records of him as a *contador,* enjoying the personal confidence and favour of both the king and Alvaro de Luna. In 1435, when the latter's eldest son was born, the Constable was actually lodging in Alfonso Alvarez's house in Madrid, and the lavish christening festivities were held there. Five years later, Alfonso Alvarez was made *contador* in the newly-established household of Prince Enrique; during Don Alvaro's last and longest exile, he helped to reconcile his new employer with the king and Constable, and so to pave the way for the victory of Olmedo. When the senior *contador,* Fernán López de Saldaña fell from favour in 1445, Alfonso Alvarez was chosen to succeed him as *contador mayor,* and to serve with the luckless Alonso Pérez de Vivero in the chief financial office of state. As a natural accompaniment to a career of this sort, Alfonso Alvarez de Toledo was also immensely rich. He is said to have owned no fewer than 380 houses in various parts of Castile. In 1447 he had a personal income from royal sources of more than 275,000 *maravedís;* the total sum which he shared with his most immediate family came to well over 400,000. No other non-titled Castilian could rival these figures, though at least a dozen *grandes del reino* comfortably surpassed

---

[4] On the Archdeacon see BELTRÁN DE HEREDIA, *Bulario.* vol. I, pp. 153-4; vol. III, pp. 502-3; ROUND, «Shadow of a Philosopher», p. 25n. His letters of the 1420s, edited in ROUND, «La correspondencia del Arcediano de Niebla en el Archivo del Real Monasterio de Santa María de Guadalupe», *HID,* 7 (1980), 215-68, give further details on him and on Juan Ramírez, for whom see also LADERO, «Los judíos», p. 426.

[5] BLAS DE SALAZAR, *Genealogía de los Condes de Cedillo* (MS Madrid, RAH, 9.120; CS, B.5), fols 4-5. For other details here see ROUND, «La correspondencia» (letter of 25th January 1427); LADERO QUESADA, *Hacienda,* p. 269; AGS, M y P, 1.445; QdC, 2.12; *CJII* (R), p. 524; *C Halc,* pp. 211-12, 336, 442, 455; FRANCISCO MÁRQUEZ VILLANUEVA, *Investigaciones sobre Juan Alvarez Gato* (Madrid, 1960), p. 92; SUÁREZ FERNÁNDEZ, «Asientos», pp. 350-1.

them. On this evidence, Alfonso Alvarez, uniquely among his fellow *conversos,* must rank with the magnates. His style of living was of a piece with this. «Noble himself and a friend to nobles», is how a writer of the next generation describes him. Ironically, and perhaps not altogether by chance, this uniquely wealthy branch of the de Toledo clan was also the only one to come under serious suspicion of Judaizing. In 1482 the Inquisition of Toledo disinterred and burned the bones of one Mayor Alvarez, who may have been —but possibly was not— Alfonso Alvarez de Toledo's mother.[6]

The only people to accuse the Relator himself of anything of that sort were the rebels of Toledo in 1449, and they were disposed to think the same of every *converso.* In fact, he seems somewhat further removed from any Jewish background than his cousins.[7] Medicine and financial administration were forms of service for which Castile had habitually looked to its Jewish minority. But Fernán Díaz followed a legal training. A Jewish family of some wealth and culture —and we may assume that a family which, once converted, could send its sons to university was that— would doubtless have seen this as a worthy profession. But the form in which Fernán Díaz as a New Christian was able to take it up was by definition something new. Because of the family's conversion he was able to attend the university at Valladolid, and to read there not only the Roman law which was the basic theoretical training for civil practitioners, but the canon law of the Church. He took his Bachelor's degree in the latter faculty in 1414, the year of his visit to Aragon. Almost certainly, by this date, he was already combining study at the university with work for the royal chancery; by the time he obtained his Doctorate, ten years later, it was necessary to grant him a special dispensation from the rules for attendance, since his professional activity now kept him permanently with the court. By this date also he had gathered together that cluster of administrative offices which was to define his role in the public affairs of the kingdom.

[6] Márquez Villanueva, p. 92 identifies the two. MS Madrid, RAH, 9.323; CS, D.49, fol. 399 points out that the «Alfonso Alvarez contador» who was Mayor Alvarez's son may have been some other *contador,* and that our Alfonso Alvarez's mother is named in his will as Mayor Fernández. Though his ancestors were certainly Jewish, these arguments have weight. Besides, neither the date nor the place seems right for disinterring the mother of a Cuencan who had himself died in 1457. Fernán Díaz's other family links with cases of Judaizing are similarly remote. Fernando Díaz de Toledo, market-overseer and *mayordomo* of Granada, listed among about a thousand other Granadinos of the 1490s whom the Inquisition would have liked to investigate (Stephen Gilman, «*Judea pequenna.* Granada ante la Inquisición», *Nueva Revista de Filología Hispánica,* 30 (1981), 591n.), may or may not have been a grandson; a Guadalajara official, married into a more obviously Jewish family, and an accuser of Judaizers in the 16th century, was perhaps a second cousin (see below, n. 15).

[7] See Benito Ruano, *Orígenes,* p. 105 (accusations in 1449); *BUS,* vol. III, p. 373 (degrees); above, Chapter 4, n. 78 (visit to Aragon).

He was, of course, a royal Secretary. This meant simply that he was available and competent to draw up documents in due form; so casual and marginal was the work that it carried no stated salary. The position of *escribano de cámara,* which he held from 1420 onwards, meant rather more: as a fully qualified notary, wholly employed in the king's service, he did merit a small but regular payment.[8] But already in 1419, he had acquired the office with which he was to become identified —that of Relator. A *relator,* in Roman legal practice, was the official who reported in summary on the arguments of both parties in cases of appeal; the post so styled in Castilian government had close associations with the royal Council. The role of that body as a legal tribunal made such a functionary useful from time to time, and of course, he had to be a *letrado*. But once such a *letrado* was in post, other tasks suggested themselves. Already, in regulations issued by Enrique III in 1406, the king's Relator was charged with keeping the Council minutes. The evidence from Juan II's reign shows Fernán Díaz as servicing every aspect of Council business: preparing its agenda; presenting each item; summarizing the petitions of outsiders; reporting debates and decisions to the king; keeping minutes and records of grants made. We cannot be certain who gave him the post in the first place, or how far all this was envisaged at the time; in 1419-20, Juan II had only just come of age, and initiative in government was delicately balanced between the Infantes Juan and Enrique of Aragón and their emerging rival, Alvaro de Luna. What does seem clear is that Fernán Díaz was destined to flourish as Relator under the last-named, and that the office grew with the man. So did that of Referendary, a title with which he was signing documents from the early 1420s onward, though he apparently received no separate payment for this office until 1435. *Referendarius* had been the usual Roman title for the official who did the work of a *relator,* but there had also been, in mediaeval times, so-called *referendarii iussi,* whose task it was to countersign and ratify official documents. That was the function which, with extraordinarily comprehensive zeal, Fernán Díaz undertook during the adult reign of Juan II.

The pivotal role in administering the kingdom which these offices came to imply was closely matched with the authoritarian political stra-

---

[8] Fernán Díaz's offices with dates of appointment and salaries are in AGS, QdC, 3.52. The post of royal Secretary gained greatly in importance in the course of the 15th century (TORRES SANZ, pp. 116-17); on *relatores* and *referendarii* see ibid, pp. 122-4; also DU CANGE, *Glossarium Mediae et Infimae Latinitatis* (Paris, 1845), vol. V, p. 651; J. MATIENZO, *Dialogus Relatoris et Advocati* (Valladolid, 1604); C. CALISSE, *A History of Italian Law* (London, 1928), pp. 56, 85; on Referendaries in Juan I's Council, SUÁREZ FERNÁNDEZ, *Historia de Juan I,* pp. 339-40; on the Relator's duties under Juan II, MS Madrid, BN, 13107, fols 21v, 147v, 149r, 150r; on Castile in 1419-20, SUÁREZ FERNÁNDEZ, *Nobleza y monarquía,* pp. 119-22; for a signature as Referendary in 1423, see *CJII* (CODOIN), 99, p. 326.

tegy of Don Alvaro de Luna. The nature of their association is spelled out at some length in Alvar García de Santa María's discussion of Don Alvaro's governmental system.[9] To record in detail the particular services of Fernán Díaz to Constable and king in the successive crises of the reign would be to write a political history of the period. But the manner in which the Relator took his reward is of some interest in itself. The office of judge of appeal, for example, which he acquired in 1423, was ancient and prestigious; though there were many such *oidores*, the salary of 30,000 *maravedís* was higher than that for any of his other appointments. Nor is it likely that Fernán Díaz ever had to serve his turn on the bench, given the full-time nature of his work in Council, and in the despatch of royal business generally. Yet the post did, in a sense, qualify him to sit as a judge on special tribunals, as he did in the case of the Count of Castro, and again in 1453. In 1429, when properties confiscated from the pro-Aragonese party were redistributed, he declined the grant to him of 500 of their vassals as inappropriate, but accepted a windfall grant in cash of 20,000 *maravedís* annually. This was a year, too, in which he received an expenses payment on a similar scale. In 1435, the attachment of a salary to his post of Referendary meant more money for the same work. When his veteran colleague Doctor Periáñez died in 1444, Fernán Díaz took over the further sinecure of *notario mayor de los privilegios rodados*. There were also minor grants to his wife Aldonza González, and to his legitimate and illegitimate children. One of the latter, Pedro de Toledo, was appointed to the king's guard; he was to end his days as Bishop of Málaga. Juana Díaz de Toledo, the Relator's daughter, was married to another royal guard; Juan Díaz de Toledo, perhaps a son, became a court notary, with a salary out of Fernán Díaz's earnings. Most important of all was the right of reversion of his offices to a successor of his choosing, granted to him in 1442, and exercised prospectively in favour of his eldest son, Luis, early in 1445. Luis did, indeed, take over the old Relator's offices and titles after the latter's death in 1457, and treated them almost exclusively as a source of income. But that is another story. What is striking about the Relator's own tale is the fact that the flow of benefits to him was not seriously interrupted either by the anti-Luna coup of 1441 or by Don Alvaro's return to dominance in 1444-6. Whatever the early patronage to which he owed his position, Fernán Díaz was essentially the servant of the king and of no one else.

The purely material aspect of his success, however, should not be exaggerated. It was an achievement on a very different scale from that

---

[9] See above, pp. 12-13. Apart from the grants of 1429 (*CJII* (R), p. 479; LADERO, *Hacienda*, pp. 269, 273), information here is from AGS: offices, QdC, 3.52; grants to wife, M y P, 2.271; to Pedro de Toledo, M y P, 192.40; to Juana Díaz, M y P, 1.455, 2.271, 7.143; to Juan, QdC, 1.12; renunciation to Luis, M y P, 7.129; QdC, 3.48.

of Alfonso Alvarez. In the 1447 *asientos,* Fernán Díaz had just under 107,000 *maravedís* annually; the total for him and his immediate family was just over 144,000.[10] These figures would put them in about the fortieth place overall among individuals and among families. They are in line with payments to other high officials, but the great *contador* and the titled magnates comfortably outstrip them. The mere circumstance of his place among Castile's ruling elite meant, of course, that the Relator was very much better off than the vast majority of his fellow-countrymen. But his place within that group remained modest. This was anomalous, given that Fernán Díaz was a high official of a very special kind.[11] The work of the Council, and indeed of the government at large, could be carried on effectively only because of the contribution which he made. When Mass was said each morning at the portable altar which he was allowed to maintain for his family and his servants, the domestic congregation was regularly swollen with petitioners, anxious not to miss the start of Council business. When an Archbishop from Castile exchanged letters with a Pope, the extraordinary qualities of the Relator were a topic on which they could easily agree. This national and international reputation rested upon his long service and his reliability, and on a prodigious energy which hardly seemed to slacken with the years. But another of its sources was Fernán Díaz's real eminence as a lawyer. The formulary which he composed —the *Notas del Relator*— remained for almost a century an influential guide to notarial practice; his other surviving work, the *Instrucción del Relator,* though written under pressure, is a notable piece of advocacy. His household had a high reputation as a legal academy; Montalvo, the greatest Castilian jurist of his age, readily acknowledged the debt which he owed to Fernán Díaz. In the light of all this, the level of reward which the Relator received from royal sources bears out Alvar García's contention that «he lived with less affluence than his labours deserved». Nor, if Alvar García and Galíndez are to be believed, did Fernán Díaz supplement that income in what, for most officials, was the normal way —by taking bribes. Whatever the motives informing

---

[10] Suárez Fernández, «Asientos», p. 362. Checklists of the 1450s (AGS, QdC, 3.50-2) add 8.400 *maravedís* as *escribano de cámara* and 2,000 as keeper of seals for Enrique IV's queen. By this time, too, Fernán Díaz held almost 75,000 *maravedís* of confiscated Luna revenues (below, pp. 198-9).

[11] See above, n. 8 (duties in Council); *BUS,* vol. III, pp. 411-12; vol. II, p. 513 (Eugenius IV to Don Gutierre, Archbishop of Toledo, 1443). Several editions of the *Notas del Relator* (some augmented) appeared between 1493 and 1548 (see Rafael de Floranes, *Vida literaria del Canciller Ayala,* CODOIN, 19, pp. 307-9; R. de Ureña y Smenjaud, *Los incunables jurídicos de España* (Madrid, 1929), pp. 31-2; Clara L. Penney, *Printed Books 1468-1700 in the Library of the Hispanic Society of America* (New York, 1965), p. 171). On the *Instrucción,* Round, «Politics, Style and Group Attitudes». On Fernán Díaz's household, Fernando del Pulgar, *Letras* (Madrid, 1929), p. 150; also Caballero, *Conquenses,* p. 347; for his incorruptibility, *CJII* (CODOIN), 100, p. 331; also CODOIN, 13, p. 32n (above, n. 3); confirmed in AGS, M y P, 55.40 (below, p. 199).

his long and arduous service of the Crown, the desire to grow rich can hardly have been foremost among them.

The desire for security is a different matter. The Relator's comparatively modest fortune was enough to see his children well provided for. Their marriages with Old Christian gentry, and the families of local notables which they founded in Seville, Ronda and Alcalá itself, are evidence of his success.[12] More immediately, his pursuit of security responded to his situation as a *converso*. Or to put the matter more exactly, it responded to the particular situation as a *converso* in which the Relator found himself. There is no evidence whatever to suggest that he was a secret Judaizer, or had close personal connections who were, or that he felt any sympathy at all for those who were in that position. But he was close enough historically to the life of the *aljamas* to know that the legal status of the Castilian Jews had been based on a special and direct relationship with the Crown —taxes for protection; the Jews were «the king's Jews». To any *converso* who remembered this, a career in the royal service made much sense. Fernán Díaz, moreover, belonged to a distinctive minority among New Christians —those who had professional talents and training to offer. That minority, in the early years of their entry into the Christian polity, were socially mobile to an unusual degree; the Díaz de Toledo clan as a whole provide a striking illustration of this. But when the resentments which this mobility could awaken were added to the existing undertow of prejudice against them, *conversos* in high office were bound to feel especially vulnerable. Their need to remain close to their patron was particularly acute. Fernán Díaz, it is clear, felt this vulnerability to the full. When his epitaph speaks of his sense of duty to «his own people», it may mean his family, but it could just as readily refer to the *conversos* as a group. He had twice written publicly and outspokenly on their behalf: first in a rebuke to Cardinal Carvajal for slighting words spoken at the Papal court, and then in his *Instrucción* on the Toledo revolt. On that occasion he had also been the target for the rebels' most violent abuse, while the support which Don Alvaro de Luna had been able to provide for the persecuted *conversos* within the city was, to say the least, disappointing. Fernán Díaz, even more than others of his caste, might have been led by these experiences to regard his links with the king as the only reliable basis for his own security.

That said, it must be added that the pursuit of security through patronage was in no sense a concern of New Christians only. Indeed, all that *conversos* in this position were trying to do was to be like other Castilians, in a society where everyone was someone's client, and the

---

[12] On Fernán Díaz's descendants see Portilla, vols I-II (Alcalá de Henares, 1725-8), passim; also *Anales Complutenses* (MS Madrid, BN 7899; dated 1652). See, too, MS Madrid, RAH, 9.300; CS, D25, fol 4, and *Instrucción*, pp. 352-3.

service of the Crown was, of all forms of clientage, the one most keenly sought. Nor need we think that the search for security, especially on the part of a man who had pondered questions of government more deeply than most, was a merely self-directed interest. The wider vision with which that search was integrated may be inferred from the other evidence which we have about Fernán Díaz as a personality. The formidable competence and the appetite for work have something to do with it; so does the refusal to take bribes. They imply a sense of the worth inherent in the offices which he held, and in the work which these involved, not as the means of private advancement but as ends in themselves. In a word, the Relator displays a new kind of professionalism in the king's service —an impression confirmed by Galíndez's observation that, though held in high esteem by the king and the magnates, he made little effort to cultivate the latter.[13] The remark, in the same account of him, that he was *pacis cupidus* —a great lover of peace— casts a similar light upon his lifelong political orientation. Not that he set his face against all conflict; indeed, the *Coplas de ¡ay Panadera!* picture him as one of the more resolute of the king's supporters on the field of Olmedo. But the political ideal which Fernán Díaz followed was something very closely related to Juan's «peace and tranquility of my realms» —a kingdom where the security which the New Christians so badly needed was not set at a further remove by lawlessness and instability.

Above all, there was the commitment to the law. When Fernán Díaz's relatives sought to record his virtues in an epitaph, they might have said that he was a just man and left it at that. Instead, they said something more specific and more emphatic: that he was *natura justus* —a just man by nature.[14] What he felt about the law —the law that he had served and expounded and administered all his long working life— is perhaps better indicated by that phrase than by any other. And in the midst of the law —*in lege positus,* as Baldus had said— there was the king. So, at all events, the Roman tradition saw it. This was the tradition which Fernán Díaz had studied in youth, and on which he had drawn for decades

---

[13] CODOIN, 13, p. 32n. (epitaph, virtues, polemic with Carvajal). Cf. also (above, n. 9) the story of his refusal of 500 vassals confiscated from Juan of Navarre and his brother in 1429, because he did not think it right for him to be their heir. Since he accepted a cash grant from the same confiscation, he was presumably objecting to the seigneurial style of the gift. See, too, *Coplas de ¡ay Panadera!* in *Cancionero de Gallardo,* ed. José María Azáceta (Madrid, 1962), p. 89; also NILDA GUGLIELMI, «Los elementos satíricos en las *Coplas de la panadera*», *Filología,* 14 (1970), 75.

[14] The phrase is in both the MS version seen by SAINZ DE BARANDA, CODOIN, 13, p. 32n., and the epitaph transcribed from the tomb by *Anales Complutenses,* p. 533. For Baldus see above, Chapter 4, n. 59. It is true that Fernán Díaz's handling of the king's testimony against Don Alvaro was in line with Jewish legal traditions. But it was also in accord with the teaching of Aquinas (above, Chapter 5, n. 52).

in helping to assert Juan II's claims to supremacy. He had used it most recently of all in drafting the documents which set out the king's position in the Luna case. We may take it that the ideology which these documents embodied was the Relator's as much as —and perhaps before— it was his master's. If his presence among the judges threatened Don Alvaro, that, and not the fact that his father had been a Jew, was the reason.

Fernán Díaz was an authoritative figure for the other commissioners; he was also, to an extent, a normative one. Much that has been said about him could also be said of several of his colleagues. At least two of them were bound to him by close personal ties. The «Doctor Pedro Dias» of the Villena record was Doctor Pero Díaz de Toledo, sometimes called «de Olmedilla», the Relator's nephew.[15] His father would appear to have been an elder brother of Fernán Díaz; it was this branch of the family which possessed the lordship of the village of Olmedilla and a substantial town house in Alcalá de Henares. Later, Pero Díaz's younger brother, the royal notary Fernando, was to become a local notable in Guadalajara while his surviving son Francisco Díaz de Olmedilla was to make a distinguished career as a judge, and in legal practice on his own account. Pero Díaz himself first appears in documents as a law student in 1433. He took his Bachelor's degree at Valladolid; later in the decade we find him enrolled at the University of Lérida. He figures in the royal registers as a Licenciate in 1440, but had attained his Doctorate in Civil Law by 1445. All of this would make him at least a score of years his uncle's junior. His promotion in the public service was rapid.[16] In 1440, he was

---

[15] CODOIN, 13, p. 32n.; also GALÍNDEZ in TORRES FONTES, *Estudio sobre la «Crónica de Enrique IV»* (Murcia, 1946), p. 86. VICENTE BELTRÁN DE HEREDIA, *Cartulario de la Universidad de Salamanca (1218-1600)*, vol. I (Salamanca, 1970), pp. 538-40 correctly distinguishes Pero Díaz from his cousin Pedro de Toledo, Bishop of Málaga, but wrongly attributes the *letrado*'s literary output to the latter. The anachronistic reference to Pedro (not Fernando) Díaz de Toledo in 1430 (*CJII* (CODOIN), 100, p. 189) suggests that the Relator had a brother of that name. Ownership in Pero Díaz's line of the Alcalá house *(Anales Complutenses*, pp. 425-6), implies descent from an elder brother. For the younger Fernando Díaz see AGS, M y P, 7.141; also PORTILLA, vol. I, p. 565; ibid., p. 587 and *Anales Complutenses*, pp. 567-8 give the joint epitaph of Pero Díaz and his son Francisco, on whom see FLORANES, *Canciller Ayala*, pp. 348-63. Pero Díaz's descendants in MS Madrid, RAH, 9.310; CS D.35, fol 199. Between 1529 and 1543 the Guadalajara market-overseer Francisco Díaz de Olmedilla made allegations of heresy against several *conversos*, including (unsuccessfully) his own brother-in-law, who had been born a Jew (F. CANTERA BURGOS and CARLOS CARRETE PARRONDO, *Las juderías medievales en la provincia de Guadalajara* (Madrid, 1975), pp. 73-4, 186-7). Not a son of Pero Díaz (for he was born in 1488), this Francisco was probably a son or grandson of the *letrado*'s brother Fernando. Though his wife's family was very recently Jewish (her parents chose exile rather than conversion), his own record is one of officious orthodoxy.

[16] BELTRÁN DE HEREDIA, *Cartulario*, pp. 538-9 (citing MS Escorial QII9) and 539-40 (early studies); AGS, M y P, 7.132; QdC, 1.10; 3.46-7; 4.253 (offices, salaries, degrees; the last-named, probably in error, reduces his salary as *alcalde de alzadas de casa y corte* by 10,000 *maravedís*). He already had the title «Doc-

appointed an appeals judge for cases arising in the king's court and household; in the following year he was raised to the main appeals bench as an *oidor* with full salary. Between them, these offices brought him an income of over 50,000 *maravedís,* with additional benefits in the royal taxes. By 1445, he was a Referendary too, though he does not seem to have been active in this role; it was a title which had brought his uncle an annual 14,400 *maravedís.* Pero Díaz also held in 1445, and may have held as early as 1440, a legal post on the personal staff of the Crown Prince. His advancement, no doubt, was eased by the fact that he was the Relator's nephew, but his own efforts and talents also played their part. He may well have served actively as a judge of appeal, for he does not seem to have travelled with the king's entourage. He was certainly a capable jurist. In the sixteenth century and thereafter the college libraries of Alcalá preserved his partial study of the *Digest,* and other juridical writings, both academic and polemical in character.[17] His other writings, too, make copious use of legal authorities. His gloss to the *Proverbios de Séneca,* for example, contains over a hundred such references, for the most part very generalized, but ranging widely among both Roman and Castilian sources.

Pero Díaz's literary work, of course, encouraged Juan II's interest in him.[18] At the king's request, probably in the first half of 1445, he translated three short ethical works, and wrote an elaborate gloss on one of them, the *Proverbia Senecae.* Later that year Juan commissioned him to write a commentary on Santillana's *Proverbios* and dedicate it to Prince Enrique. But Pero Díaz's contacts with the Marquis went back to at

tor» when he translated Pseudo-Plato *Axiochus* (late 1444-early 1445), see SCHIFF, p. 340, and ROUND, «Shadow of a Philosopher», p. 29n. Possibly he was the «licenciado Pero Díaz de Alcalá, alcaide del Príncipe» (*C Halc,* p. 367), but *CJII* (R), p. 574 refers to «Juan de Alcalá» in this role in 1440; Pero Díaz certainly held the office in 1445 (MS Madrid, BN, 13108, fol 28v).

[17] For the *Digest* see AHN, Universidades, 1091F, fol 14v (inventory, dated 1523, of Colegio Mayor de S. Ildefonso); cf. GARCÍA Y GARCÍA, *Estudios,* p. 53n. A Madrid University MS, clearly of Alcalá provenance, containing further texts, is listed as MS86 by J. VILLA-MIL Y CASTRO, *Catálogo de los manuscritos existentes en la Biblioteca del Noviciado de la Universidad Central* (Madrid, 1878); it was seen by SAINZ DE BARANDA (CODOIN, 13, p. 32n.), and in 1917 by BELTRÁN DE HEREDIA, *Cartulario,* p. 539, but is now lost. (A number of the items cited by Beltrán are concerned with the legal status of converts.) See also Pero Díaz's gloss to *Proverbios de Séneca,* MS Escorial S II 10, passim.

[18] For datings of works see ROUND, «Shadow of a Philosopher», p. 29n.; SANTILLANA, *Proverbios* (Seville, 1494), fol a. 6r. Among later works, see especially *Diálogo e razonamiento en la muerte del Marqués de Santillana,* dedicated to the Count of Alba de Tormes in the early 1460s, and *Introdución a la «Exclamación e querella de la governación»* [Gómez Manrique], dedicated to Archbishop Carrillo of Toledo *circa* 1465. Editions respectively by A. PAZ Y MELIA, *Opúsculos literarios de los siglos XIV a XVI* (Madrid, 1892) and FOULCHE-DELBOSC, *CC,* vol. II, pp. 131-47. Another untraced MS of the Biblioteca del Noviciado (no. 151) contained a version of Josephus commissioned from Pero Díaz by Carrillo (BELTRÁN DE HEREDIA, *Cartulario,* p. 540).

least a year before this, when he had translated from Latin and dedicated to the then Iñigo López de Mendoza the apparently Platonic dialogue, *Axiochus*. A more ambitious project —a version out of Latin of Plato's *Phaedo*— followed, at Santillana's request, in 1447. From about this time onward Pero Díaz was increasingly involved with literary and legal activities on behalf of the Marquis.[19] He made translations for him of many «works and treatises»; he acted as his legal representative in at least one important property transaction; he was party to the necessarily confidential business of Santillana's efforts on behalf of the imprisoned Count of Alba. Eventually, he became a habitual resident of the Marquis's great house at Guadalajara, and drew a salary from him for his services. This was something which *oidores* were not supposed to do, though many of them evidently did gravitate in similar fashion from public to private patronage. Pero Díaz's motives can only be guessed at. It was sensible for a prominent citizen of Alcalá, especially if he owned land in the area, to be on good terms with the great lord of the Henares valley. Perhaps the growing economic crisis made it less certain that Pero Díaz would receive his salaries regularly; Santillana was well known as a generous patron to men of learning. Soon, a genuine friendship had grown up between the *converso* scholar and the magnificent amateur, based on a common liking for serious talk, ancient literature, and Stoic-Christian ethics. It is hard to determine the part which political factors may have played in this. Pero Díaz, for example, reacted sharply and publicly to the anti-*converso* revolt of Toledo in 1449; for him, as for other New Christians, that event may well have precipitated a crisis of confidence in Alvaro de Luna. Yet this would not necessarily have brought him closer to Santillana, whose own anti-royalist *démarches* of the same year, though separate from the Toledo rebellion, were profoundly unhelpful. Even so, a degree of estrangement from the Constable, if not actually a cause of Pero Díaz's new relationship with his patron, must surely have been reinforced as a result of that relationship. From the late 1440s, then, Pero Díaz must be seen as somewhat detached, if not actually alienated from the regular service of the Crown. One sign of this was the fact that he was not made a member of the Council until after 1451, and probably not until after the Luna case itself. Another is the readiness

---

[19] *Diálogo e razonamiento*, pp. 248-9; 285; 250; 283-4; see also LAYNA SERRANO, vol. I, p. 332. For the impact of the Toledo revolt of 1449 on *converso* attitudes to Don Alvaro see above, p. 64. Pero Díaz's lost writings include a reply to a «sacrilegious and foolish» document issued by «los traidores apóstatas del villanaje del común de la ciudad de Toledo.» Though BELTRÁN DE HEREDIA (*Cartulario*, p. 540) relates this, inexplicably, to «la sublevación de don Enrique y del condestable», it must surely have been a counterblast to the Toledan *Sentencia-Estatuto*. For Pero Díaz's official titles as at 19th December 1451 see AHN Osuna, 1825, 6. He was not then a Councillor, but contrast his epitaph (above, n. 15).

with which, in the late 1450s and 1460s, he was to revert to the service of private patrons once more. In 1458 he was in Santillana's household; between then and his death in 1466, he worked for the Count of Alba de Tormes, and for Archbishop Carrillo. In consulting Pero Díaz on the Luna case, Juan II was consciously broadening the political base of his special commission. But he was also calling upon a *letrado* of real professional and intellectual standing. The choice might be unpromising from Don Alvaro's point of view, but it was not made on that ground alone.

Also closely associated with the Relator, though not of his family, was the Licenciate Alonso Díaz de Montalvo.[20] A close friend and pupil of Fernán Díaz, he had lived in the latter's household for a number of years. His own home was in Huete, midway between Alcalá and Cuenca. Huete had once possessed a flourishing Jewish quarter, which had suffered greatly in the pogrom of 1391; descendants of more or less forcibly converted Jews formed a great part of its present population. Montalvo, however, had been born at Arévalo in 1405, the son of a minor royal official who migrated to Huete when Alonso Díaz was still a child. The young Montalvo attended the universities of Salamanca and Lérida, paving the way for an outstanding career, both as a practising lawyer and as a legal theorist. At thirty, he was deputed by the crown to settle a boundary dispute in Galicia —not the easiest of areas in which to make the king's writ effective. In the early 1440s, he played an important part in persuading a number of potential dissidents to remain loyal to Juan II. In 1444, already a judge of appeal, he was made *corregidor* of Murcia, and held that city successfully on Juan's behalf in the campaigns preceding Olmedo. He had also held a similar governorship in Madrid, and was a member of the Council. When the anti-*converso* revolt broke out at Toledo in 1449, Montalvo wrote a critique of its legal aspects. His interest in the topic would be compatible with his being a New Christian himself, but it by no means proves the point; the work was undertaken at the king's request. Later it was interpolated in his gloss to the *Fuero real*. This, with its dedication to Fernán Díaz, must antedate the latter's death in 1457; parts of it may already have been written at the time of the Luna trial. But it would have been impossible as yet to predict in the Montalvo of 1453 the aged and vastly erudite legal eminence of the end of the century. He was, for the moment, an obviously gifted and energetic lawyer-administrator, very much after the model of his master the Relator, but with rather more of a theoretical bias. He was an obvious choice for

---

[20] See, principally, CABALLERO, *Conquenses Ilustres* and *Elogio*; also BENEYTO PÉREZ, «Science of Law», pp. 279-84; UREÑA Y SMENJAUD, *Incunábules*, pp. 19-31; EMILIO DURO PEÑA, «Catálogo de documentos reales del Archivo de la Catedral de Orense (844-1520)», *MTM*, I (1972), 70; *CCG*, pp. 125, 129; SICROFF, pp. 36-9; see also above, Chapter 5, n. 53.

a tribunal of this sort; indeed, it would have been surprising had he been left out.

The colleague of his whom the Villena document calls «el bachiller de Ferrera el viejo» is a much more elusive figure. The reference could perhaps be to Alvar Gómez de Herrera, one of the notaries of Juan II's court, who had settled in Madrid in 1405.[21] He was the father-in-law of the Relator's heir Luis Díaz, who had at one stage been Juan's envoy in the intrigues against Alvaro de Luna. His son, the *Bachiller* Fernán Gómez de Herrera, is a second possibility.[22] He too had much to do with the de Toledo family, witnessing the Relator's designation of Luis Díaz as his chosen successor in office in 1445, and engaging in business transactions with the heirs of Alfonso Alvarez in 1458-60. Between these dates we find him mentioned as the recipient of various minor grants and renunciations, which continue throughout the next decade. A person of his name —possibly not the same— was a royal notary from 1455. By 1460 Fernán Gómez was a local magistrate in Toledo; in the same year he was appointed as legal assistant to the *contadores mayores;* in 1462 he was made a judge of appeal. Over the next few years he was engaged in legal work both on behalf of the Crown and in the interest of the Pacheco family. This may not have been the first involvement of these Gómez de Herrera with magnates hostile to the Luna interest; a family of Herreras in the service of Santillana and the Count of Alba had helped to maintain contact between the two during the latter's imprisonment, very much as Pero Díaz, Fernán Gómez's relative by marriage, seems also to have done. Like the Relator's family, too, Alvar Gómez and his son may well have been *conversos;* certainly persons of their name —possibly lawyers too— were fined for Judaizing by the Inquisition of Toledo in the 1490s. But we do not know how close or how distant these connections may have been.

Nor do we know whether this family in any of its branches included a third possible «bachiller de Ferrera el viejo». This was another, and to all appearances slightly senior, *Bachiller* Fernán Gómez de Herrera.[23]

[21] *Sal Inds,* 14 (Madrid, 1956), no. 23.611 (CS, D.25, fol 150v); AGS, M y P, 63.71 and 2.271; on Luis Díaz see above, p. 44.

[22] AGS, M y P, ibid.; also 7.129; 63, 69; 8.119; QdC, 3.78 (the notary); M y P, 63.71 (*regidor* of Toledo); QdC, 3.101 (*letrado de los contadores;* granted this office in 1460 as «Bachiller Ferrando de Herrera», after death of «Bachiller Ferrando Gómez de Herrera»); Q de C, 3.79, and M y P, 8.119 (made *oidor* in 1462; therefore papers using that title for him in 1453 and 1447 respectively (M y P, 63.69; 8.119) must be wrongly filed). Legal work in 1460s: AHN, Osuna, 1.26; 35.41; *CD,* p. 75n.; LEÓN TELLO, *Duques de Frías,* vol. II, p. 42. The «Ferreras, tus criados e mios» in SANTILLANA, *Bias contra Fortuna,* in FOULCHÉ-DELBOSC, *CC,* vol. I, p. 475. CANTERA BURGOS and LEÓN TELLO, *Judaizantes del arzobispado de Toledo habilitados por la Inquisición en 1495 y 1497* (Madrid, 1969) mention in San Salvador parish the son of a servant of «el bachiller de Herrera» (p. 38), and in San Tomé a «bachiller Juan Gómez de Herrera» (p. 30).

[23] See AGS, QdC, 3.101; M y P, 63.69; 8.119 (above. n. 22). Also QdC, 1.11

He had been appointed to a judgeship in the Castilian military region as early as 1441, and became a judge of appeal in 1448. In that year too, he was named by the *contadores mayores* as the holder of a legal post which they had sought to have created to deal with taxation problems, especially those caused by irregularities on the part of certain officers in the Military Orders. (This was the post which was later to be held by Alvar Gómez's son.) For good measure, 1448 also saw this Fernán Gómez appointed as Judge-Commissary for border problems between Castile, Guipúzcoa and Navarre. In the reign of Enrique IV, he also served as the king's Latin Secretary. He died in 1459, leaving a son, Alfonso de Herrera. It was, perhaps, to the latter that Alfonso de Palencia, also a Latin Secretary from 1456, dedicated the Castilian version of his political satire, the *Batalla campal de los perros contra los lobos*.

Any of these three might have sat in the commission in 1453; any of them could have borne the epithet *el viejo* («the old», or «the elder»).[24] We know, for example, that it was sometimes used of Alvar Gómez de Herrera. The editors of the *Colección diplomática* believed that it could have been applied to his son, to distinguish him from a Licenciate of the same name, who sat in the royal Council under the Catholic Monarchs. This would be in line with fifteenth-century usage; Enrique II of Castile was sometimes known as «King Enrique the Old», by contrast with his grandson Enrique III, even though he had died at no great age. But the term could also refer to the elder of two near-contemporaries who happened to be namesakes, and in this sense it could have distinguished Fernán Gómez, the Latin Secretary, from his junior, Alvar Gómez's son.

The family links with the Relator, the possible *converso* status, and the hints of association with opponents of Don Alvaro all lend credibility to the claims of Alvar Gómez and his son, especially the latter. But there are, in either case, serious obstacles to the identification. In principle, there is no reason why Alvar Gómez, active in 1405, could not also have taken part in a trial held in 1453. The working life of Montalvo was actually longer than this, and that of the Relator was almost as long. But

---

(*alcalde en el adelantamiento de Castilla*); 3.76 (*juez comisario entre Castilla, Guipúzcoa e Navarra*; death; son Alfonso); 3.77 («un letrado que ha de ver los fechos e vejaciones de los Comendadores mayores»); 3.101 and M y P, 1.778v (Latin Secretary); also ROBERT BRIAN TATE, «Political Allegory in Fifteenth-Century Spain: A Study of the *Batalla Campal de los Perros contra los Lobos* by Alfonso de Palencia (1423-92)», *JHP*, 1 (1976-7), 171-2.

[24] See CS, D. 25, fol. 150v (*Sal Inds*, 14), above, n. 21; also *CD*, p. 75n. We do not know which Bachiller Fernán Gómez de Herrera married Sancha Vázquez, who died in Toledo in 1463 (*Sal Inds*, 13 (Madrid, 1955), no. 20.994), or acted in a Mendoza lawsuit of 1443 (ibid., 30 (Madrid, 1962), no. 47.721), or if either were the Cordovan cleric of that name, who was examined for his doctorate in 1439, while at the king's court (*BUS*, vol. II, pp. 457-8). The Bachiller Fernán Gómez de Herrera who collected taxes in Cuenca, Cartagena and Murcia in 1411 (AGS, EMdR, 1.18 and 20; MS catalogue, fols 2v, 3r) was, presumably, none of these.

it still seems unlikely that, for this important occasion, Juan II should have summoned out of long retirement someone who, when all was said, was a mere *escribano de cámara* —a very junior post indeed. As for Alvar Gómez's son, the problem with this Fernán Gómez is that he only emerges as a major figure some years after the Luna case. At the time he held no office —the few indications to the contrary are incompatible with our other evidence— and his professional experience can scarcely have been impressive. The balance of probabilities, then, favours our third candidate, Fernán Gómez de Herrera the future Latin Secretary. He had a decade of official responsibilities behind him, and his specialist experience in matters relating to taxation and to the Military Orders bore an obvious relevance to the issues in the Luna trial. The scholarly attainment which was to equip him for his Latin post may well have helped to commend him to Juan II, as the learning of Pero Díaz almost certainly did. If this Fernán Gómez and his son were, as seems likely, on good terms with Alonso de Palencia, we may take it that they, too, moved in circles which were disposed to think ill of Alvaro de Luna. And, of course, it remains perfectly possible that the Latin Secretary himself was a relative of the other Herreras, and hence, though more remotely, of Fernán Díaz the Relator.

A member of the commission who, like Fernán Díaz, had a specific official responsibility in the case was the Public Prosecutor, Doctor Juan Gómez de Zamora.[25] Amador states that he, too, was a *converso,* though on what grounds he fails to make clear. A small grant held by Juan Gómez from 1452 onwards was paid to him out of the capitation tax on Jews and Moors, but this can tell us nothing of his origins. He does, however, seem to have had some preference for holding his royal grants in Salamanca —possibly because of some family link with that city. A near-namesake, Doctor Diego Gómez de Zamora, who held a chair of Canon law at Salamanca from 1447 to 1467, could have been a relative —perhaps a brother. Another possible relation is the *Bachiller* Alonso Gómez de Zamora, who worked for the future Marqués de Santillana around 1439. Intellectually, the *Bachiller* was not one of Iñigo López's more stimulating collaborators; he translated Orosius (but only from Aragonese), and was a neat but very inaccurate copyist. Doctor Juan Gómez was certainly a more distinguished figure than that. His appointment as Prosecutor dated from 1443, and though his salary in this important office was a surprisingly low 12,000 *maravedís,* he was able to

---

[25] On the office of *fiscal* see TORRES SANZ, pp. 170-80; on Juan Gómez de Zamora, see AMADOR DE LOS RÍOS, *Judíos,* vol. III, p. 62n. Also AGS, QdC, 1.304 (appointed *fiscal);* M y P, 63.105 (grants and offices, 1452-69); *RGS* (printed catalogue), vol. I (Valladolid, 1950), p. 53; see too, *BUS,* vol. I, p. 168 (Salamancan Doctor Diego Gómez); SCHIFF, pp. 167, 424-5 (Alonso Gómez); *CD,* pp. 399; 478-9 (for Diego Gómez, Councillor).

make rather more than twice that sum in expenses. He is not mentioned as a member of the Council until 1462, some years after the Luna trial; we do not know his relationship to the Doctor Diego Gómez de Zamora who was appointed to the Council of Justice in 1465. Juan Gómez himself was made an appeals judge in that same year, and the appointment —which for someone who was also Prosecutor would have had to be a sinecure— brought him a substantial extra salary. In 1475, the Catholic Monarchs confirmed him in his offices and in his membership of the Council. The years of his advancement, then, fell mainly in the reign of Enrique IV; at the Luna trial he was a relatively junior member of the commission. Initially, the office which he held gave him a more important role, but this became less significant as the king's testimony came to take the place of an indictment.

The editors of the *Colección diplomática* identified Doctor Alonso García de Guadalajara with Juan II's Public Prosecutor Alonso García Chirino.[26] No doubt they had in mind the statement of the *Crónica de Juan II* that Chirino prosecuted in the case of Pero Sarmiento in 1451. Neither the Real Academia de la Historia nor the chronicle can be right about this; in 1453, and for ten years before that, the Public Prosecutor was Doctor Zamora. Chirino had indeed been Prosecutor, and he did use «de Guadalajara» as an alternative surname, but all that was before his death in 1431 or 1432. He was a New Christian physician who had migrated from Guadalajara to Cuenca, which city he represented in the *Cortes,* and he doubled his legal duties with the role of medical adviser to Juan II, rather as the Archdeacon of Niebla was to be both physician and chaplain at a slightly later date. One of Chirino's sons was Mosén Diego de Valera; three others are mentioned in the will which he drew up in 1429, and it was one of these, Alonso García, who was eventually to sit in judgment on Alvaro de Luna.[27] Like Montalvo, who came from much the same area, Alonso García de Guadalajara studied at both Salamanca and Lérida. In 1433, it appears, the office of Judge for the County and Lordship of Biscay, which his recently deceased father had

---

[26] *CD*, p. 75n.; *CJII* (R), p. 675. Contrast AGS, QdC, 1.304 (Doctor Zamora succeeds Alonso Fernández de Ledesma, deceased, as *fiscal*); see *CJII* (R), p. 480 and *Ref Halc,* p. 169 for Chirino's offices and his two surnames in 1430-1. Cf. CARRIAZO, *Estudio preliminar* to VALERA, *Memorial,* pp. xiv-xv; PENNA, pp. c-cii; MARÍA TERESA HERRERA, ed. *Menor daño de la medicina, de Alonso de Chirino* (Salamanca, 1973), pp. xv-xix. The identical pairs of names seem enough to identify Mosén Diego's father with the Prosecutor.

[27] CARRIAZO, p. xv; PENNA, p. ci; *BUS*, vol. II, pp. 411-12; AGS, M y P, 2.67; 12.142; 65. 115. QdC, 1.424 has Alonso García given his Biscayan post in 1423, taking the income of Doctor Juan Rodríguez de Salamanca, deceased. But the elder Chirino still held the post in 1430 (*CJII* (R), p. 480). The Simancas record, compiled in the 1450s, seems to conflate the transfer from Rodríguez, dying in 1423, to Chirino with that from the latter, dying in 1431 or 1432, to his son and near-namesake.

held, was granted to Alonso García, who as yet held only a bachelor's degree. The appointment did not immediately interrupt his studies at Lérida, for by 1436 he was a Licenciate in Canon Law of that university, but papal permission was granted in that year for him to take his doctorate while resident in the royal court. The Biscay judgeship was not a post of great distinction; it carried a salary of only 6,000 *maravedís*. It was Alonso García's practice to retain three-quarters of this sum, and to pay the rest to a deputy —in 1455 one Gonzalo García de Burgos— who actually did the work. By 1461 he had secured one of the well-remunerated judgeships of appeal. This was the year in which he sought to renounce his Biscayan appointment to the son of one of the *contadores*. If this nominee could not have it, he wrote to the king, he would prefer to hold on to the post himself. Apparently there did exist some obstacle to the transaction, for it was not until 1465 that action was taken on Alonso García's request. Then both Enrique IV and his rival, the pretender-king Alfonso, granted it. There is one further twist in this curious affair: at the time of his death in 1473, Alonso García was apparently still in post and receiving some of the financial rewards belonging to the position he had surrendered.

Of the other bearers of the surname known to us, some clearly belonged to that branch of the family which had remained in Guadalajara. Not even that is known for certain about the royal notary Fernando García de Guadalajara, witness to a Burgos document of 1416.[28] But Juan García de Guadalajara, secretary of the Constable Ruy López Dávalos, and executed in 1428 for forging the letters which had led to the latter's fall, did have some connection with the Guadalajara side of the family. His history did not prevent other members of it from finding similar employment. One Diego García de Guadalajara, besides being a local magistrate in that town, was among the royal secretaries; his son, another Diego, took a Bachelor's degree. This son may perhaps be identical with that Diego García de Guadalajara (father of yet another Diego) who was a trusted secretary of the Mendoza lords. The *Bachiller*

---

[28] SERRANO, p. 81. For Juan García see *C Halc*, pp. 19-20; *CJII* (R), p. 445. See also FRANCISCO MENDOZA Y BOVADILLA, *Tizón de la nobleza española* (Barcelona, 1880): «fué ahorcado y era confeso». But the text in JULIO CARO BAROJA, *Los judíos en la España moderna y contemporánea*, 2nd edn (Madrid, 1978), vol. III, p. 325 has «y confeso el delito». Though the family was, in fact, *converso,* the inadequacy of the *Tizón* as evidence is apparent. On the several Diego García de Guadalajara see AGS, *RGS* (printed catalogue), vol. I, pp. 218, 260; AHN, Osuna, 1860, 42; AMALIA PRIETO CANTERO, *Documentos referentes a hidalguías, caballerías y exenciones de pecho* (Madrid, 1974), p. 56. LAYNA SERRANO, vol. I, p. 338; *Sal Inds,* 19 (Madrid, 1957), no. 31.611; ibid., 17 (Madrid, 1956), no. 29.477 for descendants. The brothers Pedro García and Gonzalo García de Guadalajara, sons of the Jew Mosé el Barchilón of Guadalajara, appear as owners of property in Toledo in 1424 (PILAR LEÓN TELLO, *Judíos de Toledo* (Madrid, 1979), vol. II, p. 226). It seems possible that Alonso García Chirino may have been their brother.

Diego was murdered at some date before 1477, but the descendants of his father, the king's secretary, later married into the Mendoza line, their Jewish origins becoming a source of some embarrassment to the future Counts of Priego.

In some ways, the Doctor Alonso García of the Luna trial looks like one of the less enterprising members of an interesting if not always fortunate family. There is a certain evasiveness about his record as we have it, which is as likely to have been the product of character as of coincidence. Yet he may also have had his share of the intelligence which both his father and his brother Diego undoubtedly possessed. His presence adds one more name to the list of empanelled *conversos,* but the fact that he was Mosén Diego's brother need not imply that he shared the latter's violently anti-Luna politics. Mosén Diego's hostility to Don Alvaro was, after all, a strongly political outlook, informed less by his *converso* background than by his identification with his Estúñiga patrons. Alvar García, it seems, had other relatives who were bound in similar fashion to the Mendozas. But his own patron was the king. Perhaps the inference to be drawn from his rather colourless career was that he was likely to do what his patron wanted at the time.

Nobody could call Doctor Pero González de Avila colourless. His family, again according to Amador, were *conversos,* but they were well established locally in the town and district of Avila.[29] For some generations they had held from the crown the lordships of Villatoro, Navalmorcuende, and Atelodón. Even Gonzalo Chacón regarded them as gentry, and a leading family in their city. Yet Pero González's father, like so many *conversos,* used more than one surname, sometimes calling himself «Fernán González de Valderrábano» —a name which he passed on to his younger son, Diego. Doctor Fernán González had been raised to the Council by Enrique III; he was also a judge of appeal and a referendary. He was an active Councillor in the Castilian-Aragonese crisis of 1429, was well-rewarded out of confiscated enemy estates, and served as a delegate in the protracted peace negotiations of the early 1430s. Though he seems to have retired from active service long before the Luna trial, he survived until 1455. His own professional success can have done his son's early career nothing but good. That career itself took several decisive steps in 1429 when the Licenciate Pero González received a grant of 8,000 *maravedís* from recent confiscations, and a

---

[29] AMADOR, *Judíos,* vol. III, p. 62n. (but Alfonso Dávila, the *Reyes Católicos'* secretary, is clearly not a brother). AGS, M y P, 2.6v mentions inherited taxholdings (including Jewish taxes) in Avila; *CD,* p. 74n. suggests that the lordships belonged to Pero González's wife, but the genealogies of *Sal Inds,* 15 (Madrid, 1956), nos. 26.142, 26.133-6, imply that both partners had claims to them. (The older portions of these tables are, of course, suspect). See also *CAL* (C), p. 446, and on Doctor Fernán González, AGS, M y P, 64.50; QdC, 1.345; LADERO QUESADA, *Hacienda,* p. 273; *CJII* (R), pp. 461, 471; BOFARULL, p. 124 and passim.

judgeship of appeal (to whose salary this grant was expected to contribute); at the end of the year the new *oidor* helped to deliver the king's summons to the rebel castle of Alburquerque.[30] In the 1430s, Pero González secured his doctorate of laws from Salamanca; in 1439, he was empowered to confer the same degree on a younger *letrado* of the court —the Cordovan cleric and *Bachiller* Fernán Gómez de Herrera. (If this was one of the Herreras known to us, he never took the degree; perhaps Pero González proved hard to satisfy as an examiner.) Appointed in 1440 to the post of Referendary which his father had renounced, Doctor Pero González entered upon a series of more important public duties. He witnessed the truce sworn by the victorious Infantes de Aragón, after Alvaro de Luna been chased from Medina del Campo in 1441; within a few months, the victors themselves found that they had a use for him. Their sister, Queen Leonor of Portugal, sought Castilian armed assistance in her private war with the Regent, Pedro of Coimbra; the Infantes wanted no such entanglement. In October 1441, Pero González was one of two delegates appointed to frame a suitably evasive reply. Under the anti-Luna regime of the early 1440s, he continued to witness important royal decrees as he had done before; in the reconstituted Council of 1442, he was nominated to serve for the first six months. His official functions, though he had come to them under Alvaro de Luna's power, were not adjuncts of that power; they belonged, rather, to the king's government.

Yet Pero González's own sympathies were anything but neutral.[31] When the Luna cause reasserted itself in 1445, he was eager to defend it in arms. He fought at Olmedo as the joint captain, with one of the Commanders of Calatrava, of a troop of a hundred men, some of them, no doubt, the «men at arms of his household». At the siege of Atienza in 1446, he was one of the first to occupy, and one of the most tenacious in defending, an exposed forward position under the town wall. This feat of arms won him a grant of 15,000 *maravedís* a year, and a detailed citation in the normally laconic chancery records. From the same report we learn that Pero González was one of the «gentlemen of the household of Don Alvaro de Luna». Chacón, too, states that he lived with the Constable, though for how long and in what capacity he does not say.

---

[30] LADERO QUESADA, p. 272; AGS, QdC, 1.347; also 4.300 (though the post of *oidor* is wrongly dated at 1439); *C Halc*, p. 47; *BUS*, vol. II, pp. 457-8 (examining Fernán Gómez); QdC, 1.347; 4.300 (appointed Referendary); MS Madrid, BN, 13107, fols 22v, 54r, 127v (signatures as witness), fol. 148v (Council membership). On the Portuguese question see *C Halc*, p. 431 and RUI DE PINA, *Crónicas*, ed. M. Lopes de Almeida (Oporto, 1977), pp. 680-1.

[31] *CJII* (R), p. 628; *CAL* (C), p. 167; praise of his active service «con la gente de armas de su casa», in AGS, M y P, 64.51; the Atienza citation, ibid., 2.6v; cf. *CAL* (C), p. 446; the exclusive arrangement with the crown, M y P, 64.51.

Probably he lodged with Don Alvaro when they were both at court, and was bound to the latter by one of his numerous loyalty oaths. But the fact as reported is evidence enough, both of Pero González's political leanings, and of his seigneurial style of life. Just as striking is the arrangement which superseded it. This was a payment from the king of 15,000 *maravedís* in annual maintenance, on condition that Pero González should receive no expenses from anyone except the king or queen. The date of this provision is not known, but it must fall between 1446 and 1452. It was, from Don Alvaro's viewpoint, ominous.

The additional grant of 30,000 *maravedís*, exempted from most of the restrictions then obtaining, which Pero González received in August 1453, after the Luna trial, ought to have set the seal on his financial security.[32] But matters were less simple. The *Contadores*, totalling his holdings at this stage at an annual 67,500 *maravedís*, noted that he had been taking some of them in advance in his own fiefs. Under Enrique IV, his relations with the crown, both financial and political, were to deteriorate sharply. Payments to him, at first sporadic, were suspended altogether in 1465, as he and his Valderrábano relatives carried Avila into open support of the boy-pretender Alfonso. Pero González secured an annual 100,000 *maravedís* from Alfonso for this service, and then compounded with Enrique for the same sum when he renewed his allegiance in 1469, after the boy-king's death. Though we have a last glimpse of him as a *Cortes* delegate in 1470, swearing support for Enrique's daughter Juana as the heiress of Castile, it comes as no surprise that Pero González's son Gonzalo de Avila should have established himself on good terms with the Catholic Monarchs. A daughter, María, on whom Pero González settled a modest income in the late 1440s may have been the María de Avila who was married to Doctor Pero Díaz de Toledo.

There can be no doubt that Pero González was entitled, in terms of seniority and competence, to sit in the tribunal which judged Don Alvaro de Luna. In some respects, he was an exceptional figure there. His lordships, his armed retainers and military prowess, his taking of taxes in his own domains, all represent the assimilation of the successful *letrado* —or, if indeed Pero González was a New Christian, of the successful *converso*— to a seigneurial style of life. The Relator, with

---

[32] Despite recent prohibitions, this was a new *merced*, backdated to January 1453, perpetual and transferable. For Pero González's finances from 1453 see AGS, M y P, 64.51, 64.52, and 8.47. See also *Sal Inds*, 30, no. 48.361. On Gonzalo de Avila, *corregidor* of Chinchilla (1476), *regidor* of Avila (1477), *Cortes* delegate (1479), see AGS printed catalogues *RGS*, vol. I, pp. 201, 307; *PR*, vol. I (Valladolid, 1946), p. 92. On María de Avila see M y P, 2.6v (15,000 *maravedís* renounced to her in 1446); also Pero Díaz's epitaph (above, n. 16). Alfonso González de Avila, perhaps another relative, was living in Alcalá de Henares around 1450 (PORTILLA, vol. I, p. 218; *Anales Complutenses*, p. 450).

his self-sufficient professionalism and close identification with an official role, clearly stands for a rather different social strategy. But the contrast should not be overdrawn. Fernán Díaz was at pains to pass on his offices as heritable assets and dignities; Pero González was prepared to bind himself by contract to be under obligation to the Crown and to no one else. The *letrados* may have had a choice between different modes of social adaptation, but politically the particular group who were involved with the Luna trial shared in a common experience. In that regard, at least, Pero González is by no means set apart from his colleagues. His political trajectory is as normative as the Relator's.

The history of Doctor Gonzalo Ruiz de Ulloa is a case in point. The family administrative tradition, the strong pro-Luna orientation until shortly before the crisis of 1453, and the greater difficulties of steering a political course in the succeeding reign are all observable again here. Since Gonzalo Ruiz chose to have certain of his grants from the king located in Toro, not far from Zamora, we may with reasonable confidence connect him with the family of the Ulloas of Toro who were prominent in the royal service in his time.[33] A late and garbled source implies that they were *conversos* or had intermarried with *conversos*. Their outstanding figure was Doctor Pero Yáñez de Ulloa —the Doctor Periáñez of the chronicles— in his day as permanent a quantity in the administration as the Relator himself. And Periáñez's day was long. His signature appears on royal documents as early as 1398; he worked closely with his contemporary, Doctor Diego Rodríguez, and the somewhat younger Fernán Díaz to implement the more effectual administrative style demanded by Alvaro de Luna. Indeed, so closely did the veteran Periáñez come to be identified with the Constable and his policies that the successful rebels of the early 1440s kept him from court, with Alonso Pérez de Vivero, for longer than any other of the senior officials. He was allowed to return in 1442, and died towards the end of 1444, at a very great age, having spent most of the intervening time vigorously intriguing to bring about Don Alvaro's restoration. He left

---

[33] Grants in Toro, AGS, M y P, 102.137; 2.424. One of Periáñez's sons allegedly made a *converso* marriage, but the *Tizón* (Barcelona edition) names different sons (and different wives) on pp. 74 and 142; Caro Baroja's text (*Los judíos*, vol. III, p. 320) helps not at all. Aponte (MS Madrid, BN, 6043, fol. 164) makes Periáñez's father a Galician tanner. Gil González de Avila, *Teatro eclesiástico*, vol. IV (Madrid, 1650), p. 207 includes Periáñez among famous sons of Salamanca; presumably he studied there. See also above, Chapter 1, n. 31 and p. 13; *CJII* (R), pp. 565, 608-9, 624. For Periáñez's sons see Suárez Fernández, «Asientos», p. 358; Juan (royal guard from 1431), AGS, QdC, 1.301; Rodrigo (*contador mayor* under Enrique IV), MS Madrid, RAH, 9.329; CS, D.55, fol. 27r. Andrés Ruiz is in QdC, 1.303 (which mistakenly reports Periáñez as dead in 1439). Presumably related was the knight García Alfonso de Ulloa of Toro (renounced post as royal guard to his son Periáñez, 1440); see QdC, 1.300 and *CJII* (R), p. 466.

two sons, Rodrigo and Juan de Ulloa, whose names are known to us from the 1447 royal accounts. A nephew, Andrés Ruiz de Ulloa, became a judge of the king's household in 1439, and an appeals judge in 1442; it is a reasonable guess that Gonzalo Ruiz was another nephew. His doctorate, dating from the early 1430s, comes almost certainly from Salamanca, the nearest university to Toro, and the one attended by his famous uncle. He was appointed, while still a licenciate, to be Judge of the Province of Andalusia in 1431, and raised to the appeals bench in 1435, which made him one of the more senior judges available at the time of the Luna case.[34] Four years after Don Alvaro's fall, Doctor Ulloa was made Corregidor of Biscay —perhaps the most demanding judicial assignment in all Castile. The salary, at a handsome 48,000 *maravedís*, was in keeping with the responsibilities, and expenses were forthcoming on a similar scale; in 1458, for example, Doctor Ulloa received an additional 42,000. Undeterred by the fighting reputation of the local Basque lords, he set about earning his money with a will, successfully besieging the redoubtable Lope García de Salazar in 1456. But on the latter's return from exile, Ulloa was recalled and dismissed, dying shortly afterwards, in 1463. It is a less outstanding record, perhaps, than some other commissioners might have displayed, but Gonzalo Ruiz was plainly very far from being a nonentity.

Almost certainly the junior member of the commission was the Licenciate Alfonso Sánchez de Logroño.[35] It is hard to find any documentary reference to him before 1454, and even this is likely to be an error for a much later year. He was granted the office of judge of appeal by Enrique IV in 1459, when Alvaro de Luna's former associate Ruy García de Villalpando died. By this time, too, Alfonso Sánchez had been made Chancellor, that is to say, registrar of documents for the court of appeal. His signature on an important Pacheco family paper of 1462 suggests that he had been noticed with favour by the Marquis of Villena. The same year saw him embroiled in a private lawsuit over property in La Coruña. Shortly before 1464, he entered the royal Council, and his name occurs as that of a witness to several of the abortive provisions designed to avert the impending political crisis in 1464-5. He retained his offices into the succeeding reign, for we find him employed

---

[34] AGS, QdC, 1.302, 3.391 *(oidor);* also M y P, 1.633, 2.424 *(alcalde de la provinçia del Andaluzia);* ibid., 102.137 *(corregidor de Vizcaya);* LADERO QUESADA, *Hacienda*, p. 278; GARCÍA DE SALAZAR, pp. 329-30, 338-9; M y P, 2.518v. García de Salazar's account of Ulloa's disgrace is suspect; only in 1460 and in 1463 (the year of his death) was his salary unpaid (QdC, 3.391-2).

[35] AGS, M y P, 104.114 *(oidor, chanciller,* Councillor in «1454», but the marginal date 1474 is the more likely here). Contrast ibid., 1.107 and QdC, 2.153 (appointed *oidor* in 1459). See also *CD*, pp. 75n, 350-5 passim, 479; M y P, 12.138 (the La Coruña lawsuit); *RGS* (printed catalogue), vol. I, pp. 150 (a servant of his attached to the salt monopoly in Avilés); 189.

But he also had, as events in 1443-4 had again proved, considerable personal influence over Prince Enrique, whose tutor he had once been, and over Juan Pacheco, then his fellow-conspirator, but now Marquis of Villena and the co-ordinator of the Prince's political strategy. Barrientos' appointment was a signal that Castile was going to be governed by a consensus between its present king and the man who would be his successor. Beside this, the matter of the *conversos*, however much it may concern later historians, would not have seemed very important.

Alonso de Espina, of course, bears a considerable responsibility for the importance which it later came to assume. But the *Fortalitium Fidei*, his major polemic against Jews and *conversos*, was written between the late 1450s and early 1460s; at the time of Don Alvaro's death, he was less identified with that single theme, and perhaps less exclusively preoccupied with it himself.[56] For Chacón, he was simply «a great and famous *letrado* and Master of Theology»; he had, in fact, reached a senior position among the Franciscan scholars of Salamanca. He also had the reputation of being a «great preacher», which is enough to explain why Don Alvaro should have recognized him when they met. Nor was their meeting the result of Espina's own initiative; both Chacón and the royal chronicler imply that the Franciscan was under official instructions to make contact with Don Alvaro on the road, and to break the news of his impending execution. The provision of spiritual comfort would have been a part of these same instructions. It was characteristic of Juan II that he should seek to make Don Alvaro's end not merely an awesome spectacle of justice, but an edifying drama in a religious sense. Espina's reference to martyrdom implies not the slightest criticism of the verdict or of the means by which it was reached. It has to be taken in the context of his other exhortations: Don Alvaro is to turn from the world, which has brought him to this, and repent of his sins. If he can die serenely, supported by the faith, his exemplary end will be a witness to the mercy of God, who has allowed him this grace, so that his soul may be saved. It may well have crossed the king's mind that if Alvaro de Luna did not make a good death of this sort, he was capable of using the occasion for a demonstration of a very different nature. In this light, the choice of Espina to persuade him becomes explicable. It was far from certain how Don Alvaro might react, and a famous preacher —especially one as given to violent overstatement of his case as we know Espina to have been —might be necessary to put the fear of God into him. As it happened, the shock of the death sentence itself had that effect, and Don Alvaro played his part meekly enough— though Pérez de Guzmán still found his bearing «more courageous than de-

---

[56] NETANYAHU, p. 109n. (date of *Fortalitium Fidei*); 107n. (Espina's reputation and Salamanca post); also CAL (C), p. 429.

vout».[57] For any preacher with Espina's undoubted flair for publicity, the invitation to participate in this *cause célèbre* was the chance of a lifetime, and he made the most of it. But he was not resisting the judicial decision, or striving to mitigate it; he was helping to carry it out. It makes little sense, therefore, to see his intervention as having any particularly anti-*converso* motives.

The general lesson of all this, perhaps, is that the *converso* issue seldom, if ever, arises in isolation. Whether in the background of individual judges, or in the broader context of Don Alvaro's fall, that issue interacts with other themes, and derives its effect —where it has one— from the manner of its interaction with them. It would be an error to see the *converso* question as the deep racial and religious substance of a history whose surface alone is political. However different its underlying motives might be, such an attitude would amount to a mystification of the Old Christian-New Christian dividing-line as fertile of error as the one which prevailed at the time. The necessary task, in fact, is to rationalize the *converso* issue by establishing its relationship to its context. And that context, in the case of the Luna trial, is political through and through. Its outcome is essentially a decision about government. Like all such decisions, this one is the product of many discrete factors, the situation of some of the judges as *conversos* being one of them. But its major determinants were political, legal, constitutional. This was not a peculiarly Spanish tragedy, with the brittle coexistance of religions in the fifteenth century as its principal mover. It was a Castilian episode in the European development of the modern state and the absolute power of kings.

---

[57] *G y S*, p. 44 —a minority view. Espina himself reports with some complacency the thoroughgoing nature of Don Alvaro's penitence: «in tanta pressura ad Dominum accessit corde contrito et humiliato et pedibus meis licet indignis se per generalem confessionem totius vite sue inclinavit. Credo eum secundum signa que vidi misericordiam dei consecutum fuisse» *(Fortalitium Fidei contra Judeos Sarracenos aliosque Christiane fidei inimicos* (Lyons, 1511), fol. 339; quoted also by ADOLFO DE CASTRO, *Sobre el Centón epistolario del Bachiller Fernán Gómez de Cibdareal* (Seville, 1875), pp. 82-3n.). See also SÁNCHEZ DE ARÉVALO, *HH*, p. 235: Don Alvaro «qui tam bene mori meruit» cannot have been bad all through.

CHAPTER 7

LEGACIES

For most of Christendom 1453 was the year the Turks took Constantinople; for Castilians it was the year of Alvaro de Luna's fall. Many Castilians knew, of course, what was going on at the other end of the Mediterranean. The better-informed among them had some notion of what it might mean.[1] Thus Alonso de Palencia, interrupting his narrative of home affairs to give an account of the disaster, saw it as a threat to Christians everywhere. Fernán Pérez de Guzmán urged his friend the Marquis of Santillana, as the only poet equal to so great a theme, to mark the fall of the Eastern Empire with suitable verses. Santillana's attempt to do so, in the perhaps ill-chosen form of an Italianate sonnet, was a stirring but scarcely practical call for a new Crusade; about the eclipse of Don Alvaro he had a great deal more to say. As for Palencia, being resident in Rome at the time may well have helped him to get the two events into a proper perspective. Yet this was not quite how he himself saw the matter; rather, he excused his disgression into world affairs on the grounds that the capture of Constantinople had prevented other European nations from taking adequate notice of what had happened in Castile. On the moral and political consciousness of his fellow-countrymen, certainly, the great Constable's arrest, arraignment and death did leave an enduring mark.

It was meant to do so, of course. Above all, the execution itself was staged with that purpose. It was foreshadowed even in the Relator's report on behalf of the Councillors: «that he ought, in law, to be beheaded, and his head displayed on a spike, high on a scaffold, for several days, to be an example to all the great men of your kingdom».[2] In more senses than one, this was to be exemplary punishment; nor was

---

[1] PALENCIA, *Déc*, pp. 52-5 (*CEIV* pp. 49-52); PÉREZ DE GUZMÁN, *Requesta fecha al magnífico marques de Santyllana... sobre la estruycion de Constantynopla*, in FOULCHÉ-DELBOSC, *CC*, vol. I, pp. 677-82; SANTILLANA, *Soneto... amonestando a los grandes principes a tornar sobre el daño de Constantinopla* [Soneto XXXII], ibid., p. 524.
[2] *CJII* (R), p. 682. On ceremonious death-scenes see GARCÍA DE CORTÁZAR, p. 484.

its exemplary force to be confined to a single lesson. Those who might aspire to do what Don Alvaro had done, and were therefore in a position to take the point most directly, were, by definition, the most restricted of minorities. The rest of the noble estate —its larger part by far— the mass of their clients, the clerics and officials and *hidalgos*, who together formed the political nation, would recognize in this ritual cutting off of a head the demonstration of a great political reversal, and of the supremacy of the royal will. For the greater number of those watching, the execution was staged as the sign of something different again —the spiritual lesson that worldly fortune was fickle and dangerous, that the supreme wisdom was to live quietly and die well.

No detail was spared, that second day of June, to make the Constable's punishment memorable and its lesson effective.[3] In the main square of Valladolid, a freshly-erected scaffold stood, richly hung and carpeted. It was furnished with a cross, at which the victim might pray, and set about with lighted torches. In starkly functional contrast to this panoply, an iron hook high on a pole awaited Don Alvaro's head. He, meanwhile, had spent the night in prayer with the two Franciscans who had joined him on the road from Portillo, and who were not to leave him until the end. Early that morning he had taken the sacrament. He broke his fast with a handful of black cherries and a glass of strong wine; he dressed himself in heavy camlet cloth. It would suit neither the official notion of the spectacle to come nor his own if he were, even involuntarily, to shiver, and so give an impression of weakness. An armed escort brought him through the streets riding on a mule. Trumpets were sounded along the way, and the crier read aloud to the watching crowds the proclamation of Don Alvaro's guilt. For two of the spectators, whom he recognized, he had parting messages. He told the Prince's groom, Barrasa, to make sure that Enrique rewarded his servants better than the king was now rewarding his. And, as if to make the same point by other means, he gave his own page, Morales, the ring and the hat which he was wearing —«the last good», as he said, «that you can get of me». Plainly, Don Alvaro was making a demonstration on his own account, and one which did not entirely coincide with that which Juan II had planned for him.

It seems doubtful, even so, whether he actually made all the speeches which our various sources put into his mouth. A witness in 1497 was to remember his reaction to the proclamation: that he accepted the

---

[3] For the date see Fray Alonso de Quiriales in Foronda, pp. 178-9; also Corral, p. 45; Quintana, p. 503; *CD*, p. 77n. Primary narrative sources are *CJII* (R), p. 683 (including the words to Morales); *Abr H*, pp. cci-ccii; *CAL* (C), pp. 431-4. Further details in Corral, p. 94; literary reworkings in Palencia, *Déc*, pp. 50-1 (*CEIV*, pp. 48-9); Sánchez de Arévalo, *HH*, p. 231; Bisticci, pp. 234-5.

charge of cruel tyranny, but denied that he had ever been a traitor. This pertinent comment on the moral balance-sheet of Don Alvaro's career is rendered less credible by the failure of any text of the *pregón* to use the word «traitor» at all. And while the gesture to Morales is credible enough, it seems less likely that the Constable held forth in pathetic vein as Palencia maintains, on his desertion by all save this one page. Nor was there any real need for him to harangue the crowd around the scaffold on the mutability of fortune. The sight of what Don Alvaro now was, and the memory of what he was before, could tell that tale better than any form of words. The words ascribed to him by later historians —especially those who wrote in Latin— have to be seen as expressions of an inescapable literary topic. Yet he may, after all, have had something of the kind to say, if only because it was expected of him. Everything else that he did, marked as it was by an impressively «Roman» fortitude, was attuned to such expectations. He prayed on the scaffold before the cross, and asked those present for their prayers. He walked to and fro about the platform, discussing with his executioner the sharpness of the knife and the purpose of that ominous hook. He received with studied coolness the news that it was for his own head. Just as coolly, he bound his own hands with a light cord, and arranged his clothes so that they should not impede the fatal stroke. Then the executioner begged his forgiveness and passed the knife across his throat. The head was taken off and impaled; it was to remain on display for nine days. The crowd, many of whom must have been among those clamouring for Don Alvaro's death only the previous evening, were abashed and silent. Some wept.

Perhaps the most convincing account of what was in their minds is furnished by Pedro de Escavias —almost certainly not an eyewitness, but an annalist who often seems to catch the common mood of his time, Don Alvaro's death, he writes: «... struck terror into all who saw him... He died with a good countenance and good courage, as a knight and a faithful Christian should. May God forgive him, for he handled many great matters in the days when he enjoyed the king's favour.»[4] Don Alvaro de Luna, master of most situations in his lifetime, had not entirely relinquished his mastery over this one. He made an edifying death, and to all appearances an obedient one, but it was still not quite the end which Juan II had envisaged for him. Morally it was impressive enough; for a man deserted by fortune, Don Alvaro showed a commendable resignation to the will of God. But for a man who had, supposedly, been guilty of grave offences against the king, he did very

---

[4] ESCAVIAS, p. 343. See PÉREZ DE GUZMÁN, above, Chapter 6, n. 57; SÁNCHEZ DE ARÉVALO, ibid.; AENEAS SYLVIUS, *Descriptio Europae*, Ch. VII, quoted by CORRAL, p. 96n.

little indeed to humble himself, and nothing at all to recant his previous political record. No gesture and no word of his could be construed as admitting that he had done Juan II any wrong whatsoever. It was this political ambivalence which so exasperated Fernán Pérez de Guzmán that where others saw pious repentance, he could see only hardihood. Yet the Constable's bearing did make a deep impression on observers of every shade of sympathy. The reports reaching Aeneas Sylvius in Italy and the record transmitted by the hostile Rodrigo Sánchez de Arévalo were as fulsome on this score as Don Alvaro's own chronicle. A rare exception here is the *Lamentación de Don Alvaro de Luna*, a visionary dialogue between the imprisoned Constable and an anonymous author-narrator.[5] This presents Don Alvaro as «womanish in demeanour, clenching his fingers and wringing his hands, crying aloud and groaning beyond all reason». But this abject picture responds to a rhetorical purpose: it makes the consolation offered by the author seem urgent and effectual. The writer of the original text —composed in Latin and now lost— was almost certainly a cleric; possibly he was a connection of the Franciscan Espina, who had played a very similar role in real life to that of the narrator here. But the Alvaro de Luna of real life counts for little in this sermonizing work; what matters is his value as a topical instance of how a Christian can best be prepared to face adversity. It was as easy to abstract that single aspect from his story as any other.

This same instant exemplarity marks the response to his death at a wide variety of cultural levels.[6] Often this aspect overshadows or displaces both the record of events and any direct comment thereon. Thus it was popularly said that astrologers had told Don Alvaro he would die in Cadalso, a village on his Escalona estates. He had avoided the place all his life, only to end it on the scaffold (in Castilian, *cadalso*) in Valladolid. The tale is traditional and endlessly adaptable; Henry IV of England and the Jerusalem Chamber offer a near-contemporary instance. At the opposite extreme from this folkloric response is the scholarly Alonso de Palencia, the most insistently political of fifteenth-century

---

[5] Ed. Bertini, pp. 79-96; see esp. p. 79. The translator (p. 93) was Juan de Villafranca; that the narrator asks Don Alvaro's name (p. 80) suggests that the author was not a retainer of his; the pattern of Biblical references suggests a clerical background; for Espina see above, pp. 207-10.

[6] The Cadalso story is in *Abr H*, p. ccii, and in some later accounts, e.g. Mariana, p. 138. STITH THOMPSON, *Motif-Index of Folk Literature*, vol. V (Copenhagen, 1957), p. 57, M. 341.3, mentions Jewish, Irish and Indian analogues; for Classical and English parallels, see RICHARD CAREW, *A Survey of Cornwall*, ed. F. E. Halliday (London, 1953), p. 88. In fact, Don Alvaro had visited Cadalso on a hunting trip in 1452 (*CAL* (C), p. 290). Palencia's letter to an unknown «P. Lunensi» is in MS Burgo de Osma, Catedral, Cod. 57, fol 124r. I am grateful to Professor R. B. Tate for notice of this document, now published in ALFONSO DE PALENCIA, *Epístolas latinas*, ed. Robert B. Tate and Rafael Alemany Ferrer (Barcelona, 1982), pp. 42-3.

Spanish historians. Yet his letter to a friend reporting the news of Don Alvaro's death does not venture beyond the most anodyne of generalities: this «notable proof of the vanity of the world» illustrates the wisdom of those who «set no great store by any earthly thing, love nothing vain, covet nothing base or inflated». Perhaps Palencia was merely being tactful, for the recipient of his letter himself bore the Luna surname, and greater candour could have been out of place. But the link between the execution and topics of Stoic indifference, like that with other lines of ethical reflection, was easy to establish. It may also have been hard to resist, even at the cost of more rigorous political analysis.

This was, to some degree, the case with the Marquis of Santillana who, as an active enemy of the Constable over many years, knew well what was the political heart of the matter.[7] He even wrote minor verse about it —a sonnet on Juan II's «well-achieved liberty». But his reaction to the specifically moral dimension of Don Alvaro's fall produced two much longer poems which are, by any standards, major work. They remain, of course, strongly political poems —especially the *Coplas* beginning «De tu resplandor, o Luna,/ te ha privado la Fortuna.» Pungent, aggressive, unfair, combining raw triumph with savage inventiveness, this work has —though it does not wholly sustain them— some of the qualities of the best committed poetry. But even the *Coplas* do more than celebrate Luna's discomfiture; they also interpret that event as Fortune's revenge. The more widely admired *Doctrinal de Privados* uses artistic distance more subtly; it is Don Alvaro himself who speaks the hard lessons of his life and imminent death, and who voices his own need of forgiveness. Yet the poem is unrelentingly harsh in assessing his public record; the difference from the *Coplas* is that this assessment is here located in a richer ethical scheme. The Don Alvaro of the *Doctrinal* is still an involuntary witness to any sort of political good; his sufferings are still deserved. Yet this avowedly unworthy individual is made the bearer of universal moral experience, for all men are sinners, and all require to be forgiven. In that specific sense, this is a profounder, more reflective poem than the *Coplas*. At the same time it does not abandon its author's partisanship, any more than the *Coplas,* partisan as they are, can dispense with his moralistic vision of what Fortune is and does.

The *Doctrinal* is about political morality, not political history. That does not prevent it from being the finest single poem to take its inspira-

---

[7] SANTILLANA, *Otro soneto... al señor rey don Iohan* [Soneto XXXI], in FOULCHÉ-DELBOSC, *CC*, vol. I, p. 524; *Coplas del dicho señor marques*, ibid., pp. 497-503; *Doctrinal de privados*, ibid., pp. 503-8. For critical comment see LAPESA, pp. 225-33; DAVID WILLIAM FOSTER, *The Marqués de Santillana* (New York, 1971), pp. 39-47; MARÍA ROSA LIDA DE MALKIEL, *Estudios sobre la literatura española del siglo XV* (Madrid, 1977), p. 384n.; MICHÈLE S. DE CRUZ-SÁENZ, «The Marqués de Santillana's *Coplas* on Don Alvaro de Luna and the *Doctrinal de privados*», *HR*, 49 (1981), 219-24.

tion from Don Alvaro's death. There were other attempts at a response by other poets.[8] Fernando de la Torre wrote a prolix and classicizing *Testamento del Maestre de Santiago,* and the Catalan Berenguer Masdovelles composed an ascetic meditation of admirable bleakness on the Constable's fall. But most writers of fifteenth-century verse tended to deploy Don Alvaro as an incidental example, rather than to set down their reactions to him at length. Sometimes this tendency produces a certain narrowing of perspective: instead of learning what these authors thought about Don Alvaro, we seem to learn only what they thought they should think. Thus Don Pedro of Portugal ranges him with Midas and Croesus to prove that great riches bring great misery, and again with Haman and Seneca to show the insecure state of *privados*. Yet Don Pedro had known the man, and his awareness, at one and the same time, of the Constable's «great and singular struggle with Fortune» and of his «intolerable crimes» implies a complex personal reaction of which one would gladly learn more. Gómez Manrique's merely conventional reference to Don Alvaro's greatness and fall becomes interesting only with his wry political afterthought that later *privados* are unlikely to heed this example much in practice. And even the glamour and pathos with which Jorge Manrique imbues the vanished figure of «that great Constable/whom we knew», presents the reader with a dilemma. Was this really how Alvaro de Luna was remembered in the 1470s? Or do these associations merely serve the purposes of Manrique's own poem?

Direct memories of Don Alvaro gradually gave place to a picture which was formed in some part by these literary traditions, in part by popular tales like the Cadalso story, but most of all by the body of historical writing about him. From this last, however, there was no consensus of views to be derived, but only the tangle of conflicting testimonies to which the present study has sought to do justice. Whether Castilians of the sixteenth and later centuries thought well or ill of Don Alvaro was liable to depend on the sources which lay to their hand or, if these were in conflict, on whichever source they found most convincing. It might have been expected, then, that the received image of Alvaro

---

[8] See BARTOLOMÉ JOSÉ GALLARDO, *Ensayo de una biblioteca española*, vol. I (Madrid, 1968; 1st edition Madrid, 1863), cols 580-5; FERNANDO DE LA TORRE, *Cancionero*, pp. xxx-xxxi; also ANTONIO PÉREZ GÓMEZ, *Romancero de Don Alvaro de Luna* (Valencia, 1953), pp. 24-31; ALFRED MOREL-FATIO, *Catalogue des MSS Espagnols et des MSS Portugais de la Bibliothèque Nationale de Paris* (Paris, 1892), no. 525 (Masdovelles); CONDESTÁVEL DON PEDRO, pp. 48, 56-7; GÓMEZ MANRIQUE, [Consolación a la Condesa de Castro] in FOULCHÉ-DELBOSC, *CC*, vol. II, p. 63; JORGE MANRIQUE, *Coplas que fizo por la muerte de su padre*, in *Cancionero*, ed. Augusto Cortina (Madrid, 1929), pp. 222-3: «aquel grand condestable, /maestre que conoscimos»; other poems include items by Juan de Padilla and Juan de Valladolid (PÉREZ GÓMEZ, pp. 17, 20, 31-3); by Pero Guillén de Segovia (DUTTON, *Catálogo-índice*, p. 134); by Juan Agraz and Diego de Valera (ibid., p. 32); for an anonymous attack on the fallen Constable see ibid., p. 32.

de Luna would become less favourable as the official version of events, embodied in Galíndez's 1517 edition of the royal chronicle, gradually imposed itself on the public mind. In fact, just the opposite tendency prevailed.

One possible explanation for this is furnished by the extraordinary literary qualities of Don Alvaro's personal chronicle.[9] Projecting itself as a tribute of simple-hearted chivalresque loyalty, Gonzalo Chacón's life of his late master is a work of intense and subtly-orchestrated rhetoric. It challenges the official record of Don Alvaro's misdeeds and their punishment with the bold claim that the «virtuous and blessed» Constable suffered without cause. It adds its own tragic gloss to the usual didactic commonplaces; it is the hero's trusting nobility of soul which renders him vulnerable to Fortune. All this was immensely persuasive, but its circulation was probably limited. The *Crónica,* after all, implied much harsh criticism of Juan II, and was unlikely to be well received in the Castile of Juan's daughter, Isabel the Catholic, despite her cordial relationship with Chacón himself. Even after her death, it would have seemed tactless to present any king of Castile in quite so contemptible a public light. It may well be, then, that the work was little read outside the circle of Don Alvaro's own descendants until 1546, when his great-grandson had an edition printed in Milan. The fact that no manuscript earlier than the sixteenth century survives, and that most of those which do survive were found by Carriazo to be closely related to the printed text supports the view that few Castilians read the *Crónica de Don Alvaro* before this date. It may also indicate that later readers found some difficulty in obtaining printed copies.

Chacón's work certainly had an influence, however, on the ballads which were composed about Alvaro de Luna from the mid sixteenth century onwards, and on the seventeenth-century plays dealing with his life and downfall.[10] It was these imaginative genres which did most to propagate the view of the Constable as an innocent victim. That view, it should be stressed, was in no sense a product of surviving popular tradition about him, for while both genres have strong popular roots, the particular works in question do not. Both ballads and plays tend to be among the more sophisticated examples of their kind; Quevedo and Mira de Amescua figure in their respective lists of authors. Their subject-matter, when not actually invented, comes from the reworking

---

[9] On the Chronicle see LIDA DE MALKIEL, *La idea de la fama en la Edad Media castellana* (Mexico City, 1952), pp. 240-51; MACCURDY, pp. 99-103. See also, *CAL* (C), pp. 434 («el virtuoso e bienaventurado Maestre y Condestable»); 436-7 (Chacón and Isabel); xiii-xiv (the Milan edition); xvi-xx (the manuscripts).

[10] For the ballads see PÉREZ GÓMEZ, *Romancero.* No. XVII there (pp. 108-9) is exceptional: it antedates the Milan *Crónica* (ibid., p. 16); it is hostile to Don Alvaro, and though largely based on the royal chronicle, it has a clear grasp of the nature of the Constable's main offence as «crimen 'lese majestatis'» (p. 109). For the plays see MACCURDY, *The Tragic Fall,* passim.

of the written historical record, including, of course, the *Crónica de Don Alvaro*. Both genres, then, reflect an educated interest in Alvaro de Luna, forming rather than following his popular image. It is easy to see why such an interest should have persisted, especially in the half-century after 1600: Don Alvaro had been the prototype of royal *privados*, and the *privado* was as fascinating and problematic a figure in Spanish affairs then as he had been two centuries earlier.[11] It is less clear why these works should have opted with such near-unanimity for the most favourable view of Don Alvaro's motives and actions. Quite possibly Chacón's chronicle had less to do with it than did the need —natural to either genre— for a suitably extraordinary and dramatic story.

Certainly our non-fictional accounts of Don Alvaro from the same period are very much less predictable in tone.[12] The late sixteenth-century annalist Gonzalo de Illescas presented his fall in strongly exemplary terms: royal favourites ought to learn from it, he declared «and not get above themselves». In the following century the antiquary Gil González de Avila was well aware of the literary tradition —«his fortune and fall are widely celebrated in Spain in verse and prose»— but himself strove for a balanced view: «He loved himself well and he loved himself ill.» The great Jesuit historian Mariana regarded Don Alvaro with a temperate disfavour; the author of the early eighteenth-century *Historia de la privanza y caída de Don Alvaro* declined to pronounce at all on the vexed question of his guilt. Other similar accounts are less self-denying: the *Causa escrita a Don Alvaro,* for example, offers a forceful apologia, written with Chacón much in mind. But most of those who confronted Don Alvaro's story as a matter of historical record recognized that various elements in that record were still controversial. The arguments were kept alive, in great part, by the dispute of the Mendozas, who stood to gain property if Don Alvaro's condemnation were overturned, and the Pachecos, who stood to lose unless it were upheld.[13]

---

[11] In the early 18th century, the *privado* theme inspired two contrasting non-Spanish accounts of Don Alvaro: the French *Histoire du Connêtable*, richer in maxims of state than in historical authenticity, and the *Life of Don Alvaro de Luna* (London, 1715) of the anti-Catholic pamphleteer Michael Geddes —an astute, well-documented political biography of «the top Favorite I have anywhere met with in History» (p. 228).

[12] GONZALO DE ILLESCAS, *Segunda parte de la historia pontifical y cathólica* (Burgos, 1578), fol. 118v; GONZÁLEZ DE AVILA, *Teatro*, vol. IV, p. 35; MARIANA, *Historia de España*, pp. 138-9; *Historia de la privanza y caída*, fol. 9r; *Causa escrita*, passim. Other historical memoirs in MS include the *Nacimiento, vida, prisión y muerte de don Alvaro de Luna* (MS Madrid, BN, 11011), seen by CARRIAZO, and the unfinished *Noticia de Don Alvaro de Luna* (MS Madrid, RAH, 9.147 (CS, B.33) fols. 154-67).

[13] See above, Chapter 5, n. 35; also *Causa escrita*, fols 46-7 (innocence proclaimed under Enrique IV); ABARCA, in *CAL* (F), p. 473 (verdict overturned «much later», but Abarca could not trace the occasion); SILIÓ, p. 254 (Council decree «towards 1658»); *Consultas del Consejo... Años 1714-16,* MS Madrid,

Hence the careful preservation in the Pacheco archives of the evidence gathered in 1497 to prove that a trial had taken place. Hence, too, Salazar y Mendoza's attempted rehabilitation of Don Alvaro. Those who maintained the Constable's innocence liked to believe that this had been officially recognized in some way; there were stories of Enrique IV making such recognition public. But this did not prevent them from seeking a similar ruling from the Council of Castile in or around 1658, nor did whatever success they had then prevent the Council, some sixty years later, from using the Luna case as a precedent in its discussion of the penalties for *lesa majestad notoria*. It was still worth someone's while as late as 1755 to try to locate Alvaro de Luna's will; the attempt was, naturally, a failure.

Thus, neither the long literary tradition stemming from Don Alvaro's death nor the equally persistent legal controversy initiated by it can bring us very much nearer to the meaning of that event. A variety of didactic and exemplary concerns alter the perspective of our literary texts; vested interests mean that much of the legal argument has to be treated with caution. Don Alvaro's first and most lasting legacy to his fellow-countrymen —a legacy of topic and example for their contemplation and discussion— was liable to obscure rather than clarify the history of his life and end.

Only occasionally does it achieve more, as when Rodrigo Sánchez de Arévalo, piling topic upon topic, equates the changeable intentions of kings with Fortune in its this-worldly aspect.[14] They are perilous, he declares, but ultimately governed by God. This was a bold attempt to make ethical sense of those very aspects of the case which gave most offence to Don Alvaro's supporters —the abrupt change in the king's attitude towards him, and the fact that he was dying «at the king's command». But it was a cardinal point of orthodox wisdom about Fortune that the Fortune of this world was really Providence. Rodrigo Sánchez, in effect, was claiming that in political affairs the king's will, however capricious it might appear, was God's providence in action. We are very close indeed here to such concepts as *certa scientia* and the royal vicariate, and in fact Rodrigo Sánchez justifies his view with a Biblical quotation which was important in just this context: «the heart of the king is in the hand of God.» Once again it becomes clear

---

BN, 905, fol. 110r; León Tello, *Duques de Frías*, vol. II, p. 347 (search for will).

[14] Sánchez de Arévalo, *HH*, p. 234: «vnus ex sapientibus ait, quia vt fortuna, sic voluntas regum varia & inconstans, ac semper incerta, veluti quae semper à multis concutitur, sed tandem à Deo dirigitur. Nec enim mysterio vacat, quia scriptura sacra testante, cor regis in manu Dei est.» See above, Chapter 4, n. 13. For the topic «Fortune is Providence» see Juan de Dios Mendoza Negrillo, *Fortuna y providencia en la literatura castellana del siglo XV* (Madrid, 1973), pp. 95-209. See also, more generally, Howard R. Patch, *The Goddess Fortuna in Mediaeval Literature* (Cambridge, Mass., 1927).

how the ethical wisdom fostered by Juan II as a patron of culture served the ends of the regalist ideology which he and his chancery officials were developing in the political field. The most remarkable aspect, though, is that this is not a chancery document advancing regalist claims but a historical record of what has actually occurred. When all due allowance has been made for the fact that Rodrigo Sánchez himself was a strongly ideological historian, it remains striking that he was able to write in this way at all. What made his claim plausible was, precisely, the demonstration of Juan II's power in the execution of Don Alvaro. The beheading of 2nd June had given substance to the ideological claims of the documents issued in April and May. In that important sense, the obvious beneficiary of Don Alvaro's death was Juan II himself.

It brought him other advantages too, both in the shorter and the longer term. Most immediately, it meant that an end to the fighting around Escalona could not be long delayed. The execution, of course, was a bitter blow to the besieged, and may initially have hardened their defiance. Objectively, on the other hand, it left them with nothing to fight for, and removed any incentive for others further afield to join them. Once the rebels had acknowledged this, terms could be made.[15] In the first days of June, Fernando de Ribadeneira chose to surrender Maqueda, rather than defy his king in arms. This allowed Juan to lift a temporary levy which he had imposed on Toledo to pay for the war, and to tighten his military grip on Escalona. While the latter held out, his public stance remained intransigent; the latest document to express this attitude was his open letter of 18th June, justifying to the Castilian authorities what had been done to Don Alvaro. This ends with a stern warning against aid to the insurgents, but its main purpose was to make Juan II's definitive version of events a matter of public record. In so doing, it also implied a message for the rebels; that, whatever clemency the king might show, the accumulation of power and wealth built up by Don Alvaro was going to be broken. Hence, perhaps, the letter's timing; it is quite possible that negotiations with those inside Escalona were already in progress. Certainly by 23rd June there had been some exchange of draft terms, and a conditional settlement with Don Alvaro's widow could at last be reached. Escalona surrendered forthwith, and its defenders were pardoned. The agreement was ratified on 28th June, by which time Juan had set up his headquarters within the castle; on the 30th the financial terms of the surrender were settled.

---

[15] See above, Chapter 5, n. 20 (surrender of Maqueda); MS Madrid, BN, 13109, fols 49r-50v (Toledo levy lifted); above, pp. 153-6 (letter of 18th June); *CD*, no. XLI, p. 91 (its warning on aid to rebels); no. XLII, pp. 92-6 (conditional pardon, 23rd June, inserted in confirmation on 28th); p. 95 (earlier negotiation); no. XLIII, pp. 96-100 (detailed settlement, 30th June, inserted in confirmation and clarification —Juan had inadvertently given away some of the properties concerned— of 13th July).

In giving legal form to all this, the same conscious plenitude of royal power which had been deployed a few months earlier to dismantle Don Alvaro's formal authority was required to lift the sanctions imposed on his followers, and to protect his widow's position. The papers of the settlement are as thickly studded as their predecessors with formulae of derogation and of total sovereignty. They had to be; there was a great deal, including much earlier derogation, to be set aside. Though the issue of a pardon was one context where such formulae could be used without a great deal of specific constitutional relevance, it can seldom have been necessary to go as far as this:

> ... notwithstanding any protestations and demands... which I may have made, or might make, and... any laws... which are or may be against the foregoing... and notwithstanding the laws of my realms which require pardons to be in a certain form, and notwithstanding the laws which say that letters issued contrary to any law... must be obeyed but not complied with, even though they may contain clauses of derogation of any kind... and although valid laws... cannot be derogated except in Cortes...[16]

Juan II, of course, was pleased to assume that he was entitled to act in this way. But his willingness to do so also reflects a disposition to smooth the way to a settlement, if not actually to make things easy for Don Alvaro's widow.

The financial agreement with Juana Pimentel was neither punitive nor magnanimous; the king took his profit but left the lady with what, in her station in life, amounted to more than a competence. She was obliged to hand over the entire treasure of Escalona, of which, provided that she did so without concealment, she would retain a third. The sum, as we shall see, was considerable, but so was the corresponding forfeiture. A more detailed division was made of the grants and property which the king had confiscated from Don Alvaro. The Countess was to go on receiving many of them.[17] There was her dowry. There were also a number of other rights and inheritances of unknown value, and identi-

---

[16] CD, no. XLII, p. 94: «non embargante qualesquier protestaciones, é reclamaciones... en caso que los yo oviese fecho ó fesiese, é... qualesquier fueros é derechos... que en contrario sea ó ser pueda de lo susodicho... nin otrosí embargantes las leyes de mis regnos que dan cierta forma en los perdones, nin embargantes las leyes que dicen que las cartas dadas contra ley... deben ser obedecidas é non complidas, aunque contengan qualesquier cláusulas derogatorias... é que las leyes é fueros é derechos valederos non puedan ser derogados, salvo por cortes.» The formula *obedecidas é non complidas* was the device traditionally used in laws made in *Cortes* for invalidating particular royal acts without impugning royal authority as such.

[17] CD, no. XLIII, pp. 97-8; see also CAL (F), p. 437. LADERO QUESADA, *Hacienda*, p. 263 gives the yield of some of these revenues (Montalbán, El Colmenar, Halhamín, La Torre, El Prado, San Martín) in 1453-4. All are recorded, along with others of unknown value (Castil de la Vayuela, La Higuera) as being

fiable grants to the tune of some 770,000 *maravedís*. At a rough estimate, she may have received about a million —less than a fifth of Don Alvaro's original holding, but a very substantial recurrent income nonetheless. And if, in 1453 and 1454, many of these revenues seem to have found their way into the royal accounts, it was not long before Doña Juana was taking her cut of others. On 10th July, for example, she was authorized to receive 30,000 *maravedís* out of the proceeds of the Relator's Andalusian tax-office.

Clearly, there was no attempt made to ruin the Luna family. But it is equally clear that Juan II was concerned to undo the formidable concentration of economic power which Don Alvaro had amassed. Some, though not all, of his confiscations have a logic of their own.[18] For example, the king was bound to resume all the various local offices held by Don Alvaro. (These, of course, did not represent a clear profit, as they would eventually pass to other holders.) Again, the agreement of 30th June insists with particular force that Juan should recover the fortresses which Alvaro de Luna had held as Master of Santiago, especially those in Extremadura. Consistently with this, he also confiscated the revenues which the Constable had acquired in these same localities. But he had no coherent approach to those ecclesiastical taxes whose acquisition by Don Alvaro he had previously singled out as an abuse. Some of these *tercias* passed, with other revenues from the same areas, to Juana Pimentel; others —the majority— were retained by the king. As for the town of Montalbán, which Don Alvaro was alleged to have obtained improperly by putting pressure on the late queen of Castile, this was allowed to pass to his widow as the major element in her surviving estate. But the great castle of Escalona was to be the king's prize. The broad arc of Luna-dominated territories, the Constable's own lands and the lands of Santiago, stretching from the central mountain-ranges to the Portuguese border with its outposts elsewhere, had been erased from the political map. Besides being much richer, Juan could think himself much more secure once that was done.

It followed from this that there was to be no immediate redistribution of the confiscated properties. A good many of them subsequently found their way into Pacheco hands; the Marquis of Villena eventually came to control Escalona, for example, and the family's lawsuit with the Mendozas was to turn on the possession of Don Alvaro's old County of San Esteban.[19] But it was Enrique IV and not his father who initiated

---

paid to the crown. Doña Juana also received payments in Adarnola, Adrada, Berciana, Calera, Candeleda, Carcañosa, Noalos, Valdiitar and Villanueva. For her share of the Relator's *escribanía de rentas*, see AGS, M y P, 55.40.

[18] *CD*, p. 98 for the Santiago castles (Trujillo, Alburquerque, Montanches, Asagala, etc.). LADERO QUESADA, loc, cit., for revenues there. On the *tercias* and on Montalbán see *CD*, no. XLI, p. 85; on Escalona, *CCG*, p. 136.

[19] See TORRES FONTES, *Itinerario*, p. 234 (Escalona); LEÓN TELLO, *Duques de*

that development. Most of Juan II's dispositions that we know of had to do with minor readjustments to the Escalona estate. Juana Pimentel's Jewish physician, Rabbi Salamón, who had lost property to the king in Escalona itself, was compensated on 4th July with an olive press and various orchards from Juan's confiscations in Maqueda; apparently he had done some service for the king, whom we know to have been in poor health. On July 23rd, Juan gave orders for the village of Cadalso to be separated from the main Escalona estate. It is not likely that the popular legend about the place had anything to do with this, for Cadalso, with other minor properties, had been allocated in late June to the king's personal page Juan de Villegas. Another page, Alfonso de Illescas —perhaps a relative of the ill-fated Gómez González— received certain Escalona tolls, and property in Maqueda. Other retainers again —guards, pages, crossbowmen, a muleteer, a secretary— were similarly small-scale beneficiaries. The poet Juan de Mena, as royal chronicler, got 13,000 *maravedís* in the gaming tolls of his native Córdoba; a fellow-magistrate there got 6,000. The pattern of minor allocations to minor dependants appears well-established. For the most part, Juan seems to have been content to hold on to his confiscations and let his balances mount up. A group of forty exempted taxpayers, formerly designated by the Constable —an especially sought-after form of fiscal concession— had still not been reallocated in January 1454; a grant out of Don Alvaro's wealth to a hospital in Medina del Campo was not made until May 1455. The Simancas accounts of confiscated revenues in 1453 and 1454, published in summary by Ladero, confirm this picture in a general way. Though they present many problems of interpretation, they make it clear that most of these revenues continued from year to year. Juan II, then, was disposed to give little away. Apart from the settlement with the Countess, the most immediate call on the confiscated items was the filling of salaried offices which the Constable had held. The Relator's Andalusian post was one of these; so was a parallel office in Cuenca, which went to the king's domestic Arias Gómez de Silva in July.

Yet if there were to be no large-scale gainers —the king himself excepted— from the Luna affair, there were to be few serious losers. Juan II's mood is well caught by a story told by Rodrigo Sánchez de

Frías, vol. II, p. 255 (San Esteban); ibid., p. 185 and F. BAER, *Die Juden in christlichen Spanien,* vol. II (Berlin, 1936), p. 325 (Rabbi Salamón); MS Madrid, BN 13109, fols 83-4 (Cadalso); AGS, printed catalogue, PR, vol. II (Valladolid, 1949), p. 117 (Alfonso de Illescas); M y P, 2.500 (Don Alvaro's *escusados,* but contrast the reallocation of thirteen such concessions in November 1453 (QUINTANA, p. 503); above, pp. 198-200 (the Relator); LEÓN TELLO, p. 10 (Arias Gómez de Silva). Other minor beneficiaries included the monastery of Santa María de Valdeiglesias (ibid., p. 450). A more general picture of minor grants from June 1453 to May 1455 is in *Sal Inds,* XX 33.327 (CS F.41). See also AGS, *EMdR,* 540.676; MS catalogue, fol. 38r.

Arévalo, flattering though it is to the king's clemency.[20] Some courtiers, it seems, wanted Juan II to alter the grandiose monument which Don Alvaro had prepared for himself in Toledo Cathedral. «No», said the king «for we think it right that dying men, since they can do nothing else, should be able to write about themselves as they please.» In fact it was to be some considerable time before Don Alvaro's body was interred where he had wished it to be, but the absence of rancour in this reported episode is of a piece with Juan's conduct at the time. With the single exception of the secretary Zafra, no follower of Don Alvaro appears to have been pursued once the execution and the Escalona campaign were over. Luis de La Cerda, who had been under suspicion —indeed, under arrest at one stage— in Burgos, was actually made lieutenant of Escalona itself; Fernando de Ribadeneira appears to have gone on drawing his salary as a member of the king's guard, as he had done since 1429, without interruption. As for the imprisoned Licenciate Ruy García de Villalpando, we do not know whether it was Juan II or Enrique IV who rehabilitated him; we do know that he served Enrique as a judge of appeal until his death in 1459. Interpreting all this psychologically, we might conclude that the execution in Valladolid had assuaged Juan's need of violent revenge; once that catharsis was past, he could behave humanely once more. But if Don Alvaro's death is envisaged first and foremost as a political act, it becomes clear that, in showing forbearance now, Juan was consistently pursuing a political end. He was seeking not to work out a residual personal resentment, but to reach the kind of overall settlement in Castile to which the removal of the Constable had given him access.

The form which that settlement might take had been implicit even in the grim words with which the Relator had announced the Council's finding against Don Alvaro. The beheading was to be «an example to all the great men of your kingdom» (*CJII* (R), p. 682). It was not often that the lawyers of the administration allowed themselves a public voice in criticism of the dominant class whose affairs they were employed to order, and of its habitual political style. But this, surely, was one such occasion. In all that unanimous assembly, not one magnate would speak a word in favour of Don Alvaro's record; yet most of them, given the chance to emulate it, would have regarded the pursuit of those lands and revenues, that authority in council, that power over offices and policies, as their rightful field of activity. They might resent the *privado*, but they had nothing against *privanza;* that they understood, and the

---

[20] SÁNCHEZ DE ARÉVALO, *HH*, p. 236; see *CAL* (C), pp. 435, 437 on Don Alvaro's burial. For Zafra, La Cerda and Villalpando, see above, p. 61; on La Cerda, also *CCG*, pp. 136-7; on Ribadeneira, the entry in AGS, QdC, 3.131 (1456) mentions no recent irregularity of payments; Villalpando was *oidor* again by May 1455, *Sal Inds*, 31, no. 49.677; for his death see AGS, QdC, 2.153.

means of getting and holding it they thought they understood. Fernán Díaz, with the king's evident support, was letting them know that there was no future in this. The experiment in rule by *privado* was not going to be repeated with a change of proper names. Yet if the magnates were being advised, as individuals, not to attempt that course, they were also being invited, as a body, to seek the alternative —a tacitly agreed balance of power. That option was, in many ways, attractive; it meant less tension, less uncertainty, and in the end less resentment, for as the Marquis of Santillana was to observe, the Castilians did not take to viceroys.[21] The king's handling of Archbishop Carrillo —deeply compromised with the Constable, but allowed to extricate himself from the proceedings without embarrassment— offered an object-lesson in how things were to be managed from now on. So did the settlement on 10th June, while Escalona was still under siege, of Carrillo's long-standing dispute with the see of Burgos. The reconciliation, perhaps directly promoted by the Crown, was witnessed in the king's camp by Doctor Pero Díaz de Toledo, who had sat as one of Don Alvaro's judges. Another protracted feud involving Burgos was to take a step towards its resolution later in the summer. The wool-merchants of that city, and the shipmasters of Santander, who had been at odds over customs dues since 1451, reached a temporary agreement on 8th August. But even the general reduction of tensions went ahead cautiously. The political prisoners of the last few years were not immediately freed. Diego Gómez Manrique, Count of Treviño, for example, remained in custody until the reign of Enrique IV. So too, did the Count of Alba, though now under more relaxed conditions; Sancho Falconi of Segovia, who had plotted his escape, was given a pardon in August. Even this, however, came from Prince Enrique, not the king. The fall of Don Alvaro was not allowed to become —as a general amnesty would have made it— the triumph of some other party. Juan's extreme caution in reallocating the Constable's revenues, and still more, the fact that there was no nomination for the vacant Mastership of Santiago, confirmed the new direction of his domestic policy.

His intention was that it should be his own policy. He had been urged from many quarters —the *Cortes,* Santillana, even Alfonso of Ara-

---

[21] *Sobre la quartana del señor rey don Johan II,* in FOULCHÉ-DELBOSC, *CC,* vol I, p. 517. This exchange of verses with Juan de Mena is commonly referred to the king's serious illness of 1453-4 (MIGUEL ANGEL PÉREZ PRIEGO, ed. JUAN DE MENA, *Obra lírica* (Madrid, 1979), p. 229, but has elements of political commentary, if not of political allegory. On Carrillo see above, p. 140; also SERRANO, pp. 202-4; on Burgos and Santander, SUÁREZ FERNÁNDEZ, *Navegación y comercio en el golfo de Vizcaya* (Madrid, 1959), pp. 120-1; on the prisoners, VALERA, *Memorial,* pp. 7-8; also DIEGO DE COLMENARES, *Historia de la insigne ciudad de Segovia* (Segovia, 1969), p. 593.

gon— to take charge of affairs himself.[22] And he was willing enough to do so. The Aragonese ambassadors who met him in Tordesillas, probably in late July, found him full of the news of Don Alvaro's execution —«seeking to take great credit for it», in Zurita's phrase. But these same envoys saw his elation as unjustified. A new power-struggle with Prince Enrique seemed to be in the offing, and Juan himself looked ill-equipped to exercise much initiative of his own. Since Don Alvaro's death, «the king had gone to sleep, and people were waiting for him to wake up again». These judgments, of course, may well be coloured by the ambassadors' disappointment at the lack of any dramatic shift away from Don Alvaro's eastern policies. But they did find Juan II in dangerously poor health; he had been ill, perhaps at Escalona, certainly on his way north from there, and the quartan ague which would break his health altogether was to attack him within a few weeks of the embassy's arrival.[23] Arguably he was in no condition to assume direct charge of government. There may also have been temperamental obstacles to his doing so. The tales of Juan's melancholia in the *Crónica de Don Alvaro,* and Palencia's stories of his sensual over-indulgence doubtless serve polemic ends; they still accord reasonably well with the impression, implicit in the Aragonese narrative, of a personality subject to abrupt changes of mood. But these things did not matter as much as fifteenth-century observers sometimes thought they did. What mattered was that whoever did manage the kingdom's affairs should do so in no other interest but that of the Crown.

That consideration was fully met by Juan's choice of chief ministers.[24] Of the two men whom he had summoned to his side when he reached Avila in the course of his journey north, Bishop Barrientos of Cuenca had a background of proven loyalty. He also had a useful degree of influence over his former pupil, Prince Enrique. The single blemish on his record is the story in Zurita that, shortly after Don Alvaro's arrest,

---

[22] See above, p. 86 and 215; ZURITA, *AA,* fol. 21r (Lib. XVI, Cap. XVII); ibid., fol. 14r-v (Cap. X).

[23] It seems likely that Rabbi Salomón (above, n. 19) had had to treat Juan II in Escalona. *CJII* (R), p. 692 speaks of the king's worsening health on a journey north through Avila and Medina; its chronology is faulty, conflating events in 1453 and 1454, but this journey clearly belongs to the former year. *CCG,* p. 140 states that Juan fell seriously ill in Tordesillas, two months after Don Alvaro's death, and suffered a quartan ague for six months thereafter (i.e. August 1453-February 1454); he never fully recovered. See also *CAL* (C), p. 434; PALENCIA, *Déc,* p. 56; (*CEIV,* p. 53).

[24] On BARRIENTOS see above, pp. 207-9; also ZURITA, *AA,* fol. 21r (Lib. XVI, Cap. XVII); on Illescas, ibid., fol. 31r (Cap. XXVIII); ALBERT A. SICROFF, «The Jeronymite Monastery of Guadalupe in 14th and 15th century Spain», in HORNIK, pp. 397-422 (esp. pp. 405-6; 413n.); GERMÁN RUBIO, *Historia de Nuestra Señora de Guadalupe* (Barcelona, 1926), pp. 91, 97-9. The monastery had seen some of its revenues usurped by Don Alvaro (p. 99), but it also acted as Fernando de Ribadeneira's bank (pp. 96-7).

he had tried to set up an alliance between Enrique and Juan of Navarre, promising the latter territories in Castile. This is extraordinary, partly because Barrientos had stoutly resisted the last Navarrese invasion in 1449, and still more because Enrique could have had no intention of negotiating seriously. The assets in Castile which the Navarrese king was most anxious to recover for himself were precisely those held by Enrique and his associates. Yet the episode can hardly be pure fiction, since it left some mark in Zurita's Aragonese sources. Possibly it was a diplomatic feint, designed to probe the king of Navarre's intentions and to distract him from unilateral action against Castile in the critical months before Don Alvaro's execution. At all events, the Aragonese historical tradition is strongly hostile to Barrientos. Juan II, for his part, had no doubts about him. His colleague, Friar Gonzalo de Illescas, the Prior of Guadalupe, was the head of a unique institution. Foremost in reputation among Jeronymite monasteries, Guadalupe was subject to no episcopal authority except the Pope. A notable centre of pilgrimage, spirituality, and economic life, it enjoyed the special protection and lavish endowment of the Trastámara house; Juan II's own first wife was buried there. Yet the Prior, forbidden by statute to accept any position which would entail his absence from the monastery, was an essentially non-political figure. Only the fact that his three-year term as Prior was coming to an end enabled Friar Gonzalo to break his rule now and join Juan II at court. Once there, he was to prove himself totally the king's man. Even in Juan's last months, when most officials were busily recommending themselves to the heir apparent, the Prior, together with young Alvaro de Estúñiga and the Relator, remained single-mindedly close to the dying king.

The two ministers were at once presented with a formidable agenda. The royal chronicler (*CJII* (R), p. 692) says that Juan deputed them to carry out «many things which it was his intention to do». The two or three which this source actually mentions make it clear that nothing short of a full-scale reform programme was intended. An attempt was to be made to raise a standing army of 8,000 lances; there was a scheme to abolish tax-farming and entrust the collection of revenue to the local authorities, and it was proposed to forbid local officials of any kind to live as household clients of anyone but the king. There were foreign policy aims too, but these domestic proposals were striking enough. They implied that the king should repossess himself, in the most direct way possible, of the military initiative in Castile, of the full capacity of his revenues, and of control over administration at every level. None of them, of course, can have got beyond the stage of preliminary discussion and report. They demonstrate just how theoretical was Juan's vision of a stabilized *status quo* under a newly assertive royalty. In practice, no such programme as this was going to be implemented, least of all by a pair of middle-aged ecclesiastics, however loyal and conscientious they might be. Yet Juan II did have in his hands, as a result of Alvaro de Luna's fall, certain key elements of an altogether more modest and attainable kind of stability, on which something might yet be built. Although his more ambitious projects soon vanished from sight, while he himself was less and less able to play much active part in affairs, that stability was, by and large, achieved in the last year of his reign. More significantly, it was continued well into the next reign; the mid and late 1450s saw remarkably little active turbulence among the Castilian magnates. To bring that result about, three conditions had to be met. The *grandes* had to feel reasonably assured of their own security. The kingdom must not be overstrained by complex and ambitious foreign commitments. And the Crown must be economically strong.

The end of Alvaro de Luna, together with the studied neutrality of Juan II's subsequent conduct, meant that the principal threats to a general sense of security among the ruling nobility were already removed. The magnates had feared the Constable; they had good reason, too, to fear a period of competition between themselves, with either the king's favour or the military control of his person as the prize. It was clear by midsummer that neither threat obtained. If Juan himself had enjoyed any real prospect of getting his standing army, he too, of course, might well have appeared as a threat in the eyes of the magnates. Equally, if he had not proved himself capable of removing Don Alvaro and curbing his supporters, the claim to «rule in his own person» would have seemed derisory. But by a happy coincidence for himself, the king had established his power at just the right level of credibility. There remained, as his Aragonese visitors saw, the problem of the Crown Prince. But Enrique's interest was, in the long run, inseparable from that of the crown itself. Once there was no *privado* to complicate matters, it became a great deal easier for him to recognize this. The potential for conflict, even here, was probably less than the ambassadors believed.

In foreign affairs, too, Don Alvaro's disappearance had greatly simplified matters. He had been the chief promoter of the long-standing feud with Navarre and Aragón, and hostilities on the eastern frontiers had cooled appreciably since his fall in April. The envoys from Aragon who met Juan II in July still found resistance, both official and unofficial, to the idea of a general settlement. But they also found Juan very willing to discuss coming to a separate arrangement with Alfonso of Aragon.[25] In this, his priorities were probably well-judged. Alfonso had no claims pending to property in Castile, and no plans to intervene there; when

[25] ZURITA, *AA*, fol. 14r (Lib. XVI, Cap. X); see also ibid., fol. 22r (Cap. XVII); AGS, printed catalogue, *PR*, vol. I, p. 163; *Documentos relativos a Enrique IV de Castilla, siendo todavía príncipe de Asturias*, CODOIN, 41, pp. 6-10; VICENS VIVES, *Juan II de Aragón*, pp. 155-6.

appealed to by the Luna faction in their last desperate stand at Escalona, he had been prudent enough not to burn his fingers. With his old adversary Alvaro de Luna out of the way, only the exiled magnates at his court remained as a source of friction with Castile, and their claims might well prove to be expendable. Juan of Navarre, who wanted a great deal more out of the Castilians, presented a more difficult problem; to give him what he wanted would both provoke Prince Enrique and disrupt the painfully restored balance of power in the central kingdom. In the end, this particular embassy came to nothing. Castilian troops were still active in Navarre that summer in support of the rebel Prince of Viana. But a reconciliation was not long in coming. In late August, serious negotiations began with Aragon; on 9th September an armistice was signed in Navarre. More formal agreements involving all parties were ratified in December.

In the West, meanwhile, Juan II continued Don Alvaro's policy of resisting Portuguese claims in African waters —a policy which, after all, had some economic point.[26] In the event, the severe Castilian message of April 1454 did not wholly overawe Afonso V, whose reply, though it carefully avoided open conflict, was unaccomodating. Meanwhile, Portuguese lobbying at the Papal court went on apace, to issue —probably in January 1455— in the Bull *Romanus Pontifex*. This gave the fullest recognition to Portuguese rights in Africa, though the question of the Canaries remained problematic. By this time, however, Enrique, who had continued throughout his father's last year to pursue his own plans for a Portuguese marriage, had succeeded to the Castilian throne. With his accesion in July 1454, Castilian pressure on the Portuguese was relaxed altogether. Within two months, he had also reached a final treaty with Aragon and Navarre. Intra-Peninsular relations, though never simple, had entered a far less demanding phase with the death of Alvaro de Luna. Juan II was able to make a more deliberate choice of options —peace in the east, defiance of the Portuguese. Enrique IV could seek a general disengagement. Don Alvaro, in his long career, had made too many commitments and too many enemies for that kind of flexibility.

Of all the benefits which his death brought to the Crown, however, the most impressive was the economic reward. It is impossible to say

---

[26] See above, pp. 49-50; also PÉREZ EMBID, pp. 158-64; BOXER, pp. 21-2; DIFFIE and WINIUS, p. 94 (all on *Romanus Pontifex*); SUÁREZ FERNÁNDEZ, *Portugal y Castilla*, pp. 65-8; PÉREZ EMBID, pp. 165 ff., makes good his case for a collapse in Castile's Atlantic policy under Enrique IV, though his description of Enrique as an «ape-like figure» is mere abuse in the worst Isabeline tradition. The documents of Enrique's projected marriage are in *CD* (nos XLIV-XLV, XLVII, pp. 102-10; 127-40). On the Aragonese treaty see CODOIN, 41, pp. 8-9 and VICENS VIVES, *Juan II de Aragón*, pp. 156-7.

for certain how rich he was.[27] Pedro of Portugal, who visited him in 1445, estimated his income at 150,000 *doblas;* Fernán Pérez de Guzmán, writing after Don Alvaro's death, reckoned it at 100,000. These figures can be interpreted as converging on an estimate of 20 to 21 million *maravedís,* and thus as being derived from some common source. But that argument is weakened by the fact that they are differently based. Don Pedro had in mind Luna's income from the Crown alone; Fernán Pérez speaks of his total income, apart from royal grants of a sporadic nature and the profits from tax-farming. The 20 millions figure, in any case, greatly exceeds any credible calculation of Don Alvaro's grants from the Crown; it is still possible that with his 20,000 vassals, his Mastership of Santiago, his tax-farming ventures, and private payments to him of all sorts, his gross income from all sources was of this order. What is quite clear is that he was very wealthy indeed.

From the beginning of April 1453, all royal payments to Don Alvaro were suspended, and all his property —except the places controlled by rebel garrisons on his behalf— was sequestered. This in itself was the equivalent of a fair-sized interest-free loan to the royal finances. With the order for Don Alvaro's execution, all his holdings became definitively the property of the Crown. As regards land, buildings and vassals, we cannot begin to estimate what these confiscations were worth to the king. But an idea can be formed of the saving in payments from royal sources. The *contadores* of the time, in fact, attempted this in a paper covering the years 1453 and 1454, but the document as it stands is anomalous, and almost certainly an underestimate.[28] A common core of items, worth some 3.5 million *maravedís* in all, is registered in both years, but the totals do not square exactly. Grants to Juana Pimentel account for part of the difference; genuine fluctuations in the tax-yield may well explain the rest. Items totalling just under 0.6 millions are listed only for 1454; most of these, presumably, had been paid out for 1453 before the sequestration took effect. Others to the value of 0.9 millions appear for the earlier year only; it is less obvious what may have happened to these. Some, certainly, were allocated to other holders, but

---

[27] CONDESTÁVEL DON PEDRO, p. 57; PÉREZ DE GUZMÁN, G y S, p. 45. Using MacKay's conversion values for 1445, Don Pedro's estimate comes to 21 million *maravedís* in Castilian *doblas;* to 18.75 millions in *doblas de la banda*. In the money of the mid 1450s, Fernán Pérez's figure will make either 20 millions (*doblas castellanas*) or 15.2 millions (*doblas de la banda*).

[28] LADERO QUESADA, *Hacienda*, p. 263, summarizing AGS, EMdR, 540, 646 ant. Among Juana Pimentel's holdings, Montalbán appears for 1453 only; other items for both years; others not at all (see above, n. 17). The Relator's gate-tolls in Huete are listed for 1453; his Seville *escribanía* for 1454; Arias Gómez de Silva's similar post goes unlisted. See also SUÁREZ FERNÁNDEZ, «Asientos», pp. 328-9 listing the following unquantified items: *escribanías de rentas,* Cuenca and Toledo; *almojarifazgo,* Villa Real; commission as *notario mayor de Castilla; tercias* in Calahorra, San Esteban.

the compilers seem to have had no consistent policy as to whether these —the sums, for example, going to Juana Pimentel and to the Relator— ought to be included or not. They have certainly omitted a number of payments to Don Alvaro which are known to us from the *asientos* of 1447. A series of tax-offices listed there have no specified salary, but these, whatever they were worth, would have gone straight to other holders and need not detain us here. The offices of Constable, Lord High Chamberlain, and Chief Notary of Castile, listed with their salaries in 1447, would also have to be filled sooner or later. It is possible, too, that some of the 470,000 *maravedís* which Don Alvaro then received in lifelong grants overlapped with the items of revenue in the 1453-4 lists. But this still leaves major savings for Juan II on the maintenance paid to Don Alvaro (383,000 *maravedís* in 1447) and on the 144,000 *maravedís* of his military grant.

As for the total saved by the king, the 1453-4 accounts allow us to think of a maximum figure of 5.2 million *maravedís,* to which the 1447 record would add a further 0.5-1 million, depending on whether the lifelong grants are covered by the later figures. This would yield a total of 5.7-6.2 millions —still some way short of the «seven or eight million *maravedís* in the royal registers» which MacKay regards as a likely income for Don Alvaro.[29] Salaries, financial offices, and other rights of unspecified worth might make enough difference to justify that conjecture. For Juan II's saving in 1453, however, the identifiable cash total is the more relevant figure. From it we have to subtract the million or so restored to Juana Pimentel, together with minor outgoings to the Relator and others. The annual profit to the king, then, must have been between 4 and 5 million *maravedís;* it was probably somewhere in the middle of that range. Curiously enough, a sum of 4.5 millions would be almost identical with the amount confiscated from Juan of Navarre in 1444; the difference now was that the bulk of this sum was not at once parcelled out to new holders among the magnates.

A second element of recurrent profit arose from the vacancy which Don Alvaro's fall had created in the Mastership of Santiago.[30] Juan II was in no hurry at all to fill this, preferring to administer the Mastership himself. Indeed, he went so far as to obtain permission from Pope Nicholas V to manage its affairs for the next seven years. It is not clear how effective this management was. Some of the magnates had

---

[29] MACKAY, *Spain,* p. 180. LADERO QUESADA, pp. 261-3 notes confiscations from Juan of Navarre to the value of 4.3 million *maravedís*. MacKay sees his total income from the Crown as very much higher than this.

[30] See Juan II's will, *CD,* no. XLVI, p. 113 (seven-year royal administration); CONSUELO G. DEL ARROYO DE VÁZQUEZ DE PARGA, *Privilegios reales de la Orden de Santiago en la Edad Media* (Madrid, n.d.), p. 347 (letter of 30th August). For estimates of the *mesa maestral* see HILLGARTH, vol. II, p. 399, and LADERO QUESADA, *España en 1492* (Madrid, 1978), p. 157.

their own ideas of an appropriate response to the vacancy, and on 30th August an instruction had to be issued requiring those who had taken over property from the Order to give it back. To the extent to which he could in fact make his writ run in the territories of the Order, Juan could look to it for a valuable supplement to his recurrent income. Just over twenty years later, the price for which the Catholic Monarchs had the opportunity of incorporating the Mastership permanently in the Crown was 3 million *maravedís* a year; its value by the end of the century was estimated at 43,000 ducats —well over twice that sum. No direct extrapolation of a figure for the mid century is possible, more particularly because we do not know the extent of seigneurial encroachments. But it seems safe to think of the Mastership as worth several million *maravedís* to Juan II. Reckoned together with the confiscations, it would certainly have added at least 6 to 7 millions to his regular income. At some 6% of his annual budget, that was a very worthwhile sum indeed.

It did not, in itself, transform the economic position of the Crown. The once-for-all profit represented by the treasures in cash and kind laid up in Don Alvaro's strongholds came much nearer to doing that.[31] The spoils of Portillo and Santa María de la Armedilla between them totalled no less than 5.4 million *maravedís* —a sum comparable to the gross annual saving on Don Alvaro's former revenues. But the treasures of Escalona were of a different order again. «It was said that they were beyond count», reports Pedro de Escavias. And the detailed record in the *Cuarta crónica general* bears this out. At first sight, indeed, that record appears altogether too spectacular, especially in its story of a Moorish hoard sent to Don Alvaro by the king of Granada in 1431 and buried in the castle courtyard. An even more exotic account of a treasure uncovered in the castle at Madrid, and including the Cid's two swords, Colada and Tizón, inspires no more confidence. But even this is closely tied to real fifteenth-century personages —the exiled *contador* Fernán López de Saldaña, who told the king about the treasure, and the royal secretary Diego Romero, who wrote an inventory of it. The chronicle, moreover, was written well within living memory of the capture of Escalona, and it is especially well-informed on events in the Toledo area. Its account of the Constable's treasures deserves to be taken seriously.

Many of the items which it lists cannot be valued with any precision:

---

[31] For Portillo and Santa María de la Armedilla see above, pp. 132-3. On the Escalona treasures see Escavias, p. 343, and *CCG*, pp. 136-7; 139-40. The latter's figures are reproduced in part by Zurita, *AA*, fol. 13r (Lib. XVI, Cap. IX). Values in *maravedís* from MacKay, except for *doblas baladies moriscas* (the Moorish treasure; *CCG*, p. 139). These are taken, following Ladero Quesada, *Hacienda*, p. 42, as equivalent to *doblas de la banda*.

«... seven thousand French tapestries, and two hundred bed-hangings, and four thousand quilts, and fifteen hundred carpets... gold plate and silver beyond count... seven casks full of nobles and Alfonsine *doblas*, and Florentine florins, and ducats» (p. 136). But the chronicle also mentions a series of cash sums. One of these references is clearly corrupt as it stands: «de florines de Aragòn, e de blancas viejas, ochenta cuentos». Literally this means «of Aragonese florins and of old (i.e. undebased) silver *reales*, eighty millions». Nobody would have reckoned silver *reales* together with Aragonese florins, which were worth over seven times as much; the figure for the number of florins must have been lost. Nor can there have been eighty million *reales*, for these would amount to over a billion *maravedís*, an inconceivable sum. Of possible emendations, *ocho cuentos* (116 million *maravedís*) seems a high figure, though a credible one; *ochocientos mil* yields the most acceptable-looking total (11.6 millions), and *ochenta mil*, at just over a million, seems hardly to be a sum worth mentioning. The 300 marks of gold said to have been found in certain dishes amount to very little more, at 2.2 million *maravedís*, but gold had an intrinsic interest which silver *reales* could hardly match. A much more remarkable figure is that of 1.5 million given for *doblas de la banda*. This represents a sum of 225 million *maravedís* —a vast amount indeed, but just within the bounds of credibility. With an income in the range of twenty millions a year, it was the kind of treasure Don Alvaro could well have accumulated over several decades. From the viewpoint of the defenders of Escalona, it would have seemed worth fighting for. Juan II, too, might have thought it well worth an execution.

On these estimates, the king's two-thirds share of the treasure would have been something in excess of 160 million *maravedís* —possibly very much more. To this we may add the whole of the Moorish treasure, valued by the *Cuarta crónica general* at 84,000 *doblas baladíes moriscas* (12.6 million *maravedís*). The king's total haul, therefore (including the 5.4 millions or more from hoards elsewhere), must have been in the region of 180 millions, if not more. And this is still to say nothing at all of his non-monetary booty. The chronicler states that he generously allowed Juana Pimentel to take away her household effects, but we do not know how inclusively these were defined.

A further capital sum which stemmed indirectly from the Constable's disappearance was provided by the *cobro de albaquías* of the following year. This was the attempt to gather in tax-arrears —in this case extending to all those revenues which had bled away through the tax-farming system since 1428.[32] The Constable's fall provided a highly opportune

---

[32] See LADERO QUESADA, *Hacienda*, p. 34 (also above, p. 55). Among those exempted were Prince Enrique, Pacheco and his brother, Santillana, and Santillana's heir, Diego Hurtado de Mendoza.

moment for a settlement of this sort, for the officials and others who had made their profits under his aegis would be less anxious to defend them than to secure the continuity of their own positions under the king's newly-asserted power. If it came to that, the death of the *contador mayor* Alonso Pérez may itself have smoothed the path as well. In accordance with Juan II's conciliatory approach to the *grandes*, neither the Crown Prince nor a number of other major figures were pressed too hard, but the *cobro de albaquías* of 1454 still brought in 28 million *maravedís*.

To the approximate 6% betterment in annual revenue, therefore, we have to add a once-for-all capital sum, deriving from the *albaquías* and the various treasure-hoards, of more than 200 million *maravedís*. It is possible that the sum was higher still. That is to say, Juan's reserves were suddenly enriched by the equivalent of some two years' overall revenue. These handsome returns on the Luna affair opened up a number of possibilities, as well as restoring the inherent financial credibility of the royal government. Outstanding grants and salaries could be paid for some time to come; military adventurism on the part of the magnates could be discouraged, since the king was now able to pay for an army at need; a colourable front could be presented to the Portuguese. In the likely event of an eastern settlement, some of the money might also prove useful for paying off Juan of Navarre. Above all, this new-found economic strength could be used to effect long-term changes in the fiscal system. It might or might not prove possible to reform it on the very radical lines which Juan's latest ministers had been asked to consider. But if the Crown, with these new assets, could bring independent forces of its own to bear on cases of seigneurial abuse, or could cut free of the pattern of buying short-term support with long-term grants, then the proceeds of Don Alvaro's fall would have procured very much more than a breathing-space.

It was to Enrique IV, in the event, that most of these possibilities presented themselves. Enrique, indeed, was the residuary legatee of Alvaro de Luna's downfall as he had been, in an important sense, its cause. His pursuit of independent ends had blighted the politics of the Constable's regime ever since 1445; his negotiations with Aragón and Portugal had imposed constant strains on Castilian foreign policies. His very presence as the heir-apparent undermined the long-term allegiance of Don Alvaro's supporters. For Juan II himself, Enrique's conduct had posed a special dilemma, forcing him at every moment to choose between the *privado* whose government made his royalty effectual and the heir who could give it continuity. At first the choice had gone decisively Don Alvaro's way. But two long-term factors were on Enrique's side.[33]

---

[33] For the crisis of government see above, Chapter 2, passim. For Don Al-

The first was that, in terms of efficacy, Don Alvaro's government was beginning to exhibit a pattern of diminishing returns. The second was time itself. We do not know how long Juan II expected his reign to be. Palencia says that he trusted in foolish prophecies that he would live to be ninety, but his health gave him little reason for this confidence. The series of illnesses which began in the summer of 1453 and continued until his death must surely have had some prehistory; indeed the concern for Juan's health which Alvaro de Luna displayed in his prison of Portillo suggests that this was obvious to those of the king's immediate circle. Certainly Juan acted in the case of Don Alvaro exactly as one would expect him to have acted if the prospect of Enrique's succession were an imminent one. If Enrique were to become king with the Constable still supreme in Castilian affairs, one of two choices would confront him. He could defer to Don Alvaro; but both his own record and the aspirations of Juan Pacheco made that most unlikely. Or he could fight him —a dangerous and, as royal finances stood at the beginning of 1453, an economically precarious undertaking. His father spared him that dilemma, and at the same time resolved his own. Juan would have the kind of monarchy Don Alvaro had taught him to have, but he would make sure that it passed unimpaired to his son. The next Trastámara king would start without an excess of political or fiscal handicaps. He had, of course, plenty of others.

One possible result of these is the way in which everybody seems to have agreed that Enrique should be kept well away from the whole business.[34] For most of the time our sources do not even tell us where he was. According to Zurita, the king had to take steps to forestall any move by Enrique to come to the Constable's aid, but it is hard to imagine the prince flouting his own obvious long-term interest in Don Alvaro's removal for the sake of a piece of immediate mischief of this sort. It was, however, not quite impossible; Zurita's view may well reflect the puzzled efforts of Aragonese observers to interpret Enrique's always enigmatic motives. At all events, no such attempt was made. In May, the prince pursued quite other business; on the 11th, his divorce from Blanca of Navarre was made final. Enrique, it appears, was not present at the crucial meeting at Alcazarén, but he is unlikely to have been far away; his favourite residence, after all, was Segovia. Juan II, perhaps by more than coincidence, was in the area too. One further feature of the

---

varo's anxiety over the king's health, see above, Chapter 2, n. 14; for Juan's more recent illnesses, this chapter, n. 23.

[34] SUÁREZ FERNÁNDEZ, *Historia*, vol. II, p. 527 attributes this to the advice of Pacheco. See ZURITA, *AA*, fol. 12r (Lib. XVI, Cap. IX); also *CD*, no. XXXV, pp. 61-6. For Juan II's movements see above, p. 131. It is likely that Enrique visited Escalona after its occupation by royal forces; on 10th July 1453 he was at El Tiemblo, barely a day's ride away (Santa María de Guadalupe, Archivo del Monasterio, Legajo 3, fol. 32).

divorce proceedings is of interest to us. The non-consummation of the marriage is repeatedly attributed to the fact that the couple *estaban legados;* that is to say, they were «bound» by a spell of some kind, though they had sought by prayer and other remedies to «undo the said spell».[35] The women of Segovia who gave evidence of Enrique's virility had put this —along with much else— more bluntly: «they believed... that he was bewitched *(fechizado),* or had had some other evil done to him». And even the official sentence of divorce ends with the direct assertion that the marriage is void: «through the said cause and impediment of the said evil magic and spell» *(del dicho maleficio é legamiento).*

It was very much a part of Don Alvaro's reputation that such things were his business.[36] As early as 1440, his opponents had protested that his sway over Juan II was exercised «through magical and diabolical enchantments». Fernán Pérez de Guzmán reported the same suspicions, though he did not credit them; Rodrigo Sánchez de Arévalo, by contrast, thought them wholly reasonable, and wrote darkly of «fascination» and of «wicked arts». It was not simply the unlettered public, then, which gave credence to these tales, though they seem to have flourished with a particular exuberance in such quarters. The witnesses questioned in 1497 provided a rich vein of unlikely stories of magic rings and familiar demons in bottles; some of this material apparently antedated the execution of 1453. If anyone were looking for a spectacularly discreditable charge against Don Alvaro, here surely was the one to use, and the official record of the royal divorce offered the ideal pretext. There would be nothing against embodying such material in a political trial in the century of Joan of Arc and Gilles de Rais. Yet the documents of Don Alvaros fall contain scarcely anything which can be related with any degree of assurance to his reputation as a magician. In the report of the twelve commissioners, as incorporated in Juan II's open letter of 18th June, a long catalogue of the things which Don Alvaro has done is rounded off in these words: «... and committing many other acts of tyranny and excesses and killings and imprisonments and crimes and *maleficios* to the great disturbance and subversion of my realms and of their peaceful estate».[37] The obvious meaning of *maleficio* is the one

---

[35] *CD*, p. 62; see also pp. 64, 65.
[36] *CJII* (R), p. 562; Pérez de Guzmán, *G y S*, p. 41; Sánchez de Arévalo, *HH*, p. 233: «Arbitrati sunt itaque non abs re animum regis fascinatum, aut prauis artibus ab Aluaro diu fuisse oppressum»; Corral, pp. 60, 62, 74-5.
[37] *CD*, no. XLI, p. 90: «é fasiendo otras muchas tiranías é escesos é muertos é prisiones de omes é delitos é maleficios en grand turbacion é subversion de mis regnos é del pacífico estado dellos». For the technical meaning of *maleficio* see Round, «Five Magicians», p. 799. The word is used without apparent reference to magic in the last lines of Fernando de la Torre's *Testamento del Maestre* («por que Dios perdone a mi/mis culpas e maleficios»). A similarly neutral meaning seems to be in question in the public proclamation of Don Alvaro's

which it evidently bears in Enrique's decree of divorce: it is the fourth and the worst of the varieties of magic, in which supernatural agencies are invoked to a harmful purpose. But in this particular context, the word appears simply as an amplification of «crimes» *(delitos)* and could perfectly well mean little more than «evil deeds» —perhaps with some especial imputation of deliberate perversity. This and one other, equally doubtful, instance aside, the entire procedings have nothing to say of magic, and they contain scarcely a word which could possibly relate to Enrique's divorce.

There could be several reasons. The *letrados* handling the case may have regarded the stories of Don Alvaro as a magician as unworthy of their attention, or as incredible in themselves. In the latter event, it is true, they would have been well ahead of even the educated opinion of their time. But they may also have felt that such references would be tactless. The name of Prince Enrique, even as that of a much-abused victim, was best kept out of Don Alvaro's case, while as for the divorce, the less said about that, the better. They would take their cue from the king, who had omitted this whole area of speculation from his statement to the Fuensalida meeting. When, within a few days of that meeting, Enrique pressed his father to confer an office of some profit on the Relator, he may have known that he had more than one reason to be grateful.

Enrique, then, could expect to reap the full economic and political benefits of Don Alvaro's removal, without the damage to his own public reputation that would come from explicit reference to his personal troubles, or from too close an involvement in harrying Alvaro de Luna to his death. Thus far, the dynastic motive not only provides a wholly credible mainspring for Juan II's actions but appears to have worked itself out to some purpose through them. The history of the next few years, however, is very largely one of missed opportunities. To some extent this was sheer ill-fortune; in early August, Juan's health finally broke down, and he was seriously ill for the next six months. His absence from the conduct of affairs need not, in itself, have made much difference —it had never done so up to now. But Barrientos and the Prior of Guadalupe had been given a governmental programme so ambitious in its scope that it was unlikely to come to anything in practice, and they had little but routine and honourable service to put in its place. By the time of Juan's recovery —which was never a complete one— his sense of dynastic and political purpose had suffered some loss of clarity.[38] The

guilt: «muchos e diuersos crimines, e excesos, e delitos, e maleficios, e tiranías, e cohechos» (above, Chapter 5, n. 41).
[38] For Juan's medical history from August 1453 see *CCG*, p. 140. Of the several dates given for Prince Alfonso's birth, that of PALENCIA, *Déc*, p. 55 (*CEIV*, pp. 52-3) is compatible with *Cronicón de Valladolid*, CODOIN, 13, p. 2

factor which brought this about was the birth, on November 15th 1453, of his second son, Prince Alfonso. We need not credit the assertion in Palencia and the royal chronicle —almost certainly the product of later political developments— that the King wanted to make Alfonso his heir in Enrique's place. But the desire to make some provision for the child does seem to have overruled his judgment as to the best interests of the crown. His will, drawn up on 8th July 1454, virtually proposed to recreate for Alfonso's benefit the same concentration of offices and territories which had been the basis of Alvaro de Luna's power. The boy was to have the post of Constable and the Mastership of Santiago administered for him until he was of age to be Constable and Master himself. He was granted an entailed estate including many towns —Huete, Escalona, Maqueda, Portillo, Sepúlveda— which had formerly been Don Alvaro's. No arrangement likelier to undo the work of 1453 could have been devised, and Enrique, when he came to power, very sensibly took no notice of most of it.

In other ways, however, he himself contributed to the largely negative use which was made of the opportunities stemming from Don Alvaro's fall. The moment of relaxed tensions which followed that event and the king's refusal to exploit it in a divisive way could not be expected to last forever. It remained for the Crown to redefine in some positive and specific fashion its relationship with the magnates. If this was not attempted —if things were left simply to resolve themselves with Don Alvaro out of the way— there remained what the Aragonese ambassadors in July 1453 were quick to perceive: a power-vacuum at the heart of Castilian affairs.[39] Perhaps there was some excuse for this, within a mere couple of months of Don Alvaro's death; perhaps there was still some excuse in March 1454, when reports reaching Aragon suggested merely a drift away from the ailing king towards the faction of the expectant Crown Prince. But there was less excuse for Enrique when he came to power, with a political consensus as wide-ranging as had ever been enjoyed by his father, and the economic fruits of the Constable's fall at his disposal. Arguably it was this fortuitous financial advantage which was itself to blame. It created a temptation —not, in the event, resisted— to postpone the need for fiscal reforms. Enrique, a man of genuinely peaceable temperament, as even his many detractors admitted, took the easy way out.[40] Cushioned against necessity, first by the spoils

---

(14th November, after midnight); 16th December, the suggestion of *CJII* (R), p. 684, will not serve. See ibid., p. 692 and PALENCIA, p. 56 (*CEIV*, p. 53) for the misleading suggestion about the succession. Juan's will is *CD*, no. XLVI; the relevant clauses are on pp. 113-16.

[39] ZURITA, *AA*, fol. 14r (Lib. XVI, Cap. X); fol. 31r (Cap. XXVIII).

[40] For the shortcomings of Enrique's financial policies see LADERO QUESADA, *Hacienda*, pp. 48-50, 78-9, 228n. GARCÍA DE CORTÁZAR, pp. 474-5, and less emphatically, HILLGARTH, vol. II, pp. 326-32, take a more positive view of Enrique's

of Alvaro de Luna, and then by the proceeds of the Bull of Crusade, he allowed the magnates their way on two crucial issues. He did little to restrict grants, ignoring, for example, the rules for the suppression of vacant *mercedes*. And he legalized the direct involvement of territorial lords in the collection of taxes and the deduction of their own grants from them. The *tasa de señoríos,* introduced in 1455, produced a purely technical fall in the proportion of revenue which was budgeted for in advance. But it also surrendered the economic power of the Crown along with its fiscal functions. That power was not to be easily recovered.

Don Alvaro's fall, as we have seen, marked the break-up of a system of rule whose component elements would no longer work together save under increasingly extreme compulsion. It gathered into the hands of the king the elements of a new governmental pattern which were to offer his successor a more viable start than he could otherwise have hoped for. Conciliatory policies at home and abroad and a replenished treasury were the objective and visible components of the new situation. Just as important, however, were certain less tangible factors: a closer relationship than ever with the caste of officials, a more explicit commitment to personal rule, and an ideology of kingship in which absolutism and legalism, active politics and contemplative *ciencia moral,* were approaching a new kind of balance. These things were, very largely, what Juan II had learned from Don Alvaro. And, indeed, the Constable himself had been able to grasp the lesson on which they all converged: that to impose stability upon Castile, power and authority must come together. He had tried, though, to achieve it from the side of power, and he had failed. It would be some years before the experiment was tried again by Isabel and Fernando, this time with authority as its starting point.

For it had been Don Alvaro's great disqualification as a ruler that he was not a king. And yet, as Pérez de Guzmán put it: «... either because he enjoyed his power for a long while, and it had become, as it were, natural to him, or because his daring and presumption were great, he deployed the power of a king rather than a simple gentleman».[41] Such remarks —and there were many— imply that the contradiction between what Don Alvaro was and what he did was in itself something intolerable, if not actually monstrous. Members of Fernán Pérez's own class, of course, would have recognized no such anomaly if Don Alvaro had been

---

early years as king than that presented here. This is a proper corrective to a historical tradition too long dominated by the propagandists of the Catholic Monarchs. But if the opportunities presented to Enrique were on the scale suggested here, his fiscal and institutional failures must be taken as serious matters.

[41] Pérez de Guzmán, *G y S*, p. 45 (for *andança*, I read *audaçia*). The related class-prejudice is succinctly illustrated in Santillana's *Doctrinal de privados*, Foulché-Delbosc, *CC*, vol. I, p. 504: «Todo ome sea contento/de ser como fue su padre...»

an established magnate of one of Castile's great lineages, and not the base-born son of a middle-ranking Aragonese courtier. Yet the constitutional paradox, as opposed to the affront to class-feeling, would have been every bit as real. Indeed, it existed in the lives of virtually the whole class of *grandes,* whose notions of legitimate self-advancement were perpetually encroaching on the functions of kingship. The *tasa de señoríos,* the imposition of vassalage on free areas, the private wars, the domination of local offices —all these predicated a right to rule which limited the area of control available to the monarch. And any magnate who saw his way to making these things the foundation for a bid for *privanza* was unlikely to hesitate because of the points of principle raised by the case of Don Alvaro.

The irony of that case was that it did raise issues of principle which these more piecemeal infringements seemed able to evade. And it raised them very largely because Don Alvaro himself had helped to articulate them in the first place. He had taught Juan II what it meant to be a king, and here was that knowledge being used against him. He had taken his own role of *privado* for granted; now the absolutist outlook which he had fostered was calling that role into question. For when the king made known a change in his sovereign will, the erstwhile *privado* became, in virtue of precisely the same actions, a usurper of power. In the language of the proclamation against Don Alvaro, he became a *tirano.* This was a word to which Alvaro de Luna took strong exception. «It is a lie», he said when he heard it «for it was as a gentleman that I acted, as other gentlemen do».[42] The kernel of his potential defence lay in the claim that he had not sought to usurp what was rightfully the king's, but had merely tried to further his own fortunes in the king's service. That aim was one which any of the magnates might pursue, and Don Alvaro's methods in pursuing it had not differed greatly in kind from theirs. Ironically, it was the very scale of his success which set him apart from them; he could not plausibly claim to be acting merely «as a gentleman» when the scope of his operations made him look like a king. Least of all could he make that assertion convincing to the king himself. It was Juan's refusal to be convinced which placed Alvaro de Luna's uniquely successful pursuit of what every nobleman pursued in the category of «tyranny».

On the evidence of his actions, Don Alvaro's own analysis of events does not seem to have advanced very far beyond this point. His pursuit

---

[42] CORRAL, p. 95: «que como cavallero lo hazía, como otros cavalleros lo hazen.» For the proclamation see above, Chapter 5, n. 41; for *tirano,* ibid., n. 46. Further paradoxes of Don Alvaro's career in MARAVALL, *Estado moderno,* pp. 279-80; BERMEJO, «Soberanía», p. 286, and —surely unconscious— this, from the poet Juan de Valladolid (PÉREZ GÓMEZ, p. 32): «Tirano, queria robar/y mandar mas que no el Rey.»

of personal security through coercion, both before and after his arrest, did nothing to resolve the contradictions inherent in his position as *privado*, and in practical terms it sealed his downfall. By none of his actions did he acknowledge that the notion of kingship in which he had schooled Juan II implied a curtailment of all the other interests in Castile, his own as *privado* not excepted. But he does appear to have arrived at a clear view of what the magnates were doing to the monarchy, and to have accepted at the end that he had been doing it himself. This measure of clarity about some of the key realities in fifteenth-century Castilian history was itself rare, even in circumstances more favourable to clear thinking than those of a journey to the scaffold. Castile did not have another such head to cut off.

BIBLIOGRAPHY

This is not a full bibliography of Alvaro de Luna (or of the reign of Juan II, which would amount to much the same thing) but a list of the works cited in the present study. A few titles, of very marginal relevance to all but the particular point which they illustrate, have been omitted.

A) MANUSCRIPT SOURCES

Burgo de Osma, Biblioteca de la Catedral.
- MS 42 Alonso de Cartagena, *Duodenarium* (microfilm copy in Madrid, Archivo Histórico Nacional).
- MS 57 includes letter of Alonso de Palencia to «P. Lunensi» 1453

San Lorenzo de El Escorial, Biblioteca del Monasterio.
- MS S II 10 Pero Díaz de Toledo, *Proverbios de Séneca*

Santa María de Guadalupe, Archivo del Monasterio.
- Legajo 3 includes letter of Prince Enrique. 10th July 1453
- Legajo 55 includes letter of Juan Ramírez de Toledo. 9th May 1425

Madrid, Archivo Histórico Nacional.
- Osuna 1.26
- Osuna 35.41
- Osuna 1425.6
- Osuna 1860.42
- Universidades 1091.F
- Microfilm 1088 (R. 7238). See above, Burgo de Osma, Catedral.

Madrid, Biblioteca Nacional.
- MS 638 Papers relating to Velasco family.
- MS 773 includes *Historia que escrivió el despensero mayor de la Reina Doña Leonor hija del Rey de Aragon, mujer que fue del Rey Don Juan el primero.*
- MS 905 includes *Consultas del Consejo sobre si por delitos de lesa majestad notoria se incurre en pena ordinaria de muerte y confiscación de bienes, aunque sean de mayorazgo. Años 1714-16.*
- MS 2496 *Lamentación de Don Alvaro de Luna dum esset in vinculis.*
- MS 6043 includes Pedro Gerónimo de Aponte, *Relación de algunas personas que no van declaradas en el primer tratado* [*Adiciones al Tizón de España.*]
- MS 6185 includes *Historia de la privanza y caída de don Alvaro de Luna.*

MS 6720   *Leyes e hordenanças que fizo el señor Rey don Johan.*
MS 6765   Alonso de Cartagena, *Libros de Séneca.*
MS 7899   *Anales Complutenses y Historia Eclesiástica i Seglar de la ilustre Villa de Alcalá de Henares* (1652).
MS 9427   includes royal edict on salaries (1433).
MS 10774 includes *Causa escrita a Don Alvaro de Luna en el año de 1517* (18th century).
MS 13107 Transcripts of documents.
MS 13108 Transcripts of documents.
MS 13109 Transcripts of documents.
MS 13259 Transcripts of documents.
MS Res. 25 includes Bartolus, *De Insignis et Armis,* translated by «Ludovicus Bachelarius».
MS Vitr. 17.4   includes Plato, *Phaedo,* translated by Pero Díaz de Toledo.

Madrid, Real Academia de la Historia.
MS 9.120   Colección Salazar B. 5
MS 9.147   Colección Salazar B. 33
MS 9.300   Colección Salazar D. 25
MS 9.310   Colección Salazar D. 35
MS 9.323   Colección Salazar D. 49
MS 9.329   Colección Salazar D. 55

Santander, Biblioteca de Menéndez Pelayo.
MS M-96   Plato, *Phaedo,* translated by Pero Díaz de Toledo.

Archivo General de Simancas.

Diversos de Castilla	4.64-5	
Diversos de Castilla	38.16	
Diversos de Castilla	40.38	
Mercedes y Privilegios	1.107	1.455
	1.160	1.633
	1.445	1.778
Mercedes y Privilegios	2.6v	2.424
	2.67	2.500
	2.271	2.518v
Mercedes y Privilegios	7.129	7.141
	7.132	7.143
Mercedes y Privilegios	8.47	
	8.103	
	8.119	
Mercedes y Privilegios	12.111	
	12.138	
	12.142	
Mercedes y Privilegios	55.40	
Mercedes y Privilegios	63.69	
	63.71	
	63.105	
Mercedes y Privilegios	64.50	
	64.51	
	64.52	
Mercedes y Privilegios	65.115	

BIBLIOGRAPHY

Mercedes y Privilegios	102.137		
Mercedes y Privilegios	104.114		
	104.177		
Mercedes y Privilegios	105.123		
	105.129		
Mercedes y Privilegios	192.40		
Quitaciones de Cortes	1.10	1.300	1.331
	1.11	1.301	1.345
	1.12	1.302	1.347
	1.17-73	1.303	1.424
	1.284	1.304	
Quitaciones de Cortes	2.12	2.153	
	2.63	2.380	
Quitaciones de Cortes	3.46-7	3.77	3.391-2
	3.48	3.78	
	3.50-1	3.79	
	3.52	3.101	
	3.76	3.131	
Quitaciones de Cortes	4.253		
	4.300		

MS Catalogue: *Escribanía Mayor de Rentas. Contadurías de la Razón. Libros de Rentas ordinarios y extraordinarios.*

B) PRINTED SOURCES

ABARCA, PEDRO DE: *Anales de Aragón.* See *Crónica de Don Alvaro de Luna,* ed. Flores.
ALFONSO X OF CASTILE: *Las Siete Partidas del muy noble rey Don Alfonso el Sabio glosadas por el Licenciado Gregorio López,* vols I, II. Madrid, 1843-4.
ALVAREZ DE VILLASANDINO, ALONSO: Poems. See FOULCHÉ-DELBOSC: *Cancionero castellano del siglo XV,* vol. II.
AMADOR DE LOS RÍOS, JOSÉ: *Historia social, política y religiosa de los judíos de España y Portugal,* vol. III. Madrid, 1876.
— *Vida del Marqués de Santillana,* ed. Augusto Cortina. Buenos Aires, 1947 (1st edition, Madrid, 1852).
AMASUNO, MARCELINO V., ed.: *El «Compendio de Medicina» para Don Alvaro de Luna del Doctor Gómez de Salamanca.* Cuadernos de Historia de la Medicina Española, Monografías, 16. Salamanca, 1971.
ARROYO DE VÁZQUEZ DE PARGA, CONSUELO G. DEL: *Privilegios reales de la Orden de Santiago en la Edad Media: Catálogo de la serie existente en el Archivo Histórico Nacional.* Madrid, n.d.
AVALLE-ARCE, JUAN BAUTISTA: *Temas hispánicos medievales: literatura e historia.* Madrid, 1974.

BAENA, JUAN ALFONSO DE: *Dezir que fizo Juan Alfonso de Baena.* See *Cancionero de Baena.*
BAER, YITZHAK [FRITZ]: *Die Juden im christlichen Spanien,* vol. II. Berlín, 1936.
— *A History of the Jews in Christian Spain,* vol. II. Philadelphia, 1961.
BAHLER, INGRID: *Alfonso Alvarez de Villasandino: poesía de petición.* Madrid, 1977.
BARRIENTOS, LOPE: *Refundición de la Crónica del Halconero,* ed. Juan de Mata Carriazo. Colección de Crónicas Españolas, 9. Madrid, 1946. Includes text of *Abreviación del Halconero* for the fall of Alvaro de Luna.

BATTESTI-PÉLÉGRIN, JEANNE: *Lope de Stúñiga. Récherches sur la poésie espagnole au XVème siècle,* 4 vols. Aix en Provence, 1982.
BEINERT, B.: «La idea de cruzada y los intereses de los príncipes cristianos en el siglo xv», *Cuadernos de Historia,* 1, 45-59.
BELTRÁN DE HEREDIA, VICENTE: *Bulario de la Universidad de Salamanca* (1219-1549), 3 vols. Acta Salmanticensia: Historia de la Universidad, 12-14. Salamanca, 1966-7.
— *Cartulario de la Universidad de Salamanca (1218-1600).* Vol. I. Acta Salmanticensia: Historia de la Universidad, 17. Salamanca, 1970.
BENEYTO PÉREZ, JUAN: «The Science of Law in the Spain of the Catholic Kings», in Highfield, *Spain in the Fifteenth Century,* 276-95.
— *Textos políticos de la baja Edad Media.* Madrid, 1944.
BENITO RUANO, ELOY: «Lope de Stúñiga: vida y cancionero», *Revista de Filología Española,* 51 (1968), 17-109.
— *Los orígenes del problema converso.* Barcelona, 1976.
— *Toledo en el siglo XV. Vida política.* Madrid, 1961.
BERMEJO, JOSÉ LUIS: «La idea medieval de contrafuero en León y Castilla», *Revista de Estudios Políticos,* 187 (1973), 299-306.
— «Orígenes medievales en la idea de soberanía», *Revista de Estudios Políticos,* 200 (1975), 283-90.
— «Principios y apotegmas sobre la ley y el rey en la Baja Edad Media castellana», *Hispania,* 35 (1975), 31-47.
BERTINI, GIOVANNI MARIA, ed.: *Testi spagnoli del secolo XV°.* Turin, 1950.
BIRKENMAIER, ALEKSANDER: «Der Streit des Alonso von Cartagena mit Leonardo Bruni Aretino», in *Vermischte Untersuchungen zu Geschichte der mittelalterlichen Philosophie. Beiträge zur Geschichte der Philosophie des Mittelalters,* 20, no. 5. Münster, 1922, pp. 129-236.
BISTICCI, VESPASIANO DA: *Vite di uomini illustri del secolo XV,* ed. P. d'Ancona and Erhard Aeschlimann, Milan, 1951.
BOASE, ROGER: *The Troubadour Revival: A Study of Social Change and Traditionalism in Late Medieval Spain.* London, 1978.
BOFARULL Y DE SARTORIO, MANUEL DE: *Guerra entre Castilla, Aragón y Navarra. Compromiso para terminarla. Año 1431.* Colección de Documentos Inéditos del Archivo General de la Corona de Aragón, 37. Barcelona, 1869.
BOXER, C. R.: *The Portuguese Seaborne Empire 1415-1825.* Harmondsworth, 1973 (1st edition, London, 1969).

CABALLERO, FERMÍN: *Conquenses ilustres: El Doctor Montalvo.* Madrid, 1873.
— *Elogio del Doctor Alonso Díaz de Montalvo.* Madrid, 1870.
CABRILLANA CIEZAR, NICOLÁS: «Salamanca en el siglo xv: nobles y campesinos», *Cuadernos de Historia,* 3, 255-95.
CALISSE, C.: *A History of Italian Law.* London, 1928.
Cancionero de Baena, ed. José María Azáceta. 3 vols. Madrid, 1966.
Cancionero de Gallardo, ed. José María Azáceta. Madrid, 1962.
Cancionero de Palacio (Manuscrito N.° 594), ed. Francisca Vendrell de Millás. Barcelona, 1945.
CANTERA BURGOS, FRANCISCO: *Alvar García de Santa María y su familia de conversos: Historia de la Judería de Burgos y de sus conversos más egregios.* Madrid, 1952.
CANTERA BURGOS, FRANCISCO, and CARRETE PARRONDO, CARLOS: *Las juderías medievales en la provincia de Guadalajara.* Madrid, 1975.
CANTERA BURGOS, FRANCISCO, and LEÓN TELLO, PILAR: *Judaizantes del arzobispado de Toledo habilitados por la Inquisición en 1495 y 1497.* Madrid, 1969.

BIBLIOGRAPHY

CARO BAROJA, JULIO: *Los judíos en la España moderna y contemporánea*, 3 vols. Madrid, 1978. (1st edition, Madrid, 1961).
CARRERAS Y ARTAU, TOMÁS and JOAQUÍN: *Historia de la filosofía española. Filosofía cristiana de los Siglos XIII al XV*. Madrid, 1943.
CARRILLO DE HUETE, PERO: *Crónica del Halconero de Juan II*, ed. Juan de Mata Carriazo. Colección de Crónicas Españolas, 8. Madrid, 1946. [For the *Abreviación del Halconero* see Barrientos, *Refundición*.]
CARTAGENA, ALONSO DE: *Defensorium Unitatis Christianae. (Tratado en favor de los judíos conversos)*, ed. Manuel Alonso. Madrid, 1943. Includes FERNÁN DÍAZ DE TOLEDO: *Instrucción del Relator*.
— *Epistula ad Comitem de Haro*. See LAWRANCE: *Un tratado de Alonso de Cartagena*.
— *Proposición contra los ingleses*. See PENNA: *Prosistas castellanos del siglo XV*, vol. I.
— *Rubrica additio ex summa Episcopi Burgensis*. [*Anacephaleosis*]. See *Crónicas de los Reyes de Castilla*; also SCHOTT: *Hispaniae Illustratae Scriptores Varii*.
CASTRO, ADOLFO DE: *Sobre el Centón epistolario del Bachiller Fernán Gómez de Cibdareal y su verdadero autor el Maestro Gil González Dávila*. Seville, 1875.
Centón epistolario del Bachiller Fernán Gómez de Cibda Real. (Spuriously) Burgos, 1499.
CHIRINO, ALONSO DE: *Menor daño de la medicina de Alonso de Chirino*, ed. María Teresa Herrera. Acta Salmanticensia: Filosofía y Letras, 75. Salamanca, 1973.
CLAVERO, BARTOLOMÉ: «Notas sobre el derecho territorial castellano, 1367-1445», *Historia, Instituciones, Documentos*, 3 (1976), 141-65.
[CODOIN] *Colección de documentos inéditos para la Historia de España*, 112 vols. Madrid, 1842-95.
[*Colección diplomática*] *Memorias de Don Enrique IV de Castilla. Tomo II. Contiene la colección diplomática del mismo Rey compuesta y ordenada por la Real Academia de la Historia*. Madrid, 1835-1913.
COLLANTES DE TERÁN SÁNCHEZ, ANTONIO: *Sevilla en la baja Edad Media. La ciudad y sus hombres*. Seville, 1977.
COLMENARES, DIEGO DE: *Historia de la insigne ciudad de Segovia y compendio de las historias de Castilla*, vol. I. Segovia, 1969.
CONDESTÁVEL DON PEDRO: *Coplas del menosprecio e contempto de las cosas fermosas del mundo*, ed. Aida Fernanda Dias. Coimbra, 1976.
Coplas de ¡ay Panadera! See *Cancionero de Gallardo*.
CÓRDOBA, MARTÍN DE: *Libro del regimiento de los señores*. See RUBIO, ed.: *Prosistas castellanos del siglo XV*, vol. II.
CORRAL, LEÓN DE: *Don Alvaro de Luna según testimonios inéditos de la época*. Valladolid, 1915.
Cortes de los antiguos reinos de Aragón y Valencia y Principado de Cataluña. Madrid, 1896-1916. Vol. XII.
Cortes de los antiguos reinos de León y Castilla. Madrid, 1861-1903. Vols II and III.
Crónica de Don Alvaro de Luna, ed. J. M. de Flores. Madrid, 1784. Includes excerpts *in extenso* from SALAZAR Y MENDOZA: *Crónica del Gran Cardenal* and from ABARCA: *Anales de Aragón*.
Crónica de Don Alvaro de Luna, ed. Juan de Mata Carriazo. Colección de Crónicas Españolas, 2. Madrid, 1940.
Crónicas de los reyes de Castilla, vol. II, ed. Cayetano Rosell. Biblioteca de Autores Españoles, 68. Madrid, 1877. Includes *Crónica de Juan II*, following the edition of Lorenzo Galíndez de Carvajal (Logroño, 1517) and *Rubrica additio ex summa Episcopi Burgensis*, a vernacular version of Cartagena, *Anacephaleosis*.

Cronicón de Valladolid, ed. Pedro de Sainz de Baranda. CODOIN, 13.
CRUZ-SÁENZ, MICHÈLE S. DE: «The Marqués de Santillana's *Coplas* on Don Alvaro de Luna and the *Doctrinal de privados*», *Hispanic Review*, 49 (1981), 219-24.
Cuadernos de Historia, 1. *El tránsito de la Edad Media al Renacimiento*, ed. A. Rumeu de Armas. Anexos de la revista *Hispania*. Madrid, 1967.
Cuadernos de Historia, 3. *La sociedad castellana en la baja Edad Media*, ed. Salvador de Moxó. Anexos de la revista *Hispania*. Madrid, 1969.
Cuadernos de Historia, 6. *Estudios sobre la sociedad hispánica en la Edad Media*, ed. Salvador de Moxó. Anexos de la revista *Hispania*. Madrid, 1975.
[Cuarta crónica general]. *Continuación de la Crónica de España del Arzobispo Don Rodrigo Jiménez de Rada por el Obispo Don Gonzalo de la Hinojosa*. CODOIN, 106.

DELAVAYEN, MARTÍN: «De torrente voluptatis tue...» [Proclamation of papal indulgence.] Pamplona, 1514.
DEYERMOND, ALAN: «"Palabras y hojas secas, el viento se las lleva": Some Literary Ephemera of the Reign of Juan II», in *Mediaeval and Renaissance Studies on Spain and Portugal in Honour of P. E. Russell*, ed. F. W. Hodcroft, D. G. Pattison, R. D. F. Pring-Mill and R. W. Truman. Oxford, 1981.
DÍAZ DE MONTALVO, ALONSO: *Repertorium quaestionum super Nicholaum de Tudeschis*. Seville, 1477.
DÍAZ DE TOLEDO, FERNÁN: *Instrucción del Relator*. See CARTAGENA: *Defensorium Unitatis Christianae*.
— *Las notas del Relator*. Valladolid, 1493.
DÍAZ DE TOLEDO, PERO: *Diálogo e Razonamiento en la muerte del Marqués de Santillana*. See PAZ Y MELIA, ed.: *Opúsculos literarios*.
— *Introdución a la Exclamación e Querella de la governacion*. See FOULCHÉ-DELBOSC: *Cancionero castellano del siglo XV*, vol. II.
DI CAMILLO, OTTAVIO: *El humanismo castellano del siglo XV*. Valencia, 1976.
Documentos relativos a Enrique IV de Castilla, siendo todavía príncipe de Asturias. CODOIN, 40-41.
DIFFIE, BAILEY W., and WINIUS, GEORGE D.: *Foundations of the Portuguese Empire, 1415-1580*. Minneapolis, 1977.
DU CANGE: *Glossarium Mediae et Infimae Latinitatis*, vol. V. Paris, 1845.
DURO PEÑA, EMILIO: «Catálogo de documentos reales del Archivo de la Catedral de Orense (844-1520)», *Miscelánea de Textos Medievales*, I (1972), 9-145.
DUTTON, BRIAN: *Catálogo-índice de la poesía cancioneril del siglo XV*. Madison, 1982.

EIXIMENIS, FRANCESC: *Regiment de la cosa pública*. Barcelona, 1927.
En la España medieval: Estudios dedicados al profesor D. Julio González González. Madrid, 1980.
ESCAVIAS, PEDRO DE: *Repertorio de Príncipes de España y obra poética del Alcaide Pedro de Escavias*, ed. Michel García. Jaén, 1972.
ESPINA, ALONSO DE: *Fortalitium Fidei contra Judeos Sarracenos aliosque Christiane fidei inimicos*. Lyons, 1511.

FLORANES VÉLEZ DE ROBLES Y ENCINAS, RAFAEL DE: *Vida literaria del Canciller Ayala*. CODOIN, 19.
FORONDA, MANUEL DE: «El Tumbo de Valdeiglesias y D. Alvaro de Luna. Relación que dejó escrita Fr. Alonso de Quiriales de lo que vio y oyó en Valladolid en los días 2 y 3 de junio de 1453», *Boletín de la Real Academia de la Historia*, 41 (1902), 174-81.
FOSTER, DAVID WILLIAM: *The Marqués de Santillana*. Twayne's World Authors Series, 154. New York, 1971.

BIBLIOGRAPHY

FOULCHÉ-DELBOSC, R., ed.: *Cancionero castellano del siglo XV*, 2 vols. Nueva Biblioteca de Autores Españoles, 19 and 22. Madrid, 1912-15.

FUENSANTA DEL VALLE, MARQUÉS DE, and SANCHO RAYÓN, JOSÉ, eds.: *Cancionero de Lope de Stúñiga, códice del siglo XV ahora por vez primera publicado*. Colección de libros españoles raros o curiosos, 4. Madrid, 1872.

GALLARDO, BARTOLOMÉ JOSÉ: *Ensayo de una biblioteca española de libros raros y curiosos formado con los apuntamientos de D. Bartolomé José Gallardo*, vol. I. Madrid, 1968 (1st edition, Madrid, 1863).

GARCÍA DE CASTROJERIZ, JUAN: *Glosa castellana al Regimiento de Príncipes*, ed. Juan Beneyto Pérez, 3 vols. Madrid, 1947.

GARCÍA DE CORTÁZAR, JOSÉ ANGEL: *La época medieval*. Historia de España Alfaguara, 2. Madrid, 1973.

GARCÍA DE SALAZAR, LOPE: *Las bienandanzas e fortunas. Códice del siglo XV*, ed. Angel Rodríguez Herrero. Bilbao, 1955.

GARCÍA DE SANTA MARÍA, ALVAR: *Crónica de Juan II*. CODOIN, 99-100.

GARCÍA Y GARCÍA, ANTONIO: «Bartolo de Saxoferrato y España», *Anuario de Estudios Medievales*, 9 (1974-9), 439-67.

— *Estudios sobre la canonística portuguesa medieval*. Madrid, 1976.

GAYANGOS, PASCUAL DE, ed.: *Escritores en prosa anteriores al siglo XV*. Biblioteca de Autores Españoles, 51. Madrid, 1860.

GEDDES, MICHAEL: *Several Tracts against Popery: Together with the Life of Don Alvaro de Luna*. London, 1715.

GETINO, LUIS ALONSO: *Vida y obras de Fray Lope de Barrientos*. Anales Salmantinos, 1. Salamanca, 1927.

GILMAN, STEPHEN: *The Spain of Fernando de Rojas. The Intellectual and Social Landscape of «La Celestina»*. Princeton, 1972.

— «Judea pequenna. Granada ante la Inquisición», *Nueva Revista de Filología Hispánica*, 30 (1981), 586-93.

GIMENO CASALDUERO, JOAQUÍN: *La imagen del monarca en la Castilla del siglo XIV. Pedro el Cruel, Enrique II y Juan I*. Madrid, 1972.

GONZÁLEZ DE AVILA, GIL: *Teatro eclesiástico de las iglesias metropolitanas y catedrales de los reynos de las dos Castillas*, vol. IV. Madrid, 1650.

GRAETZ, H.: *A History of the Jews from the Earliest Times to the Present Day*. Revised edition, trans. Bella Löwy, vol. IV. London, 1892.

GUGLIELMI, NILDA: «Los elementos satíricos en las *Coplas de la panadera*», *Filología*, 14 (1970), 49-104.

HALE, JOHN; HIGHFIELD, ROGER, and SMALLEY, BERYL, eds.: *Europe in the Late Middle Ages*. London, 1965.

HIGHFIELD, ROGER: «The Catholic Kings and the Titled Nobility of Castile», in HALE, HIGHFIELD and SMALLEY: *Europe in the Late Middle Ages*, pp. 358-85.

— ed., *Spain in the Fifteenth Century. 1369-1516*. London, 1972.

HILLGARTH, J. N.: *The Spanish Kingdoms. 1250-1516*, 2 vols. Oxford, 1976-8.

Histoire du Connêtable de Lune, favori de Jean II, Roi de Castille & de Leon. Paris, 1720.

HORNIK, MARCEL P., ed.: *Collected Studies in Honour of Américo Castro's Eightieth Year*. Oxford, 1965.

ILLESCAS, GONZALO DE: *Segunda parte de la historia pontifical y cathólica*. Burgos, 1578.

Jaen, Didier T.: *John II of Castile and the Grand Master Alvaro de Luna. A Biography Compiled from the Chronicles of the Reign of King John II of Castile (1405-1454)*. Madrid, 1978.
John of Salisbury: *Joannis Saresberiensis postea episcopi Carnotensis Opera Omnia*, ed. J. A. Giles, vol. III. Oxford, 1848.
Don Juan Manuel: *Libro de los castigos*. See Gayangos, ed.: *Escritores en prosa anteriores al siglo XV*.
— *Libro de los estados*, ed. Robert Brian Tate and Ian R. MacPherson. Oxford, 1974.
— *Libro infinido y tratado de la Asunción*, ed. José Manuel Blecua. Colección Filológica, 2. Granada, 1952.
Kantorowicz, Ernst H.: *The King's Two Bodies. A Study in Medieval Political Theology*. Princeton, 1957.
Klein, Julius: *The Mesta: A Study in Spanish Economic History, 1273-1836*. Cambridge, Mass., 1920.
Laboa, Juan María: *Rodrigo Sánchez de Arévalo, Alcaide de Sant' Angelo*. Madrid, 1973.
Ladero Quesada, Miguel Angel: *España en 1492*. Historia de América Latina: Hechos, Documentos, Polémica, 1. Madrid, 1978.
— *La Hacienda Real de Castilla en el siglo XV*. La Laguna, 1973.
— «Los judíos castellanos del siglo XV en el arrendamiento de impuestos reales», *Cuadernos de Historia*, 6, 417-39.
Lamentación de Don Alvaro de Luna. See Bertini: *Testi spagnoli del secolo XV°*.
Lapesa, Rafael: *La obra literaria del Marqués de Santillana*. Madrid, 1957.
Lawrance, Jeremy N. H., ed.: *Un tratado de Alonso de Cartagena sobre la educación y los estudios literarios*. Barcelona, 1979.
Layna Serrano, F.: *Historia de Guadalajara y sus Mendozas en los siglos XV y XVI*, vol. I. Madrid, 1942.
León Tello, Pilar: *Inventario del Archivo de los Duques de Frías. II: Casa de Pacheco*. Madrid, 1967.
— *Judíos de Toledo*, 2 vols. Madrid, 1979.
Le Patourel, John: «The King and the Princes in Fourteenth-Century France», in Hale, Highfield and Smalley: *Europe in the Late Middle Ages*, pp. 155-83.
Lewis, Archibald R., ed.: *Aspects of the Renaissance: a Symposium*. Austin, 1967.
Lewis, P. S.: «France in the Fifteenth Century: Society and Sovereignty», in Hale, Highfield and Smalley: *Europe in the Late Middle Ages*, pp. 276-300.
El libro de los cien capítulos, ed. Agapito Rey. Indiana University Humanities Series, 44. Bloomington, 1960.
Lida de Malkiel, María Rosa: *Estudios sobre la literatura española del siglo XV*. Madrid, 1977.
— *La idea de la fama en la Edad Media castellana*. México City, 1952.
Linehan, Peter: «The Spanish Church Revisited: the Ecclesiastical *Gravamina* of 1279», in Tierney, Brian and Linehan, Peter, eds.: *Authority and Power. Studies on Medieval Law and Government Presented to Walter Ullmann on his Seventieth Birthday*. Cambridge, 1980, pp. 127-47.
López de Ayala, Pero: «*Libro de poemas*» o «*Rimado de Palacio*», ed. Michel García, 2 vols. Madrid, 1978.
Lucena, Juan de: *De Vita Beata*. See Bertini: *Testi Spagnoli del secolo XV°*.
MacCurdy, Raymond R.: *The Tragic Fall: Don Alvaro de Luna and Other Favorites in Spanish Golden Age Drama*. North Carolina Studies in the Romance Languages and Literatures. Chapel Hill, 1978.

BIBLIOGRAPHY

MacKay, Angus: «Las alteraciones monetarias en la Castilla del siglo XV: la moneda de cuenta y la historia política», in *En la España medieval*, pp. 237-48.
— *Money, Prices and Politics in Fifteenth-Century Castile*. Royal Historical Society Studies in History, 28. London, 1981.
— «Popular Movements and Pogroms in Fifteenth-Century Castile», *Past and Present*, 55 (1972), 33-67.
— *Spain in the Middle Ages. From Frontier to Empire, 1000-1500*. London, 1977.
McKisack, May: *The Fourteenth Century. 1307-1399*. Oxford, 1959.
Manrique, Gómez: *Consolación a la Condesa de Castro*. See Foulché-Delbosc: *Cancionero castellano del siglo XV*, vol. II.
Manrique, Jorge: *Cancionero*, ed. Augusto Cortina. Clásicos Castellanos, 94. Madrid, 1929.
Maravall, José Antonio: *Estado moderno y mentalidad social*. Madrid, 1972.
— *Estudios de historia del pensamiento español*, vol. I. Madrid, 1973 (1st edition, Madrid, 1968).
— «The Origins of the Modern State», *Journal of World History*, 6 (1961), 789-801.
Mariana, Juan de: *Obras del Padre Juan de Mariana*, vol. II. Biblioteca de Autores Españoles, 31. Madrid, 1950 (1st edition, Madrid, 1854). Includes the relevant chapters of the author's *Historia de España*.
Márquez Villanueva, Francisco: «The converso problem: an assessment», in Hornik, ed.: *Collected Studies in Honour of Américo Castro's Eightieth Year*, pp. 317-33.
— *Investigaciones sobre Juan Alvarez Gato: contribución al conocimiento de la literatura castellana del siglo XV*. Boletín de la Real Academia Española, Anejo 4. Madrid, 1960. 2nd edition, 1974.
Martín, José Luis: *La Península en la Edad Media*, Barcelona, 1976.
— «La sociedad media e inferior de los reinos hispánicos», *Anuario de Estudios Medievales*, 7 (1970-1), 555-76.
Martínez Moro, Jesús: *La renta feudal en la Castilla del siglo XV: los Stúñiga. Consideraciones metodológicas y otras*. Valladolid, 1977.
Martín Póstigo, María de la S.: *La cancillería castellana de los Reyes Católicos*. Valladolid, 1959.
Matienzo, J.: *Dialogus Relatoris et Advocati*. Valladolid, 1604.
Mena, Juan de: *Laberinto de Fortuna*, ed. Louise Vasvari Fainberg. Madrid, 1976.
— *Obra lírica*, ed. Miguel Angel Pérez Priego. Madrid, 1979.
Mendoza Negrillo, Juan de Dios: *Fortuna y providencia en la literatura castellana del siglo XV*. Boletín de la Real Academia Española, Anejo 27. Madrid, 1973.
Mendoza y Bovadilla, Francisco: *El tizón de la nobleza española o máculos y sambenitos de sus linajes*. Barcelona, 1880.
Menéndez Pidal, Ramón, ed.: *Historia de España*, vol. XV: *Los Trastámaras de Castilla y Aragón en el siglo XV*. Madrid, 1964.
Menéndez y Pelayo, Marcelino: *Antología de poetas líricos castellanos*, vol. II. Madrid, 1944.
Mitre Fernández, Emilio: «Algunas cuestiones demográficas en la Castilla de fines del siglo XIV», *Anuario de Estudios Medievales*, 7 (1970-1), 615-21.
— *Evolución de la nobleza en Castilla bajo Enrique III (1396-1406)*. Valladolid, 1968.
Morel-Fatio, Alfred: *Catalogue des Manuscrits Espagnols et des Manuscrits Portugais de la Bibliothèque Nationale de Paris*. Paris, 1892.
Moxó, Salvador de: «De la nobleza vieja a la nobleza nueva. La transformación nobiliaria castellana en la baja Edad Media», *Cuadernos de Historia*, 3, 1-210.
— «La nobleza castellana en el siglo XIV», *Anuario de Estudios Medievales*, 7 (1970-1), 493-511.

NETANYAHU, BENZION: «Alonso de Espina: was he a New Christian?», *Proceedings of the American Academy for Jewish Research,* 43 (1976), 107-65.

OLIVAR, MARÇAL: «Documents per la biografia del Marquès de Santillana», *Estudis Universitaris Catalans,* 11 (1926), 1-11.

PALENCIA, ALONSO DE: [*Décadas.*] *Alphonsi Palentini Historiographi Gesta Hispaniensa ex Annalibus Suorum Dierum Colligentis.* Madrid, 1834. (Pages 1-96 only printed, and sometimes bound with *Colección diplomática;* see above.)
— *Crónica de Enrique IV,* ed. A. Paz y Melia, vol. I. Biblioteca de Autores Españoles, 257. Madrid, 1973.
— *Epístolas latinas,* ed. Robert B. Tate and Rafael Alemany Ferrer. Barcelona, 1982.

PAZ Y MELIA, A.: «Biblioteca fundada por el Conde de Haro en 1455», *Revista de Archivos, Bibliotecas y Museos,* 1 (1897).
— ed., *Opúsculos literarios de los siglos XIV a XVI.* Sociedad de Bibliófilos Españoles, 29. Madrid, 1892. Includes PERO DÍAZ DE TOLEDO: *Diálogo e Razonamiento en la muerte del Marqués de Santillana.*

PATCH, HOWARD R.: *The Goddes Fortuna in Medieval Literature.* Cambridge, Mass., 1927.

PENNA, MARIO, ed.: *Prosistas castellanos del siglo XV,* vol. I. Biblioteca de Autores Españoles, 116. Madrid, 1959. Includes CARTAGENA: *Proposición contra los ingleses;* SÁNCHEZ DE ARÉVALO: *Suma de la política,* and VALERA: *Doctrinal de príncipes.*

PENNEY, CLARA L.: *Printed Books 1468-1700 in the Library of the Hispanic Society of America.* New York, 1965.

PÉREZ-BUSTAMANTE, ROGELIO: *El gobierno y la administración territorial de Castilla (1230-1474),* 2 vols. Madrid, 1976.

PÉREZ DE GUZMÁN, FERNÁN: *Generaciones y semblanzas,* ed. R. B. Tate (London, 1965).
— *Requesta fecha al magnifico marques de Santyllana por los gloriosos emperadores Costantyno, Theodosio, Justyniano, sobre la estruycion de Costantynopla.* See FOULCHÉ-DELBOSC: *Cancionero castellano del siglo XV,* vol. I.

PÉREZ EMBID, FLORENTINO: *Los descubrimientos en el Atlántico y la rivalidad castellano-portuguesa hasta el tratado de Tordesillas.* Seville, 1948.

PÉREZ GÓMEZ, ANTONIO, ed.: *Romancero de don Alvaro de Luna.* Valencia, 1953.

PHILLIPS, WILLIAM, D., Jr.: «State Service in Fifteenth-Century Castile. A statistical study of the Royal Appointees», *Societas,* 8 (1978), 115-36.

PINA, RUI DE: *Crónicas,* ed. M. Lopes de Almeida. Oporto, 1977.

PISKORSKI, WLADIMIRO: *Las Cortes de Castilla en el período de tránsito de la Edad Media a la Moderna. 1188-1520,* trans. Claudio Sánchez Albornoz. Barcelona, 1930.

PORTILLA, MIGUEL DE: *Historia de la ciudad de Compluto, vulgarmente Alcalá de Santiuste y aora de Henares,* 2 vols. Alcalá de Henares, 1725-8.

POST, GAINES: *Studies in Medieval Legal Thought. Public Law and the State, 1100-1322.* Princeton, 1964.

PRESTAGE, EDGAR: *The Portuguese Pioneers.* London, 1933.

PRIETO CANTERO, AMALIA: *Documentos referentes a hidalguías, caballerías y exenciones de pecho de la época de los reyes católicos, entresacados del legajo número 393 de la sección Mercedes y Privilegios del Archivo General de Simancas.* Madrid, 1974.

PROCTOR, EVELYN S.: *Alfonso X of Castile. Patron of Literature and Learning.* Oxford, 1951.

BIBLIOGRAPHY

PULGAR, FERNANDO DEL: *Letras. Glosa a las Coplas de Mingo Revulgo,* ed. J. Domínguez Bordona. Clásicos Castellanos, 99. Madrid, 1929.

QUINTANA, MANUEL JOSÉ: *Obras completas.* Biblioteca de Autores Españoles, 19. Madrid, 1898. (Ist edition Madrid, 1852.) Includes the author's biography of Alvaro de Luna in *Vidas de españoles célebres.*

RADIN, MAX: «The Conscience of the Court», *Law Quarterly Review,* 48 (1932), 506-20.

RICO, FRANCISCO: *El pequeño mundo del hombre. Varia fortuna de una idea en las letras españolas.* Madrid, 1970.

RINALDI, ODORICO: *Annales Ecclesiastici ab Anno MCXCVIII ubi desinit Cardinalis Baronius, Auctore Odorico Reynaldo,* vol. IX. Lucca, 1752.

RIZZO Y RAMÍREZ, JUAN: *Juicio crítico y significación política de Don Alvaro de Luna.* Madrid, 1865.

RODRÍGUEZ DE ALMELA, DIEGO: *Valerio de las historias de la sagrada escritura y de los hechos de España,* ed. Juan Antonio Moreno. Madrid, 1793.

ROTH, CECIL: *The Spanish Inquisition.* New York, 1964.

ROUND, NICHOLAS G.: «La correspondencia del Arcediano de Niebla en el Archivo del Real Monasterio de Santa María de Guadalupe», *Historia, Instituciones, Documentos,* 7 (1980), 215-68.

— «Five Magicians, or the Uses of Literacy», *Modern Language Review,* 64 (1969), 793-805.

— «Politics, Style and Group Attitudes in the *Instrucción del Relator*», *Bulletin of Hispanic Studies,* 46 (1969), 289-319.

— «Renaissance Culture and its Opponents in Fifteenth-Century Castile», *Modern Language Review,* 57 (1962), 204-15.

— «The Shadow of a Philosopher: Medieval Castilian Images of Plato», *Journal of Hispanic Philology,* 3 (1978-9), 1-36.

RUBIO, FERNANDO, ed.: *Prosistas castellanos del siglo XV,* vol. II. Biblioteca de Autores Españoles, 171. Madrid, 1964. Includes CÓRDOBA: *Libro del regimiento de los señores.*

RUBIO, GERMÁN: *Historia de Nuestra Señora de Guadalupe o sea: apuntes históricos sobre el origen, desarrollo y vicisitudes del santuario y santa casa de Guadalupe.* Barcelona, 1926.

RUSSELL, PETER E.: «Arms versus Letters: towards a definition of Spanish fifteenth-century humanism», in LEWIS, ed.: *Aspects of the Renaissance,* pp. 45-58. Spanish version in RUSSELL: *Temas de «La Celestina»,* 209-39.

— *Temas de «La Celestina» y otros estudios del «Cid» al «Quijote».* Barcelona, 1978.

— *The English Intervention in Spain and Portugal in the Time of Edward III and Richard II.* Oxford, 1955.

SÁEZ, LICINIANO: *Demostración histórica del verdadero valor de todas las monedas que corrían en Castilla durante el reynado del señor Don Enrique III y de su correspondencia con las del señor Carlos IV.* Madrid, 1796.

SALAZAR Y MENDOZA, PEDRO DE: *Crónica de el Gran Cardenal de España Don Pedro Gonçález de Mendoza.* Toledo, 1625. See also *Crónica de Don Alvaro de Luna,* ed. Flores.

SALVADOR MIGUEL, NICASIO: *La poesía cancioneril. El «Cancionero de Estúñiga».* Madrid, 1977.

SÁNCHEZ ALBORNOZ, CLAUDIO: *Estudios sobre las instituciones medievales españolas.* México City, 1965.

SÁNCHEZ DE ARÉVALO, RODRIGO: *Historiae Hispanicae Partes Quatuor.* See SCHOTT, ed.: *Hispaniae Illustratae Scriptores Varii.*
— *Suma de la política.* See PENNA, ed.: *Prosistas castellanos del siglo XV,* vol. I.
SANCHO IV DE CASTILLA [attributed]: *Castigos e documentos para bien vivir ordenados por el rey don Sancho IV,* ed. Agapito Rey. Indiana University Humanities Series, 24. Bloomington, 1952.
SANTILLANA, MARQUIS OF [IÑIGO LÓPEZ DE MENDOZA]: *Bias contra fortuna Coplas del dicho señor marqués. Doctrinal de privados. Sobre la quartana del señor rey don Johan II. Sonetos.* See FOULCHÉ-DELBOSC: *Cancionero castellano del siglo XV,* vol. I.
— *Proverbios.* Seville, 1494.
SCHIFF, MARIO: *La Bibliothèque du Marquis de Santillane.* Bibliothèque de l'Ecole des Hautes Etudes, 153. Paris, 1905.
SCHOTT, ANDREAS, ed.: *Hispaniae Illustratae seu Rerum Urbiumque Hispaniae, Lusitaniae, Aethiopiae et Indiae Scriptores Varii,* vol. I. Frankfurt, 1603. Includes CARTAGENA: *Anacephaleosis,* and SÁNCHEZ DE ARÉVALO: *Historiae Hispanicae Partes Quatuor.*
SEARS, HELEN L.: «The *Rimado de Palacio* and the «De Regimine Principum» Tradition of the Middle Ages», *Hispanic Review,* 20 (1952), 1-27.
SERRANO, LUCIANO: *Los conversos Don Pablo de Santa María y Don Alfonso de Cartagena, Obispos de Burgos, gobernantes, diplomáticos y escritores.* Madrid, 1942.
SEVERIN, DOROTHY S., ed.: *Cancionero de Martínez de Burgos.* Exeter Hispanic Texts, 12. Exeter, 1976.
SHAW, K. E.: «Povincial and Pundit: Juan de Castrojeriz's Version of *De Regimine Principum*», *Bulletin of Hispanic Studies,* 38 (1961), 55-63.
SICROFF, ALBERT A.: *Les Controverses des Statuts de «pureté de sang» en Espagne du XVe au XVIIe siècle.* Paris, 1960.
— «The Jeronymite Monastery of Guadalupe in 14th and 15th century Spain», in HORNIK, ed.: *Collected Studies in Honour of Americo Castro's Eightieth Year,* pp. 397-422.
SILIÓ, CÉSAR: *Don Alvaro de Luna y su tiempo.* Buenos Aires, 1939.
Archivo General de Simancas. Printed catalogue:
Diversos de Castilla (Cámara de Castilla), 972-1716. Madrid, 1969.
Patronato Real (834-1851), vols. I-II. Valladolid, 1946-9.
Registro General del Sello, vol. I. Valladolid, 1950.
SOBREQUÉS CALLICÓ, JAIME: «La Peste Negra en la Península Ibérica», *Anuario de Estudios Medievales,* 7 (1970-1), 67-101.
SORIA, ANDRÉS: *Los humanistas de la corte de Alfonso el Magnánimo (según los epistolarios).* Granada, 1956.
STÉFANO, LUCIANA DE: *La sociedad estamental de la baja Edad Media española a la luz de la literatura de la época.* Caracas, 1966.
STELLA-MARANCA, F.: *Seneca giureconsulto.* Studia Juridica, 8. Rome, 1966 (1st edition, Lanciano, 1926).
SUÁREZ FERNÁNDEZ, LUIS: *Historia de España antigua y media,* 2 vols. Madrid, 1976.
— *Historia del reinado de Juan I de Castilla,* vol. I. Madrid, 1977.
— *Juan I, rey de Castilla (1379-1390).* Madrid, 1955.
— «Un libro de asientos de Juan II», *Hispania,* 68 (1957), 323-68.
— *Navegación y comercio en el golfo de Vizcaya. Un estudio sobre la política marinera de la Casa de Trastámara.* Madrid, 1959.
— *Nobleza y monarquía. Puntos de vista sobre la historia política castellana del siglo XV.* Valladolid, 1975 (2nd edition, with additions and corrections).

— *Relaciones entre Portugal y Castilla en la época del Infante Don Enrique, 1393-1460*. Madrid, 1960.

TATE, ROBERT BRIAN: *Ensayos sobre la historiografía peninsular del siglo XV*. Madrid, 1970.
— *Joan Margarit i Pau, Cardenal e Bisbe de Girona. La seva vida i les seves obres*. Barcelona, 1976.
— «Political Allegory in Fifteenth-Century Spain: A Study of the *Batalla Campal de los Perros contra los Lobos* by Alfonso de Palencia (1423-92)», *Journal of Hispanic Philology*, I (1976-7), 169-86.
THOMPSON, STITH: *Motif-Index of Folk Literature*. Revised edition. 6 vols. Copenhagen, 1955-8.
TORREÁNAZ, CONDE DE: *Los Consejos del Rey durante la Edad Media*, 2 vols. Madrid, 1884-90.
TORRE, FERNANDO DE LA: *Cancionero y obras en prosa*, ed. A. Paz y Melia. Gesellschaft für Romanische Literatur, 16. Dresdren, 1907.
TORRES, JUAN DE: *Pregunta a Juan de Padilla*. See FUENSANTA DEL VALLE and SANCHO RAYÓN, eds.: *Cancionero de Lope de Stúñiga*.
TORRES FONTES, JUAN: *Estudio sobre la «Crónica de Enrique IV» del Doctor Galíndez de Carvajal*. Murcia, 1946.
— *Itinerario de Enrique IV de Castilla*. Murcia, n.d.
TORRES SANZ, DAVID: *La administración central castellana en la baja Edad Media*. Valladolid, 1982.

ULLMANN, WALTER: *A History of Political Thought: The Middle Ages*. Harmondsworth, 1965.
— *The Medieval Idea of Law as Represented by Lucas de Penna. A Study in Fourteenth-Century Legal Scholarship*. London, 1946.
UREÑA Y SMENJAUD, R. DE: *Los incunables jurídicos de España*. Madrid, 1929.

VALDEAVELLANO, LUIS G. DE: *Curso de historia de las instituciones españolas. De los orígenes al final de la Edad Media*. Madrid, 1968.
VALDEÓN BARUQUE, JULIO: *Los conflictos sociales en el reino de Castilla en los siglos XIV y XV*. Madrid, 1976 (1st edition, 1975).
— «Las Cortes castellanas en el siglo XIV», *Anuario de Estudios Medievales*, 7 (1970-1), 633-44.
— *Enrique II de Castilla: la guerra civil y la consolidación del régimen (1366-1371)*. Valladolid, 1966.
VALERA, MOSÉN DIEGO DE: *Doctrinal de príncipes*. See PENNA, ed.: *Prosistas castellanos del siglo XV*, vol. I.
— *Memorial de diversas hazañas. Crónica de Enrique IV, ordenada por Mosén Diego de Valera*, ed. Juan de Mata Carriazo. Colección de Crónicas Españolas, 4. Madrid, 1941. Includes relevant sections of the author's *Crónica abreviada de España*.
VAN KLEFFENS, E. H.: *Hispanic Law until the End of the Middle Ages*. Edinburgh, 1968.
VARGAS ZÚÑIGA Y MONTERO DE ESPINOSA, A. DE, and CUARTERO Y HUERTA, B., eds.: *Indice de la colección de Don Luis de Salazar y Castro*. The following volumes:
13. Madrid, 1955.
14. Madrid, 1956.
15. Madrid, 1956.
19. Madrid, 1957.
20. Madrid, 1957.
28. Madrid, 1961.

29. Madrid, 1961.
30. Madrid, 1962.
31. Madrid, 1962.
32. Madrid, 1963.
33. Madrid, 1964.

VICENS VIVES, JAIME: *Juan II de Aragón (1398-1474). Monarquía y revolución en la España del siglo XV.* Barcelona, 1953.

VICENS VIVES, JAIME, and NADAL OLLER, JORGE: *Manual de historia económica de España.* Barcelona, 1964.

ZURITA, JERÓNIMO: *Los cinco libros postreros de la segunda parte de los Anales de la Corona de Aragon: compuestos por Geronimo Çurita Chronista del Reyno.* Zaragoza, 1579.

INDEX

ABARCA, Fray Pedro de, historian, 135n, 218n.
Abreviación de la crónica del Halconero, 71, 135.
ACUÑA, Luis de, Administrator of Diocese of Segovia, 131.
ACUÑA, Pedro de, brother of Archbishop Alfonso Carrillo, 131n-132, 138.
ADARNOLA, 222n.
adelantado, see MANRIQUE, Diego; MANRIQUE, Pedro; RIBERA, Perafán de.
Admiral of Castile, see ENRÍQUEZ, Fadrique (1).
ADRADA, 222n.
AEGIDIUS ROMANUS, political theorist, 111-12, 116, 124, 128.
AENEAS SYLVIUS, later Pope Pius II, 213n-214.
AFONSO V, King of Portugal, 47n, 48-50, 229.
AFRICA, 48-50, 229.
AGRAZ, Juan de, poet, 216n.
AGREDA, 198n.
ALBA DE TORMES, count of, see ALVAREZ DE TOLEDO, Fernando.
ALBERT II, Holy Roman Emperor, 122.
ALBURQUERQUE, 148-9, 189, 222n.
ALBURQUERQUE, Count of, see LUNA, Juan de.
alcabala (sales tax), 53, 54, 58.
ALCALÁ DE HENARES, 171, 177, 179, 181, 182, 190, 203.
ALCALÁ DE HENARES, University of, 180n.
ALCALÁ, Juan de, «alcaide del Príncipe», 180n.
alcaldes de casa (judges of royal household), 145, 146n.
ALCAZARÉN, 131, 235.
ALFARROBEIRA, 48.
ALFONSO V, King of Aragon, 1, 7, 34n, 225-6, 228-9.
ALFONSO X, King of Castile, 94, 102, 104-8, 111, 116, 119, 120n, 122, 123-5, 152, 160.
ALFONSO XI, King of Castile, 109n, 126n.
ALFONSO VI, King of Leon-Castile, 123.
ALFONSO VII, King of Leon-Castile, 123.
ALFONSO, Prince, second son of Juan II, 48, 187, 190, 237n-238.
ALVAREZ, Alfonso, *contador*, son of Mayor Alvarez, 173n.
ALVAREZ, Mayor, condemned for Judaizing, 173, 204.
ALVAREZ DE TOLEDO, Alfonso, *contador mayor*, 62, 172-3, 176, 183, 202, 203.
ALVAREZ DE TOLEDO, Fernando, Count of Alba de Tormes, 19, 36, 180n, 181-2, 183, 200n, 225.
ALVAREZ DE VILLASANDINO, Alfonso, poet, 24, 201.
AMADOR DE LOS RÍOS, José, historian, 63, 139n, 185, 188, 204-6.
ANDALUSIA, 6, 53-4, 79, 192, 198n-199, 222, 223.
ANDREAE, see JOHANNES ANDREAE.
ANDREAS OF ISERNIA, jurist, 110n, 128, 162.
apoderamiento (usurpation), 40-1, 101, 144, 151-8, 162.
APONTE, Pedro Gerónimo de, genealogist, 204.
AQUINAS, see THOMAS AQUINAS, ST.
AQUINAS (PSEUDO), see THOMAS AQUINAS (PSEUDO).
ARAGON, 1, 6, 7, 13n, 24, 29, 34, 35, 38, 87, 88, 89, 93n-94, 116, 118, 126, 127, 172, 173, 193, 195-6, 226, 228, 229, 234, 235.
ARAGÓN, Fadrique de, Count of Luna, 25n.
ARAGON, Infantes of (see also JUAN, King of Navarre; ENRIQUE, Infante, Master of Santiago), 7-10, 24, 29, 46, 174, 193.
ARÉVALO, 18n, 24, 63, 130, 131, 137, 149, 182, 195.
ARIAS DE AVILA, Diego, *contador mayor* under Enrique IV, 203.

257

ARJONA, Duke of, see ENRÍQUEZ, Fadrique (2).
ASAGALA, 222n.
ASTUDILLO, 34, 36n-37.
ASTURIAS-LEON, 164n.
ATELODÓN, 188.
ATIENZA, 37, 78, 189.
audiencia (Court of Appeal), 2, 16, 63, 175 (see also *oidor*).
AVILA, 49, 188, 190, 203, 226.
AVILA, Alfonso de, secretary of Fernando and Isabel, 188n.
AVILA, Bishop of, see FONSECA, Alonso de.
AVILA, Gonzalo de, son of Pero González de Avila, 190.
AVILA, María de, daughter of Pero González de Avila, 190.
AVILÉS, 192n-193.
AYLLÓN, 88, 92, 97, 101.
ayudas de costa (expense allowances), 51, 57.

BABILAFUENTE, 166, 196.
BALDUS (BALDO DEGLI UBALDI), jurist, 105, 116, 125n, 128, 178.
BARBARY, 49.
EL BARCHILÓN, Mosé, Jew of Guadalajara, 187n.
BARRASA, Prince Enrique's groom, 212.
BARRIENTOS, Lope, Bishop of Cuenca, 207-9, 226-7, 237.
BARTOLUS (BARTOLO DI SASSOFERRATO), jurist, 93-4, 105, 116, 122-3, 125, 128, 152n.
BARZIZZA, Guinforte, Humanist, 41n.
BASLE, 126n-127.
BASSIANUS, see JOHANNES BASSIANUS.
BÉJAR, 37, 69, 70.
BENAVENTE, Count of, see PIMENTEL, Rodrigo.
BENEDICT XIII, Antipope, 94, 98n, 127.
BERCIANA, 222n.
Bias contra Fortuna (Marquis of Santillana), 200n.
BIENVENISTE, Abraham, Jewish tax-farmer, 172.
BISCAY (VIZCAYA), 186-7, 192.
BISTICCI, Vespasiano da, biographer, 68.
Black Death, 3, 31.
BLANCA, Princess of Navarre, first wife of Prince Enrique, 8, 48, 131, 235.
BOLOGNA, University of, 125.
BONAVENTURE, ST., 106.
BRACTON, Henry of, jurist, 103, 116n.
BRIVIESCA, *Cortes* of (1387), 119, 120.
BUELNA, Count of, see NIÑO, Pero.
BURGOS, 22, 36n-37, 53n-54, 60, 61, 64-5, 67-86, 88, 89n, 90, 108, 130, 131, 134, 135n, 171, 194, 200, 204, 205, 224, 225.
BURGOS, Bishop of, see CARTAGENA, Alonso de; SANTA MARÍA, Pablo de.
BURGOS, *Cortes* of (1453), 60, 69, 86, 87, 130, 199-200, 225-6.
BURLEY, Walter, anthologist, 124n.

caballeros moriscos, 18.
CADALSO, 214-15, 223.
CÁDIZ, 199.
CALAHORRA, 230n.
CALATRAVA, Order of, 193, 194.
CALERA, 222n.
CALLÍS, Jaime, jurist, 93-4.
camarero mayor (Chamberlain), see LUJÁN, Pedro de.
CANARIES, 48-9.
CANDELEDA, 222n.
CANTERA BURGOS, Francisco, historian, 64.
CARCAÑOSA, 222n.
CARLOS, Prince of Viana, son of Juan King of Navarre, 196, 229.
CARRILLO-ACUÑA, family, 134.
CARRILLO DE ACUÑA, Alfonso, Archbishop of Toledo, 36, 53, 65, 69, 131n-132, 134, 139-40, 144, 180n, 182, 225.
CARRILLO DE HUETE, PERO, chronicler (see also *Abreviación de la Crónica del Halconero*), 17.
CARTAGENA, 184n.
CARTAGENA-SANTA MARÍA, family, 64-5, 85, 194, 203.
CARTAGENA, Alonso de, Bishop of Burgos, 21n, 40, 64-5, 68, 70, 77n, 78n-80, 83, 102, 122, 126-7, 128, 206.
CARTAGENA, Alvaro de, son of Pedro de Cartagena, 64, 76, 97.
CARTAGENA, Pedro de, brother of Alonso de Cartagena, 64n-65, 72, 76-7, 82, 85, 107, 109.
CARVAJAL, Juan de, Cardinal of St. Angelo, 177.
Casa de las Cuentas (Treasury), 14.
CASTIL DE LA VAYUELA, 221n.
CASTILE, 1-3, 11, 14, 29-30, 33, 35, 48-50, 60n, 61n, 87, 94, 99, 102, 103, 109-10, 118, 119, 122-4, 127, 164, 184, 228-9.
CASTILLA, King-at-arms, 44-5.
CASTRO, Count of, see GÓMEZ DE SANDOVAL, Diego.
CASTROJERIZ, Juan de, translator, 124n.
CASTRONUÑO, 8, 9.
CATALONIA, 121, 126.
Catholic Monarchs, see FERNANDO II, King of Aragon and ISABEL I, Queen of Castile, *Reyes Católicos*; also, se-

INDEX

parately, ISABEL I, Queen of Castile.
Causa escrita a Don Alvaro de Luna (anonymous), 136n, 169, 218.
causa regni, 162.
certa scientia, see *cierta ciencia*.
CHACÓN, Gonzalo, in Alvaro de Luna's household; later his chronicler 41, 74-6, 80-2, 89, 132-3, 138, 140, 147, 149, 169, 188, 189, 209, 217-18.
Chamberlain, see LUJÁN, Pedro de, *camarero mayor*.
CHARLES I, King of England, 164n.
Chief Justice, see ESTÚÑIGA, Pedro de, Count of Plasencia, *justicia mayor*.
CHINCHILLA, 190.
CHIRINO, family (see also GARCÍA DE GUADALAJARA), 64.
cierta ciencia (certa scientia), 93-5, 101, 104, 120, 160, 163, 167n, 219.
CLEMENT VI, Pope, 93n.
CLEMENT VII, Pope, 93n, 94n.
cobro de albaquías (recovery of tax arrears), 55, 233-4.
common knowledge, see *cosa notoria*.
conscience, of the Court, 158n, 163-4, 166; of the King, 117-18, 142, 147n, 155, 160.
Consejo (royal Council), of Aragon, 195; of Castile, 2, 4-5, 9, 13, 16, 25-6, 28, 63, 114, 120, 135-44, 145-6, 147-8, 149, 157, 161, 162, 165, 169-70, 174-6, 181, 184, 186, 188, 189, 193, 194, 199-200, 202, 207, 211, 224; of Navarre, 61n.
Consejo secreto, 13, 25.
Constable, see LÓPEZ DÁVALOS, Ruy, LUNA, Alvaro de.
CONSTANTINOPLE, 211.
contadores mayores (heads of Treasury), 14, 20, 184, 190, 193.
contadores mayores de cuentas (second tier of Treasury officials), 193, 195.
conversos (converted Jews or their descendants), 11, 18, 21-2, 29, 63-5, 77, 80, 85, 171-210 passim.
Coplas de ¡ay Panadera! (anonymous), 178, 202n.
Coplas: «De tu resplandor, o Luna...» (Marquis of Santillana), 41, 215.
CÓRDOBA, 7, 53n, 184n, 189, 223.
CÓRDOBA, *Cortes* of (1455), 56n.
CORRAL, León de, historian, 149n.
Cortes (Castilian assembly of estates), 2, 4, 8, 10, 14, 16-17, 22-3, 26, 28, 51, 54, 55-7, 58, 60, 63, 69, 86, 87, 91, 92n, 96, 99, 104, 106, 107n, 111, 117, 119-20, 123, 130, 158n, 186, 190, 199-200, 221, 225-6.
Cortes subsidy, 54, 56-7, 58-9.

Corts (Catalan assembly of estates), 106n, 107, 126.
LA CORUÑA, 192.
cosa notoria (common knowledge), 40, 136, 151, 156, 157.
Council, see *Consejo; Consejo secreto*.
Crónica de Don Alvaro de Luna, 29, 39, 42-3, 44, 64, 67-8, 71, 79-82, 84, 89, 132, 136, 138, 140, 151, 209, 217, 226.
Crónica de Juan II, 32, 38, 42-3, 45, 46-7, 49, 78, 80-1, 136, 138-40, 152, 166, 209, 217, 227.
Cuarta Crónica General, 40, 232-3.
CUENCA, 64, 172, 173, 182, 184n, 186, 203, 223, 230n.
CUENCA, Bishop of, see BARRIENTOS, Lope.
CURIEL, 69, 73-5.
currency debasement, 15-16, 26-7, 51, 52n, 58-9.

DÁVILA, Alfonso, see AVILA, Alfonso de.
Decretum gloss, 164.
«De tu resplandor, o Luna...» (Marquis of Santillana) see *Coplas*: «De tu resplandor, o Luna...».
Dialogus de Scaccario, 104.
DÍAZ DE ALCALÁ, Pero, in Prince's houseold; possibly=Pero Díaz de Toledo, 180n.
DÍAZ DE MENDOZA, Ruy, *mayordomo mayor*, 73n, 78-80, 81n, 82, 85, 88, 90, 131, 134, 138-9, 195.
DÍAZ DE MONTALVO, Alonso, Licenciado, judge at trial of Alvaro de Luna, 122, 125n, 147-9, 159-60, 161, 163, 164n-165, 165n-166, 171, 176, 182-3, 184, 186, 197, 198, 201, 203, 204, 207.
DÍAZ DE OLMEDILLA, Fernando, see DÍAZ DE TOLEDO, Fernando, brother of Dr Pero Díaz de Toledo.
DÍAZ DE OLMEDILLA, Francisco (1), Dr, *oidor*, son of Dr Pero Díaz de Toledo, 179.
DÍAZ DE OLMEDILLA, Francisco (2), market overseer (Guadalajara), 173n, 179n, 204-5.
DÍAZ DE OLMEDILLA, Pero, Dr, see DÍAZ DE TOLEDO, Pero, Dr.
DÍAZ DE TOLEDO family, 177, 207.
DÍAZ DE TOLEDO, Fernán, Dr, Relator, judge at trial of Alvaro de Luna, 13, 16, 17, 20, 42, 44-5, 62, 70, 78n-80, 82, 90, 92, 100-101, 126n-127, 129, 134, 137, 139-40, 144, 145, 146-7, 148, 151, 158-60, 164n, 165, 169, 171-9, 180, 182, 183, 184, 185, 190-1, 197, 198-200, 201, 202, 203, 204-5, 206, 208, 211, 222-3, 224-5, 227, 230n-231, 237.

DÍAZ DE TOLEDO, Fernando (1), Dr, Archdeacon of Niebla, cousin of Relator, 172, 186.
DÍAZ DE TOLEDO, Fernando (2), royal notary, brother of Dr Pero Díaz de Toledo, 179.
DÍAZ DE TOLEDO, Fernando (3), *converso* of Granada, 173n, 205.
DÍAZ DE TOLEDO, Juan, son of Relator, 175.
DÍAZ DE TOLEDO, Juana, daughter of Relator, 175.
DÍAZ DE TOLEDO, Luis, eldest son of Relator, 44-5, 62, 79n, 175, 183.
DÍAZ DE TOLEDO, Pedro, possibly brother of Relator, 179n.
DÍAZ DE TOLEDO, Pero, Dr, *oidor*, nephew of Relator, judge at trial of Alvaro de Luna, 23n, 63, 113n, 179-82, 183, 185, 190, 197, 198, 200, 201, 203, 204, 225.
diezmos de la mar de Castilla (Burgos customs dues), 53n.
Digest, 110, 121.
Digest commentary (Pero Díaz de Toledo), 180.
Doctrinal de privados (Marquis of Santillana), 215-16, 239n.
Dominican Order, 207.
DUEÑAS, 131n-132, 134, 139.
Dum Diversas (Bull), 48n-49.

EDWARD III, King of England, 167n.
EIXIMENIS, Francesc, Franciscan, 121, 126n.
ENGLAND, 2, 29, 103, 104, 116, 126, 164, 167, 214.
ENRIQUE II, King of Castile, 1, 3, 94, 106, 120n, 126, 184.
ENRIQUE III, King of Castile, 3, 51, 94, 96, 120n, 174, 184, 188.
ENRIQUE, Prince, eldest son of Juan II; later Enrique IV, King of Castile, 8, 10, 11, 24, 27n, 33-4, 35-6, 38-9, 43, 47n-48, 50-1, 55, 63, 64, 66, 88, 89, 95, 99, 102, 131, 172, 176n, 180, 184, 186, 187, 190, 191, 192, 194n-195, 198, 199-200, 209, 212, 219, 222-3, 224, 225, 226, 227, 228, 229, 233n-234, 234-9.
ENRIQUE, Prince of Portugal («Henry the Navigator»), 48.
ENRIQUE, Infante, Master of Santiago (see also ARAGON, Infantes of), 10, 172, 174.
ENRÍQUEZ family, 18, 34n.
ENRÍQUEZ, Fadrique (1), Admiral of Castile, 35, 56n, 88, 200.
ENRÍQUEZ, Fadrique (2), Duke of Arjona (died 1430), 154n.
ESCALONA, 49, 61, 65, 89, 108, 115, 117, 118, 130, 131n, 133, 134, 135, 136, 137, 138, 139, 140-4, 147, 148, 153, 167, 169-71, 220-3, 224, 225, 226, 229, 232-3, 235n, 238.
ESCAVIAS, Pedro de, chronicler, 40, 136, 213, 232.
escribano de cámara (royal notary), office of, 174.
ESPINA, Alonso de, Franciscan, 207-8, 209-10, 214.
estates, see *Cortes*.
ESTÚÑIGA family, 32, 34, 35, 36-9, 42, 43-5, 54, 65, 72, 76, 77, 78, 85, 87-9, 134, 188, 200.
ESTÚÑIGA, Alvaro de, son of Count of Plasencia, 44n-45, 69-71, 73-7, 79, 81n, 85, 87-8, 129, 134, 227.
ESTÚÑIGA, Beatriz de, Countess of Ribadeo, 42, 45, 69.
ESTÚÑIGA, Diego de, cousin of Alvaro de Estúñiga, 134, 137, 138-9, 144.
ESTÚÑIGA, Iñigo de, brother of Count of Plasencia, 37, 74, 77.
ESTÚÑIGA, Lope de, son of Iñigo, 36n-37.
ESTÚÑIGA, Pedro de, Count of Plasencia, *justicia mayor*, 32, 36-9, 43-4, 69, 87, 134.
ESTÚÑIGA, Sancho de, *mariscal*, 37.
EUGENIUS IV, Pope, 94, 176n.
EXTREMADURA, 193, 222.

FALCONI, Sancho, supporter of Count of Alba, 225.
favourite, see *privado*.
FERNÁNDEZ, Mayor, mother of Alfonso Alvarez de Toledo, 173n.
FERNÁNDEZ, Sancho, *contador*, 25n, 193, 206.
FERNÁNDEZ GALINDO, Juan, in household of Alvaro de Luna, 74.
FERNÁNDEZ DE LEDESMA, Alonso, *fiscal*, 186n.
FERNÁNDEZ DE MIRANDA, Gómez, Dr, judge, 195.
FERNÁNDEZ DE VELASCO, Pero, Count of Haro, 33n, 38, 53n, 62.
FERNANDO I, King of Aragon («Fernando de Antequera»), 6, 7, 24, 196.
FERNANDO II, King of Aragon and ISABEL I, Queen of Castile, *Reyes Católicos* (see also ISABEL I, Queen of Castile), 21, 29, 184, 188n, 190, 232, 239.
FERRÁNDEZ DE LORCA, Pero, royal secretary, 90.
fiscal (public prosecutor), see FERNÁNDEZ DE LEDESMA, Alonso; GARCÍA CHIRINO, Alonso, Dr; GÓMEZ DE ZAMORA, Juan, Dr.

INDEX

FONSECA, Alonso de, Bishop of Avila, 74, 83.
FRANCE, 29, 40, 96, 122, 123, 126, 127.
FRANCO, Dr, see GONZÁLEZ FRANCO, Diego, Dr.
FRANCO family, 195, 205.
FRANCO, Alfonso, Bachiller (later Licenciado), son of Dr Franco, 194-5.
FRANCO, García, son of Dr Franco, 194-5.
FRANCO, Gonzalo, son of Dr Franco, 195.
FRANCO, Pedro, son of Dr Franco, 194.
FRANCO, Pedro, illegitimate son of Dr Franco, 195.
FRANCO, Pero, brother of Dr Franco, 193.
FREDERICK II, Holy Roman Emperor, 106n, 116.
FUENSALIDA, 137-43, 149, 151, 155-6, 160, 165n, 166, 169, 237.
FUENTIDUEÑA, 139n.
Fuero real gloss (Alonso Díaz de Montalvo), 159-60, 182.

GALICIA, 182, 191n, 193.
GALÍNDEZ DE CARVAJAL, Lorenzo, chronicler, 138, 171n, 176, 178, 217.
GARCÍA DE BURGOS, Gonzalo, deputy for Judge of Biscay, 187.
GARCÍA CHIRINO, Alonso, Dr, *fiscal*, 44, 186, 188, 203.
GARCÍA DE GUADALAJARA, Alonso (1), Dr, see GARCÍA CHIRINO, Alonso.
GARCÍA DE GUADALAJARA, Alonso (2), Dr, judge at trial of Alvaro de Luna, 186-8, 197, 201, 203, 204.
GARCÍA DE GUADALAJARA, Diego (1), magistrate in Guadalajara and royal secretary, 187-8.
GARCÍA DE GUADALAJARA, Diego (2), son of (1), 187-8.
GARCÍA DE GUADALAJARA, Diego (3), secretary of Mendoza family, possibly=(2), 187.
GARCÍA DE GUADALAJARA, Diego (4), son of (3), 187.
GARCÍA DE GUADALAJARA, Fernando, royal notary (1416), 187.
GARCÍA DE GUADALAJARA, Gonzalo, son of Mosé el Barchilón, 187n.
GARCÍA DE GUADALAJARA, Juan, secretary of Ruy López Dávalos, 187.
GARCÍA DE GUADALAJARA, Pedro, son of Mosé el Barchilón, 187n.
GARCÍA DE ILLESCAS, Gonzalo, treasurer of Alvaro de Luna, 90n.
GARCÍA DE MAZARAMBROZ, Marcos, Bachiller, leader of Toledo revolt, 22n.
GARCÍA DE SALAZAR, Lope, annalist, 40, 43n-44, 45, 136, 192.

GARCÍA DE SANTA MARÍA, Alvar, chronicler, 12-19, 22, 25, 33, 34, 175, 176.
GARCÍA DE VILLALPANDO, Rui, Dr, Councillor of King of Navarre, 61n.
GARCÍA DE VILLALPANDO, Ruy, Licenciado, magistrate in Toledo, 61, 192, 202n, 224.
GEDDES, Michael, biographer of Alvaro de Luna, 218n.
Genoese (in Seville), 53.
GERONA, Bishop of, see MARGARIT I PAU, Joan.
GERSON, Jean, jurist and theologian, 121n-122, 125.
GHENT, see HENRY OF GHENT.
GIRÓN, Pedro, brother of Juan Pacheco, 233n.
GÓMEZ DE HERRERA, Alvar, royal notary, father-in-law of Luis Díaz de Toledo, 183-5.
GÓMEZ DE HERRERA, Fernán (1), Bachiller, *oidor*, son of Alvar Gómez de Herrera, 100n, 183-5.
GÓMEZ DE HERRERA, Fernán (2), Bachiller, *oidor*, Latin Secretary of Enrique IV; died 1459; possibly judge at trial of Alvaro de Luna, 183-5, 201, 203, 205, 207.
GÓMEZ DE HERRERA, Fernán (3), Bachiller, royal notary, possibly=(2), 183.
GÓMEZ DE HERRERA, Fernán (4), Bachiller, tax collector, 184n.
GÓMEZ DE HERRERA, Fernán (5), Bachiller, in orders, examined for doctorate, 184n, 189.
GÓMEZ DE HERRERA, Fernán (6), Bachiller, husband of Sancha Vázquez, 184n.
GÓMEZ DE HERRERA, Fernán (7), Licenciado, Councillor of Catholic Monarchs, 184.
GÓMEZ DE HERRERA, Juan, Bachiller, 183n.
GÓMEZ DE SANDOVAL, Diego, Count of Castro, 18, 145, 148, 161n, 175.
GÓMEZ DE SILVA, Arias, in household of Juan II, 223, 230n.
GÓMEZ DE ZAMORA, Alonso, Bachiller, in household of Marquis of Santillana, 185.
GÓMEZ DE ZAMORA, Diego (1), Dr, Councillor, 185n-186.
GÓMEZ DE ZAMORA, Diego (2), Dr, Professor of Canon Law at Salamanca, 185.
GÓMEZ DE ZAMORA, Juan, Dr, *Fiscal*, judge at trial of Alvaro de Luna, 89, 107, 136, 150, 151, 166, 185-6, 201, 203, 204.

González, Aldonza, wife of Relator, 175.
González de Ávila, Alfonso, of Alcalá de Henares, 190n.
González de Ávila, Fernán, *oidor*, father of Pero González de Ávila, 188.
González de Ávila, Gil (1), father-in-law of Alonso Pérez de Vivero, 202.
González de Ávila, Gil (2), antiquary, 166, 218.
González de Ávila, Pero, Dr, judge at trial of Alvaro de Luna, 188-91, 197, 198, 201, 203, 204, 207.
González del Castillo, Pero, Dr, Referendary, 196.
González Franco, Diego, Dr, judge at trial of Alvaro de Luna, 64, 138, 143, 159, 161, 165, 193-5, 196, 197, 201, 202, 203, 204-6.
González de Illescas, Gómez, notary, 150, 223.
González de León, Alonso, lieutenant of castle of Portillo, 131.
González de Orihuela, Inés, wife of Dr Franco, 194.
González de Toledo, Diego, Dr, see González Franco, Diego, Dr.
González de Valderrábano, Diego, brother of Dr Pero González de Ávila, 188.
González de Valderrábano, Fernán, Dr, see González de Ávila, Fernán.
González de Valladolid, Pero, *contador*, 149n-150.
Graetz, Heinrich, historian, 205-6.
Granada, city and kingdom, 7, 8, 11, 23-4, 29, 54, 57, 154, 173n, 205, 232.
grants, see *ayudas de costa, mercedes, juros.*
Guadalajara, 20, 102n, 173n, 179, 181, 186, 187.
Guadalajara, *Cortes* of (1390), 102n.
Guadalupe, 226n-227.
Guadalupe, Prior of, see Illescas, Gonzalo de.
Guadarrama mountains, 54, 130,
Guinea, 49.
Guipúzcoa, 183.
Gutiérrez de Corral, Alonso, in household of Relator, 42.
Guzmán, Inés de, second wife of Alonso Pérez de Vivero, 202n.
Guzmán, Juan de, Duke of Medina Sidonia, 48.

Halhamín, 221n.
Haro, Count of, see Fernández de Velasco, Pero.
Henry IV, King of England, 214n.

Henry of Ghent, theologian, 104n-105.
Herrera family, 183, 203, 204, 205.
Herrera, Alfonso de, son of Fernán Gómez de Herrera, Latin Secretary, 184-5.
La Higuera, 221n.
Hillgarth, Jocelyn, historian, 33.
Histoire du Connêtable de Lune (anonymous), 50, 207, 218n.
Historia de la privanza y caída de Don Alvaro de Luna (anonymous), 149n.
Hohenstaufen Emperors, 105, 106.
Huete, 182, 198, 230n, 238.
Hurtado de Mendoza, Diego, eldest son of Marquis of Santillana, 233.
Hurtado de Mendoza, Juan, brother of Ruy Díaz de Mendoza, 73n, 85, 131, 134.

Illescas, Alfonso de, page of Juan II, 223.
Illescas, Gonzalo de (1), Hieronymite, Prior of Guadalupe, 207, 226n-227, 237.
Illescas, Gonzalo de (2), annalist, 218.
inalienabilia, 103, 154, 162.
indictment, see *proceso*.
Infantado, Duke of, 149n.
Innocent IV, Pope, 116n, 152n.
Innocent VI, Pope, 94n.
Inquisition, 173, 179n, 183, 195, 204-5.
Instrucción del Relator (Fernán Díaz de Toledo), 176, 177, 203, 205, 206, 208n.
Isabel I, Queen of Castile, 103, 125n, 217.
Isabel, Princess of Portugal, later Queen of Castile, second wife of Juan II, 40-2, 45-7, 50, 69, 190.
Isernia, see Andreas of Isernia.
Isidore of Seville, St, 106.
Italy, 214.

Jaén, 53n.
Jews, 15, 18, 21, 54n, 63-4, 158n, 171, 172, 173, 177, 179, 182, 185, 187n-188, 204-5, 206, 207n, 223.
Joan of Arc, 236.
Johannes Andreae, jurist, 125, 128, 148.
Johannes Bassianus, glossator, 158n.
Johannes de Deo, canonist, 105, 106.
Johannes Teutonicus, jurist, 110n, 123.
John of Salisbury, political theorist, 112, 114, 116, 121, 124, 128.
John of Wales, encyclopaedist, 106, 114, 124.
Juan I, King of Castile, 2-3, 4n, 21, 96, 102, 109n, 111-12, 119, 126n.
Juan II, King of Castile: absolutism,

101-18, 121n, 122, 125-6, 134, 153, 159, 178-9, 210, 220, 239, 241; adult reign summarized, 6-11; cultural policies and patronage, 22-4, 127-9, 220; currency debasement, 15-16, 26-7, 51, 58-9; derogation, 91-7, 99-101, 104, 108-9, 114, 115-16, 119-21, 159, 221; foreign policy: Aragon and Navarre, 228-9, Portugal, 48-50; and Alvaro de Luna: allegedly bewitched by, 8, 25, 236, first hostility to, 45, changing attitudes to, 39-40, 45-6, 66, 72, 83-5, marriage and L, 40-2, 45-7, L's parsimony with him, 42, 51-2, intrigues against L, 42, 45, 67, 69-70, conduct before arrest of L, 68-76, during arrest, 77-83, administrative moves against L, 90-3, arrangements for custody of L, 85, 131-2, 134-5; for trial, 136-44; conduct at trial, 146-68; and L's execution, 209-10, 211-13, 224; and L's wealth, 89, 130-1, 132-3, 230-4; and L's family and partisans: aware of their revolt, 108-9; exchanges letters with them, 115-18, 140-3, 153, 170; settlement with them, 220-2; leniency towards them, 223-4; *mercedes*, 57-8, 60, 61; offices, filling of, 12-14, 19, 61; officials, relations with, 20, 22, 61-2, 73, 197-204, 206-7, 210, 220; revenues, 54-9; succession, 50-1, 63, 228, 234-8; also, 1, 3, 4n, 16, 18, 21, 28, 29, 33, 36, 65, 86, 87, 88, 120, 123-4, 125, 126, 130, 133, 145, 172, 174, 175, 180, 182, 183, 185, 186, 187, 188, 189, 190, 193, 194, 195, 196, 205, 208, 214, 215, 217, 219, 225, 226, 227, 240.

JUAN, King of Navarre, later Juan II, King of Aragon, 1, 9-11, 18, 35, 61, 62, 88, 126n, 174, 178n, 194, 227, 229, 231, 234.

JUAN MANUEL, Infante of Castile, 102, 114, 122, 123.

JUANA, Princess of Portugal, later Queen of Castile, second wife of Enrique IV, 48, 176n.

JUANA, Infanta, daughter of Enrique IV, 190.

Judge of Appeal, see *oidor*.
juros (state bonds), 57.
justicia mayor, office of, 134.
JUSTINIAN, Emperor, 22, 110, 121.

LA ASPERILLA, 130 n, 137.
LA CERDA, Luis de, lieutenant of castle of Toledo, 61, 90, 224.
LADERO QUESADA, Miguel Angel, historian, 14-15, 30, 223.

laesa majestas, 154, 157, 162, 166.
Lamentación de Don Alvaro de Luna (anonymous), 214.
LANZAROTE, 48.
LEÓN, 11.
LEONOR, Dowager-Queen of Portugal, 46-47, 189.
LÉRIDA, University of, 179, 182, 186-7, 197, 201.
letrados (officials), 2, 5, 20-2, 30, 61-4, 73, 82, 92, 105, 106, 108, 118-19, 120, 123-7, 141, 145-6, 160, 167, 169-71, 171-207, 220, 237.
Lex Regia, 121.
LISBON, 49.
LOAISA, Juan de, annalist, 135n.
LÓPEZ DÁVALOS, Ruy, Constable, 187.
LÓPEZ DE AYALA, Pero, chronicler, 2, 128n.
LÓPEZ DE MENDOZA, Iñigo, Marquis of Santillana, 36, 38, 41, 63, 113n, 124, 128, 180-2, 183, 185, 198, 200, 211, 215, 225, 233.
LÓPEZ DE SALDAÑA, Fernán, *contador mayor*, 13, 172, 232.
LOUIS IX (Saint Louis), King of France, 96, 122, 226.
LUCAS OF TUY, chronicler, 123.
LUCENA, Juan de, author of *De Vita Beata*, 121-2.
LUJÁN, Pedro de, *camarero mayor*, 76.
LUNA, family, 88, 110, 143, 169, 217, 222.
LUNA, Alvaro de, Constable, Master of Santiago: career as *privado* summarized, 6-11; his government in 1430s, 11-21; after Olmedo, 33-4; opposition to him in early 1450s, 35-6, 38-9, 42-5; changing relations with Juan II, 39-40, 45-6, 66, 72, 83-5; and J's marriage, 40-2; parsimony towards J, 42, 51-2; overconfidence before arrest, 73-4, 76; behaviour during arrest, 77-83; safeconduct to him, 80-3; appeals to J, 83-4; letters to partisans, 89, 108; arrangements for captivity, 85, 131-2, 134-5; his trial: nature of proceedings, 135-44, legality, 144-6, evidence taken, 148-50, role of King, 146-68, possible defence statement, 149, judges' report, 153, 155-6; trial reported to Council (text), 147; proclamation of his guilt (text), 152; execution, 1, 137, 151-2, 209-10, 211-14, 240-1; disposal of properties, 222-223; political settlement after his death, 224-30; alliances and loyalty oaths, 24, 33n, 34, 90-1, 91-2, 102-3, 109; L and *conversos*, 63-5, 77, 80, 171, 177, 181, 205-10; economic policies,

14-16, 26-8, 51-2, 58-62; L and Prince Enrique, 50-1, 228, 234-7; feud with Estúñigas, 32, 35, 36-8, 87, 188; L and Jews, 63-5, 205-6; his literary image, 214-18; as Master of Santiago, 10, 38n, 54, 106, 143, 147-8, 151n, 185, 222, 230; offences alleged against L: *apoderamiento*, 40-1, 101, 144, 151-8, 162, black magic, 8, 25, 236-7, ecclesiastical offences, 25, 148, murders and acts of violence, 25, 46-7, 150-1, 236, other crimes and abuses, 24-5, 36, 57n; officials, relations with, 12-14, 21-2, 44-5, 61-3, 73, 171-5, 178-9, 183-184, 189-94, 202-6; with Alonso Pérez de Vivero, 41-5, 62, 66, 67-73, 82, 89-90, 101, 131, 150, 154, 156-7, 162, 202, 203-4, 206, 208; and Portugal, 47-50; wealth, 89, 130-3, 230-4; also 23, 29, 30, 31, 53, 54, 55, 75, 86, 87, 88, 92, 96, 97, 98, 99, 105, 107, 108, 110, 113, 114, 115, 116, 117, 118, 119, 121n, 122, 129, 130, 169, 170, 186, 192, 196, 221, Evaluations of him, 28-9, 58-62, 218-20, 239-41.
LUNA, Count of, see ARAGÓN, Fadrique de.
LUNA, Juan de (1), Count of Alburquerque, son of Alvaro de Luna, 89, 172.
LUNA, Juan de (2), son-in-law of Alvaro de Luna, 72.
LUNA, María de, daughter of Alvaro de Luna, 149.
LUNA, Martín de, illegitimate son of Alvaro de Luna, 50.
LUNA, P. de («P. Lunensis»), 214n-215.
LUNA, Pedro de, illegitimate son of Alvaro de Luna, 74, 77n-78, 89, 139n.

MACKAY, Angus, historian, 14, 26, 30, 51, 58, 60, 230n, 231, 232n.
MADRID, 102n, 172, 182, 183, 203, 232.
MADRID, *Cortes* of (1392), 102n; (1435), 16n.
MADRIGAL, *Cortes* of (1438), 16n, 17n.
MÁLAGA, 175, 179n.
MALDONADO, Francisco, page of Alvaro de Luna, 149n-150.
mandate, royal, 138, 143, 151, 159, 161, 162, 163-6, 167, 169.
MANELLI, Luca, Bishop of Cito, 128.
MANRIQUE family, 34n.
MANRIQUE, Diego, *adelantado*, 34n.
MANRIQUE, Diego Gómez, Count of Treviño, 225.
MANRIQUE, Gómez, poet, 180n, 216.
MANRIQUE, Jorge, poet, 216.
MANRIQUE, Pedro, *adelantado*, 8.

MANRIQUE, Rodrigo, Count of Paredes, father of Jorge, 99n.
MAQUEDA, 130, 137, 141, 143, 220, 223, 238.
MARGARIT I PAU, Joan, Bishop of Gerona, 126.
MARÍA, Infanta of Aragón, Queen of Castile, first wife of Juan II, 14n, 46, 47, 151n, 222, 227.
MARIANA, Juan de, historian, 84, 152, 218.
mariscal, see ESTÚÑIGA, Sancho de; RIBERA, Payo de.
MARTIN V, Pope, 94, 127.
MARTÍN, José Luis, historian, 33.
MARTÍNEZ MORO, Jesús, historian, 30.
MASDOVELLES, Berenguer, poet, 216.
mayordomo mayor (Steward of King's Household), see DÍAZ DE MENDOZA, Ruy.
MEDINA DEL CAMPO, 8-9, 93, 96, 99, 189, 193n-194, 223, 226n.
MEDINA SIDONIA, Duke of, see GUZMÁN, Juan de.
MENA, Juan de, poet, 23, 223, 225n.
MENDOZA family, 34n, 38, 41, 73n, 78, 134, 149n, 184n, 187, 188, 195, 200, 218, 222.
MENÉNDEZ Y PELAYO, Marcelino, historian, 29.
mercedes, 3, 27-8, 57-8, 60, 61, 156-7.
Mesta (Castilian graziers' guild), 53.
MILAN, 217.
military commands, see *adelantado*; Constable; *mariscal*.
MIRA DE AMESCUA, Antonio, dramatist, 217.
MIRAFLORES, 148n, 151n.
MITRE FERNÁNDEZ, Emilio, historian, 30.
MONREAL, 193.
MONTALBÁN, 151n, 221n-222, 230n.
MONTALBÁN, Deputy Prior of, 83.
MONTANCHES, 222n.
MONTEMAYOR, 37.
MONTIEL, 1.
Moorish knights, see *caballeros moriscos*.
MOORS, 141; see also GRANADA.
MORALES, page of Alvaro de Luna, 148n, 212-13.
MORELLA, 126n-127.
MOROCCO, 49.
MOXÓ, Salvador de, historian, 30.
MURCIA, 11, 53n, 182, 184n.

NAPLES, 38.
naturaleza (natural vassalage), 18, 102-3, 109, 110, 112-13, 127.
NAVALMORCUENDE, 188.

INDEX

NAVARRE, 1, 7, 11, 13n, 35, 37, 61n, 87, 131, 183, 198, 227, 228-9.
NEW CASTILE, 54, 132, 134, 171, 203.
New Christians, see *conversos*.
NICHOLAS V, Pope, 49, 94n, 205-7, 231.
NIEBLA, Archdeacon of, see DÍAZ DE TOLEDO, Fernando (1).
NIÑO, Pero, Count of Buelna, 195.
NOALOS, 222n.
notary (royal), see *escribano de cámara*.
notario mayor de los privilegios rodados, office of, 175.
Notas del Relator (Fernán Díaz de Toledo), 176.
NÚÑEZ DE HERRERA, Pero, correspondent of King of Aragon, 34n.

ODOFREDUS, jurist, 110n, 125n.
officials, see *letrados*.
oidor (judge of appeal), office of, 175, 203.
OLD CASTILE, 54, 203.
OLMEDILLA, 179.
OLMEDO, battle of, 10, 11, 12, 33, 35, 51, 54, 57, 62, 66n, 91-2, 119n, 172, 178, 182.
OLMEDO, *Cortes* of (1445), 56, 91, 96, 104, 105n, 106, 107n, 111, 117, 119n, 123, 158n.
OROSIUS, 185.
OSMA, 151n.
OSMA, Bishop of, 205-6.

PACHECO family, 41, 53, 55, 137, 149, 164n, 183, 192, 218-19, 222.
PACHECO, Juan, Marquis of Villena, 10, 11, 24-5, 34, 38-9, 192, 209, 222, 233n, 235.
pacífico estado (King's peace), 103-4, 118, 134, 156, 162, 178.
PADILLA, Juan de, poet, 216n.
PALENCIA, Alfonso de, chronicler, 41, 42, 43, 45, 49, 184, 185, 211, 214-15, 226, 235, 238.
PALENZUELA, *Cortes* of (1425), 22-3.
PAREDES, Count of, see MANRIQUE, Rodrigo.
Partidas, see ALFONSO X, King of Castile.
Partidas gloss (Alonso Díaz de Montalvo), 147-9, 161.
PEDRO, King of Castile, 1, 2, 3, 124.
PEDRO, Constable of Portugal, 35, 216, 230.
PEDRO, Duke of Coimbra, 46n-48, 189.
PENNA, Lucas de, jurist, 96, 109n, 110, 111, 114n, 125, 158n, 162, 163.
PEÑAFIEL, 69, 79n.
PERE IV, King of Aragon, 121.

PÉREZ DE GUZMÁN, Fernán, poet and biographer, 40, 42, 43, 68, 135, 136, 151, 209-10, 211, 214, 230, 236, 239.
PÉREZ DE VIVERO, Alonso, *contador mayor*, 37-8, 41, 42-5, 62, 64, 66, 67-73, 78n-79, 82, 89, 101, 118, 131, 136, 150, 154, 156-7, 162, 167, 172, 191, 202, 204, 206, 208, 234.
PERIÁÑEZ (1), Dr (Pero Yáñez de Ulloa), 13-14, 17, 21, 175, 191, 196, 202.
PERIÁÑEZ (2) (Pero Yáñez de Ulloa), son of García Alfonso de Ulloa, 191n.
PETIT, Jean, jurist, 121n.
PIMENTEL family, 17n, 34n.
PIMENTEL, Juana, wife of Alvaro de Luna, 17n, 89, 132, 198n, 220, 221-3, 230, 231, 233.
PIMENTEL, Rodrigo, Count of Benavente, 36, 48.
PISTOIA, Cino de, jurist, 162n-163.
PIUS II, Pope, see AENEAS SYLVIUS.
PLASENCIA, Count of, see ESTÚÑIGA, Pedro de.
PLATO, 181, 200n.
plenitudo potestatis, 96, 119.
poderío real absoluto, 92n, 93, 95, 96, 101, 116, 120, 158, 160.
PORTILLO, 41, 83, 108, 130-1, 133, 134, 135, 136-8, 139, 141, 143, 149, 208, 212, 232, 235, 238.
PORTUGAL, 2, 11, 29, 36, 40, 46, 47-50, 53, 60n, 66, 189, 193, 229, 234.
EL PRADO, 221n.
PRIEGO, Counts of, 188.
princeps legibus solutus, 95n, 115-16, 121n-122.
privado («favourite»), 5-6, 218, 224-5, 240.
proceso (indictment), 135-6, 144, 161, 166.
propio motu, 93, 101, 120.
Proverbios (Marquis of Santillana), 180.
Proverbios de Séneca gloss (Pero Díaz de Toledo), 180.
PTOLEMY OF LUCCA, see THOMAS AQUINAS (PSEUDO).
public prosecutor, see *fiscal*.

QUEVEDO, Francisco de, 217.
QUINTANA, Manuel José, biographer of Alvaro de Luna, 137, 150n.
QUIRIALES, Alonso de, Cistercian, 152n.
quod principi placuit, 121-2, 159.

RAIS, Gilles de, 236.
RAMÍREZ DE GUZMÁN, Vasco, Archdeacon of Toledo, 128n-129.
RAMÍREZ DE TOLEDO, Juan, brother of Archdeacon of Niebla, 60n, 172.

referendario, office of, 174-5, 203.
relator, office of, 174, 203 (see also DÍAZ DE TOLEDO, Fernán).
RESTRE, herald, 78.
RÉVIGNY, Jacques de, jurist, 112.
rex imperator, 93n, 105, 122, 126-7.
rex legibus solutus, see *princeps legibus solutus*.
Reyes Católicos, see FERNANDO II, King of Aragon and ISABEL I, Queen of Castile, *Reyes Católicos*; also, separately, ISABEL I, Queen of Castile.
RIBADENEIRA, Fernando de, in household of Alvaro de Luna, 70, 71, 83n, 137, 141n, 220, 224, 226n.
RIBADEO, Countess of, see ESTÚÑIGA, Beatriz de.
RIBERA, Payo de, *mariscal*, 198n.
RIBERA, Perafán de, *adelantado*, 78n-81.
RICHARD II, King of England, 126.
RIZZO Y RAMÍREZ, Juan, biographer of Alvaro de Luna, 145-6, 150n.
RODRÍGUEZ, Juan (1), Dr, judge at trial of Alvaro de Luna, 166-8, 196-7, 198, 201, 203, 204.
RODRÍGUEZ, Juan (2), Dr, magistrate in Seville, 196.
RODRÍGUEZ DE ALMELA, Diego, pupil of Alonso de Cartagena, 40, 83.
RODRÍGUEZ DE SALAMANCA, Juan, Dr, Councillor, 186n, 196.
RODRÍGUEZ DE VALLADOLID, Diego, Dr, royal secretary, 13-14, 17, 191, 196.
ROJAS, Fernando de, 195.
Romanus Pontifex (Bull), 229.
ROME, 127, 147-8, 207, 211.
ROMERO, Diego, royal secretary, 232.
RONDA, 177.
RUEDA, Martín de, criminal, 18.
RUIZ DE ULLOA, Andrés, judge, nephew of Dr Periáñez, 192.
RUIZ DE ULLOA, Gonzalo, Dr, judge at trial of Alvaro de Luna, 191-2, 201, 203, 204.

SAHARA, 48n-49, 50.
SALAMANCA, 17-18, 36n-37, 166n, 185, 196, 203.
SALAMANCA, University of, 172, 182, 185, 189, 191n-192, 196, 197, 208.
SALAMANCA, Vicar-general of, 205-6.
SALAMÓN, Rabbi, physician of Juana Pimentel, 223, 226n.
SALAZAR Y MENDOZA, Pedro de, biographer of Cardinal Mendoza, 135n, 144, 152, 170-1, 197, 205, 219.
SALISBURY, see JOHN OF SALISBURY.
SALUTATI, Coluccio, Humanist, 116n, 152n.

SÁNCHEZ DE ARÉVALO, Rodrigo, historian, 45, 114, 122-3, 127, 136, 214, 219-20, 223-4, 236.
SÁNCHEZ DE ARRIBA, José, antiquary, 165n.
SÁNCHEZ DE LOGROÑO, Alfonso, Licenciado, judge at trial of Alvaro de Luna, 192-3, 197, 204.
SÁNCHEZ ZURBANO, Juan, Dr, judge at trial of Alvaro de Luna, 138, 143, 159, 161, 165, 195-6, 197, 198, 202n, 204.
SAN CUGAT, *Corts* of (1419), 107, 126.
SANDOVAL family, 34n.
SAN ESTEBAN, County of, 222, 230n.
SAN MARTÍN, 221n.
SANTA MARÍA family, see CARTAGENA family.
SANTA MARÍA, Pablo de, Bishop of Burgos, Chancellor, 22.
SANTA MARÍA DE LA ARMEDILLA, 133, 232.
SANTA MARÍA DEL CAMPO, 130n.
SANTA MARÍA DE VALDEIGLESIAS, 223n.
SANTANDER, 225.
SANTIAGO, Order of, 10, 38n, 54, 106, 143, 147-8, 151n, 222, 225, 230, 231-2, 238.
SANTILLANA, Marquis of, see LÓPEZ DE MENDOZA, Iñigo.
SAPERA, Bishop, 126n.
SARMIENTO family, 34n.
SARMIENTO, Pero, leader of Toledo revolt, 65, 145, 148.
SASSOFERRATO, Bartolo di, see BARTOLUS.
secretary, royal, office of, 174.
SEGOVIA, 20, 130, 225, 235, 236.
SENECA, Lucius Annaeus, 106, 111, 128, 216.
SENECA, Annaeus, the Elder, 128.
sentence (of court), 138, 143, 160-1, 163-166, 167.
SEPÚLVEDA, 238.
servicio y montazgo (tax on flocks and herds), 53-4.
SEVILLE, 36n-37, 42, 48n, 50, 53, 90, 177, 194, 196, 199, 230n.
SIGÜENZA, José de, historian, 166.
SILIÓ, César, historian, 29, 135, 149n.
SIMANCAS, 14, 196, 223.
status regis et regni, 104.
Steward of King's Household, see *mayordomo mayor*.
STRATFORD, John, Archbishop of Canterbury, 167n.
SUÁREZ FERNÁNDEZ, Luis, historian, 29, 30, 33.

tasa de señoríos (taxation of magnates self-administered), 55, 239, 240.

INDEX

taxation, see *alcabala, cobro de albaquías, Cortes* subsidy, *diezmos de la mar de Castilla, servicio y montazgo, tasa de señoríos, tercias, tomas.*
tercias (ecclesiastical taxes), 148n, 222, 230n.
TEUTONICUS, see JOHANNES TEUTONICUS.
THOMAS AQUINAS, St, 158n, 178n.
THOMAS AQUINAS (PSEUDO), Ptolemy of Lucca, 95n, 114, 128.
EL TIEMBLO, 235n.
Tizón de España, 204.
TOLEDO, Archbishop of, see CARRILLO DE ACUÑA, Alonso; TOLEDO, Gutierre de.
TOLEDO, 36, 53n-54, 61, 89-91, 92, 100, 101, 129, 130, 134, 141, 150, 172, 183, 184n, 187n, 193, 195, 203, 205, 220, 224, 230n, 232.
TOLEDO, *Cortes* of (1436), 16n.
TOLEDO, Gutierre de, Archbishop of Toledo, 176n.
TOLEDO, María de, mother of Relator, 171.
TOLEDO, Pedro de, illegitimate son of Relator, Bishop of Málaga, 175, 179n.
TOLEDO revolt (1449), 11, 22n, 34, 51, 60, 62, 64, 65, 107, 173, 177, 181, 182, 205, 206, 207, 208.
tomas (usurpation of tax revenues), 55, 190.
TORDESILLAS, 67n, 226.
TORO, 191-2.
TORQUEMADA, 89n, 130, 132n.
LA TORRE, 221n.
LA TORRE, Fernando de, poet, 216, 236n.
TORRES, Juan de, poet, 41.
Treasury, see *Casa de las Cuentas, contadores mayores, contadores mayores de cuentas.*
TREJO, Francisco de, messenger from Escalona, 141, 144.
TREVIÑO, Count of, see MANRIQUE, Diego Gómez.
TRUJILLO, 95, 99, 222n.

UBALDI, Baldo degli, see BALDUS.
ULLOA family, 191-2, 204.
ULLOA, Dr, see RUIZ DE ULLOA, Gonzalo.
ULLOA, García Alfonso de, knight of Toro, 191.
ULLOA, Juan de, son of Dr Periáñez, 191n-192.
ULLOA, Rodrigo de, son of Dr Periáñez, 191n-192.
ULPIAN, jurist, 116, 121.
usurpation, see *apoderamiento*; of taxes, see *tomas.*

VALDEÓN BARUQUE, Julio, historian, 28, 30.
VALDIÉTAR, 222n.
VALERA, Diego de, chronicler, 32, 36-7, 40, 42, 43, 44, 45, 51, 62, 73n-74, 80, 81n, 87-8, 114, 153n, 164-5, 166, 186, 188.
VALERIUS MAXIMUS, 163n.
VALLADOLID, 1, 14, 38, 43-5, 49, 73, 111n, 131n, 134, 137, 151-2, 208, 212-214, 224.
VALLADOLOD, *Cortes* of (1442), 28, 63n, 119; (1447), 10, 51, 57, 60, 63, 119; (1451), 55, 57, 60.
VALLADOLID, Juan de, poet, 216n, 240n.
VALLADOLID, University of, 21n, 173, 179, 197.
VALLEJO, Juan de, servant of Archbishop Carrillo, 140.
VÁZQUEZ, Sancha, wife of Fernán Gómez de Herrera (6), 184n.
LA VEGA, Leonor de, mother of Marquis of Santillana, 195.
VEGETIUS, 109n, 128n.
VELASCO family, 34n.
VELÁZQUEZ DE CUÉLLAR, Juan, Dr, lawyer, 165n-166.
VENEGAS, EGAS, knight of Córdoba, on treason charge, 7.
VENICE, 29.
VICENS VIVES, Jaime, historian, 29.
VICENTIUS HISPANUS, canonist, 105, 122.
VILLAFRANCA, Juan de, translator of *Lamentación de Don Alvaro de Luna*, 214n.
VILLALBA, Marcos de, jurist, 107, 114.
VILLANUEVA, 222n.
VILLA REAL, 230n.
VILLATORO, 188.
VILLEGAS, Juan de, page of Juan II, 223.
VILLENA family, see PACHECO family.
VILLENA, Marquis of, son of Juan Pacheco, 149n.
VIVERO, 64.
VIVERO family, 90n, 134-5.
VIVERO, Juan de, son of Alonso Pérez de Vivero, 71-2.
VIZCAYA, see Biscay.

WALES, see JOHN OF WALES.
WARREN, W. L., historian, 167.

YÁÑEZ DE ULLOA, Pero, see PERIÁÑEZ.

ZAFRA, Bartolomé de, secretary, 61, 141n, 224.

Zamora, 16n, 191.
Zamora, *Cortes* of (1432), 16n.
Zamora, Dr, see Gómez de Zamora, Juan.
Zamora, Juan Gil de, chronicler, 109.
Zurbano, Dr, see Sánchez Zurbano, Juan.

Zurita, Jerónimo, historian, 29, 84, 88, 226-7, 235.

The author wishes to acknowledge the assistance of the University of Glasgow Hetherington Language Centre in providing technical facilities for the making of this Index.